OPEN WORLD

Jessica Smith

Cambridge University Press
www.cambridge.org/elt

Cambridge Assessment English
www.cambridgeenglish.org

Information on this title: www.cambridge.org/9781108627061

© Cambridge University Press and Cambridge Assessment 2019

This publication is in copyright. Subject to statutory exception
and to the provisions of relevant collective licensing agreements,
no reproduction of any part may take place without the written
permission of Cambridge University Press.

First published 2019

20 19 18 17 16 15 14 13 12 11 10 9 8 7 6 5 4 3 2 1

Printed in Spain by GraphyCems

A catalogue record for this publication is available from the British Library

ISBN 978-1-108-62706-1 Teacher's Book with Downloadable Resource Pack

The publishers have no responsibility for the persistence or accuracy
of URLs for external or third-party internet websites referred to in this publication,
and do not guarantee that any content on such websites is, or will remain,
accurate or appropriate. Information regarding prices, travel timetables, and other
factual information given in this work is correct at the time of first printing but
the publishers do not guarantee the accuracy of such information thereafter.

CONTENTS

Exam letter	4
Exam journey	5
How to use the Student's Book	6
Component line-up	8
Exam information	9
Starter Who I am	10
Unit 1 A busy life	16
Unit 2 Changing world	28
Progress check 1	39
Unit 3 Free time, screen time?	40
Unit 4 Keep fit, feel good	51
Unit 5 More than a holiday	62
Progress check 2	73
Unit 6 Time for food	74
Unit 7 Live life!	83
Unit 8 Feels like home	93
Progress check 3	102
Unit 9 Getting along	103
Unit 10 Out and about	113
Unit 11 Saving and spending	124
Progress check 4	135
Unit 12 Through life	136
Unit 13 About me	147
Unit 14 Play it, watch it, love it	157
Progress check 5	168
Grammar reference answer key	169
Phrasal verb bank answer key	172
Writing bank answer key	172
Speaking bank answer key	174
Workbook answer key and audioscripts	177
Links to Student's Book video and Push Yourself audio	191

CAMBRIDGE

DEAR TEACHERS

I'm delighted that you've chosen our official preparation materials to prepare for a Cambridge English Qualification.

We take great pride in the fact that our materials draw on the expertise of a whole team of writers, teachers, assessors and exam experts. These are materials that you can really trust.

Our preparation materials are unique in many ways:

- They combine the skills and knowledge of the teams at Cambridge Assessment English, who create the tests, and the teams at Cambridge University Press, who create the English Language Teaching materials.

- They draw upon the experience of millions of previous exam candidates – where they succeed and where they have difficulties. We target exercises and activities precisely at these areas so that you can actively 'learn' from previous test takers' mistakes.

- Every single task in our materials has been carefully checked to be an accurate reflection of what test takers find in the test.

In addition, we listen to what you tell us at every stage of the development process. This allows us to design the most user-friendly courses, practice tests and supplementary training. We create materials using in-depth knowledge, research and practical understanding. Prepare for Cambridge English Qualifications with confidence in the knowledge that you have the best materials available to support you on your way to success.

We wish you the very best on your journey with us.

With kind regards,

Pamela Baxter
Director
Cambridge Exams Publishing

PS. If you have any feedback at all on our support materials for exams, please write to us at cambridgeexams@cambridge.org

THE OPEN WORLD EXAM JOURNEY

The unique exam journey in Open World Key allows learners to build their confidence and develop their skills as they progress through each unit, ensuring they are ready on exam day. Along the journey there are ...

Two 'training' exam tasks in every unit, with guidance and tips to ensure students have the skills necessary to understand and do the exam task

Opportunities to fine-tune and practise each exam task again in the Exam focus pages at the end of each unit, confident in the knowledge that the material is checked by the same team who writes the exams

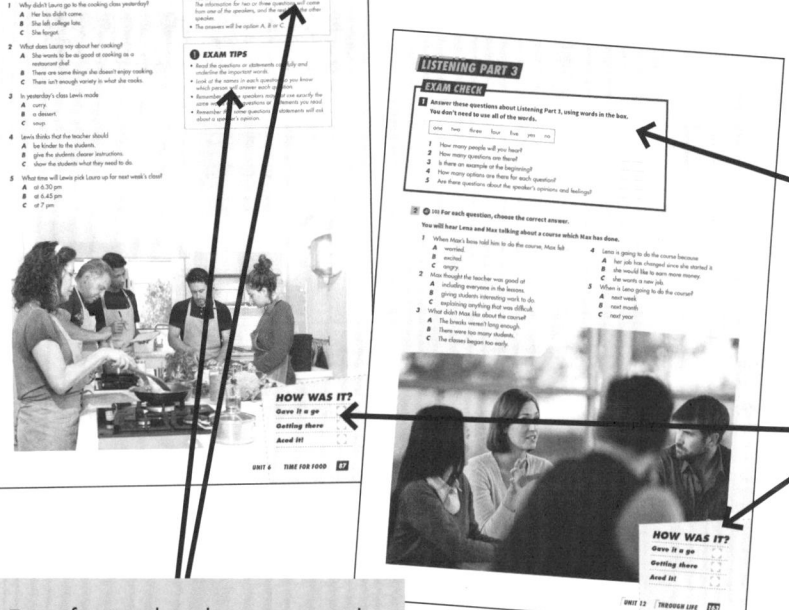

Exam check boxes where students can check their understanding before doing an exam task for the second time in the Exam focus pages

How was it? boxes on every Exam focus page to allow your students to assess their results as they progress through the exam tasks

Exam facts and tips boxes to remind students how to approach each exam task when doing the task for the first time in the Exam focus pages

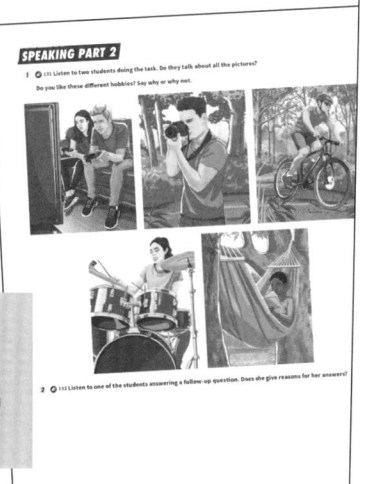
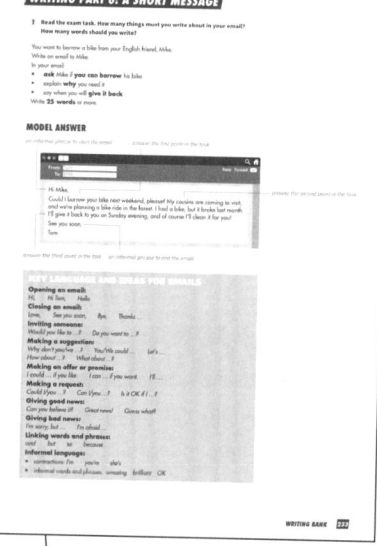

Extra practice sections for speaking and writing exam tasks at the back of the book, with preparation exercises and model exam tasks for students to follow

HOW TO USE THE STUDENT'S BOOK

WELCOME TO OPEN WORLD
THE COURSE THAT TAKES YOUR STUDENTS FURTHER

Learn about the features in the Student's Book

Large images at the start of each unit introduce the topic and get students talking

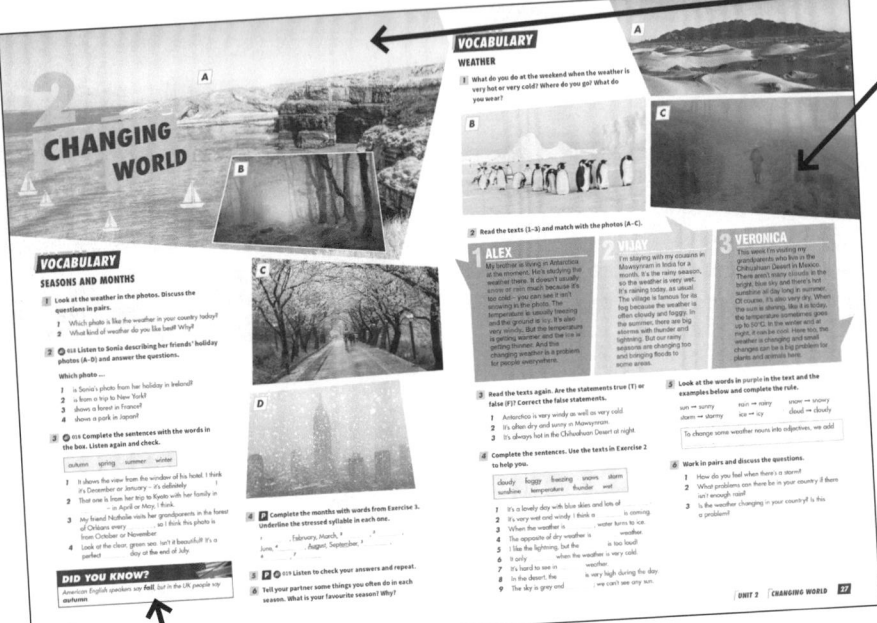

EXAM TRAINING

'Training' exam tasks provide guidance and tips on each part of the exam

DID YOU KNOW?

Students learn the differences between British English and American English

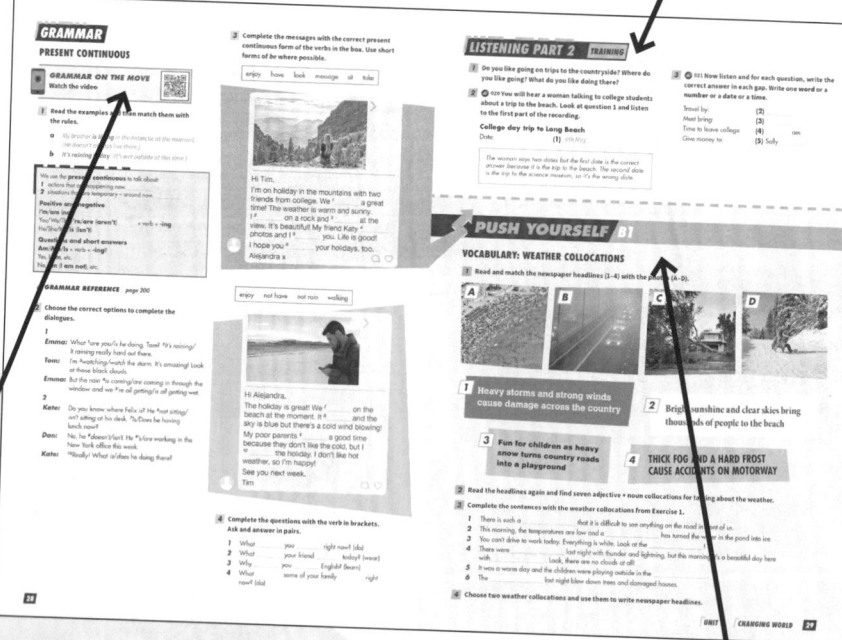

GRAMMAR ON THE MOVE

Students scan the QR codes to watch grammar animations in their free time to learn about each grammar point

PUSH YOURSELF

Students learn and practise more challenging language and skills that take them to the next level

EXAM FOCUS

Students read exam tips and facts and do two complete practice exam tasks after every unit

EXAM CHECKS

test what students remember about the exam

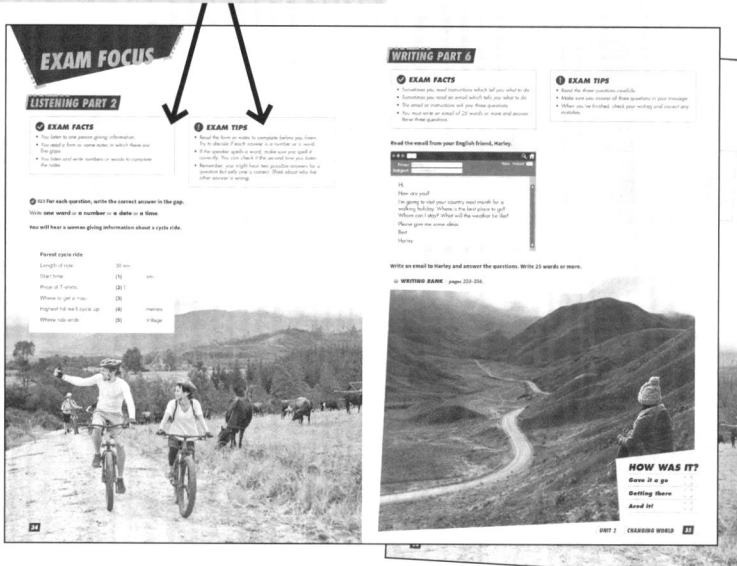

REAL WORLD

pages take students outside the classroom and into the real world

PHRASES YOU MIGHT USE AND HEAR

Students learn and practise phrases they might use and hear when they are using English in the real world

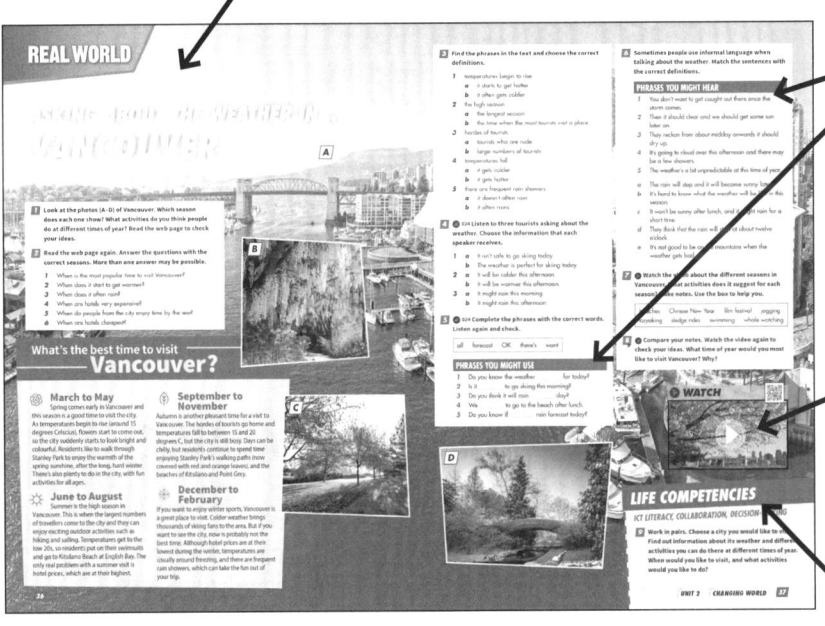

Students scan the QR codes to watch videos of different locations around the world on their mobile phone

LIFE COMPETENCIES

Students develop important skills, knowledge and attitudes that they can use in their daily life

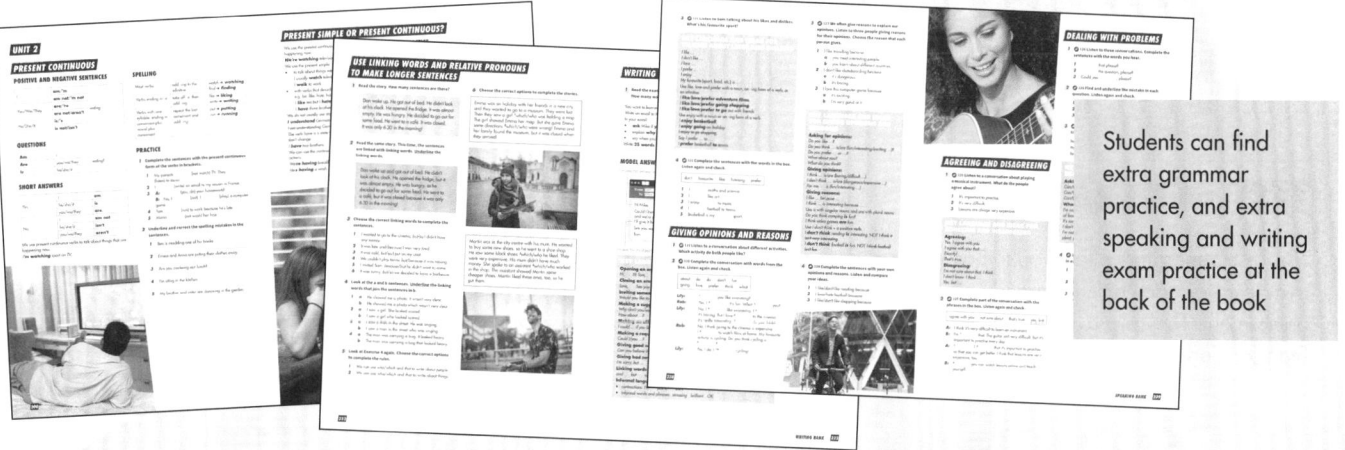

Students can find extra grammar practice, and extra speaking and writing exam practice at the back of the book

HOW TO USE THE STUDENT'S BOOK | **7**

COMPONENT LINE-UP

WORKBOOK WITH AND WITHOUT ANSWERS WITH AUDIO DOWNLOAD

The activities in the Workbook consolidate the language presented in the Student's Book. It also includes extra exam practice in every unit. Students can access and download the audio files using the QR code or the code in the book.

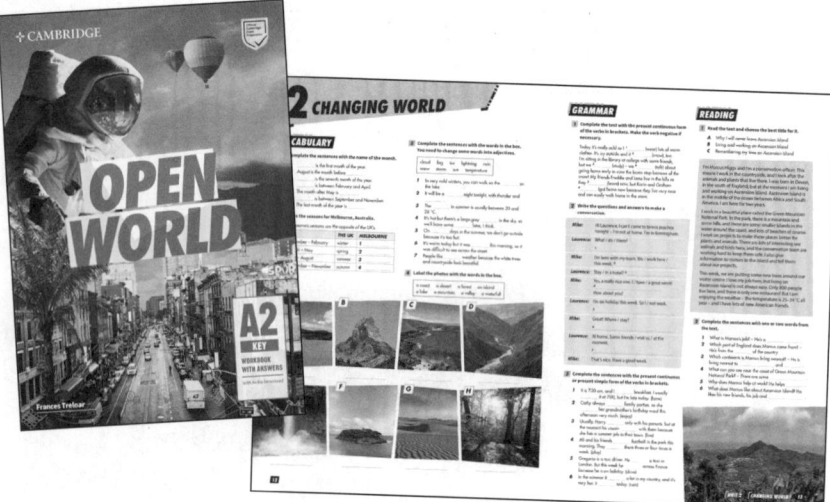

ONLINE WORKBOOK

The Online Workbook is a digital version of the print Workbook and allows you to track your students' progress, highlighting areas of strength and weakness for ongoing performance improvement.

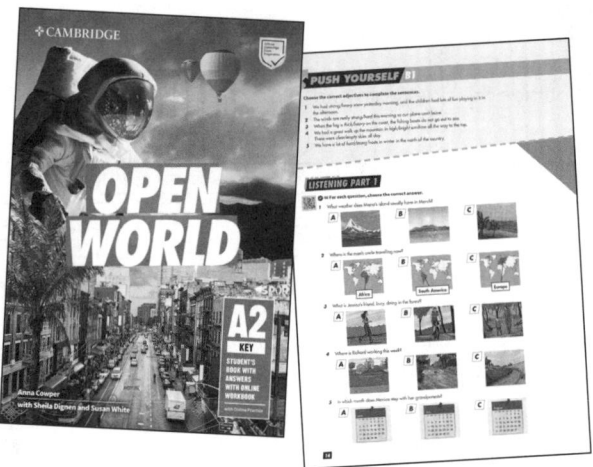

TEACHER'S BOOK WITH DOWNLOADABLE RESOURCE PACK

This Teacher's Book includes step-by-step activities for each stage of the lesson, with answer keys, background information, model answers and extension tasks. The Teacher's Book also provides access to:
- The Class Audio
- Extra teacher photocopiable resources
- Speaking videos
- Two practice tests

TEST GENERATORS

The Test Generators allow you to build your own tests for each unit, term and end-of-year assessment. They are available at two levels: Standard and Plus.

PRESENTATION PLUS

Presentation Plus is easy-to-use, interactive classroom presentation software that helps you deliver effective and engaging lessons. It includes the Student's Book and Workbook content and allows you to present and annotate content and link to the online resources.

A2 KEY EXAM INFORMATION

PART/TIMING	CONTENT	EXAM FOCUS
1 **Reading and Writing** 60 minutes	**Part 1:** Discrete three-option multiple-choice questions on six short texts. **Part 2:** Matching. There are three short texts with seven items. Candidates are asked to decide which text an item refers to. **Part 3:** Three-option multiple choice. Candidates read a text and are asked to choose the correct answer from five multiple-choice questions. **Part 4:** Three-option multiple-choice cloze. A text is followed by six questions. Candidates select the correct word from each question to complete the text. **Part 5:** Open cloze. Candidates complete gaps in one or two short texts. **Part 6:** Writing – short message **Part 7:** Writing – story	**Part 1:** Candidates focus on overall understanding of emails, notices and messages. **Part 2:** Candidates read for specific information and detailed comprehension. **Part 3:** Candidates read for detailed understanding and main ideas. **Part 4:** Candidates read and identify the appropriate word. **Part 5:** Candidates read and identify the appropriate word with the focus on grammar. **Part 6:** Candidates write a communicative note or email of at least 25 words. **Part 7:** Candidates write a narrative of at least 35 words describing the people, events and locations that are shown in three pictures.
2 **Listening** approximately 30 minutes	**Part 1:** Five short dialogues with three-option multiple-choice questions with pictures. **Part 2:** Longer dialogue. Five gaps to fill with words or numbers. **Part 3:** Longer informal dialogue with five three-option multiple-choice items. **Part 4:** Five three-option multiple-choice questions on five short dialogues or monologues. **Part 5:** Matching. There is a longer informal dialogue. Candidates match five items with eight options.	**Part 1:** Candidates are expected to listen and identify key information. **Part 2:** Candidates are expected to identify and write down key information. **Part 3:** Candidates listen to identify specific information, feelings and opinions. **Part 4:** Candidates listen to identify the main idea, message, gist, topic or point. **Part 5:** Candidates listen to identify specific information.
3 **Speaking** 8–10 minutes per pair of candidates	**Part 1 Phase 1:** Each candidate interacts with the interlocutor, giving factual information of a personal nature. **Part 1 Phase 2:** A topic-based interview where the interlocutor asks each candidate two questions about their daily life. **Part 2 Phase 1:** A discussion based on topic-based artwork prompts. Candidates discuss the objects and activities in the artwork with each other. **Part 2 Phase 2:** The interlocutor leads a follow-up discussion on the same topic as in Phase 1. Each candidate is asked two questions.	**Part 1:** Candidates focus on interactional and social language. **Part 2:** Candidates focus on organising a larger unit of discourse.

WHO I AM

UNIT OBJECTIVES	
Topic:	personal identification
Grammar:	be; have got; can; present simple – he/she/it
Vocabulary:	countries and nationalities; families
Listening:	listening for specific personal information: a short dialogue
Reading:	reading for detail: two personal profiles
Speaking:	asking and answering personal questions; numbers and dates
Writing:	a profile
Pronunciation:	pronouncing the letters of the alphabet

Ask your students to watch the Grammar on the Move videos on pages 10 and 11. You can use these to present or reinforce *have got* and *can*.

GRAMMAR
SB P8

BE

LEAD-IN

With books closed ask students what they talk about when they meet someone new and try to elicit some ideas such as age, hobbies and interests.

1 Open books and ask students to work in pairs to ask and answer the questions, giving true answers for themselves. They should try to suggest the actual words they might use, e.g. *How old are you? Where are you from? What's your favourite football team?*

2  002 Tell students they are going to hear some people meeting for the first time. Look at the pictures together, covering up the conversations and asking students to say where they think the people are and what they are doing there. With a stronger group, students can listen to the conversations without reading them and match the name of the place with each conversation. Check answers.

A at a sports centre, photo 1   **B** on holiday, photo 3
C in an English class, photo 2

AUDIOSCRIPT 002

A
Ben: Hi, I'm Ben. What's your name?
Jim: Hello Ben. My name's Jim. Nice to meet you.
Ben: Nice to meet you, too, Jim. Is this the basketball club?
Jim: No, it isn't. It's five-a-side football.

B
Man: Are you British?
Woman: No, we aren't. We're Canadian.
Man: Oh, that's interesting. Where are you from in Canada?

C
Girl 1: Is he our English teacher?
Girl 2: Yes, he is. His name is Mr Robinson. He's very nice. Are you a new student?
Girl 1: Yes, I am. This is my first lesson.
Girl 2: Where are you from?

3 002 With a weaker class elicit the verb *to be* and write it on the board. Include contractions (*I am/'m, he/she/it is/'s*, etc.). Allow students to work individually to complete the gaps in the dialogue using the correct form of the verb *to be*. Remind them the words can be used more than once. Repeat the recording so students can check their answers with a partner before class feedback.

| **1** 'm | **2** 's | **3** Is | **4** isn't, 's | **5** Are | **6** Aren't, 're |
| **7** 's, are | **8** Is | **9** is, 's, Are | **10** am | **11** are | |

⊕ EXTENSION

Encourage students to underline the questions in each dialogue and then model the correct intonation (or use the recording as the model) for each one. Drill the questions chorally and then individually. Allow students to practise reading the dialogues with a partner, focusing on intonation. Go around the class listening and giving feedback on intonation styles.

➡ **GRAMMAR REFERENCE** / Page 196

VOCABULARY
SB P8

COUNTRIES AND NATIONALITIES

LEAD-IN

With books closed, write *Country* on the board and brainstorm students' suggestions to make a list of countries they know. Then add a second column with the heading *Nationality*, and ask students to complete it. Highlight the stress patterns and changes from noun to adjective, e.g. *Japan* /dʒəˈpæn/ and *Japanese* /ˌdʒæp.ənˈiːz/ and drill the words as necessary.

Look at the words in the box and ask students if the words are countries or nationalities (nationalities). Allow students to work in pairs to complete the dialogues. Check answers.

1 Italian, American
2 Spanish, Mexican
3 French, Chinese

READING
SB P9

1 Look at the pictures together and establish that they show one extended family. Ask students to guess the relationship between the people. You can start by saying, e.g. *I think this man is married to this woman.* Ask students to guess who Karl is.

Then ask students to read the text to check their answers (Karl is number 1). Allow students to work individually to write the names of the other people next to the numbers by reading the text again. Check answers, establishing if any of their initial guesses were correct.

1 Karl 2 Robert 3 Adam 4 Zadie
5 Adi   6 Lily   7 Marco 8 Leroy

2 Ask students to read the text again, if necessary, and in pairs to match the questions and answers. Check as a class.

1 b 2 c 3 a 4 f 5 d 6 e

FAST FINISHERS

Students can try to write one or two further questions about the text and ask their partner to answer them.

3 Focus students' attention on the question words in bold in Exercise 2. Look at the first question together and ask the class to answer, e.g. *When the question is 'Who…?'* (the answer is always a person). Then students do the rest of the exercise individually. Check answers together.

1 who   2 where   3 what   4 how old
5 whose 6 how many

⊕ EXTENSION

Tell students to close their books as they are going to play a memory game. Divide the class into two teams and tell them you are going to ask them questions to see what they can remember about Karl's family. Start with the questions in Exercise 2 and continue asking other similar questions about the family, e.g. *Who is Robert? He's Karl's father. How old is Leroy? He's 28, etc.* Teams can either nominate a student to write the answers down, or take turns to say the answer. Award one point for the correct answer and another point if they say/write it using a complete sentence.

➔ **GRAMMAR REFERENCE** / Page 197

VOCABULARY
SB P10

FAMILIES

WARMER

With books closed, elicit some names of different family members and write them on the board. For example, you could write *me* in the centre, then a line to *my mother* and ask students to help you complete the family tree as you write other lines leading to *grandmother, father, brother, aunt,* etc. Encourage students to ask questions about the people in your family. For example: *What's your mother's name? How old is your aunt? Where are your grandparents from?*

1 Look at the family tree on page 10 of the Student's Book together and ask students to read the texts below. As they read, encourage them to identify the position of the people described in the diagram. Students work in pairs to complete the sentences and then check together.

LANGUAGE NOTE

It may be helpful to focus on the difference between *grandchildren* (children of your children) and *nephews* and *nieces* (sons and daughters of your brothers/sisters) as in some languages the same word is used for both. Point out that there is no general term for *nephews* (male) and *nieces* (female) whereas *cousins* can be male or female.

The term *sibling* exists but is not appropriate for students at this level, so remind them to use *brothers* and *sisters* in the same way as *nieces* and *nephews*. *Parents* and *grandparents* can be used generically, but there is no equivalent in English for *uncles* and *aunts*. This is different in some other languages.

Relatives refers to all the members of a person's extended family (*cousins, grandparents, brothers, sisters,* etc.) whereas *parents* is used only for a person's mother and/or father. It is a false friend in some languages.

1 grandparents 2 nephew 3 uncle 4 nieces
5 aunt 6 cousins 7 granddaughter, grandson

2 With a stronger class, students may be able to do this exercise with the words in the box covered. They can then uncover and check before you give feedback to the class.

1 Mum 2 Dad 3 Grandma/Granny
4 Grandad/Grandpa

LANGUAGE NOTE

Students may have heard or seen *mom* or *mam* as alternatives to *mum*, which are generally used more commonly in the US and Ireland.

There is no difference between *grandma* and *granny* and some people also use *nana* (or *nanna*) or *nanny*. It depends on use within individual families. You could have a short discussion about whether there are similar terms in the students' language(s).

SB P10

HAVE GOT

LEAD-IN

Write a sentence on the board about yourself using *have got*, e.g. *I've got one brother and two cats, but I haven't got a dog*. Then try to elicit some similar sentences, first from two or three stronger students, then two or three weaker ones, using your sentence as a model.

Open books and look at the table together, pointing out the third person singular form.

1 A weaker group can do the exercise in pairs or work individually before feedback as a class.

> **1** 's **2** haven't **3** Have, I have **4** Has, has

→ **GRAMMAR REFERENCE** / Page 196

2 Draw students' attention to the question forms in the table and highlight that the two parts of the verb (*have got* / *has got*) are separated by the subject when making questions, e.g. *Have you got ...?* / *Has she got ...?*

Students complete the questions and after a quick check round the class they practise asking and answering them in pairs. Encourage students to use the complete short answers, *Yes, I have/No, I haven't*, rather than *Yes/No*, and where possible, to extend their answers using another sentence.

Use the first question to demonstrate the rule by asking three or four students for answers, trying to elicit, e.g. *Yes, I have. I've got one brother and two sisters*, or, *No, I haven't, but I have got a cat!*

FAST FINISHERS

Students can think of two or three more questions to ask their partner using *have got*.

> **1** Have, got **2** Has, got **3** has, got **4** has, got

SB P11

1 Ask students to cover the text and look at the photo and the questions. Brainstorm ideas and encourage students to speculate about where he's from and which languages he speaks. Write all the suggestions on the board.

2 Give students no more than a minute to read the text to find the answers. As a class, check whether any of the answers on the board were correct.

> He works at a dance school; He can speak English and Portuguese.

3 Ask students to read the questions below the text and choose the correct answer individually. Encourage students to compare their answers with a partner and point to the part of the text which explains why their answer is correct. Check as a class, again asking students to say reasons for their answers using the information in the text.

> **1** Porto **2** two languages **3** a dance teacher
> **4** two sisters **5** dance

GRAMMAR
SB P11

CAN

1 Direct students' attention to the three sentences from the text about Miguel above the Grammar box. Remind them that *can* is used here to talk about ability.

Highlight the two forms used for the negative (*can't* and *cannot*) which can be used interchangeably, and the question forms.

> **1** can **2** can't **3** Can **4** can't

→ **GRAMMAR REFERENCE** / Page 197

2 Students look at the examples in speech bubbles and then work in pairs to ask and answer questions. Encourage students to make questions about other people and if necessary provide an example such as, *Can your friend speak English?*

> **Suggested answers**
> Can your parents speak English? / Can your dad dance? / Can your teacher swim? / Can your brother/sister play tennis? / Can you cook?

PRESENT SIMPLE *HE/SHE/IT*
SB P11

LEAD-IN

Ask students some questions about Miguel to elicit sentences in the present simple. For example, *Where does he come from?* (*He comes from Porto.*); *Where does he live?* (*He lives in New York.*); *Where does he work?* (*He works in a dance school.*).

If they don't remember the answers, give them time to look back at the text. Then ask students some direct questions, e.g. *Where do you come from?* (*I come from Rome.*); *Where do you live?* (*I live in Milan.*). Write some of the answers on the board and highlight the *s* on the third person singular verb forms.

Then ask some more questions about Miguel to elicit the short answers, such as, *Does Miguel like living in New York?* (*Yes, he does.*); *Does he like his job?* (*Yes, he does.*); *Does he work in a shop?* (*No, he doesn't.*). Remind students of the use of *does* for third person singular questions and *doesn't* for negative sentences and short answers.

3 Allow students a few minutes to read the sentences and complete the examples in the box with the correct form of the verb *like* or an auxiliary verb. Check answers as a class.

> **1** likes **2** doesn't like **3** Does **4** like **5** does
> **6** doesn't

➡ GRAMMAR REFERENCE / Page 197

4 Ask students what they can guess from the picture without reading the information. If necessary, use questions to elicit ideas, e.g. *Where does she work? How old is she?*

Then write these words on the board: *computers, snakes, cooking, cars, bicycles, films, music, cats.* Ask students to guess whether Polly likes or dislikes these things after explaining any vocabulary they don't understand.

Give students two minutes to read the profile to check whether they were right.

Then students read more carefully to complete the sentences with the correct form of the verbs in the box.

Give students a few minutes to do the task and check answers in pairs before class feedback.

> **1** lives **2** comes **3** likes **4** works

5 In pairs students match the questions and answers. Check as a class.

> **1** c **2** a **3** b

6 Ask students to look back at the three Grammar boxes (*have got, can*, present simple) to remind themselves of the question forms before completing the questions with the verbs given. Students work individually to write questions and answers where required. Check as a class.

> **1** doesn't live **2** Can, speak, Yes, she can.
> **3** Has, got, Yes, she has.
> **4** does, work, She works at a pizza restaurant.
> **5** Does, like, Yes, she does. **6** doesn't like

LISTENING
SB P12

PERSONAL INFORMATION

WARMER

Ask three or four students to spell the name of someone they know while you write what they spell on the board. If they pronounce a letter incorrectly it is important that you write the *actual* letter they pronounce, or ask them to repeat it correctly in order to highlight when they make a mistake. Ask students if they know how many letters there are in the English alphabet (26) and if that is a different number to their own language.

1 Students work in pairs to read and say the alphabet and make a note of any letters they don't know how to pronounce.

2 003 Use the recording as a model for the pronunciation and drill any letters that students have difficulty pronouncing.

AUDIOSCRIPT 003

A B C D E F G H I J K L M N O P Q R S T U V W X Y Z

3 004 Write *UN* on the board and ask students to pronounce it (/ˌjuːˈen/). Remind students that they should pronounce the two letters separately.

Then ask if anyone knows what the letters stand for (United Nations). Students work in pairs to say the abbreviations and write what they think they stand for before listening to the recording to check their answers.

> **1** UK – United Kingdom **2** USA – United States of America **3** EU – European Union **4** DOB – date of birth **5** LOL – laugh out loud

AUDIOSCRIPT 004

1 UK (United Kingdom)
2 USA (United States of America)
3 EU (European Union)
4 DOB (date of birth)
5 LOL (laugh out loud)

⊕ EXTENSION

Ask students if they know any other abbreviations used in English. Some examples may include: ASAP (as soon as possible), FYI (for your information), VIP (very important person), BW (best wishes), BRB (be right back).

Read the *Did you know?* box with the class to highlight the difference between the American and British pronunciation of the letter 'z'.

With books closed write the title of the lesson (Personal information) on the board and ask students where they can find personal information about someone. Try to elicit *driving licence*, *passport* and *identity card*. Students may also suggest other documents such as a health card or a student card. Write all their suggestions on the board.

4 Students answer the questions in groups of three. If they have the document with them, allow them to show it to their partners and talk about the information in English. For example, *This is my date of birth. This is my photo, and this is my address*.

> **Suggested answer**
> Your first name, surname, address and date of birth

5 🎧 005 Direct students' attention to the photo at the bottom of the page and ask them where they think the people are. Listen to the recording to check answers.

> at a sports club

AUDIOSCRIPT 🎧 005

George: Hello, I'd like to become a member, please.
Woman: OK, that's no problem. Which sports are you interested in?
George: Tennis and swimming – and I'd also like to use the gym.
Woman: That's fine. Can I take some personal information? What's your name, please?
George: George Smithson.
Woman: How do you spell that?
George: George G-E-O-R-G-E and my surname is Smithson – S-M-I-T-H-S-O-N.
Woman: Could you spell your surname again, please?
George: Yes, it's Smithson – S-M-I-T-H-S-O-N.
Woman: Thank you, Mr Smithson.

6 🎧 005 Look at part 1 of the membership form and ask students what information they need to listen for to complete the gaps (a first name and a surname).

After listening to the recording again, students check answers in pairs.

Ask one student to spell the surname (Smithson) for the class.

> First name: George   Surname: Smithson

7 🎧 006 Tell students they are going to hear the same two people continuing their conversation.

Ask students to say what information they need to listen for to complete the form in part 2 (a date of birth (a day, a month and year), an address (a house number, road name, town and postcode), and a phone number).

Students compare answers with a partner before listening a second time to check or complete their answers. Then check as a class.

> **Date of birth:** 17 June 1995
> **Address:** 16 Redwood Road, New Town, NW4 8JG
> **Phone number:** 06819 772 3451

AUDIOSCRIPT 🎧 006

Woman: OK, could you tell me your date of birth, please?
George: Oh, yes. It's the 17th June, 1995.
Woman: The 17th June … 1995.
George: Yes, that's right.
Woman: Thank you. And now I just need your contact details. What's your address please?
George: It's sixteen – that's one six, Redwood Road R-E-D-W-O-O-D Road, New Town and the postcode is NW4 8JG.
Woman: NW4 8JG.
George: Yes, that's right.
Woman: OK and finally, what's your phone number?
George: It's 06819 772 3451.

8 Students work in pairs to complete the questions then check answers as a class.

> **1** name   **2** spell   **3** old   **4** date of birth
> **5** address   **6** phone number

9 Make sure students know how to ask for the spelling of a word they don't know, (*Can you spell that please?/How do you spell that?*) and remind students to ask for spellings if necessary. Other useful questions to elicit before students start are, *Can you repeat that please?* and *Sorry?* if they want something repeated.

FAST FINISHERS

Students can ask their partner some extra questions about a member of their partner's family. For example, *What's your father's name?*; *How old is your brother?*, etc.

SPEAKING
SB P13

PERSONAL INFORMATION

> **WARMER**
>
> Ask the class to count back from 30 or 40 depending on the size of the group, with each student saying the number before the previous student (30, 29, 28, etc.). You could set this up by counting from 33 to 31 and asking students to continue.
>
> Listen carefully to stress patterns of 30 /ˈθɜː.ti/ and 13 /θɜːˈtiːn/ and if necessary model the differences between 19 and 90, 18 and 80, etc.

1 Students ask and answer the questions in pairs but may need support with vocabulary. Allow them two or three minutes to answer the questions, then feedback by eliciting as much information as possible about the people in the photos. Take the opportunity to revise nationalities asking, *What's his/her nationality?* (American, Mexican, British). Ask, *What's his/her job?* If necessary teach vocabulary such as *tennis player*, *champion*, *singer*, *actor*, *actress*.

> Beyoncé, famous singer and songwriter. USA
> Diego Boneta, famous actor and singer. Mexican-American
> Millie Bobby Brown, actress, England

2 007 Give students a minute to look at the dates of birth and check they know how to pronounce them (the fourth of September, nineteen eighty-one). In pairs, students guess which person the dates match to, then play the recording to check answers.

> **1** Beyoncé: 4 September 1981
> **2** Diego Boneta: 29 November 1990
> **3** Millie Bobby Brown: 19 February 2004

AUDIOSCRIPT 007

Beyoncé is a very famous American singer. She was born on the 4th September 1981 in Houston. Beyoncé has got two daughters and a son.
Diego Boneta is Mexican-American. He's an actor, but he can also sing. He was born in Mexico City on 29 November 1990. He's got a brother and a sister.
Millie Bobby Brown is a young British actress. She was born on the 19th February 2004 in Marbella. She's got a brother and two sisters.

3 Write a date on the board and ask a student to read it out using the correct pronunciation. Then model the task by encouraging students to ask you questions about the date starting with the example questions in the Student's Book until the students guess the significance of the date. While students do the exercise in pairs, move around the classroom checking question forms and pronunciation.

WRITING
SB P13

A PROFILE

1 Brainstorm information students can remember about Miguel (page 11), as a class. Then, students complete as much of the form as they can before looking back at the original text to check and complete their answers.

> **Name:** Miguel
> **Likes:** New York and his job
> **Lives:** New York
> **Age:** 30
> **Family:** his parents and two sisters
> **Is from:** Porto
> **Languages:** English and Portuguese
> **Things he can do:** dance, speak English and Portuguese

2 Students can work individually or in pairs to brainstorm ideas for a person to write a profile about. They don't have to choose the same person. If you have internet access, students could use it to find information about their choice in the classroom. Alternatively, they could choose a person they know or already know about.

3 The writing task can be done in the classroom or at home. Encourage students to look at the text about Miguel as a model and revise the language in the grammar and vocabulary sections of the unit. The finished texts could be presented with a photo and displayed in the classroom, or some students could read their texts to the class.

> **⊕ EXTENSION**
>
> Students could complete another table similar to Exercise 1 without writing the name of the person. Other students can then practise question forms by asking for the information, e.g. *Where does he/she live?; What languages does he/she speak?; How old is he/she?*, etc. Then students can guess who is being described.

→ **WORKBOOK** / Starter Unit, page 4

1 A BUSY LIFE

UNIT OBJECTIVES

Topic:	daily life
Grammar:	present simple; question forms; adverbs of frequency
Vocabulary:	things I do; jobs; applying for a job
Listening:	Part 1: choosing the correct picture with short dialogues; routines
Reading:	Part 2: multiple-choice questions about night jobs
Speaking:	asking questions about people
Writing:	an email about a job
Pronunciation:	pronouncing times
Exam focus:	Reading Part 2; Listening Part 1
Real world:	talking about yourself in Mexico City

Ask your students to watch the Grammar on the Move videos on pages 16 and 19. You can use these to present or reinforce the present simple and adverbs of frequency.

SB P14

THINGS I DO

LEAD-IN

With books closed ask the question, *What do you do in your free time?* to brainstorm activities. Write students' suggestions on the board. Help students with vocabulary as necessary, and try to elicit some of the activities from the book by asking additional questions such as, *Who do you spend your free time with?*; *Where do you go?*

1 Draw students' attention to the photos A–F in the Student's Book and ask them to work in pairs to answer the questions about a perfect day.

Ask two or three students to tell the class about their perfect day.

2 Students match the activities in the box with the photos on the page. Remind them to use each activity only once. Students check answers in pairs before checking as a class.

A spend time alone	B spend time with friends
C play video games	D relax at home
E go shopping	F play or watch sport

3 🎧 008 Read the instructions, as a class, and make sure students understand that they will hear four short monologues. Play the first recording (Speaker 1).

Check answers as a class.

Once this has been completed, ask students to match the pictures as they listen to the other recordings. Repeat if necessary. Check as a class.

Speaker 1: B;   Speaker 2: F;   Speaker 3: A;
Speaker 4: C

AUDIOSCRIPT 🎧 008

Narrator: Speaker 1
Woman 1: My perfect day …? Well, on my perfect day, I spend time with my friends. We go to the beach and swim, talk and have fun. We probably go home at about half past seven.
Narrator: Speaker 2
Boy: For me, a perfect day is about sport. I meet my friends at the park when it opens at quarter past eight and we play basketball. When we get tired, we watch sport on TV and eat ice cream.
Narrator: Speaker 3
Man: My perfect day is when I can spend time alone. I like getting up early and going for a long walk in the countryside. I can walk for 15 or 20 kilometres in the fresh air. Perfect!
Narrator: Speaker 4
Woman 2: For me, a perfect day is playing video games for hours with my friends. We play all day and stop at about half past nine in the evening to go for a pizza.

4 🎧 008 Read the questions as a class, checking understanding as necessary. A stronger group could try to answer the questions before they listen to the recording again to check their answers. Otherwise, students listen again and try to answer the questions as they listen. Then check answers in pairs before checking as a class. With a weaker class it may be necessary to play one or more recordings more than twice.

1 at the beach
2 They watch sport on TV and eat ice cream.
3 going for a long walk alone
4 go out for a pizza

5 Look at the photos in Exercise 2 again, and provide students with an example by telling them something about yourself. For example, *I go shopping on Saturdays. I usually go to clothes shops and bookshops.*

Students then work in pairs to answer the questions. A stronger group can try to add an extra sentence, giving more detail as in the example above. If necessary, write some time expressions on the board to help students talk about when they do the activities. For example, *on Monday, Tuesday, at the weekend.* Point out that we use *on* before days of the week but *at the* before *weekend*. Remind students that *on Saturdays* means *every Saturday* whereas *on Saturday* refers to Saturday *this week*. Ask four or five students to tell the class about the activities they do.

16

FAST FINISHERS

Students can add some more sentences about other activities they do. Encourage them to say where and when they do them and if they are alone or with friends or family.

⊕ EXTENSION

The task can be extended by encouraging students to talk about other activities they do at different times of the year, using *in the spring/summer/autumn/winter*. For example, *I go skiing in the winter.*

ROUTINES

1 If necessary, revise the time in English by writing several examples on the board and asking students, *What's the time?* Students work in pairs to match the times with the clocks. Check answers.

CULTURAL INFORMATION

In most English-speaking countries, the 12-hour clock is used in most situations. When it is necessary to specify, people say *8 am* or *8 pm* or *10.30 in the morning* or *evening*. However, the 24-hour clock is always used for plane, bus and train timetables.

> 1 one o'clock   2 half past nine
> 3 quarter past eight   4 quarter to six

2 🔊 009 With books closed, tell students they are going to listen to *times*. Play the first recording and have students repeat as a class. It helps students focus on the sounds if they do not read the words on the page and become distracted by the spelling. Drill chorally and individually if necessary. Play the second recording and ask students to repeat as a class, then ask three or four students to repeat the time individually. Continue in this way for the other recordings. Repeat the recordings as necessary.

AUDIOSCRIPT 🔊 009

at half past six
at half past two
at quarter to four
at quarter to seven
at quarter past nine
at quarter past eleven

3 🔊 009 Ask students to open their books and read the questions. Play the recordings again. Students read the times and listen to answer the questions. Students compare answers in pairs before checking as a class.

> **1** at **half** past **six**
> at **half** past **two**
> at **qua**rter to **four**
> at **qua**rter to **sev**en
> at **qua**rter past **nine**
> at **qua**rter past e**lev**en
> **2** the /l/ is silent
> **3** They are both pronounced /ə/ (like the final sound in *America* or *teacher*)

⊕ EXTENSION

Encourage students to take turns reading the times in exercises 1 and 2 aloud to a partner, remembering to apply the pronunciation rules. Move around the class listening and checking.

4 Read the questions and then give an example answer for yourself, e.g. *I am in the car at 8:00 in the morning.* Then ask one or two students to say where they are at 8:00 to check understanding of the task. Students then work in pairs to answer the questions.

5 🔊 010 Tell students they will hear Amy describing her typical day. Encourage students to read the questions before listening to the recording. Remind students to continue listening even if they don't catch the answer to a question. After listening, students compare their answers with a partner before repeating the recording (if required) and checking as a class.

> **1** She's a teacher.
> **2** She's a police officer.
> **3** They live in a small village.

AUDIOSCRIPT 🔊 010

Interviewer: So, Amy, what job do you do?
Amy: I'm a teacher.
Interviewer: Can you tell me about your day? What time do you get up?
Amy: I usually wake up at quarter past seven, but I don't get up! I always stay in bed until half past seven and then I get up! Then I have breakfast with my sister, Olivia. She's a police officer, and we live together.
Interviewer: What do you have for breakfast?
Amy: I usually have toast and Olivia has cereal. We both drink coffee for breakfast. We don't like tea. After breakfast, I have a shower and get dressed. Then I get my bag, put on my coat and leave the house to go to work.
Interviewer: How do you get to work?
Amy: By bus. We live in a small village and it's the quickest way to get into town.
Interviewer: How does Olivia get to work? Does she go by bus, too?
Amy: No, she doesn't catch the bus. She goes by car.

6 🔊 011 Encourage students to read the statements in pairs and to ask you for help with any words they don't understand, before listening to the recording again. Remind students that the information is in the same order as the statements, so if they miss an answer they should continue listening. If necessary, the recording – or parts of it – can be repeated. On the second listening, ask students to listen for the reason why the false statements are false.

> **1** F She wakes up at 7.15. **2** T **3** T **4** F Lessons start at nine o'clock. **5** T **6** T **7** F She sometimes watches TV.

AUDIOSCRIPT 🔊 011

Interviewer: So, Amy, what job do you do?
Amy: I'm a teacher.
Interviewer: Can you tell me about your day? What time do you get up?
Amy: I usually wake up at quarter past seven, but I don't get up! I always stay in bed until half past seven and then I get up! Then I have breakfast with my sister, Olivia. She's a police officer, and we live together.
Interviewer: What do you have for breakfast?
Amy: I usually have toast and Olivia has cereal. We both drink coffee for breakfast. We don't like tea. After breakfast, I have a shower and get dressed. Then I get my bag, put on my coat and leave the house to go to work.
Interviewer: How do you get to work?
Amy: By bus. We live in a small village and it's the quickest way to get into town.
Interviewer: How does Olivia get to work? Does she go by bus, too?
Amy: No, she doesn't catch the bus. She goes by car.
Interviewer: So, Amy, can you tell me about your day at work?
Amy: I arrive at work at quarter to nine. Lessons start at nine o'clock and lunch is at half past twelve.
Interviewer: Where do you have lunch? Do you have lunch at college?
Amy: No, I don't. I have lunch in a café. Sometimes, if it's a nice day, we buy sandwiches and go to the park.
Interviewer: Who do you have lunch with?
Amy: I often have lunch with some of the other teachers from college, but I like having lunch alone sometimes. In the afternoon, lessons finish at half past three. I do some work and get the bus back. I usually get home at about quarter past five.
Interviewer: What do you do when you get home?
Amy: I take off my work clothes and put on my jeans and go outside for some fresh air! I take my dog for a walk and when we get home, I have dinner. Then I sometimes watch TV.
Interviewer: And when do you go to bed?
Amy: I usually go to bed at about half past ten.

7 Ask students to complete the sentences, then check their answers in pairs.

> **1** get dressed **2** take off **3** get on **4** wake up
> **5** put on **6** get up

FAST FINISHERS

Students can write sentences about themselves using some of the verbs from Exercise 7.

BEFORE AND AFTER

Read the sentences with the class and ensure that the meanings of the two terms are understood completely.

⊕ EXTENSION

Brainstorm vocabulary for other things that students do every day. For example, *have a shower/bath, clean my teeth, catch a train/bus*, etc. Help students with any vocabulary they don't know. Students work in pairs to talk about their day. Encourage them to use complete sentences and *before* and *after*. Ask two or three students to repeat their answers to the class.

GRAMMAR

SB P16

PRESENT SIMPLE

WARMER

With books closed, write some sentences on the board using the present simple. For example, *I usually wake up at 8.00 on Sundays, but my brother always wakes up at 7.30.*; *Julie goes to the cinema on Saturday evenings, but she doesn't like watching TV.* Ask the students questions about the present simple, e.g. *When do we add -s or -es to the main verb? How do we make the negative, questions and short answers?*

1 Open books and check answers by looking at the Grammar box. Encourage students to read the example sentences and give them two or three minutes to choose the correct options to complete the rules.

> **1** regularly **2** always true

➡ **GRAMMAR REFERENCE** / *Page 198*

2 Ask students to look at the picture and tell you what they can see. Try to elicit *police officer* and if necessary explain that a police officer can describe a man and/or a woman in the police force. Give students five or six minutes to choose the correct options in the text and then check answers in pairs. Check answers as a class.

> **1** don't **2** get up **3** meet **4** doesn't **5** feels
> **6** have **7** go **8** don't

3 Remind students that they may have to use question and short answer forms to fill the gaps in the sentences. Point out that three of the verbs will be in the negative. Students work in pairs to do the exercise and then check answers as a class.

> 1 doesn't get dressed   2 has, doesn't eat   3 walks
> 4 Do, go, catch   5 don't write

4 Read the instructions together and, if necessary, give an example to make sure students understand the task, e.g. *I go to work during the week, but I stay at home at the weekend.* Encourage students to give more than one example.

With a weaker group it may be helpful to brainstorm ideas and vocabulary on the board for things they do during the week and things they do at the weekend before asking them to tell their partner about themselves.

With a stronger group, students could then be asked to make new pairs and tell their new partner about their previous partner, using the third person, e.g. *Julio goes to football training during the week, but he plays a match at the weekend.*

QUESTION FORMS

LEAD-IN

With books closed, write the possible answers to the example questions on the board, e.g. *at half past seven, by car, in a café*. Encourage students to tell you which question word we use for each answer (*What time/When, How, Where*).

Brainstorm other question words students know, and add them to the list on the board with example answers (*Who…? Maria… Why…? because…*).

5 Then open books and read the example questions and answers. Ask students to focus on the questions to answer 1 and 2 in the box.

> 1 does   2 How/What

➡ **GRAMMAR REFERENCE** / Page 198

6 Students work in pairs to match the questions and answers. Check as a class by asking one student to read each question and another student to read the corresponding answer.

> 1 e   2 f   3 b   4 a   5 c   6 d

7 Look at the picture with the students and ask them some questions about it, e.g. *What's his name? How old is he? What job does he do?*, etc.

With a weaker class try to elicit the first question, *What job does he do?* and write it on the board before having students complete the other questions about Sergio.

Remind students to use the third person form and check the word order in questions. Check answers as a class.

> 1 What job does he do?   2 Where does he study?
> 3 Where does he live?   4 Who does he live with?
> 5 How does he get to work?   6 What time does he start and finish work?   7 What does he do in the evening?   8 Why does he like his job?

SPEAKING
SB P17

WHAT YOU DO AND WHAT YOU LIKE

1  012 Read the instruction together and encourage students to read the sentences and try to predict which words fill the gaps.

Write all the suggestions on the board. Play the recording and ask students to listen for the answers. Check answers together.

If they are on the board, underline any answers to show students that trying to predict answers can be a useful skill. Remind them that they should try to predict answers when reading through the questions before listening in the exam.

> 1 watching, listening   2 studying, walking

AUDIOSCRIPT 🔊 012

Interviewer:	So, Sergio, what do you like doing in the evening?
Sergio:	I like watching TV and I love listening to music.
Interviewer:	And what don't you like doing?
Sergio:	I don't like studying for my job in the evenings. And I hate walking.

2 Ask students to complete the rule in the box. Check as a class.

> -ing

3 Encourage students to read the whole text first and ask you for help with any vocabulary they don't understand. Then students work individually to complete the text. Remind them to use the correct form of the verbs.

> 1 staying   2 listening to   3 having   4 meeting
> 5 dancing   6 playing   7 watching   8 shopping

4 Remind students to talk about what they don't like as well as what they like or love.

5 Ask students to use the questions in the speech bubbles to interview a partner. Then exchange roles.

Encourage students to ask some other questions using the ideas in Exercise 5. Remind students to change the questions to the first person, and to use complete sentences in their answers.

UNIT 1   A BUSY LIFE   **19**

With a weaker group, it may be necessary to transform the questions in Exercise 5 from third person to first person as a class before starting.

⊕ EXTENSION

Students work with another partner to report the information they learned about their first partner. Remind them to use the third person form of the verb.

6 Look at the photos with the students and elicit answers to the questions.

> **A** in a garden, a gardener
> **B** on an oil rig, a mechanic

7 Tell students they are going to read some more information about each of the people in Exercise 7. Divide the class into groups, A and B and tell student As to turn to page 192 and student Bs to turn to page 194.

With a weaker group:

- Ask students to pair up with another student who has the same letter (A+A and B+B).
- Students work together to complete the questions for their text using the question words given. Remind them to use information in the Grammar box to help with question forms (5–6 mins).
- Students read the text about the other person. Allow time for them to check vocabulary they don't understand with you (2–3 mins).
- Finally, students pair up with another student, this time someone who was working on the other text (A+B) and they take turns to ask the questions in order to complete the gaps in their own text (7–8 mins).

With a stronger group:

- Give students time to read the two texts and think about possible questions.
- Students can then pair up with another student (A+B) and take it in turns to ask questions in order to complete the gaps in their text.

NB: It's important that students don't read their partner's text, so it may be helpful to remind students of expressions such as, *Can you repeat that please?*; *Can you speak more slowly please?*; *Can you spell that please?*

> Karen
> **1** 7.00 am   **2** big, old house in her village
> **3** a cup of tea and a sandwich   **4** eats her breakfast
> **5** she works in the garden   **6** 2.00 pm   **7** the owner of the garden   **8** 5.00 pm
> Roman
> **1** in the Gulf of Mexico   **2** for a week   **3** 10.00 pm
> **4** the gym   **5** table tennis   **6** his friend Pepe
> **7** it's very cold on the oil rig   **8** 9.45 pm

READING PART 2 TRAINING
SB P18

✓ EXAM INFORMATION

Part 2 of the Reading paper is a matching task. Students have to read three short texts on the same topic and answer seven questions by choosing the correct option. The task in the Student's Book is simplified with six questions instead of seven. This section teaches students that they have to read for specific information and detailed comprehension. Students should allow about ten minutes to do Part 2 in the exam.

1 Ask students to answer the questions and write the good and bad things they suggest on the board. This language may be useful for Exercise 4.

2 In pairs, students match the jobs with the pictures, then read the texts quickly to check their answers. Tell students they don't have to understand every word at this point.

> **A** the nurse   **B** the nightclub DJ   **C** the security guard

3 Read question 1 as a class and point out that the question is negative (*Which person **doesn't** always work …*).

Ask students to read the texts again to find information to answer the question. In pairs, students choose the correct answer and say why.

Then read the exam tip as a class to check answers. Students then read the other questions and answer them in the same way. A stronger class can be encouraged to say why the other two answers are not correct.

Check answers as a class and ask students to say why they chose the answer they did.

> **1** C Pablo   **2** B Tobi   **3** B Tobi   **4** A Bridget
> **5** C Pablo   **6** A Bridget

4 Brainstorm other jobs and write them on the board. Then ask students to work in pairs to discuss the questions.

GRAMMAR
SB P19

ADVERBS OF FREQUENCY

1 Read the example sentences as a class, and ask students to choose the correct options in the summary. Check answers.

> **1** before   **2** after   **3** between

➡ **GRAMMAR REFERENCE** / Page 199

2 Encourage students to look at the Grammar box showing the adverbs of frequency before they complete the sentences in pairs. Remind students of the rules about the position of adverbs in a sentence and to think about the differences in meaning. Check answers.

> 1 sometimes 2 never 3 always
> 4 usually/often 5 often/usually

3 With a weaker group, students can look back at the free-time activities on page 14, before completing the sentences about themselves. Then students read their sentences to a partner.

ONCE/TWICE A ...

4 Ask one student to role play the part of Tobi and another student, the interviewer, and read the interview to the rest of the class.

Then read the rules as a class and ask students to complete the gaps.

Check answers and if necessary model the pronunciation of *once* (/wʌns/).

> 1 once 2 twice

5 Elicit the first question from the class and write it on the board as a model, (*How often do you go running?*).

Then highlight the example answers in the speech bubbles. Read the information in the box and remind students they can use adverbs of frequency, *once a*, *twice a*, etc.

Ask two or three students to answer the question as a model for the class, then put students in pairs to ask and answer the questions.

With a stronger group, encourage students to extend their answers to say why or to give a little more information.

Move around the class helping with vocabulary as necessary.

At the end of the activity write all the new vocabulary on the board for the whole class to check and note down if it is new.

FAST FINISHERS

Students can ask each other some more 'how often' questions using their own ideas. They can then report back the extra information they found to the class at the end of the activity.

SB P19

JOBS

LEAD-IN

With books closed, brainstorm names of jobs on the board. If possible, try to elicit the jobs in Exercise 1 using questions such as, *Who takes photographs? Who flies planes?*

Focus on pronunciation when students give you the answers, modelling the correct sounds if necessary.

Point out the stress pattern in *photographer* (/fəˈtɒg.rə.fər/) and the vowel sound in *pilot* (/ˈpaɪ.lət/).

Leave the names on the board as they may be useful for the Extension task after Exercise 2.

1 🔊 013 Ask students to look at the pictures and tell them they will hear the people talking about their jobs. Students write a number next to each photo in the order of the recordings.

Repeat the recording if necessary to check answers.

> 1 photographer D 2 police officer C
> 3 mechanic A 4 pilot B

AUDIOSCRIPT 🔊 013

1
Man 1: I'm a photographer. My job is taking interesting photographs of things, places and people.
2
Man 2: I'm a police officer. My job is to keep people safe. I work in a police station.
3
Woman 1: In my job, I repair machines, like cars, when they go wrong – or I try to! I'm a mechanic.
4
Woman 2: I'm a pilot. My job is to fly planes. I work for an airline.

2 Students complete the sentences using the jobs from the box in Exercise 1. Check answers as a class.

> 1 mechanic 2 photographer 3 pilot
> 4 police officer

⊕ EXTENSION

With a stronger group, students can work in pairs to write short sentences similar to those in Exercise 2 for the other jobs which were suggested at the start of the lesson.

Then they read their sentences to another pair without saying the name of the job (*An X repairs cars*).

The other pair has to guess the job.

UNIT 1 A BUSY LIFE

PUSH YOURSELF — B1

SB P20

VOCABULARY: APPLYING FOR A JOB

1 Students read the text and then work in pairs to match the two parts of the definitions. Point out that it is helpful to read the words before and after the word being defined to try to understand the meaning.

Check answers as a class by asking students to read out the complete definitions.

| **1** f | **2** d | **3** a | **4** b | **5** c | **6** e |

LISTENING PART 1 TRAINING

SB P20

✓ EXAM INFORMATION

In Part 1 of the Listening paper students hear five short recordings. Students have to choose the correct answer A, B or C from the three visual options which are provided. Students also hear an example. Students need to listen to identify key information. In the exam they hear each recording twice.

This section in the Student's Book teaches students to focus on and underline important information in the question before they listen. The task in the Student's Book is simplified with only three questions.

1 Read the questions to the class and invite a class discussion on what is important in a job and why. Try to elicit ideas from the class, but if necessary the following can be written on the board to help generate discussion: *money, holidays and free time, working with people, travelling for your job, using technology, helping people*.

Help students with any vocabulary they do not know.

Read the *Did you know?* box with the class. Model the different pronunciations of *clerk* in American (/klɜːk/) and British (/klɑːk/) English.

Point out that in British English a clerk works in an office.

2 🔊 014 Read the instructions together to highlight that students need to read the instructions carefully, underlining the important part of the question as shown here (*when she finishes her studies*). This helps focus on exactly what information they are listening for.

Ask students to identify the jobs in the pictures before they listen to the example recording (A – nurse, B – teacher, C – DJ). Then play the recording. Ask students if they can tell you the correct answer before reading the explanation in the book. If necessary, repeat the recording.

AUDIOSCRIPT 🔊 014

Narrator:	One. What job does the woman want to do when she finishes her studies?
Interviewer:	You're studying to be a nurse, aren't you?
Student:	Yes, but I've decided that's not the job I want. After my course ends, I want to become a DJ.
Interviewer:	Wow! Are your parents OK about that?
Student:	Well, they're a bit worried but I've told them I'll become a teacher if I can't make any money as a DJ, and they're happy with that.

3 🔊 015 Ask students to read the instructions for questions 2 and 3 and underline the important information. Students can compare what they have underlined, in pairs, and describe what they can see in the pictures to their partner. Compare ideas as a class before playing the recording.

Suggested answers
2 do first when he gets home
3 what time … get up

Remind students they may hear two or three of the pictures mentioned in the recording, but only one will be the answer to the question. Repeat the recording as necessary.

Check answers as a class. With a stronger group, students can try to say why the other pictures are wrong.

| **2** B | **3** C |

AUDIOSCRIPT 🔊 015

Narrator:	Two. What does the police officer do first when he gets home from work?
Interviewer:	Now, you're a police officer. What do you do when you get home from work? Do you have something to eat?
Police officer:	I usually have a sandwich in my afternoon break, so I'm not hungry when I get home. I go and read in the garden.
Interviewer:	Don't you eat any dinner?
Police officer:	Yes, but I cook dinner later. And then I watch TV for a while before I go to bed.
Narrator:	Three. What time does the man get up in the morning?
Interviewer:	You're a DJ on an early morning radio programme, aren't you? What time do you have to get up in the morning?
DJ:	Well, I wake up at quarter to four most days.
Interviewer:	That IS early. Is that difficult?
DJ:	Yes, but I then have a coffee in bed at four and I don't usually get out of bed until quarter past four. Then I have a shower and get dressed.

WRITING

SB P21

AN EMAIL ABOUT A JOB

LEAD-IN

With books closed, brainstorm different ways of communicating with people. If necessary write *text message*, *audio message*, *video call*, *phone call*, *postcard*, *letter*, *email* on the board.

1 Encourage students to answer the questions in a class discussion.

2 Tell students they are going to read an email from Tori, the woman in the picture, to her friend. Ask students to predict what she may write in the email. Accept any suggestions and help with vocabulary as necessary. Students read the email to see if their predictions were accurate and to answer the questions.

> She's a waitress. She likes talking to customers.

3 Ask students to look at the email again and underline the words and phrases used at the start and end of the email. Point out that this is an email to a friend, so the expressions can be used in informal emails. Students write the expressions in the correct position in the box.

> Expressions for beginning an email: Hi, How are you?
> Expressions for ending an email: Love, Write soon!

4 Make sure that students understand the instructions by asking some questions, e.g. *What job do you do? I'm a shop assistant. When do you work? At weekends. What do you like about the job?*, etc. Tell students to choose a job they would like to do in the future. They can choose computer programmer or any other job and should complete the table with notes. This does not have to be true; students can invent the information.

5 Encourage students to look back at Tori's email and tell you what information is included in each paragraph before they read the email plan.

Explain that it is important to use paragraphs when writing in English, and that each paragraph should contain information on one topic as shown in the plan.

Students can then write their email using the notes in the table (Exercise 4) and the plan.

Remind them also to use the language for starting and finishing the email from Exercise 3.

As they are writing, move around the class to help with vocabulary as necessary.

Allow students to exchange emails with a partner when they have finished writing to check each other's work.

They should make sure their partner has answered all the questions, used paragraphs as suggested in the plan and hasn't made spelling or grammar mistakes.

If necessary, you can write a checklist on the board which students can copy down and use every time they do a piece of writing to check their own work:

Did I answer all the questions?
Did I use paragraphs?
Did I use correct spelling?
Did I use correct grammar?
Did I use the right words to start and finish the email?

> **Suggested answer**
> Dear Tori,
> Thanks for your email. I'm fine thanks!
> Let me tell you about my job. I work as a shop assistant in a games store at the weekends. I work from 9 am to 5 pm. I wear a uniform and I work with the other shop assistants and the shop manager. I like playing the new games, but I don't get a lot of money.
> In the future I want to go to university because I want to be a computer programmer. I love computers and I want to work in an office with other people who love computers.
> What do you do at the weekends when you're not working? Do you like playing computer games? I like going to the cinema. What about you?
> Write soon!
> Best wishes,
> Mario

EXAM FOCUS

SB P22

READING PART 2

Read through the Exam facts and tips boxes carefully with the class. Remind students that they have 60 minutes to answer 30 reading questions and two writing questions in the exam. They can divide the time as they wish but a suggestion could be 1.5 minutes to answer each reading question, then five minutes and ten minutes for the two writing tasks.

Tell students that they have just over ten minutes to complete Part 2 of the Reading exam. Encourage them to read the questions through carefully before looking at the texts and underlining the important words.

Set the task under exam conditions and when 10 or 11 minutes are up, go through the answers with the class.

Ask students to explain which words or phrases in the texts gave them the answers.

> **1** C   **2** A   **3** B   **4** C   **5** B   **6** A   **7** C

UNIT 1 · A BUSY LIFE

LISTENING PART 1

SB P23

Read through the Exam facts and tips boxes with the class. Remind students that they can underline the important words in the questions before they listen. They should also look at the pictures and think about the words that can be used to describe them. They have a few seconds before listening to each recording. They should try to choose an answer the first time they listen and then listen again to check their answers.

Tell students they are going to do the listening under exam conditions, i.e. without conferring with a partner. Allow a few seconds for students to look at the first question. Then play the recording.

Elicit answers around the class.

| 1 B | 2 A | 3 A | 4 C | 5 C |

AUDIOSCRIPT 016

Narrator: For each question, choose the correct answer. One. What time does the man start work?
Woman: How's your new job, Luca? Do you have to start at seven in the morning, as you did before?
Man: That's one of the things I like about this job – the shop opens at half past nine.
Woman: Great! But you have to arrive before then, don't you?
Man: Oh yes. I'm there from nine, but that's much better than seven!
Narrator: Two. Where did the woman go with her friend?
Man: Did you see that film you wanted to see yesterday, with your friend Sara?
Woman: There weren't any seats left when we got to the cinema. Sara works in a restaurant, and she finished work late.
Man: Oh, that's a pity. So what did you do?
Woman: We just walked around the centre of town, chatting, until it was time to come home.
Narrator: Three. How should the man contact Eva?
Man: Do you know how I can contact Eva? I've called her several times this morning, but she never answers.
Woman: She's not good at answering calls. I send her emails. She checks those on her phone when she's working.
Man: OK, I'll try that. I thought about going to her office.
Woman: She's not always there. Sometimes she goes out to meet customers.
Narrator: Four. What does the man need to buy?
Man: I'm going to the supermarket later. Shall I get some bread? I don't think we've got much.
Woman: I got that this morning at the shop on the corner. I wanted some fruit as well, but they didn't have any.
Man: I'll get some then. And what about some fish, for dinner?
Woman: We're going out for dinner tonight. Have you forgotten?
Narrator: Five. Why was the woman late for work?
Woman: I'm really sorry I'm late.
Man: Don't worry, it's only a few minutes. Was the traffic bad this morning?
Woman: Actually, it was fine, but I couldn't start my car. I tried to get a taxi, but there weren't any, so I had to wait for a bus.
Man: Oh, well let me know if you need a lift tomorrow.

Finally, read through the options in the *How was it?* section and elicit the meaning of each one: *gave it a go* (I tried hard but didn't feel it went particularly well); *getting there* (I'm improving but I'm not perfect yet) *aced it* (I feel I did really well). Ask students to tick the appropriate box.

You might like to ask students to share how they felt about the task to get an indication of your students' confidence. Depending on your class, you might like to do this openly or allow students to give their feedback without their classmates seeing. For example, give students a piece of A4 paper each with the *How was it?* scale written in large letters. Allow students to tick the relevant box then hold up their papers at the same time so that you can see how well students think they are doing.

REAL WORLD

SB P24

TALKING ABOUT YOURSELF IN ... MEXICO CITY

> ### WARMER
> Ask students to brainstorm a list of things they know about Mexico in groups. Set a time limit of two minutes. The team with the most ideas, wins.

1 Direct students' attention to the photos of Mexico City and give them a few moments to look at the different aspects of the city, then elicit brief descriptions of them, supplying vocabulary as necessary.

Ask if students know anything else about Mexico City and make notes of useful vocabulary on the board for students to copy down.

Elicit suggestions about what life for a typical Mexican family might be like. If appropriate, you could ask what differences students think there might be between life in their home town and life in Mexico City as shown in the photos.

> ### CULTURAL INFORMATION
> Mexico City is one of the largest cities in the world, with a population of nine million people. It is located at an altitude of over 2,000 metres and is surrounded by mountains on three sides. It has a rich cultural heritage and has preserved many of its historical monuments and architecture while embracing modernity.
>
> Teotihuacán, also known as the City of the Gods, is a UNESCO World Heritage Site about 50 km from Mexico City. It is the most important and largest city of pre-Aztec central Mexico. It is famous for its well-preserved murals, the two-kilometre Avenue of the Dead and the pyramids.

2 Ask if anyone in the class has experienced a homestay. If so, encourage them to tell the class where they went and when. If not, briefly explain that homestay involves living with a host family in their home.

Students discuss the questions in pairs for two or three minutes and then feed back to the class. Note down the suggestions on the board. Then students read the text to see if any of the suggestions are mentioned.

3 Tell students they are going to read some information about host families in Mexico City. Read through the questions with the class, helping with vocabulary if necessary. Students work in pairs to find the answers. Feed back as a class by asking students to read the words in the texts which gave them the answers.

| 1 D | 2 C | 3 B | 4 A |

4 Students work in pairs to do the exercise then feed back as a class.

| 1 b | 2 a | 3 b | 4 a | 5 a | 6 b |

5 017 Tell students they are going to listen to three conversations with a student in different places in the city. With a weaker class try to elicit some suggestions about the type of conversation they might hear in each of the places. For example, at a party: a conversation about food, drink, music or preferences, or at an airport: a conversation about luggage, security or travel arrangements, etc.

Then play the conversations and ask students to identify the places. Ask students to tell you some of the words which helped them decide.

| 1 b | 2 d | 3 a |

AUDIOSCRIPT 🔊 017

1
Official: Passport, please. Thank you. What's the purpose of your visit?
Student: I'm here for a holiday and also to learn Spanish.
Official: How long are you planning to be in the country?
Student: I'll be here for five weeks.
Official: OK. When do you fly back?
Student: I'm flying home on the 28th of August.
Official: And where are you staying?
Student: I'm staying with a family in Mexico City.

2
Maria: Hello. You must be Charlie. Welcome to Mexico City.
Student: Thanks.
Maria: Come in. I'm Maria, and this is my husband, Raul.
Student: Pleased to meet you.
Maria: And you. You'll meet our children later, but they're at school at the moment.
Raul: Here, let me take your bags for you. So, how was your flight?
Student: Fine, thanks. No delays.
Maria: Good. Come in and sit down.
Student: Thanks.
Maria: So, you're from the UK?
Student: Yes. I live in Harrow.
Maria: And do you come from a big family?
Student: No. I've got one brother. I'm the oldest.
Raul: That's nice. And is this your first time in Mexico?
Student: Yes. I'm very excited to be here.
Maria: That's perfect. Now, before I show you your room, I'd just like to ask you a few questions. First, about food. Is there anything you don't eat?
Student: No, I like everything.
Maria: Good. Do you have any food allergies? Any foods that make you ill?
Student: No, I'm not allergic to anything.
Maria: That's nice and easy. We usually eat at around 8 o'clock in the evening. Is that convenient for you?
Student: Yes, that's fine for me.

3
Girl: Hi. I'm Eva.
Student: Hi, Eva. I'm Charlie. Nice to meet you.
Girl: Nice to meet you too. Where are you from?
Student: I'm from Harrow, in the UK. I'm staying with Maria and Raul for a few weeks.
Girl: Cool. I'd love to visit the UK one day. What do you do?
Student: I'm a student. I'm studying Spanish and business at university.
Girl: Wow. That's great. And what do you think of Mexico City?
Student: I really like the city. It's very lively and there's lots to do.

Girl: Great. And what about Mexican food?
Student: I love spicy food, so I really like the food here.
Girl: That's good. So, maybe we should go and get some food, then?
Student: Yes, good idea!

PHRASES YOU MIGHT USE

6 🔊 017 Students work in pairs to complete the phrases from the conversations. Play the recording to check answers.

1 I'll	2 I'm staying	3 I've got	4 very excited
5 allergic	6 from	7 student	8 really like

PHRASES YOU MIGHT HEAR

7 Point out that the expressions and questions here are all extracts from the conversations in Exercise 5. Students work in pairs before feedback as a class.

1 a	2 b	3 a	4 b

⊕ EXTENSION

Photocopy audioscript 017 and ask students to work in pairs to find and underline the words and phrases 1–8 from Exercise 6 in the conversations. By reading what is said before and after each one they can decide which answer, a or b, is correct in each case.

WATCH

8 and **9** ▶ With books closed tell students they are going to watch a video about Mexico City. Ask them which topics they think might be covered. Write their suggestions on the board. Then play the video without any sound and ask students if they think their topic suggestions were covered or not.

Alternatively, with a stronger group, tell students they are going to watch a short video about Mexico City. Ask them if they have any questions they would like answered about the four topics listed in the book. Elicit some questions and write them on the board. Students watch the video to find out whether their questions were answered.

While watching, ask them to note down any information they hear about the four topics. It is important for students to understand that they need to make brief notes, one or two words, rather than trying to write sentences, as otherwise they will miss the next part of the video. With a weaker group it may be helpful to pause the video after the first section, about Mexico City, and to go through the notes students have made together.

After watching the rest of the video, students work in pairs to compare notes. If necessary, the video can be repeated to give students the opportunity to check and complete their notes.

Feed back by asking students to tell the class the information they learned from the video.

Mexico City: capital of Mexico; first buildings there in 1300s; Spanish explorers built a new city when they arrived in 1500s; lots of old colonial buildings in the city centre.
family life: in the past, Mexican families were large, and grandparents, parents and children all lived together; most modern families now just parents and children; family life and traditions still important, for example, a quinceañera is a celebration when a girl turns 15 and has a big party with family and friends.
homestays: a good way to learn about family life and culture and learn the language; there are official websites.

VIDEOSCRIPT ▶ Mexico City

Mexico is just to the south of the USA, and Mexico City is the capital. Mexico City has lots of beautiful old buildings. There was an Aztec city here from about 1300 AD, but when Spanish explorers arrived in Mexico in the 1500s, they built a new city here. Many of the old colonial buildings in the city were built by the Spanish. Nowadays Mexico City is a busy, modern city where lots of families live and work.

However, you can still see examples of Mexico's amazing past in and around the city. This is Teotihuacán, an ancient city built around 100 BC. It has amazing pyramids, and tourists can visit it and climb them. In the past, Mexican families were large, with parents, grandparents and children all living together or very close by.

These days, it is usually just parents and children who live together. But family life and traditions are still as important as in the past. For example, quinceañera is a very important family celebration. It takes place on a girl's 15th birthday, to celebrate that she is now an adult. The girl wears a special dress, and there's usually a big party, with family and friends.

Learning about national traditions is very interesting if you are learning the language of the country. Understanding the culture of a language helps you become a better student.

If you are learning a language, it is a good idea to visit a country where they speak it. A homestay is a good way to do this. You learn about family life and culture there, and you can practise speaking the language every day. Check out official homestay websites for more information.

LIFE COMPETENCIES
SB P25

COMMUNICATION, UNDERSTANDING AND CULTURE

10 Students work in groups of three or four and decide together what information they would include in a video, leaflet or presentation for someone who is coming to live in their city. They can use the headings and notes they made in the previous exercise as a model. With a weaker class it may be helpful to brainstorm some ideas on the board together before separating the class into groups but it might be more interesting if each group was given the flexibility to choose the topics themselves.

If you have the facilities, students could be asked to make a short video about their city. This could be done outside the classroom after doing the preparation in class. Alternatively, they can prepare a leaflet or give a presentation to the rest of the class. They can include photos or other visuals to make it more engaging. While students are preparing the project, move around the classroom offering vocabulary or other support they may need.

When they have finished, students can share their work with the class, showing the video, giving the presentation or displaying the leaflet. Other students can be encouraged to give feedback on the parts they liked best or found most interesting and, if appropriate, there could be a class vote to choose the best project.

➡ **WORKBOOK** / Unit 1, page 8

2 CHANGING WORLD

UNIT OBJECTIVES

Topic:	the natural world and weather
Grammar:	present continuous; present simple or present continuous?
Vocabulary:	seasons and months; weather; continents; geography and the natural world; weather collocations
Listening:	Part 2: gap-fill: a monologue about a trip to the beach
Reading:	reading for detail: short texts about living in a different country
Speaking:	describing a photo
Writing:	Part 6: writing a short email
Pronunciation:	pronouncing months
Exam focus:	Listening Part 2; Writing Part 6
Real world:	asking about the weather in Vancouver

Ask your students to watch the Grammar on the Move videos on pages 28 and 31. You can use these to present or reinforce the present continuous and the present simple or the present continuous.

VOCABULARY

SB P26

SEASONS AND MONTHS

LEAD-IN

Draw students' attention to the photos and ask them to say what they can see in each of the photos. Write any new and interesting vocabulary on the board for students to use in their discussion in Exercise 1.

1 Students work in pairs to discuss the questions. Encourage them to say why they like their favourite type of weather and why they don't like the others.
If necessary, extra support can be given by asking them to think about activities they can or can't do in different weather conditions.

2 018 Tell students they are going to hear Sonia talking about some photos she and her friends posted of their holidays. Give them a minute to match the photos (A–D) with the numbers (1–4).

Students listen to the recording to check their answers.

> 1 A   2 D   3 B   4 C

AUDIOSCRIPT 018

1
Sonia: My friends love to share photos of their trips on social media. These photos are from their holidays at different times of the year. Sam's photo is this winter one with all the snow. It's from his trip to New York and it shows the view from the window of his hotel. I think it's December or January – it's definitely winter!

2
Sonia: My Japanese friend Keiko posts photos every day. That one is from her trip to Kyoto with her family in spring – in April or May, I think. They're walking through a park in the rain, but you can see from the flowers on the trees that it's spring.

3
Sonia: My friend Nathalie visits her grandparents in the forest of Orléans every autumn, so I think this photo is from October or November. This is what a French forest looks like on a foggy day in autumn!

4
Sonia: The last one is from our summer holidays in Ireland. Look at the clear, green sea. Isn't it beautiful? It's a perfect summer day at the end of July.

LANGUAGE NOTE

Read the *Did you know?* box as a class and point out that the word *fall* was originally used in England (taken by English settlers to the American colonies). It was short for *fall of the leaf*. It continued to be used in America, but was replaced by *autumn* in the UK.

3 018 Students work in pairs to complete the sentences from the recording and then listen again to check their answers.

> 1 winter   2 spring   3 autumn   4 summer

⊕ EXTENSION

If students are allowed to use their phones in the classroom, they could find a photo of their own or a friend's holiday and describe it to their partner, using the descriptions on the recording as a model. Alternatively, some photos could be projected onto the whiteboard for students to describe. If there are three or four photos on the board, their partner could listen and guess which one they are talking about.

4 Ask students how many syllables there are in *February* (four – /ˈfeb.ru.ər.i/), then point out the symbol which tells them the stress is on the first syllable. Drill individually then chorally.

This could be an opportunity to show students how stress is marked in dictionaries too. If you have paper dictionaries in the classroom, ask students to look up the word and/or if you encourage students to use certain online dictionaries you could look up the word and check the stress symbol there.

Then do the same for *August* and *September*. Elicit why *March* and *June* do not have a stress marked (because they only have one syllable).

Students work individually to add the names of the months which are missing from the list and mark the stress on the correct syllable.

5 019 Students listen to the recording to check their answers. It may be helpful to repeat each word twice. To check this activity, ask individual students to read the words and then drill the correct pronunciation chorally.

It may be necessary to point out that months always start with a capital letter in English.

1 January	**2** April	**3** May	**4** July
5 October	**6** November	**7** December	

AUDIOSCRIPT 019

January, February, March, April, May, June, July, August, September, October, November, December

6 Students discuss the questions. Ask two or three pairs to tell the class their answers.

VOCABULARY
SB P27

WEATHER

LEAD-IN

Write *Weather* on the board and brainstorm any vocabulary students can remember to talk about it. Try to elicit *sun*, *rain*, *hot*, *cold*, etc. Leave these words on the board as you may use them again in the Extension task after Exercise 3.

1 Students discuss the questions in groups of three. Move around the classroom helping with vocabulary as necessary. Ask two or three students to tell the class about one of their partners, e.g. *Pablo goes to the beach when it's very hot and he wears a T-shirt and shorts.*

2 Ask students to look at the pictures and try to guess where they were taken. Then give them about four minutes to read the texts to check their suggestions.

1 B **2** C **3** A

3 Read the three statements and ask students to read the texts for a second time to find out whether they are true or false. Then students compare answers in pairs. If their answers are different, encourage them to show their partner where they found the information in each text and then work together to correct the statements which are false.

1 T   **2** F It's wet and often cloudy and foggy.
3 F At night it can be cool.

⊕ EXTENSION

Look back at the words associated with *weather* which you wrote on the board at the start of the lesson. Ask students to think about other words they can find in the text which connect to the weather and create a mind map on the board. Write *weather* in the centre of the board and draw lines coming from it leading to *sun*, *rain*, *snow*, *storm*. Allow students five or six minutes working in small groups to list words and short phrases under each of the sub-headings by referring back to the texts. If they wish they can add other sub-headings too.

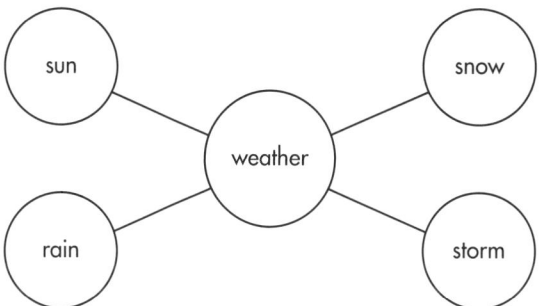

Suggested answers
Sun: the sun is shining, sunshine, it's sunny, it's (very) dry, blue sky
Rain: it's raining, the weather's / it's wet, it's the rainy season
Snow: it's snowing, it's cold, the temperature's / it's freezing, it's icy
Storm: it's windy, thunder, lightning, clouds

4 If you did not use the extension idea above, students may need to find the words in the box in the texts above to check meaning in context. Otherwise, allow students five or six minutes to do the exercise individually and then check as a class.

1 sunshine	**2** storm	**3** freezing
4 wet	**5** thunder	**6** snows
7 foggy	**8** temperature	**9** cloudy

UNIT 2 CHANGING WORLD

5 Close books. Write two sentences on the board: *Don't look at the sun – it's dangerous. Today it's sunny – can we go to the park?* Underline *sun* and *sunny* and ask students if they can tell you the difference between the two. Try to elicit *noun* and *adjective*.

Students open books and work individually to complete the rule. Students check answers with a partner before class feedback.

Check answers before asking students to use some of the words to do Exercise 6.

-y

6 Ask students to suggest words to describe how they feel when it snows. Try to elicit a range of adjectives, e.g. *happy, great, strange, bored*. Then ask students to say why they feel like this. For example, *I feel great because I can go skiing*, or *I feel bored because I can't go out*.

Then students work in pairs to answer the questions in the book. Encourage them to use full sentences when they answer and move round the class helping with vocabulary. Ask two or three students to tell their answers to the class.

GRAMMAR
SB P28

PRESENT CONTINUOUS

1 Direct students' attention to the sentences in bold in the texts on page 27. Try to elicit the name of the tense (present continuous), then point out the time expressions (*today, at the moment, for a month*) and ask students when we use the present continuous.

They may be able to tell you we use the present continuous for something happening now. If they can't, ask them to look at the rules in the Grammar box and match the two examples *a* and *b* to the rules.

Point out the form of the tense, using the examples in the box. Remind students that questions are formed by inverting the subject and the verb *to be* and that contracted forms, e.g. *I'm*, cannot be used in the positive short answers, e.g. *Yes, I am*, NOT *Yes, I'm*.

1 b   **2** a

➡ **GRAMMAR REFERENCE** / Page 200

LANGUAGE NOTE

Most verbs: add *-ing* to the base form of the verb, e.g. *rain – raining*

Verbs which end in *-e*: remove the *-e* and add *-ing*, e.g. *live – living*

Verbs which end in one vowel and one consonant: double the consonant and add *-ing*, e.g. *sit – sitting*

Ask students if they can think of any other examples of each type of verb.

2 Students choose the correct form of the verbs in each of the options. Encourage them to read the complete dialogue before they decide on their answers and to use the information in the box to help if necessary. Check answers as a class.

1 are you	**2** It's raining	**3** watching
4 is coming	**5** 're all getting	**6** isn't sitting
7 Is	**8** isn't	**9** 's working	**10** is

3 Ask students to look at the two photos and say where they think the people are and if they think they are enjoying themselves. Then students read the messages to find the answers (*in the mountains, at the beach; they are both having a great time*). Check understanding of the verbs in the boxes and ask students to complete the gaps. Students compare their answers with a partner. If their answers are different, encourage them to explain their answers using the information in the box if necessary. Feed back as a class.

1 're having	**2** 'm sitting	**3** looking	**4** is taking
5 'm messaging	**6** 're enjoying	**7** 're walking
8 isn't raining	**9** aren't having	**10** 'm enjoying

4 Students complete the questions individually, check together then ask and answer. Move round the room to monitor as they do the task.

1 are, doing	**2** is, wearing	**3** are, learning
4 are, doing

FAST FINISHERS

In pairs, one student mimes an action while the other guesses what they are doing. If necessary you can give one or two suggestions to start them off (*you're sleeping, you're texting a message, you're chewing gum*, etc).

LISTENING PART 2 TRAINING
SB P29

✓ EXAM INFORMATION

In Part 2 of the Listening paper, students listen to a longer monologue. They have to complete five gaps with one word, number, date or time. One word is always dictated and the spelling of that word has to be correct. Students listen for names, places, numbers, dates or times. In the exam, the recording is played twice.

1 Ask the class to suggest places in the countryside near them that can be visited. Note down some places on the board and brainstorm ideas for what activities people can do in these places (e.g. *walking, hiking, having a picnic, swimming*). Allow students two or three minutes to discuss the questions before getting feedback from the class.

2 🔊 020 Direct students' attention to the form on the page and read the instructions together as a class, up to '… *a trip to the beach*'. Then check students' understanding by asking some questions such as, *Who is talking?* (a woman); *Who is she talking to?* (some college students); *What is she talking about?* (a trip to the beach).

Read the example and highlight that the answer is a date (6th May). Read the information and play the first part of the recording. With a stronger group you could ask students to listen for the date of the trip to the Science Museum (29th April) as well.

Ask students to look at the rest of the form and suggest what type of answers they are listening for in each case. For example, (2) *Travel by …*, tells us a means of transport. Elicit suggestions, e.g. *bus, train, coach,* etc.

Try to elicit what they are listening for in (3) by asking students to guess what they must bring for a trip to the beach, e.g. *swimming costume, sun cream, towel,* etc.

Ask students to suggest a time for (4) and ask students what they think they are listening for in (5) (a surname).

You could write all their suggestions and guesses on the board before listening so that students can see that sometimes it is possible to predict the correct answer before listening.

AUDIOSCRIPT 🔊 020

Woman: Hello, everyone. As you know, we're going on a trip to Long Beach soon. It's on the 6th of May – that's one week after the trip to the Science Museum on the 29th of April.

3 🔊 021 Before playing the recording remind students that they need to ensure they listen for the correct answer as there may be more than one answer which could fit logically, as in the example.

After the first listening, students compare their answers with a partner and then play the recording again for them to check.

LANGUAGE NOTE

In the UK the term *college* refers to an educational institution where students study or train to get knowledge and/or skills after the age of 16. For example, at a sixth-form college, students study for A levels prior to going to university to take a degree, while at an art college students study a range of artistic subjects. In the US the term *college* refers to university. This is a false friend with some other languages.

2 coach **3** towel **4** 9.45 **5** Burrell

AUDIOSCRIPT 🔊 021

Woman: Hello everyone. As you know, we're going on a trip to Long Beach soon. It's on the 6th of May – that's one week after the trip to the Science Museum on the 29th of April.

We usually travel by train on our trips. But we're taking a coach this time, because there isn't a station near Long Beach.

If you want, you can bring beach balls or games to play. It's possible to rent sunbeds at the beach, but you will need to take a towel.

The journey from college to Long Beach takes only one hour. We're going at 9.45 but can everybody be outside school at 9.15? We'll be back at 4.30. If you'd like to join this trip, please pay Sally Burrell in the college office. If Sally's not there, put the money in an envelope and leave it for her. Sally's surname is spelled B-U-double-R-E-double-L. Now, any questions?

UNIT 2 CHANGING WORLD 31

PUSH YOURSELF B1

SB P29

VOCABULARY: WEATHER COLLOCATIONS

1 Students look at the pictures and describe what they can see to their partner. Remind them to use the weather vocabulary from page 27. Then ask students to match the newspaper headlines with the photos. Check answers as a class.

> **1** C **2** A **3** D **4** B

2 Look at the first headline again together, and ask students to underline the nouns which talk about the weather, e.g. *storms, winds,* etc. Then ask them to identify the adjectives which describe these nouns (*heavy, strong*). Tell students that two words which go together in this way are called *collocations* (e.g. *heavy + storms*) and learning them can help make their descriptions more interesting and natural sounding. Students work in pairs to underline the adjective + noun combinations in the other sentences. Check as a class.

> heavy storms, strong winds, bright sunshine, clear skies, heavy snow, thick fog, hard frost

3 Students complete the sentences and check their answers with a partner before class feedback.

> **1** thick fog **2** hard frost **3** heavy snow
> **4** heavy storms, clear skies **5** bright sunshine
> **6** strong winds

4 Students work in pairs to write their headlines. Then they read their answers to another pair. Ask one or two pairs to read their headlines to the class.

⊕ EXTENSION

Give out a set of 14 small pieces of paper to each group of four or five students and ask them to write each of the individual words from the collocations in Exercise 1 onto individual pieces of paper: *thick – fog – hard – frost – icy – roads – heavy – storms – clear – skies – bright – sunshine – strong – winds*

Then students mix the pieces of paper up and lay them face down on the desk to play a memory game (they take turns to turn over two pieces of paper – if they make a collocation they can keep them and win a point, if not, they must put them back on the table and the next student tries to remember where they are).

READING

SB P30

LEAD-IN

Tell students about your experience living in another country or city. For example, *I went to live in Berlin for a year after university because I wanted to learn German* or *I'm from Madeira but I went to live in Lisbon for university.*

1 Put students into small groups to discuss the questions and monitor them, listening for interesting ideas and opinions to elicit during feedback. You could extend the discussion by asking students if they know anyone who has taken a gap year and why they think some young people prefer to move away from their family home.

CULTURAL INFORMATION

Young people in the UK, US, Australia and New Zealand often leave home as soon as they finish school. Students often choose to move away from their home town to go to university and share accommodation with other students. Many choose to take a gap year between school and university or between university and work. Typically they will work for a part of it to raise money to go travelling or they may choose a working holiday or volunteering.

Young people in their first jobs often share a house or flat with other people of a similar age in order to reduce costs.

2 Tell students they are going to read about two people who are spending time living in another place to their home town. Look at the pictures and ask students to guess where they are. Allow five minutes to read the texts quickly to find answers to the questions and then check their answers with a partner. Check answers as a class.

> **1** Koon-Sung usually lives in Singapore. Now he's living in Turin, Italy.
> Carla usually lives in Mexico City. Now she's living in the United Arab Emirates and is on holiday.
> **2** Koon-Sung is in Turin for his job. He is working on a big engineering project / making a road in the mountains.
> Carla is in the United Arab Emirates because she is on a student exchange programme.

3 Encourage students to read the questions and the options before they read the texts again to choose the correct answer. Students check their answers with a partner and try to explain why their answer is correct if they have different answers. Check as a class. If necessary, ask students to find the part of the text which gives each answer.

> **1** c **2** b **3** b **4** a

32

FAST FINISHERS

Students can talk to another fast finisher about which of the two places described they would prefer to live in. Encourage them to think about the activities described to say why they prefer one or the other.

SB P30

GEOGRAPHY AND THE NATURAL WORLD

WARMER

Ask students to look back at the texts in the reading section and find the words *north* and *east*. Draw the four points of the compass on the board and ask students which position the two words should be in. Elicit the other two directions (*south* and *west*).

Then ask students to use the words to describe towns and cities in their country. For example, Lyon is in the south of France, Calais is on the north coast of France. Point out the use of the prepositions *in the* and *on the* (coast) in the two examples.

1 Tell students to underline the words in colour in the texts. Encourage them to read the sentences around the words in the text to help them understand the meanings and then match the two parts of the definitions.

Students use the words from the texts to fill the gaps, remembering that there is one word they don't need. Check answers in pairs before class feedback.

| 1 mountains | 2 Islands | 3 valley | 4 coast |
| 5 hill | 6 forest | 7 lake | 8 waterfall |

2 Students work in pairs to answer the questions. Monitor as the class does the task, helping with vocabulary as necessary. As a class, decide which other places in their country students would recommend to a visitor and encourage them to explain why.

3 Elicit opinions from the class to answer the question. Encourage students to say why.

⊕ EXTENSION

Students work in groups of three or four to make a poster advertising a popular destination. They can draw pictures or print photos from the internet and then write a short description saying why it is a good place to visit. Encourage them to think about the best time of year to go and to mention the weather conditions. They can also describe where the place is in their country. If necessary, students can research the information on the internet or in books or guides. The finished posters can be shared with the rest of the class.

SB P31

PRESENT SIMPLE OR PRESENT CONTINUOUS?

LEAD-IN

Elicit how we form the present continuous (subject + *to be* + verb+*ing*) and what we use it for (actions that are happening now and temporary situations). Ask students to give you some example sentences using the present continuous, e.g *I am speaking English at the moment. I'm staying at work until 7 pm today.*

1 Read the four example sentences as a class and ask students to identify the present simple (1, 2) and the present continuous (3, 4). Then students work in pairs to read the rules (a–d) and to match the sentences with the correct rule.

| **a** 2 | **b** 4 | **c** 1 | **d** 3 |

➜ **GRAMMAR REFERENCE** / Page 201

2 Students work individually to choose the correct answer. Then, working in pairs, encourage them to tell their partner which rule (a–d) each sentence is an example of. Check answers as a class.

| 1 rains | 2 'm staying | 3 's snowing | 4 live |

3 Ask students what they can see in the photo and what she is doing (she is at a rock concert, and singing).

Students complete the text. Encourage them to read the whole text before they start. Check answers as a class. A stronger class could be asked to explain why they used each tense using the rules in the box.

1 plays	2 travels	3 's staying
4 's practising	5 're learning	6 goes
7 doesn't like	8 's wearing	

4 Students discuss the questions in pairs. Encourage them to use complete sentences in their answers and remind them to use the correct tense. Monitor the discussions and ask two or three students to tell the class their answers.

UNIT 2 | CHANGING WORLD | 33

WRITING PART 6 TRAINING
SB P32

INVITATIONS AND REPLIES

✓ EXAM INFORMATION

In Writing Part 6, students have to write a short message, for example, a note or email, in response to a brief text or instruction. There are always three pieces of information to include or three prompts to answer. Students should write 25 words or more.

The whole Reading and Writing paper lasts 60 minutes and has 30 reading questions (Parts 1–5) and two writing questions (Parts 6 and 7). Students should spend about five minutes on Part 6.

1 Tell students how you invite friends to go out, e.g. *I usually call or send a text if it is a dinner, but if I want to invite more than one friend to a more important event like a birthday celebration I write an email. This weekend I am going to see a film with some friends. We organised it by text message.* Initiate a class discussion to answer the questions. Help students with vocabulary and make sure they use the present simple to answer the first two questions and the present continuous for the third.

2 Tell students they are going to read three short emails. Give them one or two minutes to look at them and decide whether they are invitations or replies (invitations). Read the questions with the class and ask students to read the first email to find the answer to the first question (go out for a pizza). Students then read the emails more carefully and answer the three parts in the questions for each email. Remind them to write short phrases rather than complete sentences. Then they compare their answers with a partner. Check answers by asking questions, e.g. *What are they doing? When/Where are they meeting?*

> **Email 1:** go out for a pizza, in the Arum Café, at 6 pm
> **Email 2:** go to the beach and go camping, in the supermarket car park, at 10 am
> **Email 3:** go to a football match, at Rose's house, at 4.30

3 Write two headings on the board: *Beginning an email / Finishing an email*. Ask students to copy the examples from the emails in the book and suggest any other language they know to start and end an email. If they cannot answer, you could write some suggestions on the board (not under the headings) and ask students to decide whether they can be used to begin or finish an email. For example, *Hello, Best wishes, All the best, Good morning, Hi, everyone, See you soon.*

Check answers together and ask students if there are any differences in use between the expressions. Elicit or supply that, *Hey* and *Hi* are more informal than *Dear*, and *Best wishes* is the most formal ending, but all of them are appropriate for an email to a friend.

> **1** *Hi* + name; *Hey* + name; *Dear* + name; Name only
> **2** Name only; *Love* + name; with a question; *Let me know; Hope you can make it!*

4 Tell students they are going to read some answers to the email invitations. Ask them to read each one and match it with the correct email.

> **a** 3   **b** 2   **c** 1

LANGUAGE NOTE

Highlight the use of *instead* in answer *a* which is an adverb and means *in place of something else*.

5 Elicit which email accepts the invitation (b) and which emails do not (a, c). Then ask students to identify the language used to say *yes* and *no* in the replies and complete the table.

Phrases for saying 'yes'	Phrases for saying 'no'
I'd love to come …	Thanks for asking but …
Thanks, that sounds great.	I'd love to come, but I'm afraid …

⊕ EXTENSION

Ask students to look at replies *a* and *c* again and find the reasons why the writers say *no* and the suggestions they make. (*a*: I've got a music exam, meet for a coffee after the match; *c*: I'm babysitting, pizza next week?)

6 Students complete the invitations and replies using the words in the box. Check answers as a class.

> **1** interested   **2** about   **3** like   **4** afraid
> **5** sounds   **6** come

LEAD-IN

Direct students' attention to the exam question and check understanding by asking questions such as, *What do you have to write?* (an email); *Who do you have to write to?* (Morgan, your English friend); *What information do you have to include?* (the three points in the prompt); *How many words do you have to write?* (25 or more).

7 Ask students to read the model answer and point out the underlined phrases which correspond to the three content points in the question.

> Yes, it does.

8 Check understanding by asking similar questions to those in the lead-in on page 34 and then remind students to use the language they have seen in the example emails in Exercise 1 and the model answer. The writing can be done as homework or in class. Encourage students to check they have answered the question by underlining the answers to the three content points and counting the words.

> **Suggested answer**
> Hi Jo,
> Do you want to play tennis next Saturday? I'm going to the new sports club in town. I want to go by bus, so we can meet at the bus stop at 2 pm.
> Hope you can make it!
> Julia

SB P33

DESCRIBING A PHOTO

1 Allow three or four minutes for students to discuss the questions and then ask some students to tell the class their answers.

2 Ask students to look at the pictures in the book and the questions in 1. Elicit answers to the questions about picture A. Ask students to take turns to say one sentence about the picture and help with vocabulary as necessary. Then students repeat the task for the other picture, in pairs, taking turns to say a sentence about the picture.

3 022 Tell students to listen to the description and identify which photo Irina is talking about.

> Photo B – the man by the waterfall

> **AUDIOSCRIPT** 022
>
> **Irina:** In this photo I can see a man who is standing next to a big, beautiful waterfall. He is quite young and he's got dark hair and a beard. He's wearing a black T-shirt and jeans and he's holding his phone on a selfie stick and he's taking a photo. He's smiling and he looks happy. The man is in the middle of the picture and he is alone. Maybe he is visiting the waterfall with friends but we can't see them. Behind him, at the bottom of the picture, we can see a fence. I think it is to stop people from falling into the river. Behind the fence is the river with the waterfall. It's very big. On the left, at the top of the photo, we can see the trees of a big forest.

4 022 Students read the extracts from the recording and then listen again to complete the gaps. It may be necessary to point out the *selfie stick* and the *fence* in the photo if they do not know the words.

> **1** dark hair, beard
> **2** black T-shirt and jeans, happy
> **3** taking a photo
> **4** waterfall, friends
> **5** into, water

5 Students read the sentences in Exercise 4 again to identify the phrases used to give your own ideas.

> **1** He/She/It looks … **2** Maybe he's visiting …
> **3** I think it is to stop …

6 Students look at photo A again to complete the sentences and if necessary listen to the recording again to check their answers.

> **1** next **2** middle **3** bottom **4** Behind **5** top

7 Divide the class into two groups, A and B. Then ask group A and group B to look at page 192. Students work in groups of two or three to make notes about the ideas (1–6) in the book for their photo. Help with vocabulary as necessary while students are working. When they have completed their notes, pair students up with a partner who looked at the other photo (A or B). Then students take turns to describe their photo using the notes, without showing the photo to their partner.

⊕ EXTENSION

If students have access to other photos in their books, on their phones or on the internet they can take turns to describe a different photo to their partner. The listening student can try to draw the photo from the description (no drawing skills are required – they can use stick people for example).

UNIT 2 CHANGING WORLD 35

EXAM FOCUS

LISTENING PART 2

SB P34

Read through the Exam tips and facts boxes with the class carefully. Focus on the first tip in the Exam tips box and tell students they will have a short time to read the notes or form and remind them that it is a good idea to try to decide if they are listening for a number, a date, a time or a word in each gap. Look at the last point in the Exam tips box: tell students that even if they are sure they have the right answer on the first listening, they should use the second listening to check their answers.

Do the task under exam conditions, reminding students that they should work alone. Play the recording twice and then allow students to compare answers with a partner before class feedback.

> **1** 8/eight **2** 6/six **3** (the) office
> **4** 75/seventy-five **5** Albury

AUDIOSCRIPT 023

Narrator: For each question, write the correct answer in the gap. Write one word or a number or a date or a time. You will hear a woman giving information about a cycle ride.

Woman: Welcome to the visitor centre at Redhill Forest. I hope you're all ready for your thirty kilometre cycle ride! It's now seven thirty, and we'll be on our bikes and away at eight. We ask everyone to arrive well before the ride starts because someone's always late – but not me! I was here at six! As you're all early, you've got time to visit the shop! For £3 you can buy a hat, or if you prefer a T-shirt, they're £6 each. I hope you've all brought water, but if you haven't it's £1 per bottle. We did send everyone maps, but if you've forgotten or lost yours, go to the office, which is just behind me, opposite the café. As you know, this forest does have some hills. The highest is 300 metres! Don't worry – we won't be cycling up that one today! The highest we'll go is 75 metres, which isn't too bad. The ride ends at Albury village. You spell that A-L-B-U-R-Y. Albury. Right any questions …?

WRITING PART 6

SB P35

Read the Exam tips and facts boxes carefully with the class checking understanding. Remind students that there could be three questions to answer or there may be three bullet points with information to include.

Remind students that this is an exam-style task and they should work alone without talking. Allow students five or six minutes to read the question and write their email individually. They should leave some time to check their answer when they finish. Then ask them to exchange their work with a partner for peer feedback. Students can use the exam tips to comment on their partner's work.

> **Model answer**
> Hi Harley,
> Good to hear from you. The best place to go walking is in the mountains. There are lots of hotels that you can stay in. The weather is hot at this time of year. (36 words)

Read through the options in the *How was it?* section and elicit the meaning of each one that they learned in the first unit.

Ask students to tick the appropriate box. You might like to ask students to share how they felt about the task to get an indication of your students' confidence. Depending on your class, you might like to do this openly or allow students to give their feedback without their classmates seeing. For example, give students a piece of A4 paper each with the *How was it?* scale written in large letters. Allow students to tick the relevant box then hold up their papers at the same time so that you can see how well students think they are doing. Finally, ask students if they found it easier, harder or the same as the exam practice in Unit 1.

➡ **WRITING BANK** / *Pages 233–234*

REAL WORLD

SB P36

ASKING ABOUT THE WEATHER IN … VANCOUVER

WARMER

Write *Vancouver* on the board and brainstorm anything students know about the city. If there is little response, write on the board: *USA/Canada, east/west coast, mountains/sea/lakes/desert* and ask students to choose the words which can describe Vancouver (a city on the west coast of Canada on the Pacific Ocean and is surrounded by mountains).

1 Direct students' attention to the photos. Elicit the season which is shown in each one. Students work in pairs to suggest activities for each of the seasons in Vancouver and then feed back with the whole class. Accept all suggestions and if students need support, ask them to look carefully at the photos for ideas (*cycling, swimming, skiing*, etc.). Write ideas on the board.

Divide the class into four groups and allocate each group one of the paragraphs. Ask the members of each group to read their paragraph and underline the activities that they read about. Then they compare answers with the other members of their group.

Next, form new groups of four students who have each read a different text. Each member of the group tells the other three which time of year and which activities they have read about.

Finally, compare the information from each season to highlight the similarities and differences between the texts.

| A spring | B summer | C autumn | D winter |

CULTURAL INFORMATION

Vancouver is a city on the west coast of Canada in the province of British Columbia. It is surrounded by water on three sides and mountains to the north. Stanley Park is the largest urban park in North America and is located in downtown (central) Vancouver. Vancouver often ranks highly in worldwide quality-of-life surveys.

2 Read the questions with the whole class and allow students time to read the complete web page to find the answers. Remind them that sometimes there is more than one correct answer. Students correct answers in pairs before class feedback.

| 1 summer | 2 spring | 3 winter | 4 summer |
| 5 summer/autumn | 6 winter |

3 Students work in pairs to find the phrases in the text and choose the correct answer. Feedback as a class.

| 1 a | 2 b | 3 b | 4 a | 5 b |

⊕ EXTENSION

Ask students in small groups to brainstorm places in the world with 'extreme' weather. Check what *extreme* means and then allow one to two minutes for groups to think of different places and types of weather. Elicit ideas from the groups and ask them what type of weather and temperatures these places have.

4 024 Tell students they are going to hear three conversations about the weather between tourists and hotel receptionists. Look at the two options, 1a and 1b, and check understanding of the difference by asking some questions. For example, in 1a, *Is it a good idea to go skiing today?* (no); *Is it dangerous to go skiing?* (yes); in 1b, *Is it a good idea to go skiing today* (yes). Ask students, *What type of weather is it dangerous to ski in?* (storms, too much snow, wind); and, *What type of weather is perfect for skiing?* (sun, light snow). Then students listen to the conversations and select the correct answers. Check the answers after playing the recording once or twice.

| 1 a | 2 b | 3 b |

AUDIOSCRIPT 024

1
Guest: Good morning. Do you know the weather forecast for today? We want to go skiing.
Receptionist: Oh, I don't think you'll have much luck with that today. They're forecasting a big storm coming in from the north about mid-afternoon, with gale-force winds and a lot of snow.
Guest: Oh. So, is it OK to go skiing this morning?
Receptionist: No, I think they'll be closing the slopes all day because you never quite know when the storm will hit, and you don't want to get caught out there once the storm comes.

2
Receptionist: Good morning. Not such a good day today.
Guest: No. Do you think it will rain all day?
Receptionist: No. The forecast is for rain till lunchtime, then it should clear and we should get some sun later on.
Guest: Oh, that's good. We want to go to the beach after lunch.
Receptionist: Yeah, well they reckon from about midday onwards it should dry up, and once the sun comes out, it'll soon warm up.

3
Receptionist: Hi. Good morning. Can I help you?
Guest: Yes. Do you know if there's rain forecast today?
Receptionist: Yes. The morning's going to be fine, quite bright and sunny, but then it's gonna cloud over this afternoon, and there may be a few showers, so you might want to take an umbrella with you.
Guest: OK. Thank you.
Receptionist: Yeah. The weather's a bit unpredictable at this time of year, so you never know what's going to happen.

PHRASES YOU MIGHT USE

5 024 Encourage students to work in pairs to complete the sentences with the words from the box to make expressions from the recording. Then play the recording to check answers.

| 1 forecast | 2 OK | 3 all | 4 want | 5 there's |

PHRASES YOU MIGHT HEAR

6 Read through the definitions (a–e) as a class, helping students with understanding, if necessary, and then ask students to work in pairs to match the phrases with the correct definition. Feed back as a class.

> 1 e 2 a 3 d 4 c 5 b

WATCH

7 ▶ Before watching the video, encourage students to read the words and phrases in the box and ask them to decide which season they might match in Vancouver. For example, *I think Chinese New Year and sledge rides are in the winter, but you can go swimming in the summer.*

Play the video while students check their answers. With a less able group it may be helpful to play the first part of the video about spring, then stop and check answers about that season before watching the rest of the video.

> **spring:** kayaking and whale watching, **summer:** beaches and swimming, **autumn:** jogging and film festival, **winter:** sledge rides and Chinese New Year

> **VIDEOSCRIPT** ▶ Vancouver
>
> Vancouver is a big, modern city. Over 600,000 people live there. It's also a world city because many nationalities live there. More than half its population do not speak English as their first language, and more than a quarter have Chinese origins. Spring is a beautiful season in Vancouver. The winter snow goes away, and it's often sunny and warm. The city is full of spring flowers, and people enjoy going for walks in the park. It's a great time for enjoying the water. It's too cold to swim in the sea, but you can go kayaking. It's a great way to get away from the noisy city and enjoy some peaceful time. Or why not try a boat trip? Spring is also a great time to see whales. They come nearer to the shore and it's amazing to get close to them, and watch them as they jump out of the water. Kitsilano Beach is one of the most popular beaches in Vancouver, and in the summer lots of people go there to lie on the sand and relax in the sunshine. The water is also warm enough for swimming. You can swim in the sea, or in a pool like this one. In the autumn, Vancouver is beautiful. In Stanley Park, the leaves on the trees turn orange and red, and it's still warm enough to go jogging in the park or walking in the mountains. There's also lots to do in the city. For example, the Vancouver Film Festival takes place every year. It's the biggest film festival in North America. In winter, it usually snows and gets pretty cold, so why not go for a sledge ride? And Vancouver's large Chinese population celebrate the Chinese New Year in winter. There's a big street celebration with music and dancing – and, of course, dragons! The celebration ends with a big firework show.

8 ▶ Students discuss in pairs what they remember from the video. Repeat the video and ask students to take notes about the times of year for each activity. Then discuss in pairs and decide which time of year they would like to visit. Feed back by asking students to explain to the class the reasons why they chose the season.

LIFE COMPETENCIES
SB P37

ICT LITERACY, COLLABORATION, DECISION-MAKING

9 Students work in pairs. Encourage students to choose a city they have never visited before. If you have internet access in the classroom students could do a web search for information about a city to visit, or they could do the research at home.

Students should make notes under the headings of *weather* and *activities* at different times of year and then talk about their preferences.

Each pair should make a two-to-three-minute presentation to the rest of the class.

The class listens to check that they talk about at least one activity in each season and can ask questions at the end of the presentation. At the end, hold a vote to decide which city would be their favourite place to visit and why.

➡ **WORKBOOK** / *Unit 2, page 12*

PROGRESS CHECK 1
STARTER UNIT TO UNIT 2

SB P38

1

1 wakes up, quarter past seven
2 get up, half past seven
3 gets dressed, quarter to seven
4 puts on, eight o'clock
5 gets on, quarter to nine
6 takes off, four o'clock

2

1 grandmother
2 niece
3 uncle
4 nephew
5 cousin
6 grandfather

3

1 has got
2 have got
3 is
4 are
5 hasn't got
6 Has … got

4

1 **A** mountain **B** winter
2 **A** coast **B** summer
3 **A** forest **B** autumn
4 **A** spring **B** lake

5

1 island
2 west
3 valley, hills
4 waterfall
5 north
6 desert

6

1 France
2 Italian
3 Mexico
4 Spanish

7

1 Nurses *often* have to work at night.
2 Musicians need to practise *every day*.
3 Teachers *never* go to school at the weekend.
4 Some school children *always* wear a uniform.
5 Is your shop *usually* busy at weekends?
6 Business people *sometimes* travel to other countries.

8

1 I drink
2 it's raining
3 I wake up
4 it never snows
5 Is he playing
6 We go

9

1 ~~coming~~ come
2 She ~~have~~ has (got) green eyes
3 The people there ~~is~~ are very friendly
4 I usually ~~can~~ write
5 The club is always open ~~always~~.
6 ~~I sell~~ I'm selling a bike

10

1 C
2 B
3 A
4 C
5 B
6 A
7 B
8 C

3 FREE TIME, SCREEN TIME?

UNIT OBJECTIVES

Topic:	entertainment and media
Grammar:	past simple of *to be*; past simple
Vocabulary:	the internet; TV and time expressions
Listening:	Part 5: matching information about weekend activities
Reading:	Part 3: three-option multiple choice about a professional gamer
Speaking:	talking about the weekend
Writing:	a review of a series
Pronunciation:	pronouncing *-ed* endings
Exam focus:	Reading Part 3; Listening Part 5
Real world:	buying tickets for a show in New York

Ask your students to watch the Grammar on the Move videos on pages 42 and 43. You can use these to present or reinforce the past simple of *to be* and the past simple.

VOCABULARY
SB P40

TV AND THE INTERNET

LEAD-IN

Write the title *Free time, screen time?* on the board. Ask students how many screens they use and the names of the devices they prefer, e.g. phone, computer, TV, tablet, games console, etc.

1 Students discuss the questions in pairs then feed back as a class deciding who spends the most and the least number of hours.

2 Direct students' attention to the diagram and explain that it shows the percentage of free time spent on each activity by the average person. It may be necessary to supply the pronunciation of '%' (/pə ˈsent/). Students match the activities in the box with the correct percentage and then compare answers with a partner.

3  025 Students listen to the recording to check their answers to Exercise 2. Initiate a discussion around the answers. Ask students if they also spend so little time on outdoor sports and activities and whether they think the diagram reflects their free time in general. Ask students if they think younger or older people would have similar answers to them and why.

> 54% watching TV 20% using social media
> 12% watching videos online 8% playing video games
> 6% playing sports and doing exercise

AUDIOSCRIPT 025

Woman: So, how do we spend our leisure time? Well on average, we spend 54% of it watching TV. That's still everybody's favourite free-time activity. We spend 20% of our time using social media and 12% watching videos online. On average we spend 8% of our free time playing video games, but some people probably spend more. In total we only spend 6% of our time outdoors playing sports or doing exercise.

4 026 Show students the quiz and point out the answer options for each question. Check understanding of *once* (one time) and *several* (two or three, but not specific). Tell students they are going to listen to a conversation between Roz and her friend. Her friend is asking the quiz questions and Roz is answering them. Students listen to answer the two questions, then check answers in pairs.

> **1** chat online – 5; messaging friends – 5; upload photos – 3; download films – 3; watch an episode/series – 4; write or follow a blog – 3; stream music – 5
> **2** Her final score is 28. She's a screen fan.

AUDIOSCRIPT 026

Friend: So how often do you chat online, Roz?

Roz: Er, that's number five – several times a day. You know that! I chat online with you every evening!

Friend: Yes, that's true! So what about messaging? Is that five, too?

Roz: Well, I message my friends all day: that's how we talk to each other if we aren't together. So I think the score should be five here.

Friend: OK and how often do you upload photos?

Roz: Mm, I like uploading photos to social media sites to share them with my friends, so that's probably number three. And it's also three for 'How often do you download films?' I watch most films online.

Friend: And what about series? How often do you watch them online?

Roz: I usually watch an episode from my favourite series every day, so that's four.

Friend: And blogs and vlogs. Do you have any time to watch those?

Roz: I probably look at them … once or twice a week. So that's three.

Friend: OK, and finally, what about streaming music?

Roz: I stream music all the time. It's how I listen to music, so that's another score of five.

Friend: So, let's see, that gives you a total score of … 28. So, you spend a lot of time in front of screens. It's the way you like to spend free time and talk to people.

5 🎧 026 Students complete the sentences then listen and check as a class.

> 1 chat online   2 message, friends
> 3 uploading photos   4 watch, episode   5 stream

LANGUAGE NOTE

Students may be familiar with the term *season* which is used in the US with the same meaning as *series* in the UK.

6 Students work in pairs and take turns to ask and answer the questions in the quiz. They should keep a note of their partner's score and then read the interpretation of the score on page 192 to them. Feed back as a class to find out how many students are in each of the four categories and who is a 'net-head'. Then look at the questions in the speech bubbles and elicit some follow-up questions students could ask about the other activities. For example, *Who do you chat to online?*; *Where do you post your photos?* Encourage students to ask and answer the questions in groups of three. Ask some groups to report back, telling the rest of the class about the people they spoke to. For example, *Anna listens to rap music and watches American TV series.*

7 With books closed, brainstorm TV programme and film genres by asking, *What's your favourite type of programme/film?* Then open books and ask students to suggest the name of one film or TV programme for each genre in the box. For example, action film: *Avengers*.

Tell students about your own favourite TV programme. Include answers to the questions in 2 and some useful vocabulary for students which you can write on the board. For example, *My favourite programme is called …*; *I watch it twice a week.*; *The star is …*; *The actors are …*; *I like it because it's funny/interesting.* Students discuss the questions. Move around the classroom helping students with vocabulary as needed. Ask some students to present their answers to question 2 to the class.

PUSH YOURSELF B1

SB P41

VOCABULARY: ADJECTIVES TO DESCRIBE FILMS

LEAD-IN

Ask students how they decide which films to watch. Accept all suggestions, e.g. *friends' recommendations*, *famous actors*, etc. and elicit or supply *reviews*. Ask where they might see a written review and try to elicit *online*.

1 Tell students they are going to read three short reviews. Give students two or three minutes to read the reviews quickly to find the answers to the questions. Students should be encouraged to read quickly so that they learn how to read a text for 'gist' or general idea. It is not necessary for them to understand every word of the text to answer the questions here. This is a useful skill for the exam and when reading in a more general sense. When checking answers, ask students to say which words were the clues to tell them their answer was correct:

> 1 science-fiction film = 3; horror film = 2; comedy = 1
> 2 The writer enjoyed the comedy and the science-fiction film but not the horror film.

2 Students work in pairs to match the sentence parts to complete definitions. They may not know all the words, so suggest they match the ones they know first and then try to work out the other meanings by looking at the words as used in the reviews. Check as a class.

> 1 d   2 b   3 j   4 i   5 h   6 c   7 e
> 8 f   9 a   10 g

FAST FINISHERS

Students can write one or two sentences of their own using some of the adjectives.

SB P42

PAST SIMPLE OF *TO BE*

1 Ask students to do the exercise and then point out the information in the box, highlighting that there are only two past forms of the verb *to be* (*was* and *were*) and that *was* is also the past of *am*.

> 1 was   2 were

→ **GRAMMAR REFERENCE** / Page 202

2 Students work in pairs to fill the gaps, deciding whether they need a positive or negative, singular or plural form.

> 1 wasn't   2 Were   3 were   4 Was   5 wasn't
> 6 weren't

3 Ask one or two questions, using the prompts in the book, e.g. *Where were you on Saturday?*; *Where were your parents at 10 o'clock yesterday evening*? Elicit answers in full sentences (*I was at the park with my cousin. They were at home*). With a weaker group, ask students to write three or four questions using the prompts before they start speaking. A stronger group may be able to make questions without writing them down. Feed back by asking students to report some information about their partner to the class. For example, *Rebecca was at football training at lunchtime.*

UNIT 3 FREE TIME, SCREEN TIME? **41**

LISTENING PART 5 TRAINING
SB P42

✓ EXAM INFORMATION

In Listening Part 5 students listen to an informal conversation between two people about an everyday topic such as travel, free-time activities, daily life. Students listen to identify specific information such as objects, places, feelings etc. and have to match five items with a choice of eight options e.g. people with the food they like to eat or the places they like to go. There is always an example and the recording is played twice. In the example in the Student's Book there are only four questions with seven options and the focus is on listening carefully for the correct information rather than just listening for the words in the options.

LEAD-IN

Briefly talk about the photo with the class, telling students it was taken last weekend. Elicit what the people in the photo did last weekend (had fun, maybe watched a sports match, enjoyed themselves, etc.). Then answer the question yourself as a model (*I enjoy going to the cinema at the weekend but last weekend I was at my friend's house*) etc.

CULTURAL INFORMATION

Students in the UK and the US do not usually go to school on Saturday or Sunday so the weekend is often an opportunity for spending time with friends and doing other free-time activities such as gaming, or watching or doing sports.

1 Then students work in threes to answer the two questions. Encourage them to use full sentences. Feedback to hear a range of activities.

2 027 Read the question with the class and check understanding by asking questions, e.g. *Who is speaking on the recording?* (Abby and Sophie). *What are they talking about? What they and their friends did on Saturday. How many friends do they talk about?* Read the information about the example (Sophie) and then play the first part of the recording to demonstrate how to choose the correct answer.

> Abby was at a barbecue and Sophie was visiting her cousin.

AUDIOSCRIPT 027

Abby: Hi, Sophie. You didn't come to the barbecue on Saturday. Were you ill?
Sophie: No, I went to see my cousin. She's just had a baby. She's got an apartment near the football stadium.

3 028 Play the full recording. Students compare answers with a partner before listening again. If necessary, stop the recording after each answer to elicit or supply the words which provide the answer.

| **1** D | **2** C | **3** E | **4** A |

AUDIOSCRIPT  028

Abby: Hi, Sophie. You didn't come to the barbecue on Saturday. Were you ill?
Sophie: No, I went to see my cousin. She's just had a baby. She's got an apartment near the football stadium. Was the barbecue fun?
Abby: Yes, but a few people couldn't come.
Sophie: I suppose Alice was at work.
Abby: Actually, she had to go and buy a present for her older brother. He's getting married next week.
Sophie: Wow! Was Meg at the barbecue?
Abby: No, she phoned me to say she was feeling sick. She didn't get up at all on Saturday. I hope she's better soon – she starts her new job as a games designer in two weeks.
Sophie: Oh dear. Did you see Ben?
Abby: No. He was at home. He had some important homework to do and he didn't even have time to play his favourite video game.
Sophie: Really?
Abby: And James was missing, too. He went to see his favourite team play – he just loves football. But it was a shame I didn't see him. I want to ask him which is the best sports shop in town.
Sophie: Send him a text.

GRAMMAR
SB P43

PAST SIMPLE

LEAD-IN

Ask students questions to elicit and practise the short answer form of the past simple. For example, *Did you watch TV last night, Janis?* (*Yes, I did.*) *Did Janis watch TV last night?* (*Yes, she did.*) Point out that the question and answer forms are similar to the present simple but there is no different form for the third person singular (compare with -*s* and *does* in the present simple). The exception is the verb *to be* (*was/were*).

1 Ask students to look at examples and complete the rules. Then point out that in English many verbs are irregular. This means that the past simple tense form of the verb does not end with -*ed*. Each irregular verb is different, and students have to learn them.

> **2** -*ed*
> **4** didn't / did

LANGUAGE NOTE

There are some spelling rules for forming past simple regular verbs.

If the verb ends in -e: add -d (e.g. *decide – decided*)

If the verb ends in a vowel and a consonant: double the consonant and add -ed (e.g. *stop – stopped*)

If the verb ends in a consonant and -y: take off the *y* and add -ied (e.g. *carry – carried*)

If the verb ends in a vowel and -y: add -ed (e.g. *play – played*)

→ **GRAMMAR REFERENCE** / Page 202

2 Ask students to write the past tense forms of these irregular verbs. Check answers together.

> **1** saw **2** got up **3** came **4** went
> **5** said **6** had

3 Remind students that question forms and negatives are formed using *did* and *didn't* for irregular verbs in the same way as regular verbs. For example, *Did you make a cake? No, I didn't make a cake – I made a pizza!*

Look at sentence 1, and elicit the answer from the class before asking students to continue with the exercise individually. Then ask them to check answers in pairs before class feedback.

> **1** She said 'good morning' when she saw us.
> **2** I didn't see her there.
> **3** They had a really good time.
> **4** Did she stay with you last week?
> **5** No, she didn't.
> **6** He played video games until midnight.

FAST FINISHERS

Students can write some more sentences using the past simple to talk about what they did last weekend/week or last summer.

4 Students read the text and write the correct simple past form of the verbs into the gaps. Remind them that some of the verbs are irregular. When they have finished, ask them to check answers in pairs before class feedback.

> **1** visited **2** didn't stay **3** got **4** worked
> **5** helped **6** didn't stop **7** came **8** made
> **9** cleaned **10** didn't finish

5 🔊 029 Tell students there are three different pronunciations of the -ed ending.

Read the first rule in the book and model the sound /d/.

Then play the first part of the recording asking students to listen for the /d/ sound. Then drill the pronunciation chorally, repeating the recording as a model if necessary.

Repeat for the second and third sounds.

Point out that the third sound is the most important one to remember as it is completely different and students at this level may have more difficulty identifying the difference between 1 and 2.

AUDIOSCRIPT 🔊 029

1 I phoned my friend. We loved the film.
2 She cooked lunch. I helped my grandmother.
3 She invited my cousins. We downloaded a film.

6 🔊 030 Students use the rules in Exercise 5 to work out the pronunciation of the past tense verbs in the phrases and then read them to a partner. Play the recording for students to check and repeat and drill pronunciation as necessary.

AUDIOSCRIPT 🔊 030

1 I uploaded lots of photos.
2 We cooked lunch.
3 They started early.
4 He streamed some music.
5 I liked the film.
6 We enjoyed the party.

⊕ EXTENSION

Read out a list of regular simple past verbs to students and ask them to say 1 (for /d/), 2 (for /t/) or 3 (for /ɪd/), according to which sound they hear at the end.

As they answer, confirm and write the verbs on the board in a list, without separating them into categories.

Then ask students to take turns reading the list to a partner, and then writing them into three categories.

A list could include: *closed, climbed, walked, watched, repaired, missed, played, rested, opened, stayed, collected, painted, practised.*

7 Students make questions. Check the questions are correct as a class before students ask and answer with a partner.

> **1** What did you do last weekend?
> **2** Where did you go on your last holiday?
> **3** How did you come to class today?
> **4** What was the last really good film you saw?

FAST FINISHERS

Students can write one or two more questions using the past simple to ask another fast finisher.

UNIT 3 FREE TIME, SCREEN TIME?

VOCABULARY
SB P44

TIME EXPRESSIONS

LEAD-IN

Ask some questions to several students in the class on the model of the questionnaire. For example, *When was the last time you went swimming?*; *When was the last time you ate ice cream?* Ask one or two follow-up questions to elicit more detail, if necessary. For example, *Who did you go with?*; *Where did you go?* etc.

1 Ask students to read the questions in the questionnaire and tell them to write the questions she answered. Check answers.

> 1 When was the last time you downloaded a great song?
> 2 When was the last time you phoned a friend?
> 3 When was the last time you watched a film that made you cry?
> 4 When was the last time you walked more than 5 km?

2 Read the questions as a class to check understanding first and then students read the texts to find the answers. Compare in pairs before class feedback.

> 1 a new song by a Turkish singer.
> 2 She wanted to speak to him because it's his birthday and birthdays are special.
> 3 sad films
> 4 walk

3 Look at the example together. Ask students to find the expression *last week* in the first answer. Then students continue to complete the exercise. Check as a class, pointing out that all the time expressions talk about a finished time in the past which is why Maria uses the past simple tense.

> 2 five minutes ago   3 two years ago   3 last year

4 Copy the first *timeline* onto the board. Above *now* write the actual time and then ask students what to write above *five minutes ago* (the actual time five minutes ago). Try to elicit the correct position for the other two expressions in the box from the class and then ask them to suggest the actual time each expression corresponds to. Students continue in pairs to complete the second timeline in the book with the expressions from the box. When you check answers, ask for the corresponding day/time/year for each expression. Explain to students that they can use the time expressions to substitute the actual time.

> 1 yesterday afternoon   2 an hour ago   3 last year
> 4 last month   5 the day before yesterday

5 Read through the questionnaire with the class, checking vocabulary as necessary. For example, *Can you give me an example of 'exercise'?* (e.g. *football, swimming, physical activity*, etc.). *What are the names of some 'social media'?* (e.g. *Facebook, Instagram*, etc.). Highlight the question students need to ask to find someone who went to bed after 11 pm last night (in the first speech bubble).

Ask two or three students the question to demonstrate the activity and elicit some answers (*Yes, I did. / No I didn't.*).

Next, elicit the question students need to ask for the second point in the questionnaire: *Did you use social media yesterday?* Ask students to continue writing questions for the rest of the points, reminding them of the simple past question form. Check the questions as a class.

Once this has been completed, direct students' attention to the follow-up questions in the speech bubbles and ask students if they can think of a further follow-up question, e.g. *Why did you go to bed at 12 pm?* Then elicit or supply a possible answer (*I wasn't tired.*).

Encourage students to ask one or two follow-up questions whenever they receive a positive answer to the question. Students should try to speak to four or five different people, rather than asking one person all the questions.

6 Students then work with a partner to tell him/her about what they found out about their classmates.

Feed back by asking the questions and eliciting the names that students collected. Then ask one or two students to tell you something more about some of the people.

READING PART 3 TRAINING
SB P45

✓ EXAM INFORMATION

In Reading Part 3, students read a text and answer five three-option multiple-choice questions about it. They read for detailed understanding and main ideas. In the example here there are only three questions. The focus in the Student's Book is on encouraging students to find the correct answer by thinking about why the other answer options are incorrect.

They should allow about eight minutes to do Part 3 in the exam.

1 Initiate a class discussion about video games using the questions in the book. Encourage students to explain why they enjoy playing, or why they don't, and help with vocabulary as necessary.

2 Ask students if they know what *e-sports* are. If any students know, allow or help them to explain to the rest of the class. If not, ask students what they think the picture shows. Then students read the text and discuss the answers to the questions in pairs before class feedback.

BACKGROUND INFORMATION

In recent years e-sports (electronic sports) using video and computer games have become mainstream spectator sports with many teams and individual players enjoying major sponsorship deals just as traditional sports professionals do. Competitors play video games while being watched by a live audience and millions more online. There are various tournaments held across the world. Many professional gamers also focus on fitness levels and diet in the same way as a more traditional sportsperson.

3 Students discuss the meaning of the words in the box. If necessary, students can find the words in the text to see how they are used in context. Check answers as a class.

> **a competition** – a situation in which someone is trying to win something or be more successful than someone else
> **prize** – something valuable, such as an amount of money, that is given to someone who succeeds in a competition or game, or that is given to someone as a reward for doing very good work
> **professional** – used to describe someone who does something as their job
> **win** – to achieve first position and/or get first prize in a competition, election, fight, etc.

4 Read the rubric with the students and then ask one or two questions to check understanding. For example, *Who are you going to read about?* (Haiyun Tang); *What does she do?* (She's a professional gamer.); *Which question do you have to answer?* (Which games does she play?). Allow students about a minute to read the text quickly to find the answer. Encourage students to read quickly as it is not necessary to understand every word to find the answer. In the exam there may be vocabulary which is above A2 level, but students will not need to understand it in order to answer the questions. Not being put off by 'unknown' words is an important reading skill. Feed back as a class.

> World of Warcraft, Hearthstone

5 Read question 1 with the class and encourage them to re-read the first paragraph to find the answer. Demonstrate why B is the correct answer by reading the explanation in the book together. Point out that it can be helpful to try to think about why options are incorrect as well as choosing the correct answer. Students read the rest of the questions and try to answer them. Then, in pairs, encourage them to explain why they think those are the correct answers using 1 as a model. Check answers as a class and encourage students to justify their answers.

> **2** C **3** B

6 Students work in pairs to answer the questions. Monitor the discussions, helping with vocabulary as necessary, and then open the discussion to the whole class to compare ideas. If necessary you can suggest they think about strategic skills, creativity, physical activity, international events, prize money.

SB P46

A REVIEW

1 Students discuss the questions in pairs for two or three minutes then ask the class for feedback and compare opinions.

2 Allow students two minutes to read the review quickly to find the answer to the question. Encourage students to continue reading even when they don't understand a word to demonstrate to them that it's not always necessary to understand every word of a text in order to answer a question.

> The characters, because they are like real people

3 Ask students to look again at the words in blue and to re-read the sentences around them if necessary, in order to match the words with their definitions. Feed back as a class.

> **a** plot **b** dialogue **c** character
> **d** scene **e** setting

4 Encourage students to read the questions before they read the text again for the answers. Feedback as a class.

> **1** *The Originals* **2** Madrid **3** science students
> **4** science fiction comedy **5** Valeria – she's clever and funny but does silly things **6** when Valeria finds out that she can fly **7** It's funny and exciting.
> **8** The characters say interesting things that make the writer think and laugh at the same time.

UNIT 3 FREE TIME, SCREEN TIME?

5 Redirect attention back to the review. Ask students what the title is (The Originals) and how many paragraphs there are (three). Show students the table and ask them to re-read the first paragraph to find the sentence which talks about the setting (The setting is the city of Madrid (place) in the future (time)). Look at the box again and ask students to read the rest of the paragraph to decide what else is described.

Feed back as a class, asking students to read out the words or phrases which correspond to the genre, characters and plot. Then students continue the activity, in pairs, completing the chart for paragraphs two and three. Feed back in a similar way to ensure that everyone has an accurate chart.

Explain that it is important to separate different ideas into separate paragraphs when writing any text in English and that it is helpful to plan the order of the ideas before starting to write to help the reader understand what is written.

		Key words (suggested answers)
paragraph 1	setting genre plot	Madrid in the future science-fiction comedy-drama students studying science experiment, something strange happens, special powers
paragraph 2	character favourite scene	out of a window, special powers, can fly
paragraph 3	why the writer likes it	unusual difficult funny exciting characters like real people

6 Students can work in pairs or groups of three to select a series to write about. Move around the class helping with vocabulary, as necessary, while they are writing their plans into the table.

7 The writing can be done at home or in class. Encourage students to use the example review in the book as a model and to follow the plan they have prepared. Ask them to check their writing for grammar and spelling mistakes before exchanging texts with a partner who chose a different series. Encourage students to use the questions in the book to check the writing again. Remind them that it is always important to check work through when you finish writing.

SB P47

TALKING ABOUT THE WEEKEND

LEAD-IN

If you have personal experience of friends or family abroad tell students about it. For example, *My brother lives in London but we usually speak every two weeks. We talk about family and work.*

1 Ask students to read the questions and work in groups of three to answer them. Then ask three or four students to tell the class about their experience.

2 031 Students read the instructions. Ask some questions to check understanding. For example, *Who is speaking on the recording?* (Sara); *Where does she live?* (England); *Who is she talking to?* (Her sister who lives in New York). Read the *Did you know?* box with the class and point out the difference between American and British English. Ask students if they know any other differences between the two. They may know *football* (UK) and *soccer* (US) or *rubber* (UK) and *eraser* (US). Write *flat* on the board and ask students if they know the American equivalent (*apartment*) as this is in the recording. Read the question and ask students to predict who had a fun weekend, then play the recording. Students listen to find out if they were right.

Sara had a fun weekend.

AUDIOSCRIPT 031

Sara: Hi, Iman! How are you?

Iman: Hi, Sara, I'm fine. How are you? Did you have a nice weekend? Did you go to the cinema to see that new film?

Sara: No, I didn't, but my weekend was still really good, thanks. I went shopping on Saturday and I got a really nice new top, then, well, do you remember Sam who was at school with us? Well, he's started his own restaurant, so I went there for dinner.

Iman: Of course I remember Sam! Do you often see him?

Sara: No, but I'm friends with some of his friends and he invited us all for food at his new place. We had a party till late. It was great! What about you? How was your weekend?

Iman: Well it wasn't great, to be honest. It was really quiet on Saturday. I stayed at home and finished some work. I didn't really want to work this weekend, but it was good to finish it! After that I cleaned the apartment and watched TV.

Sara: And what about Sunday? What did you get up to on Sunday?

Iman: Not much. I was really tired. I went for a run in the park. I tried to call you, but you were out! What did you do on Sunday?

Sara: This and that. It was quite busy. A group of us went for a bike ride. The weather was great and we had a picnic. Then we watched films at mine.

Iman: Your weekend sounds great. Mine was so boring! I'm coming home next month, little sister, so I hope you take me out at the weekend with you then!

3 Tell students that in the recording Sara and Iman used different questions to ask each other about their weekend. Students work in pairs to order the questions. Check as a class.

LANGUAGE NOTE

In 3, the phrasal verb *get up to* is used. This means *to do something*.

1 Did you have a nice weekend?
2 How was your weekend?
3 What did you get up to on Sunday?
4 What did you do at the weekend?

4 031 Read through the answers and play the recording again for students to identify who said them. It may be necessary to stop the recording after each one to check.

Sara = really good, quite busy, this and that
Iman = not great, really quiet, not much

5 Read question 1 to the class and then ask students to look at a–f for the answer. If necessary, offer support by asking whether it is in the present or past tense (past).

Students match the questions and answers, using a process of elimination in the same way.

Move around the classroom helping with vocabulary as required, then check answers as a class.

1 c 2 d 3 a 4 f 5 b 6 e

6 Encourage students to re-read the different types of question presented in Exercise 6, and then write a minimum of five questions of their own to ask a partner. Stronger students can write more additional follow-up questions. Monitor students while they are writing and, if necessary, check the questions before students ask and answer in pairs.

Feed back by asking students to report what they learned about their partner to the class.

⊕ EXTENSION

Refer students back to the *Did you know?* box and tell them they are going to play a game using British and American vocabulary. Put them into groups of three or four and ask them to each think of two pairs of words. Each pair will have the British and the American name for something. For example, *TV* and *telly*, *apartment* and *flat*. They should write each word on a small piece of paper. Then they put the paper face down in the middle of the table and take turns to turn over a piece of paper and say the British or American equivalent of each word.

EXAM FOCUS
READING PART 3
SB P48

Read through the Exam facts and tips boxes with the class and answer any questions they may have. Remind students that the answers can be found in the text in the same order as the questions, with the exception of the question which may ask about the whole text (usually the last question). Encourage students to read the questions carefully before focusing on the part of the text where they can find the answer.

Remind students they have about 1.5 minutes per question in the Reading part of the exam, so allow 7.5 or 8 minutes for students to complete the task under exam conditions, individually, without speaking.

When checking answers, encourage students to explain *why* their answer is correct and if possible why the other two are wrong, e.g. 1 is B because the text says, *I've got a friend who does make-up in a small theatre so I contacted her*. It is not A because she did not get the job because she saw the advertisement – it just gave her the idea. It is not C because her friend was not at university – she worked in the theatre.

1 B 2 C 3 A 4 B 5 A

LISTENING PART 5
SB P49

Read through the Exam facts and tips boxes with the class. Check understanding of the task. Remind students that if they miss the answer to a question they should continue listening for the other answers and try to hear the one they missed when they listen for a second time.

032 Then read the question and tell students to complete the task under exam conditions, i.e. without talking to the other students. Play the recording twice for students to complete and check their answers. Feed back as a class.

1 E 2 A 3 H 4 C 5 G

UNIT 3 FREE TIME, SCREEN TIME?

AUDIOSCRIPT 032

Narrator: For each question choose the correct answer. You will hear Luis talking to his friend about a weekend trip to the city. What activity is each person going to do?

Woman: Hi, Luis. Are you ready for your weekend trip with your friends? What activity are you going to do on Saturday morning – visit a museum?

Luis: That's what I usually do, isn't it! Actually, I'm seeing a friend who I met on holiday.

Woman: Great! And Stella's going with you, isn't she?

Luis: Yes. She's going to do a bus tour, because it's her first time in the city. She said that's more important than concerts or shopping!

Woman: Is that what Marco's going to do – shopping?

Luis: That's his plan. He wants to go to the music shops in the area where the theatres are.

Woman: Who else is going?

Luis: Lili. She wanted to take a river trip, but it's too cold, so she's going to do a walking tour with a guide. She wants to see the museums, concert halls and other famous buildings from the outside.

Woman: And Richard?

Luis: He has a friend who's in a play, so he's going to see that.

Woman: What's Clara going to do?

Luis: There's a new art museum near the river that she's decided to go to.

Woman: Well I hope you're all going to eat together in the evenings!

Finally, read through the options in the *How was it?* section and elicit the meaning of each one: *gave it a go* (I tried hard but didn't feel it went particularly well); *getting there* (I'm improving but I'm not perfect yet) *aced it* (I feel I did really well). Ask students to tick the appropriate box.

You might like to ask students to share how they felt about the task to get an indication of your students' confidence. Depending on your class, you might like to do this openly or allow students to give their feedback without their classmates seeing. For example, give students a piece of A4 paper each with the *How was it?* scale written in large letters. Allow students to tick the relevant box then hold up their papers at the same time so that you can see how well students think they are doing.

REAL WORLD

SB P50

BUYING TICKETS FOR A SHOW IN … NEW YORK

LEAD-IN

Read the title together and ask students if they can tell you the name of a show. Accept all their suggestions.

1 Direct students' attention to the photos and brainstorm ideas to answer the questions.

> **Suggested answers**
> at the theatre, acting/performing, queueing for tickets

LANGUAGE NOTE

show can refer to a theatre, television or radio programme which is entertaining and fun rather than serious. We can talk about a quiz show or a game show but usually when we say just *show* we are referring to live theatre.

In American English the spelling is *theater* while in British English it's *theatre*.

2 Write *Broadway* on the board and ask the class if anyone knows what it is. Read through the paragraph headings in the box with the class to make sure they understand the vocabulary and then ask students to read the text and write the headings in the right place. Check answers as a class.

CULTURAL INFORMATION

Broadway is the name of a road in Manhattan, New York City, around which most of the large theatres of New York are located. The equivalent area in London is known as *the West End* or *Theatreland*. These two areas are famous across the English-speaking world for representing the highest level of professional theatre. You can watch everything, from Shakespeare to contemporary drama to musicals. The longest running show in London is *The Mousetrap* by Agatha Christie, which opened in 1952.

> **1** What to see   **2** Where to get tickets
> **3** Where to sit   **4** Where to eat before the show
> **5** What to buy

3 Read the statements as a class and then students read the texts to find out whether they are true or false. Encourage students to correct the false statements. Check as a class.

> **1** T
> **2** F It's more expensive to watch a show in the evening.
> **3** F Sometimes you want to be further away to get a bigger picture of what's happening.
> **4** F Restaurants around Times Square are usually expensive.
> **5** T

4 Encourage students to underline the phrases in the text and read carefully before and after them to help decide on the correct definition. Students work in pairs before class feedback.

| 1 a | 2 b | 3 b | 4 b | 5 a |

⊕ EXTENSION

Ask students to find the names of two different seating positions in the theatre in paragraph 3 to elicit *orchestra* and *mezzanine*. If possible, project or show a theatre seating plan on the board to identify where in the theatre these seats are. Ask students if they know the names of the seats which are higher up than the *mezzanine* (*balcony*) and then tell them that these are all American English names. If students have access to the internet ask them to find out what the British English equivalent names are – *stalls* (*orchestra*), *circle* or *dress circle* (*mezzanine*) and *upper circle* or *grand circle* (*balcony*). Students will need to use some of these names for the listening task in Exercise 5.

5 🎧 033 Tell students they are going to hear three conversations in which a tourist is buying a ticket for a Broadway show. Look at the table together and check understanding of *matinee* by asking students to suggest what time the matinee performance could be (usually in the afternoon, between 2 and 4 pm). Point out that the conversations are in New York so the names for the theatre seats will be in American English (*mezzanine*, *orchestra*, *balcony*).

Play the first recording and then give students a minute or so to check answers with a partner. Then repeat the recording if necessary. Check answers as a class.

Then play the second and third recordings twice. Give students time to compare answers before class feedback.

Speaker	Show	Day	Evening or matinee	Seats
1	Wicked	Thursday	evening	balcony
2	School of Rock	Tuesday	evening	orchestra
3	Charlie and the Chocolate Factory	Saturday	matinee	mezzanine

AUDIOSCRIPT 🎧 033

1
Tourist: I'd like to book four tickets for *Wicked* on Thursday.
Clerk: OK. Matinee or evening?
Tourist: Matinee if possible, please.
Clerk: Let's have a look. Hmm. No, the matinee's sold-out, I'm afraid. I have tickets for the evening.
Tourist: OK, the evening is fine.
Clerk: I have tickets in the balcony and the mezzanine.
Tourist: OK. Probably the balcony, I think. How much are the tickets?
Clerk: For the balcony, they're $69.
Tourist: Yes, that's fine.
Clerk: OK. How would you like to pay?
Tourist: By card, please.
Clerk: OK. The machine's ready for you. If you could put your number in, please.
Tourist: Thanks.
Clerk: And here's your receipt and your tickets. Enjoy the show.

2
Tourist: Do you sell tickets for *School of Rock* here?
Clerk: Yes, we do. When are you looking to go?
Tourist: On Tuesday evening, if possible.
Clerk: And how many tickets do you need?
Tourist: Four, please.
Clerk: OK. I don't have four in a block. Is that a problem?
Tourist: What have you got?
Clerk: I have two twos in the orchestra, for $89 each. There's the plan, do you see?
Tourist: Yes, I think that would be OK. I've got a student card. Is there a discount for students?
Clerk: No, sorry. We don't offer any concessions.
Tourist: OK. No problem. I'll take the four tickets.
Clerk: Thank you. That'll be $356 in total.

3
Tourist: Can I book tickets for *Charlie and the Chocolate Factory* here?
Clerk: You certainly can. When would you like to go?
Tourist: Next Saturday, the matinee performance.
Clerk: Let's have a look. It's pretty full. OK, I have some in the mezzanine. Do you mind the back row?
Tourist: No, that's fine. I need two tickets.
Clerk: OK. I have two tickets in the back row at $120 each.
Tourist: That's great. Can I use these vouchers to pay for the tickets?
Clerk: Let me see the date on them. Yes, you can use these. They give you 20% off, so your tickets will come to $192 in total.
Tourist: Thanks.

PHRASES YOU MIGHT USE

6 🎧 033 Students work in pairs to complete the sentences, then listen to the recording to check answers.

> **1** I'd like   **2** Do you sell   **3** Is there
> **4** Can I   **5** these vouchers

PHRASES YOU MIGHT HEAR

7 Students could be supported in this exercise by looking at a photocopy of the audioscript from Exercise 5 and reading the words in context. They can work in pairs to decide which definition is correct. Check answers as a class.

> **1** c   **2** a   **3** d   **4** e   **5** b

WATCH

8 ▶ Tell students they are going to watch a video about Broadway. Before watching, students work in pairs to guess the answers to the exercise by matching the numbers to the facts. As they do this, help with pronunciation of the numbers as necessary. Play the video and encourage students to listen to check their answers.

> **1** c   **2** e   **3** a   **4** b   **5** f   **6** d

VIDEOSCRIPT ▶ New York

Welcome to Broadway! This is New York's Theater District where you'll find most of the city's theatres. It's always busy. There are 40 theatres in this area, but there are actually only four theatres on Broadway Street itself.

The Gerschwin Theatre opened in 1972. It has 1,933 seats, and it's the biggest theatre on Broadway.

The Majestic Theatre is famous for the musical *The Phantom of the Opera*, one of the most popular shows ever on Broadway. It opened in 1988, and there have been over 11,400 performances!

The Lyric Theatre is also well-known. It's the theatre where you could see the most expensive show ever, *Spider-Man: Turn off the Dark*. It cost $79 million. But it wasn't a popular show, so the theatre lost money!

There are lots of different seats inside most theatres, such as the orchestra, the mezzanine and the balcony. Many people who visit New York come for the Broadway experience, and tourists buy 70% of Broadway show tickets.

You can buy tickets at the box office in each theatre, or, of course, you can buy them online. This is the best way to buy tickets in advance.

But you can go to the TKTS booth in Times Square if you want to buy tickets for the same day. You will probably have to queue. But you can often get a discount of 20–50%, so it's worth waiting for.

However you buy your tickets, there's nothing like the excitement of Broadway. Enjoy the show!

9 ▶ Students read the questions and discuss what they remember from the video. Play the video again for students to check their answers and add extra detail to their ideas. Then feed back as a class.

LIFE COMPETENCIES
SB P51

MAKING NOTES AND GIVING INFORMATION

10 Students work in groups of three or four. Ask them to find out which shows are on in their area and talk together for three or four minutes about which one they would like to see and why.

Then encourage students to make a list of headings which they can use to search for information about the show. For example, *prices*, *discounts*, *times*, etc.

If they have access to the internet they can do the research in class. Otherwise, they can do it at home or use a local newspaper.

Students make a short (one or two minutes) presentation to the rest of the class about the show they have chosen. There could be a class vote at the end of the presentations to decide the most popular show.

➡ **WORKBOOK** / Unit 3, page 16

4 KEEP FIT, FEEL GOOD

UNIT OBJECTIVES	
Topic:	health, exercise and illness
Grammar:	*can* and *can't*; *could* and *couldn't*; *should/shouldn't* for giving advice
Vocabulary:	the body; illness and injury; linking words; parts of the body
Listening:	Part 4: identifying the main idea in short dialogues
Reading:	reading for detail: two texts about amazing athletes
Speaking:	giving advice; telling a story about an accident
Writing:	Part 7: a story with picture prompts
Pronunciation:	stressed and unstressed *can* and *could*
Exam focus:	Listening Part 4; Writing Part 7
Real world:	if you're ill in Dublin

Ask your students to watch the Grammar on the Move videos on pages 54 and 56. You can use these to present or reinforce *can*, *can't*, *could* and *couldn't*, and *should/shouldn't* for giving advice.

READING

SB P52

> **WARMER**
>
> Ask the question, *Do you do any physical exercise?* Elicit names of activities and sports.

1 Then students work in pairs to ask and answer the questions in the book. Feed back by asking three or four students to report what their partner does to the class.

2 Write the word *amazing* on the board and ask students if they can think of another way of saying it. Elicit or supply *surprising* or *incredible*.

Students quickly read the quiz. Tell them they do not need to answer the questions the first time they read, just match each question with a photo. Then they work in pairs to read the questions more carefully and guess the answers.

Compare suggestions as a class without giving the right answers. It may be necessary to help them with pronunciation. For example, km = kilometre /ˈkɪl.əˌmiː.tər/, m = metre /ˈmiː.tər/, kg = kilogram /ˈkɪl.ə.ɡræm/; 284 (two hundred and eighty-four), 2,850 (two thousand eight hundred and fifty), 28,400 (twenty-eight thousand, four hundred).

| 1 A | 2 D | 3 B | 4 C | 5 E | 6 F |

3 034 Play the recording to check answers. Encourage students to comment on anything surprising. You could encourage the discussion by asking them some questions, e.g. *How long do you think you can stay under water?* (one or two minutes); *How fast can you run?* (15 to 20 kph).

| 1 a | 2 c | 3 b | 4 b | 5 c | 6 b |

AUDIOSCRIPT 034

Man: The fastest runners can run up to 44 kilometres per hour.

Woman: Professional basketball players and dancers can jump nearly one point three metres.

Man: The fastest cyclists can cycle up to 54 kilometres in one hour.

Woman: Some divers can stay under water for over 20 minutes.

Man: Some skiers can ski up to 250 kilometres per hour.

Woman: It's possible for a person to lift 2,840 kilos.

4 Direct students' attention to the pictures and ask the class the first two questions. Then give students two minutes to read the texts. Tell students it is not necessary to understand every word. They should learn to scan the texts to find the information. Elicit students' answers in feedback.

5 Read through the statements as a class, helping with understanding as necessary. Students do the task, correcting the false statements. Move around the class offering support as necessary, while students work through the exercise.

For a less able group this task could be broken down so that small groups of students read one text each and answer the questions referring only to that text (1–3 for Mikhail, 4–6 for Oscar). They then explain their answers to students who read the other text.

1 T	2 F Only the women dancers dance on their toes.
3 T	4 F They can. Small athletes run a lot.
5 T	6 F He couldn't play for three months.

6 Ask students if they remember any of the answers and then encourage them to re-read the texts quickly to check.

| 1 their feet | 2 their knees, neck and shoulders |

VOCABULARY
SB P53

THE BODY

WARMER
Brainstorm parts of the body on the board starting with those in the previous reading text.

1 Students work in pairs to label the diagram and then check answers as a class.

> 1 neck 2 back 3 stomach 4 toe 5 brain
> 6 finger 7 heart 8 knee

2 Students complete sentences before class feedback.

> 1 toes 2 back 3 neck 4 stomach 5 heart
> 6 fingers 7 brain 8 knee

⊕ EXTENSION
Write on the board: *On my hand I have five …*,
When you eat, the food goes down to your …

Elicit answers from the class to complete the sentences. Then ask students to work in pairs to write three or four more gapped sentences about body parts. Students then change partners to ask and answer. Remind them not to use gestures when speaking so that their partners have to listen carefully to the complete sentence. Monitor the activity helping with vocabulary as necessary.

GRAMMAR
SB P54

CAN AND CAN'T; COULD AND COULDN'T

LEAD-IN
Ask the class some questions using *can* and *could* to try to elicit short answers. For example, *Can you ski?* (*Yes, I can./ No, I can't.*), *Can you play tennis?* (*Yes, I can./ No, I can't.*), *Could you swim when you were four years old?* (*Yes, I could./ No, I couldn't.*).

1 Direct students' attention to the example sentences. Use the information in the box to highlight the form of the verbs and point out that there is no difference for the third person form (compared to the simple present tense) and that questions are formed by inverting the subject and verb. Ask students to complete the rules.

> 1 can   2 could

➡ **GRAMMAR REFERENCE** / Page 204

2 Students match the two parts of each sentence. Remind them to check whether the sentence refers to the present or the past.

A weaker group could be supported by looking for the question forms first and matching them before attempting the positive sentences. You may need to explain the expression *stand on my head* which you can do by drawing a quick stick figure on the board. Check answers as a class.

> 1 b   2 f   3 e   4 d   5 a   6 c

3 Ask students to read the first sentence. Elicit whether the word in the gap will refer to the present or the past (past – *When I was young*). Then, point out that the connector *but* is used to give contrasting information. Ask whether the word will have a positive or negative meaning (negative to contrast with the positive *I was a good guitar player*). Elicit which word is the past negative form (*couldn't*). Students continue to fill the rest of the gaps using similar reasoning, working in pairs. Check answers as a class. For the first two or three responses ask students similar questions to the above.

> 1 couldn't   2 could   3 can't   4 could   5 can't
> 6 couldn't   7 can

4 🔊 035 Look at the photo and ask students if they remember how to say what the person is doing. If your stick figure is still on the board pointing at it may help students remember the expression (*stand on your/my head*).

Ask students to read and listen to the first dialogue focusing on the stress pattern. The stressed words are marked. Then repeat for the second recording. If students have difficulty hearing the stress pattern you can clap your hands on the stressed words to help them identify the rhythm. Now ask students to circle the *can* and *could* which are unstressed in the dialogues. Repeat the recording for students to hear the pronunciation of the unstressed *can* and *could*.

Finally, students practise reading the two dialogues, focusing on stress patterns and the difference in the individual sounds. Move around the classroom to offer extra support as required.

> *Can* and *could* are unstressed:
> • in the second question in each dialogue (*Can you? / Could you?*);
> • in the positive statements in the last line of each dialogue (*I can walk on my hands, too / I could write quite well, too*).

AUDIOSCRIPT 🔊 035

1
A: <u>Can</u> you <u>stand</u> on your <u>head</u>?
B: <u>No</u>, I <u>can't</u>. Can <u>you</u>?
A: <u>Yes</u>, I <u>can</u> and I can <u>walk</u> on my <u>hands</u>, <u>too</u>!

2
A: <u>Could</u> you <u>read</u> when you were <u>six</u> years <u>old</u>?
B: <u>Yes</u>, I <u>could</u>, a <u>little</u>. Could <u>you</u>?
A: <u>Yes</u>, I <u>could</u> and I could <u>write</u> quite well, <u>too</u>.

5 Read the speech bubbles as a class and then ask one or two students the two questions, encouraging them to give their own answers, and modelling or correcting pronunciation as necessary. Students work in pairs, asking questions and answering them using the prompts in the box. Remind them to use the appropriate pronunciation.

VOCABULARY
SB P55

ILLNESS AND INJURY

> ### WARMER
> Brainstorm on the board names of illnesses or injuries that the students know. To get them started you could mime a few examples such as *headache* and *toothache*.

1  036 Tell students they are going to listen to each person in the photos talking about their problems. They match the people with the photos, decide what problems they have and decide who hasn't got a health problem. Check answers as a class.

> **1** C (Jack) has a headache **2** G (Alissa) has a broken arm **3** H (Mina) has backache
> **4** D (Luca) hurt his knee **5** F (Harry) has a cold
> **6** A (Jenna) has a stomach ache and feels sick
> **7** B (Daniel) has a toothache **8** E Sally hasn't got a health problem

AUDIOSCRIPT 036

1
Woman: Are you OK, Jack? What's the matter?
Jack: I've got a headache. I think it's because of the sun. I was outside without a hat.

2
Man: Oh Alissa! How did you break your arm?
Alissa: I broke it when I was playing tennis with my friends.
Man: What happened?
Alissa: A friend called an ambulance and I went to hospital.

3
Woman: What's the matter, Mina?
Mina: I've got backache. I just need to sit down and have a rest.

4
Boy: Hi Luca. How's your knee?
Luca: It's OK. I hurt it when I was playing football last weekend! Luckily, I didn't break it.

5
Woman: Have you got a cold, Harry?
Harry: Yes, I have.
Woman: Can I get you some medicine?
Harry: Oh no, it's OK. I went to the pharmacy and I got some already.

6
Man: Where's Jenna?
Woman: She's in bed. She ate some bad fish last night and now she's got a stomach ache and she feels sick.
Man: I'm sorry to hear that. I hope she gets better soon.

7
Woman: Have you got a headache, Daniel?
Daniel: No, I haven't. I've got toothache. It really hurts!
Woman: You should go to the dentist.

8
Man: How are you, Sally? Are you well?
Sally: I'm very well, thank you. I feel great!

2 036 Students listen again to complete the information. Then students work in pairs to check their answers. Then check answers as a class.

> **1** head **2** arm **3** backache **4** hurt **5** cold
> **6** stomach ache / feels **7** ache **8** fine

3 036 Give students a few minutes to read the sentences and match the parts. Repeat the recordings to check answers.

> **1** e **2** d **3** g **4** f **5** a **6** c **7** b

> ### LANGUAGE NOTE
> In British English *chemist* or *chemist's* is also used to describe a shop where you can buy medicine as well as other things such as make-up. In American English the equivalent is *drugstore*. Both use *pharmacy* to describe the place where medicines are prepared and sold.

4 Point out that the expressions come from the previous recording. Students work in pairs to complete the gaps. Check as a class.

> **1** matter **2** well **3** hurt **4** sorry
> **5** better **6** your

5 Do the exercise as a class.

> **1** 1, 2, 3, 6 **2** 4, 5

6 Students work together to ask and answer the questions. Monitor as they talk, moving around the class to help with vocabulary as necessary. Feed back by asking one or two students each question to tell the whole class their answers.

UNIT 4 KEEP FIT, FEEL GOOD 53

GRAMMAR
SB P56

SHOULD/SHOULDN'T FOR GIVING ADVICE

1 Initiate a class discussion to answer the question, *Do you think you have a healthy lifestyle?* Ask students to tell you reasons why they feel that way. Supply any vocabulary they need. Then students continue, in pairs, to discuss questions 1–4. Feed back as a class by encouraging students to compare their answers.

2 Read the title of the fact file and ask students to predict what will be included in it. Elicit or supply *advice*. Ask students to cover the numbers in the box and read the fact file in pairs guessing the missing numbers. Then uncover the numbers and ask them to select the answers from the list.

| **1** 5 | **2** 25g | **3** 1.6 | **4** 10 | **5** 9 | **6** 30 |

3 Complete rule 1 as a class and then direct students' attention to the box before they complete the other rules.

| **1** should | **2** shouldn't | **3** Should | **4** shouldn't |

➡ **GRAMMAR REFERENCE** / *Page 205*

4 With a weaker group go through 1 together asking students to read the sentence and then ask, *Is he hungry?* (yes); *What should he do?* (eat). Elicit the answer: *should eat*. Students complete the other sentences. Check answers as a class.

| **1** should eat |
| **2** Should, exercise, should |
| **3** should drink |
| **4** shouldn't drive, should walk |

5 Encourage students to think about what they do and the advice in the fact file as well, as any other ideas they have. Read the example sentences together and ask for one or two more suggestions from the class before students continue working in pairs to make other suggestions. Ask two or three students to tell the whole class what they *should* and *shouldn't* do.

SPEAKING
SB P56

GIVING ADVICE

1 🔊 037 Read the questions next to the photos with the class. Brainstorm some advice that each person might receive, helping students with vocabulary.

With a weaker group play the first part of the recording and ask students if they can identify which person the expert is giving advice to. Feed back as a class asking students which words helped them decide.

Then play the second part of the recording and ask the same questions.

AUDIOSCRIPT 🔊 037

1
Woman: First of all, it's great that you are trying to start exercising, but perhaps you should start exercising more slowly! To begin with, what about walking for half an hour every day? Walking is great exercise. Also, running isn't the only way to keep fit. Why don't you try some different types of exercise like dancing and swimming as well? It's important to do exercise that you enjoy.

2
Woman: Well, it's OK to eat fast food sometimes, but you shouldn't eat it all the time. It's bad for you because it has too much fat, salt and sugar in it. Why don't you try some other types of food? Healthy food tastes good too! And if you really want a burger, how about having a salad with it, or some fruit as a dessert?

2 🔊 037 Encourage students to read the sentences before listening again to complete the gaps. After listening, students discuss their answers in pairs. If necessary, the recording can be repeated before class feedback.

| **1** you should | **2** how about | **3** Why don't you |
| **4** you shouldn't | **5** Why don't you | **6** how about |

LANGUAGE NOTE

After *Why don't/doesn't I/you/he/she/we* we use the infinitive of the verb, e.g. *Why don't you cook dinner?* After *How about …?* we use the verb + *ing*. For example, *How about cooking dinner?*

3 Students work in pairs, taking turns to role play each situation, where one student is asking for advice and the other student is the expert offering advice.

Encourage students to listen carefully to their partner to make sure they are using the phrases in the right way.

Feed back by asking one or two students to repeat their advice for each photo.

LISTENING PART 4 TRAINING

SB P57

✓ EXAM INFORMATION

In Part 4 of the Listening paper, students listen to five short monologues or dialogues. They have to choose the correct answer from three multiple-choice options by listening for the main idea/gist/topic. In the exam students hear the recording twice.

This section in the Student's Book teaches students to focus on and underline important information in the question and answer options before they listen. They are encouraged to think of different ways of expressing the ideas in the answer options. The task here has only two questions.

1 038 Read the question and the options as a class and check understanding. Then read the information in the box, up to *feel stressed*, together. Encourage students to suggest alternative ways of expressing the ideas in A, B and C.

Play the recording, asking students to listen to identify the phrases which confirm the answer is A. If possible, elicit the language from students before reading the explanation in the Student's Book.

AUDIOSCRIPT 038

Narrator: One. Annie is talking to her friend at work. What's the matter with Annie?
Man: Are you OK, Annie? You look unwell.
Annie: I ate something yesterday that made me sick. I didn't sleep at all last night.
Man: Shall I help you with your work? I know you've got loads to do.
Annie: No, it's OK. I've finished everything for today. My stomach feels better today but I'm going home now – I just can't keep my eyes open.

2 039 Students read the questions and underline the important information. Then play each recording twice while students listen for the answers. Feed back as a class.

> 2 C   3 C

AUDIOSCRIPT 039

Narrator: Two. You will hear Victor phoning his friend Karen. Why is Victor phoning?
Victor: Hi, Karen. It's Victor.
Karen: Hi, Victor. Do you still want to go for a walk after lunch?
Victor: I'd really like to, but I've got a problem with my leg. Whenever I try to walk, I'm in so much pain. I've made a doctor's appointment for 3 o'clock.
Karen: Oh dear. Then I'll fetch you from your house and drive you there.
Victor: Thanks.
Narrator: Three. You will hear Jake talking to his friend Naomi. What's the matter with Jake?
Naomi: What's the matter, Jake? Have you got a headache?
Jake: Hi, Naomi. No, I was at the dentist yesterday. She took one of my teeth out.
Naomi: Ouch! Was it giving you a lot of pain?
Jake: It was, but not anymore. The thing is, I've hurt my neck. Probably my head was in the wrong position when I was lying in the dentist's chair.
Naomi: Poor you!

PUSH YOURSELF B1

SB P57

VOCABULARY: PARTS OF THE BODY

WARMER

Tell students they are going to read an interview with a sports doctor who is talking about the parts of the body that people injure when doing sport.

Draw the outline of a body on the board with lines for labelling and encourage students to name the different parts of the body, e.g *ankle, elbow, shoulder, wrist, hips, bone, muscle, lungs*.

1 Give students two or three minutes to read the interview to answer the question. Encourage them to look for the information about parts of bodies that sports people injure, and tell them not to worry about the other information in the text at this stage. Check answers as a class.

> No, sports people often injure the parts of the body they use in their sports.

UNIT 4 KEEP FIT, FEEL GOOD 55

2 Students work in pairs to complete the sentences with the words in orange in the text. Feed back as a class.

> **1** ankles **2** lungs **3** shoulders **4** muscles
> **5** wrists **6** Bones **7** elbows **8** hips

FAST FINISHERS

Students can write definitions for other parts of the body, e.g. *toes, mouth, arm*, etc.

VOCABULARY
SB P58

LINKING WORDS

1 Initiate a class discussion to answer the questions. Be aware that some students may be reluctant to talk about accidents so allow them to listen rather than participate in the discussion at this stage. As an alternative students could describe an accident scene from a film they have seen. For example, *It was at night in a big city. There were two fast cars and one crashed into a tram.* Provide vocabulary to help students describe situations as necessary.

2 Direct students' attention to the photos and ask them to say what they can see and predict what might happen in the stories. If necessary help students with vocabulary when they describe their suggestions.

Accept all suggestions. Give students two or three minutes to read the texts to see if anyone's prediction was correct.

Read through the questions with the class. Divide the class into two groups. Each group re-reads one text and answers the questions about that text. Then students pair up with someone who read the other text and tell them about the situation they read about. Feedback as a class.

> **1 A** on holiday in the mountains **B** in the garden
> **2 A** last year **B** one afternoon
> **3 A** A man skied in front of her and she bumped into him. **B** He was helping his nephew who was stuck in a tree and he got stuck too.
> **4 A** her leg **B** his arm

3 Draw attention to the words in blue in the two texts and ask students which phrase in the text about Sam answers the first question (when the story happened). Elicit *One sunny afternoon*. Then read questions 2 and 3 with the class. Encourage students to suggest answers to the questions. Finally, allow students two or three minutes to answer the questions for the second text.

> **1** last year, one day, one sunny afternoon
> **2** then, after that, so, when
> **3** suddenly

4 Encourage students to underline the verbs from the box when they find them in the texts. Ask which verb is regular (*bump into*). Encourage students to read all the sentences before deciding which verb fits in the gap. Go over answers as a class.

> **1** fell over **2** hit **3** got stuck **4** bumped into

FAST FINISHERS

Students can write some more sentences using the verbs in Exercise 4.

⊕ EXTENSION

Hand out a piece of paper to each pair of students. Tell them they are going to write a story together. Ask each pair to write one sentence introducing the story and saying when it happened. Then they pass their piece of paper to the pair next to them and write another sentence to continue the second story. Remind students to use the words and expressions in Exercise 3 and if appropriate the verbs in Exercise 4. Continue passing the pieces of paper along so that each sentence or two is written by another pair. Students need to make sure the sentence they write connects to the rest of the story on the page. At the end, students take turns to read the finished stories to the class. They can hold a vote to choose the best story.

WRITING PART 7 TRAINING
SB P59

✓ EXAM INFORMATION

In Reading and Writing Part 7, students have to write a short story based on three pictures. They should write 35 words or more.

The focus in the Student's Book is on using linking words and time expressions. Students should spend nine to ten minutes on Part 7. There is an example exam-style question on page 61 in the Student's Book.

WARMER

Go over the information about this part of the exam and ask the class some questions to check understanding. For example, *How many pictures are there?* (three); *Can you use the past tense?* (yes, or the present); *What should you do when you finish writing?* (check spelling).

1 Go over the instructions with the class. A weaker class could be supported by doing this exercise in groups. First, form groups of three or six students and hand out six strips of paper to each group. Each student copies one or two of the sentences in the book onto a strip of paper. Then students work together to put the sentences in order on the desk to make the story. Remind them to use the words in bold to help decide the correct order. Check answers as a class by reading the story.

Finally, ask students which tense the writer has used (past). Point out the use of time expressions and linking words (in bold). Highlight that the writer has given names to the people in the pictures to make the story more interesting.

1 c **2** e **3** a **4** d **5** f **6** b

2 Go over the instructions as a class. Encourage students to look carefully at the pictures before they start.

Point out the list of useful words for each picture in the box and check understanding, if necessary. Tell students that in the exam it is a good idea to think about vocabulary for the story before they start writing and it may be helpful to make a list of words they want to use. Students write their story. When they have finished, encourage them to check their writing using the instructions in the box above Exercise 1. Alternatively, you could write a checklist on the board. For example:

Did you write 35 words or more?
Did you use linking words and time expressions?
Did you write full sentences?
Did you check spelling?

> **Suggested answer**
> **One day**, Tom went to the swimming pool to play water volleyball with his friends. He didn't look at the sign behind him that said *No Running*. **Suddenly**, he fell on the wet floor and hurt his arm. **After that**, an ambulance took him to hospital because his arm was broken. The next week Tom was back at the swimming pool. He couldn't swim. He had to sit and watch his friends having fun in the water. Tom was so bored!

TELLING A STORY

1 🔊 040 Go over the instructions as a class. Then encourage students to read the questions in the box.

Play the recording, asking students to listen for the answers to the questions without writing anything. Before listening, for a second time, students discuss any answers they think they heard with a partner.

Then play the recording again and ask students to take notes for each answer.

Point out that it is not necessary to write complete sentences while they are listening. With a weaker class the recording can be played for a third time.

Check answers as a class.

When/Where?	winter holidays, in the mountains
Who with?	cousin Gemma
What did they do?	They went ice skating.
How did he feel?	worried, frightened
What happened?	A duck landed in front of him and he couldn't stop – he fell and hurt a finger.
What happened after that?	They didn't go skating again – his finger ached for the rest of the holiday.

AUDIOSCRIPT 🔊 040

Alex: Last winter holidays, I went to visit my cousin Gemma in the mountains. It was very cold and the lake near her house was covered in thick ice, so we decided to go ice skating. I felt a bit worried because I'm not very good at ice skating, but Gemma said it would be OK. When we got to the lake, I put on my ice skates and went on the ice for the first time.
I was frightened, but I started skating slowly across the lake. Soon, I began to skate faster, and it was actually quite fun! Then suddenly a duck flew down and landed on the ice in front of me. I tried to stop but I couldn't! I lost control and I fell hard onto the ice! I didn't hit the duck, because it flew away, but I did hit my hand and I hurt one of my fingers. I didn't break anything, but my finger ached for the rest of the holiday and we didn't go skating again.

2 Go over the instructions and explain that the story does not have to be true. Give three or four minutes for students to think about an idea and make notes. Move around the classroom while students are preparing and help with vocabulary as necessary.

3 Students take turns to tell their story. Their partner listens and asks at least one question.

> **FAST FINISHERS**
> Students write the story they told in class or at home, adding linking words and time expressions.

EXAM FOCUS
LISTENING PART 4

SB P60

Read through the Exam facts and tips boxes with the class and answer any questions they may have. Remind students that they can underline important words before they listen and that they should think about other ways to express the same ideas. Students have a few seconds before each recording to read the question and answer options. They should try to choose an answer the first time they listen and then listen again to check their answers.

🎧 041 Tell students they are going to do the listening under exam conditions, i.e. without conferring with a partner. Allow a few seconds for students to look at the first question. Then play the recording. Elicit answers around the class.

| 1 A | 2 B | 3 C | 4 B | 5 C |

AUDIOSCRIPT 🎧 041

Narrator: For each question, choose the correct answer. One. You will hear two friends talking about doing exercise. What does the man say about it?

Woman: I swam three kilometres yesterday!

Man: Wow, that's incredible! I can't swim that far. But don't you ever find swimming boring?

Woman: No, I love it. I like having time alone to think.

Man: I work harder when I do exercise with friends. That's why I like football or tennis.

Narrator: Two. You will hear a woman leaving a message for a doctor's receptionist. Why did the woman call?

Woman Hello, this is Lily Williams. I called yesterday, and made an appointment to see the doctor next Monday. Now my boss says I have to work that day, so I was wondering if I could come on Tuesday instead. The time you gave me was 4 pm. Can I come at that time on Tuesday? Call me back, please.

Narrator: Three. You will hear a woman called Lara talking to a friend about going shopping. What does Lara want her friend to do?

Man: I'm looking forward to going to the new shopping centre, Lara. Is there plenty of parking there?

Woman: Yes, but my car's broken down. Can we go in yours? I'll pay you for the petrol.

Man: No problem and don't worry about the money! I'll pick you up at ten.

Woman: Thanks! I'm going to get a dress for Helena's wedding. I've seen the perfect one!

Narrator: Four. You will hear a man talking about his new job. How does the man feel about his new job?

Woman: How's the new job, Daniel?

Man: Pretty good. At first I wasn't sure, because the boss shouts, and he's always talking about how much money the company is or isn't earning. But I guess that's his job – he's the boss! And there's no real end time. When we finish the day's work, we just go, so my days are shorter now, which is great.

Narrator: Five. You will hear two friends talking about an exhibition of photographs. Where will the exhibition be?

Woman: Lucy's chosen a great place for her photography exhibition!

Man: I know! A few of the photos will be behind the reception desk, so people will see them when they arrive, or as they're paying. There'll be others in the restaurant, too.

Woman: What about in the guest's rooms?

Man: No, but there'll be some on the walls between the lifts and the rooms.

WRITING PART 7
SB P61

Read through the Exam facts and tips boxes carefully with the class. Remind students to think about some useful vocabulary before they start writing. Then allow students ten minutes to write their story individually under exam conditions, i.e. without using a dictionary or comparing ideas with a partner. They should leave some time to check their answer when they finish. They can exchange finished texts with a partner for peer feedback when they finish. Students can use the points in the tips box to check their partner's work.

> **Suggested answer**
> A man had a toothache, so his wife phoned the dentist to make an appointment. He didn't want to see the dentist, so she pushed him into the room. She waited for him. When the man came out, he was smiling and didn't have toothache anymore. (45 words)

Read through the options in the *How was it?* section and elicit the meaning of each one that they learned in the first unit.

Ask students to tick the appropriate box. You might like to ask students to share how they felt about the task to get an indication of your students' confidence. Depending on your class, you might like to do this openly or allow students to give their feedback without their classmates seeing. For example, give students a piece of A4 paper each with the *How was it?* scale written in large letters. Allow students to tick the relevant box then hold up their papers at the same time so that you can see how well students think they are doing. Finally, ask students if they found it easier, harder or the same as the exam practice in previous units.

➡ **WRITING BANK** / *Pages 235–236*

REAL WORLD

SB P62

IF YOU'RE ILL IN ... DUBLIN

> **WARMER**
>
> Ask students where they go if they are sick or have an accident. Try to elicit *pharmacy / chemist's*, *doctor's* and *hospital*.

1 Draw attention to the photos and encourage students to suggest reasons why people go to the places. For example, *You go to the pharmacy if you have a headache. You go to the hospital if you break your leg.* Encourage students to suggest as many reasons as possible, helping with vocabulary as necessary. It may be helpful to provide extra vocabulary for students such as *medical centre, doctor's surgery, GP, ambulance, A&E, drop-in centre.*

> to get help with health problems / if they are sick

> **CULTURAL INFORMATION**
>
> Dublin is the capital city of Ireland. All the inhabitants speak English, although street signs are also in Irish Gaelic.

2 Read the introductory question with the class and ask students if they know any other ways of saying *being sick*. Elicit or supply *feeling/being ill/unwell*. Allow students two or three minutes to read the text quickly and match the photos to the paragraphs. Feed back as a class.

> 1 C   2 A   3 B

3 Students work in pairs to match the definitions with the words. Encourage them to read the sentence around the word in the text again before deciding on the definition. Feed back as a class.

> 1 c   2 f   3 a   4 h   5 g   6 d   7 e   8 b

4 Students work in pairs to find the answers to the questions in the text.

Feed back as a class, encouraging students to tell you if the answers are the same or different for their country.

> **Suggested answers**
> 1 from a supermarket, small shop or petrol station
> 2 from a supermarket, small shop or petrol station
> 3 from a pharmacy
> 4 find your nearest GP and phone to book an appointment
> 5 find out which doctor is on call and go to the medical centre
> 6 go to the A&E department of a hospital, or call 112 or 999 and ask for an ambulance

5 042 Go over the instructions with the class and elicit suggestions for what type of information or language they might hear in each place. For example,

- at a hotel: a guest asking about where the hospital or pharmacy is;
- at a pharmacy: advice about medication or buying some medicine;
- in a GP's waiting room: a conversation about an appointment or how someone is feeling;
- at an emergency department: questions and answers about an accident.

Play the first conversation and then ask students to check their answer with a partner before checking as a class. If possible, ask students to say why they chose the answer they did.

> 1 b

AUDIOSCRIPT 042

1
Assistant: Hello. Can I help you?
Tourist: Yes. I have a prescription from the doctor.
Assistant: OK. Let me see … Yes, we can do this for you. Are you taking any other medicines?
Tourist: No, I'm not taking any medicines at the moment.
Assistant: Any other medical conditions?
Tourist: No.
Assistant: And have you taken this medicine before?
Tourist: Yes. In my own country.
Assistant: And you didn't have any side effects?
Tourist: No.
Assistant: That's good. Well, take a seat. It'll be about five minutes.
Tourist: Thank you.
Assistant: Here's your prescription. Take one tablet three times a day, with food. And you must finish the whole course.
Tourist: OK. Thank you.

Students listen to the other two recordings and check answers with a partner before checking as a class.

> 2 d   3 a

UNIT 4   KEEP FIT, FEEL GOOD

AUDIOSCRIPT 042

2

Nurse:	Maria Baldini, please. Could you come this way?
Nurse:	OK. Just take a seat for me. Can I check your name first?
Maria:	Yes, it's Maria Baldini.
Nurse:	And what's your date of birth, Maria?
Maria:	The tenth of December, 1999.
Nurse:	So, can you tell me what's happened?
Maria:	Yes. I was getting off a bus and I fell, and I've hurt my arm.
Nurse:	And when was this?
Maria:	About one hour ago.
Nurse:	OK. Can I take a look?
Maria:	Yes, of course.
Nurse:	OK. Does this hurt here?
Maria:	Ah, yes.
Nurse:	Sorry. And what about this?
Maria:	Yes, but that's not so bad.
Nurse:	Can you move your fingers?
Maria:	No, not really.
Nurse:	OK, well I think we need to get it X-rayed. Any other medical problems?
Maria:	No.
Nurse:	Do you take any medicines regularly?
Maria:	Yes, I take tablets for headaches.
Nurse:	OK. Do you know the name?
Maria:	I have it here.
Nurse:	OK. Thanks. And where are you from, Maria?
Maria:	I'm from Italy.
Nurse:	Do you have your EHIC card with you?
Maria:	Yes, it's in my bag. Here it is.
Nurse:	Thanks. Are you in pain at the moment?
Maria:	No, I'm OK, thanks.
Nurse:	That's great. If you could wait back in the waiting area, you'll see a doctor within an hour, and they'll do an X-ray to see if anything's broken. Then they'll decide what to do next. There will be a charge for the emergency consultation, but you can probably claim that back when you get home.
Maria:	OK. thanks.

3

Receptionist:	Hi. How are you doing?
Tourist:	OK, thanks, but I have a really bad sore throat and I need to get something for it.
Receptionist:	OK. Do you think you need to see a doctor?
Tourist:	No, I think it's OK. I just need some painkillers.
Receptionist:	OK. Well, it's best to try the pharmacy on Argyle Street. It's only a five-minute walk from here. If you go out of the hotel and turn right, then first left, that's Argyle Street.
Tourist:	OK. Thank you.

PHRASES YOU MIGHT USE

6 042 Point out that the sentences are from the conversations in Exercise 5. Students work in pairs to complete the sentences, then play the recording for them to check their answers.

> **1** prescription **2** medicines **3** tablets
> **4** sore **5** painkillers

PHRASES YOU MIGHT HEAR

7 Go over the instructions with the class and point out that the phrases come from the audio track 042 in Exercise 5.

Students work in pairs to do the exercise. If necessary, when checking answers you can ask some follow-up questions to check understanding. For example, for item 2, *Give me an example of a side effect* (a medicine causing a headache).

> **1** c **2** d **3** a **4** b

WATCH

8 Read through the bullet points with the class and ask them to predict any information that might be in the video about Dublin and its health services. Note the suggestions the class makes on the board.

Tell students they are going to watch the first part of the video. Ask them to listen to see whether the ideas on the board are mentioned and whether they learn anything else about Dublin.

Students discuss answers in pairs before class feedback.

> **the city:** the capital of the Republic of Ireland, and also the biggest city; on the East coast of Ireland; has many old buildings and also modern buildings

VIDEOSCRIPT ▶ Dublin

Dublin is the capital city of the Republic of Ireland. It's also the biggest city in the country. It's on the east coast of Ireland, and has many old buildings, and lots of modern buildings, too. There are lots of pharmacies in the city. Look for this green cross sign outside if you need one.

You can go there to buy medicines, such as painkillers, and also to collect medicines if you have a doctor's prescription. If you need to see a doctor, you usually need to make an appointment at a medical centre. At some big medical centres, you can just 'drop in', without an appointment. At the medical centre, you see a GP, a general doctor, to discuss your problem.

If you need to see a specialist doctor, you have to go to a GP first. The GP then sends, or 'refers', you to a specialist. Most medical centres are open all day, but at night only one or two doctors are on call.

If you need to see a doctor at night, you can ask at your hotel to find out which doctors are on call. Of course, hospitals are open 24 hours a day. You can go to the A&E (Accident and Emergency) department at any time.

If you are seriously ill, or there is an emergency, you can also dial 999 to call for an ambulance. The ambulance will take you to the hospital Accident and Emergency department, and here, specialist doctors and nurses will look after you until you are better.

Now students listen to the rest of the video and make notes about the other places in the list. With a weaker class it may be helpful to pause the video after each section to give students time to complete their notes and/ or discuss their ideas with a partner.

9 ▶ Students discuss their notes with a partner before watching the video again to check answers.

pharmacies: have a green cross outside; you can buy medicines such as painkillers and also collect medicines when you have a prescription

medical centres: usually need to make an appointment to see a doctor, but at some medical centres you can go without an appointment. You will see a GP, a general doctor.

doctors on call: medical centres all open during the day; at night only one or two doctors are on call. Ask at your hotel to find out which doctors are on call.

hospital emergency departments: hospitals open 24 hours a day; you can go to the emergency department at any time, or dial 999 to call an ambulance if you are seriously ill or there is an emergency. Specialist doctors and nurses will look after you.

LIFE COMPETENCIES
SB P63

SHARING IDEAS AND PROBLEM-SOLVING

10 Divide the class into groups of three or four. Go over the instructions and highlight that students need to find the answers to the questions for visitors to the city, not themselves.

Encourage students to read through the questions in their groups and note down any answers they think they know.

As they are working, help with vocabulary as necessary.

If you have internet access in the classroom, students can then start researching the rest of the information. Otherwise, they can do this at home. If necessary, they could decide who will look for which information.

Once students have gathered the information, encourage them to think about the design and layout of an effective leaflet. They should think about the visuals, e.g. photos, pictures, colours; the type of language, e.g. sentences, notes, questions and answers; and the quantity of information, e.g. maps, addresses, telephone numbers.

11 Then each group makes its leaflet and presents it to the class.

➡ **WORKBOOK** / *Unit 4, page 20*

5 MORE THAN A HOLIDAY

UNIT OBJECTIVES

Topic:	travel and holidays
Grammar:	past continuous; past simple and past continuous; *when, while* and *as*
Vocabulary:	travel; easily confused words
Listening:	listening for general understanding and detail: short monologues about travelling; listening for specific information: a talk about an explorer
Reading:	Part 4: 3-option multiple-choice cloze about a pioneering pilot
Speaking:	Part 2: discussing pictures about holidays
Writing:	an email about something that happened on holiday
Pronunciation:	*was* and *were*
Exam focus:	Reading Part 4; Speaking Part 2
Real world:	going on a sightseeing tour in Berlin

Ask your students to watch the Grammar on the Move videos on pages 66 and 68. You can use these to present or reinforce the past continuous and the past simple and continuous.

VOCABULARY
SB P64

TRAVEL

WARMER

Pre-teach *tourist* and *destination*. Write or say the following sentence: *Millions of tourists visit New York City every year.* Elicit or supply a definition of *tourist*: *someone who visits a place when they are on holiday.* Then use this sentence: *Rome is a popular holiday destination* and elicit or supply the definition of *destination*: *the place where someone goes on holiday.*

1 Students work in groups of three to discuss the questions. Encourage them to think about which areas are most popular and why. It may be necessary to prompt them when thinking about problems, e.g. pollution, traffic, crowds. Then ask one or two groups to tell the class their answers and ideas.

2 Look at the title of the quiz with the class. Pre-teach *adventurous* (an adventurous person is someone who is happy to try new or difficult things). Brainstorm suggestions of some of the things an adventurous traveller might do. For example, try new food or a new activity, stay in an unusual place, visit places which are difficult to get to, etc.

Students match the photos A–E with the quiz questions. Make this into a race by giving a time limit (two minutes). It is not necessary for students to read all the questions and answer options to complete the task.

Feed back as a class.

| 1 B | 2 A | 3 C | 4 D | 5 E |

3 Students work in pairs to ask and answer the quiz questions and then evaluate their partner's responses using the answer key on page 193.

Hold a show of hands to see the results for the whole class. Ask who are the most and least adventurous. Discuss as a group whether they think the results accurately describe how adventurous the class is.

CULTURAL INFORMATION

Students may be interested to know that other English-speaking countries such as Australia, New Zealand and Canada tend to follow the same spelling rules as British English.

LISTENING
SB P65

LEAD-IN

Go over the instructions and read the destinations (the city, the beach, the mountains) with the class. Ask students to suggest what type of activity people might enjoy doing in each of them. For example, going to museums and restaurants in the city.

1 🔊 043 Play the recording and encourage students to match the people with their ideal destinations. Tell students it is not necessary for them to understand every word of the recording.

Feed back by asking the class if they remember any words they heard that helped them choose their answers.

Loli – the beach
Chloe and Lisa – the mountains
Jamie – the city

62

AUDIOSCRIPT 043

Loli: I love the beach but I'm a student and don't have much money at the moment, so I always try to find cheap destinations. If the weather is sunny and I can go swimming in the sea, I'm happy! My friends and I look for cheap flights and places to stay online. Some of them dream about staying in expensive hotels, but for me, staying with local people in their houses is the best kind of holiday accommodation.

Chloe: Well, for Lisa and me, a true holiday is when we are outside in nature. We like going to places where there aren't many tourists – or even any other people at all. We often go walking and camping in the mountains. We don't take much luggage – just a tent to sleep in and a backpack with food and water.

Lisa: Yes, that's right. Chloe loves camping like this and I do too, but I'm also happy when we can stay in a campsite where there are toilets and showers. I like meeting the local people and trying to talk to them. We enjoy going to places where we can't speak the language, but we do try to learn some important words before we go!

Jamie: An interesting city with lots of museums and restaurants is always a good destination for me! I work long hours in a bank and I like to pack a small suitcase on Friday night and fly to a city for the weekend. I always stay in the best hotels because I want to be really comfortable. When I visit a city for the first time, I take a proper city tour with a tour guide, so I can learn all about its history. In the evenings, I enjoy going to music concerts and I think that asking at the tourist information centre is a good way to find out about what's on. They can tell you about the best plays and concerts and book tickets for you.

2 043 Read the statements and help with vocabulary, as necessary. With a stronger group, give students a minute or two to discuss the answers in pairs before they listen as they may have already heard some of the answers.

Play the recording again. With a weaker group it may be helpful to pause after each speaker and give students the opportunity to discuss their answers with a partner.

Students go over answers in pairs before class feedback.

> **1** F She likes swimming.
> **2** T
> **3** F She's happy when they can stay in a campsite where there are toilets and showers.
> **4** F They often go to places where they can't speak the language, but they try to learn some important words before they go.
> **5** T
> **6** F He goes to the tourist information centre to find out about concerts.

3 A stronger group can be encouraged to try to complete the sentences without looking back at the words in the quiz.

Otherwise, encourage students to read the sentences together and decide whether the missing words are verbs or nouns and singular countable or uncountable (an article before the space will help students decide).

Brainstorm the words from the quiz and write them on the board. Then categorise them into three lists: verbs, countable nouns and uncountable nouns.

Students work with a partner to complete the sentences. Feed back as a class.

> **1** accommodation   **2** miss, delay
> **3** luggage, tent, backpack   **4** destination
> **5** suitcase   **6** tour guide   **7** tourist information centre

4 Students work in pairs to match the two parts of the questions. Feedback as a class before students ask and answer. A stronger group can be encouraged to ask and answer the follow-up question *Why?*, where appropriate. Monitor as students do the activity by moving around the room and listening for interesting and unusual answers to elicit during class feedback.

> **1** d   **2** e   **3** f   **4** a   **5** c   **6** b

READING

1 Initiate a class discussion to answer the questions. Encourage students to think about whether the experience of riding a camel might be similar or different to horse riding and why. Ask students to name some countries where they might see a camel.

BACKGROUND INFORMATION

Taking an excursion on a camel is a popular activity for tourists in countries with areas of desert such as Morocco, Egypt and Australia. Guides can take you on short trips of an hour or treks across the desert lasting a few days, staying overnight in traditional camps.

2 Tell students they are going to read a text about a person who has an adventure while on holiday in Morocco. Check understanding of the questions and give students two or three minutes to look for the answers in the text. Encourage students to scan the text quickly to find the answers and not to worry if they don't understand some of the other words at this stage. Feed back as a class.

> **1** He wanted something exciting to do. No.
> **2** He started to feel sick / was feeling bad.

3 Read the questions as a class and then ask students to work in pairs to read the text again and find the answers. Discuss the answers as a class.

> 1 Camels are very friendly and they love their owners.
> 2 The camel didn't look friendly and made strange, loud noises.
> 3 She was saying hello to Jon.
> 4 so that people can get on to them
> 5 because riding a camel was like being in a boat
> 6 She was a nice animal.

GRAMMAR

SB P66

PAST CONTINUOUS

1 Ask comprehension questions about the two sentences: a) *Were they driving to the coast at 2 o'clock?* (yes); b) *Were they trying to find something to do when they were visiting Morocco?* (yes), to elicit the information in the rules.

> 1 an action in progress at a time in the past
> 2 at the same time

➡ **GRAMMAR REFERENCE** / Page 206

2 Direct students' attention to the box and remind them of the spelling rules to form the *-ing* form of the verb.

Then students complete the sentences. Go over the answers as a class.

> 1 were, doing   2 wasn't raining, was snowing
> 3 were lying, watching   4 was packing, was doing
> 5 wasn't living, was studying   6 Was, looking for, wasn't

3 Students complete the sentences in pairs.

> 1 Where were you going yesterday afternoon?
> 2 The children weren't playing on the beach this morning.
> 3 'Was she trying to take a photo?'
> 4 Your friend wasn't staying at this hotel.
> 5 'Was he looking at her?' 'No, he wasn't.'
> 6 Which city were they visiting?

LEAD-IN

Read out some of the sentences from Exercise 3, above, to the class and ask them to listen carefully and underline the stressed words. It may be necessary to slightly exaggerate the stressed words to help students hear them.

4 044 Go over the instructions and make sure students understand they only have to underline *was/were* when they are stressed.

Play the recording and check answers as a class.

AUDIOSCRIPT 044

A: Where were you last night? Were you at the party?
B: Yes, we <u>were</u>.
A: Was it good?
B: Yes, it was great! <u>Weren't</u> you invited?
A: Yes, we <u>were</u>. But we couldn't go because my mum was cooking us dinner.

LANGUAGE NOTE

It may be helpful to highlight the differences in the pronunciation of *was* and *were* when they are stressed and unstressed:

was = /wɒz/ when stressed   *was* = /wəz/ when unstressed
were = /wɜː/ when stressed   *were* = /wə/ when unstressed

5 045 Read the rules as a class and then allow students two or three minutes to choose the options with a partner. Encourage students to say the words out loud in order to listen to the sounds and decide on the answers. Then play the recording to check.

Play the recording again, pausing after each sentence to allow students to repeat, focusing on stress. If necessary, ask individual students to read some of the sentences to the class.

> 1 A unstressed, B stressed
> 2 A unstressed, B stressed
> 3 unstressed

AUDIOSCRIPT 045

1 **A:** Was it hot that day?
  B: No, it <u>wasn't</u>.
2 **A:** Was the exam really three hours long?
  B: Yes, it <u>was</u>.
3 The actors in the play were really funny.

If necessary, repeat the recording and then let students practise reading the dialogue in pairs.

6 Remind students to use the correct word stress when asking and answering the questions.

LISTENING
SB P67

CULTURAL INFORMATION
Benedict Allen is a British explorer and writer who is famous for travelling to remote places without the use of technology such as a phone or GPS. His objective is to immerse himself in challenging environments and live with indigenous people.

WARMER
Ask the class to imagine they are explorers. Which parts of the world would they like to explore? Why? Brainstorm ideas.

1 Direct students' attention to the photo and the information about Benedict Allen in the rubric (supplementing this with the cultural information above, if necessary). Elicit answers to the questions. If you have a map in the classroom or internet access you could ask them to show you where the Gobi Desert is.

BACKGROUND INFORMATION
The Gobi Desert is in Central Asia and covers large areas of both Mongolia and China. The name comes from the Mongolian 'gobi' which means 'waterless place'. Most of the desert is rock rather than sand and there is very little vegetation.

> **1** Mongolia and China   **2** Students' own anwers

2 046 Ask students what they think the weather was like in the desert, before listening to check.

> cold

AUDIOSCRIPT 046
Benedict Allen began to cross the Gobi Desert in Mongolia and China in August 1997. It was a journey of 1,600 kilometres and he was alone and on foot. He took three camels with him to carry his things and he decided not to use any modern technology to help him. He preferred to use a map.

He only had three months to make the journey because the Gobi Desert can be very cold and he needed to cross it before the beginning of winter. Many people thought that it was an impossible journey and one of Benedict Allen's camels did too. As they were doing the most difficult part of the journey, the camel decided that it didn't want to continue and it ran away. So, Benedict Allen had to continue his journey with only two camels.

He never got lost but sometimes he didn't meet or speak to other people for weeks.

During his journey, one of Benedict Allen's biggest problems was the cold. Sometimes his food turned to ice before he finished eating it. On the 12th of October 1998, he reached the end of his journey and became one of the few people to cross the Gobi on foot.

3 046 Read through the questions as a class and check pronunciation of dates and distances as well as vocabulary. Tell students that the answers are in the same order as the questions, so it is important to keep listening if they miss an answer.

Students check answers with a partner before listening to the recording again if necessary.

> **1** b   **2** b   **3** c   **4** b   **5** c   **6** b

4 Students discuss the questions in pairs. The discussion could be extended by asking some further questions such as *What type of person chooses to become an explorer?* To conclude, the class could vote on the most popular place to explore.

⊕ EXTENSION
Students choose one of the places they talked about in Exercise 4 above and do some research on it. They can find out how to get there, how to travel around, what the climate is like, etc. This could be done in class in small groups or at home and students can write a short text with visuals about their chosen destination.

GRAMMAR
SB P68

PAST SIMPLE AND PAST CONTINUOUS

1 Read the example sentences and elicit the rules. It may be helpful to draw a time line on the board to show the relationship in time between the different actions.

> **1** in the middle of   **2** after each other

➡ **GRAMMAR REFERENCE** / Page 207

2 Students work in pairs to underline the verbs.

> **1** the dog ran out of the house
> **2** I realised I didn't have my passport

3 With a less able group, work through the first sentence as a class using the information in the rules in Exercise 1. Ask questions to help students choose the answers. For example, *Which action continued for a period of time?* (visit); *Which action happened in the middle of it?* (lose). You could draw a time line on the board to demonstrate the relationship between the two actions (a long, horizontal line to show 'were visiting', with a vertical line indicating 'now', to highlight that these actions are in the past, and then another horizontal line interrupting 'were visiting' showing when she 'lost' her purse).

Students continue to choose the answers with a partner, using the rules to help. Students could be asked to draw a time line for each sentence, showing the relationship between the two actions described by the verbs.
Feed back as a class.

> 1 were visiting, lost   2 stopped, got off
> 3 was having, reading   4 met, was walking

4 Point out that it is important to read the full sentence and decide whether each action continued for a period of time or not, before filling in the gaps. Students complete the sentences.

> 1 were, going   2 were sailing, started
> 3 were driving, ran   4 was shining, came out

PUSH YOURSELF B1
SB P68

GRAMMAR: WHEN, WHILE AND AS

LEAD-IN
Draw attention to the photo and ask students what they think Helen Skelton is famous for (travelling down the Amazon river alone by boat and crossing Antarctica. She generally enjoys challenges).

Students read the text quickly to find out if their predictions were correct. Encourage students to scan the text to find the answer without worrying about understanding all the detail at this stage.

1 As a class, read the sentences with words in bold and ask students to underline the verb forms in those sentences. (While: was working / asked, as: filmed / was doing, when: were waiting / finished).

Students complete the rules using the text to help decide. Check answers as a class.

> 1 at the same time   2 after

➡ **GRAMMAR REFERENCE** / Page 207

2 Pre-teach the verb *trip* (to fall after hitting your foot on something). Students match the sentence parts in pairs before class feedback.

> 1 d   2 f   3 e   4 c   5 b   6 a

FAST FINISHERS
Students can be asked to think about what they were doing last weekend or yesterday and to use the rules in the box to describe something that happened when, while or as they were doing something else.

VOCABULARY
SB P69

EASILY CONFUSED WORDS

LEAD-IN
Write the title *Travel* on the board and explain that we often use *travel* as a general term to describe going from one place to another, but that *to travel* is also a verb.

Ask students if they know any other words to describe going from one place to another. Brainstorm suggestions on the board.

1 Draw attention to the photo and ask students to suggest answers to the questions.

Students read the text quickly to find the answers. Allow about two minutes for this, encouraging students to focus on the answers to the questions without trying to understand every word of the text at this point.

> She works for a hotel company. She doesn't enjoy cruises.

2 Ask students to look again at the words in bold in the text. Are there any words which were already written on the board? Add these words to the list and then ask, *Which word is the odd one out?* (*travel* is used as a verb in the text, all the others are nouns).

Students read the text again and match the beginnings and endings of the definitions. Encourage them to read the words in the text to understand the differences in meaning.

Feed back as a class and then ask students some questions using the words. For example, *When was the last time you went on a flight/journey?*; *Did anyone go on a cruise last year?*

> 1 e   2 b   3 d   4 f   5 a   6 c

3 Students work in pairs to choose the correct answer using the definitions in Exercise 2 if necessary. Feed back by asking the students to explain why the other word is incorrect.

> 1 journey   2 trip   3 travel   4 cruise
> 5 flight   6 crossing

READING PART 4 TRAINING
SB P69

✓ EXAM INFORMATION

In Reading and Writing Part 4, students read a text from which six words have been removed. Students choose the appropriate words to fill the gaps from six three-option multiple-choice options. The main focus is on vocabulary, but there may be one or two questions which test grammar. In the example in the Student's Book there is one example and four other questions.

Students should allow about nine minutes to do Part 4 in the exam.

LEAD-IN

Go through the instructions with the class and point out the gapped text with multiple-choice options as an example of the task. Tell students that in the exam there will be six gaps.

Ask if anyone knows who Antoine de Saint Exupéry is. Accept all suggestions and then ask students to quickly read the text without worrying about the gaps to find out (a French pilot and writer).

1 Read the sentence with the first gap and the question together and point out that it is necessary to read the words before and after the gap to be able to identify the answer. In this case the verb *fly* is the correct answer as it collocates with *a plane*.

2 Ask students to work in pairs to choose the other answers. Encourage them to discuss why the other answers are incorrect as they work.

> **1** B **2** C **3** A **4** B **5** C

SPEAKING PART 2 TRAINING
SB P70

DIFFERENT TYPES OF HOLIDAY

WARMER

Tell students about your favourite type of holiday. For example, *I like visiting cities.* Encourage students to brainstorm words that they associate with that type of holiday. These can be adjectives or nouns. For example, *busy, crowded, sightseeing, museums.* Write the words on the board.

Then put students into groups of three or four and allocate a different type of holiday to each group, e.g. *camping holiday, mountain holiday, beach holiday, cycling holiday, backpacking holiday.* Students work in their groups to brainstorm words associated with their type of holiday.

Each group reports back to the rest of the class. Encourage students to make a note of any new vocabulary.

1 Check understanding of the words in the box by asking students if they generally have a positive or negative meaning, pointing out that some could be either (positive: *relaxing, popular, fantastic, lovely* / negative: *tiring, noisy, terrible* / either: *crowded, quiet*).

Draw attention to the photos in the book and ask students to work in pairs to discuss the questions, using any new vocabulary they have just learned.

Hold a class vote to decide which type of holiday would be most popular.

2 🔊 047 Point out the names of the people in the photos and tell students they will hear each of them talking about their holiday.

Students listen to match the people with the holidays in the photos.

> Pablo – picture C   Julia – picture D
> Arturo – picture A   Teresa – picture E
> Picture B isn't mentioned.

AUDIOSCRIPT 🔊 047

Pablo: My last holiday was in my country, in Mexico. I went to the beach with my family and some of our friends for a week and we had a great time. The weather was fantastic – really warm and sunny so there were lots of other people there. Sometimes the beach was very crowded but we didn't mind and we went swimming every day. I think that the best holidays are when you are with your friends.

Julia: Well I didn't have a good time on my last holiday. I went walking in the mountains with my boyfriend and it was really tiring. The weather was OK for the first two days and then it rained all the time. It was terrible! I hate being out in the rain.

Arturo: I came back from holiday last week. I went to New York with some friends. I didn't really enjoy it. For me, a holiday is a time to relax but New York is too noisy and crowded for that. My friends just wanted to go shopping and buy clothes but I'm not really interested in walking around shops so I was bored.

Teresa: In summer, I went camping for a week in the country. We were on a campsite by a lake. It was lovely – we lay on the grass under the trees all day or went swimming. The place was so quiet – it was really nice.

3 🔊 047 Tell students they will hear Pablo again. Ask them to listen and try to remember the words which tell them whether he enjoyed his holiday or not (*great, fantastic*). Then play the other three speakers to answer the same question for each.

> Pablo and Teresa had a good time. Julia and Arturo didn't enjoy their holiday.

4 Draw attention to the speech bubbles and remind students the people are all talking about the good and bad things about their holidays. Students work in pairs to complete the expressions using the phrases in the box.

When checking answers, ask students if they can identify the speaker from the recordings they heard (see audioscript for answers).

> 1 I didn't have a good time
> 2 It was lovely.
> 3 For me, a holiday is a time to relax.
> 4 The weather was fantastic.
> 5 I think that the best holidays are

5 Direct students' attention to the pictures, and brainstorm vocabulary to describe what the people are doing. For example, *relaxing/sleeping by the swimming pool, swimming, hiking, trekking, walking, looking at the view, sightseeing, taking a photo, having fun, visiting an amusement park / a funfair, going on a slide.* Encourage students to make a note of any new vocabulary.

Read through the information about this part of the exam with the class and ask some questions to check understanding.

For example, *What do you do in the first part?* (talk about some pictures with your partner); *How much time do you have?* (one or two minutes); *What happens in the second part?* (the examiner asks you one or two questions); *What do you have to remember?* (to give reasons for your answers).

Point out that it is important for students to ask their partner questions in the first part of the discussion.

Elicit some ideas for general questions that could be used. For example, *Do you like…?, Do you agree?; What about you?*

6 Read the first question to the class (as if you are the examiner) and allow students to talk about the pictures in pairs for at least two minutes, asking questions and giving opinions.

Ask one or two students to tell the class their opinions about each picture.

Then put students into groups of three. One student is the examiner and asks the other two students questions 2–5. Remind 'examiners' that they only use the why / why not questions if a student does not give a reason for their answer.

7 048 Read the checklist with the class before playing the recording. Point out that the pictures being discussed are the ones in the book.

After listening, students compare their checklists with a partner. Highlight that this is an example of two students doing the exam well.

> The candidates: ask each other questions; give reasons using *because*; use phrases like *I think* and *In my opinion*. They don't give longer answers.

AUDIOSCRIPT 048

Examiner: Now, in this part of the test you are going to talk together. Here are some pictures that show different things to do on holiday. Do you like these different things to do on holiday? Say why or why not. I'll say that again. Do you like these different things to do on holiday? Say why or why not. All right? Now, talk together.

Elena: Let's talk about the first holiday, Ricardo – the people spending their holiday by the hotel swimming pool. Do you like doing this on holiday?

Ricardo: I like swimming – in the pool or in the sea – but I don't enjoy doing this every day on holiday. It's a bit boring for me.

Elena: I think swimming and sunbathing are very relaxing.

Ricardo: And what about the next picture? The people walking in the mountains.

Elena: Oh, I think it's fantastic to enjoy nature on holiday. It could be tiring to climb a mountain.

Ricardo: Yes, but you can see interesting things.

Elena: In my opinion, you can see more interesting things when you visit old cities on holiday, like in this picture. Do you agree?

Ricardo: Yes, but I don't enjoy visiting cities when they're crowded. It's terrible.

Elena: That's true.

Ricardo: Do you enjoy visiting amusement parks on holiday?

Elena: Yes, why not?

Ricardo: I think amusement parks are noisy. I don't want to spend a whole day there.

Examiner: Do you think walking in the mountains is good for you, Ricardo?

Ricardo: Yes, the air is clean and you can stay fit.

Examiner: Do you think going to an amusement park is exciting, Elena?

Elena: Yes, because the rides are scary.

Examiner: So, Elena, which of these things to do on holiday do you like best?

Elena: I like going sightseeing.

Examiner:	And you, Ricardo, which of these things to do on holiday do you like best?
Ricardo:	Probably, walking in the mountains.
Examiner:	Thank you. Now, do you prefer to go on holiday with your friends or your family, Ricardo?
Ricardo:	With my friends, because it's more fun.
Examiner:	What about you, Elena?
Elena:	I like going on holiday with my family. My mum always goes shopping with me and buys me lots of things!
Examiner:	What will you do on your next holiday, Elena?
Elena:	I don't know. I'll probably visit my grandparents' house. I'll go swimming and windsurfing because they live by the beach.
Examiner:	And you, Ricardo?
Ricardo:	Sorry?
Examiner:	What will you do on your next holiday?
Ricardo:	I'll probably go sailing on a lake and ride my bike in the countryside.
Examiner:	Thank you. That is the end of the test.

AN EMAIL ABOUT SOMETHING THAT HAPPENED ON HOLIDAY

1 049 Read through the questions with the class and ask students to make notes of the answers while they listen to the recording. Students check answers in pairs. With a less able group repeat the recording.

> 1 on holiday in the mountains, camping
> 2 with her friends Thomas and Jo
> 3 No, she hates it.

AUDIOSCRIPT 049

Lily:	Hi, Carla, it's Lily here.
Carla:	Lily! Where are you? You sound far away.
Lily:	I am! We're in the mountains with my friends Thomas and Jo and I can't phone or text any of my friends most of the time – there's no signal. It's terrible. I have to sleep in a tent and it's really cold and uncomfortable.
Carla:	Oh dear … So you don't enjoy camping then?
Lily:	No, I hate it! I hate not having an indoor bathroom and I don't like walking or climbing up mountains like Thomas and Jo do. I prefer shopping and going to see interesting places when I'm on holiday.
Carla:	What's the weather like there? Can't you go swimming? Or at least do some sunbathing?
Lily:	Well it's sunny but it's not warm enough for sunbathing. And the water in the lake is REALLY cold.

2 Pre-teach *souvenir* (something you buy to help you remember a holiday) and *damage* (to harm or make something no longer functional). Read the question as a class and elicit ideas about what might have changed since the conversation.

Then students read the email to answer the question. Feed back as a class.

> It's now cold and raining. She isn't camping any more, she's staying in a hotel. She's enjoying her holiday.

3 Read the instructions and find the answer to the first question, as a class, by encouraging students to find the expression in the text and then try to substitute it with one of the phrases in a–f. Then allow students a few minutes to complete the exercise with a partner. Feed back as a class.

> 1 c   2 a   3 d   4 b   5 e   6 f

4 Students work individually before checking answers in pairs. Then feed back as a class.

> 1 in the evening   2 yesterday   3 right now
> 4 This morning   5 After that   6 Today

5 Go over the instructions with the class.

Refer students back to Lily's email and point out how she starts and finishes it. Ask students if they remember any other expressions for starting and finishing an email.

Ask students to read through the questions which refer to each paragraph and decide whether Lily has answered them, and if so, how. Students discuss the answers in pairs.

Next, students start planning their own email. They can write about a real experience or something that is not true. Encourage them to make brief notes, not full sentences, at the preparation stage to answer the questions.

As students are making notes, move around the classroom helping with vocabulary as necessary.

The writing can be done in class or at home.

6 Students swap emails and check their partner's work. They should check that paragraphs have been used appropriately, that the right expressions for starting and finishing have been used, that time expressions have been included and that most of the questions have been answered. They should also check spelling.

EXAM FOCUS

SB P72

READING PART 4

Read through the Exam facts and tips boxes with the class. Remind students to quickly read the text through before they try to choose the answers. Students have about 1.5 minutes per question in the Reading part of the exam, so allow no more than nine minutes for students to do the task under exam conditions. Tell them they should leave some time to check through their answers when they finish. Check answers as a class, asking students which words in the text helped them choose the answers.

> **1** C   **2** A   **3** C   **4** A   **5** B   **6** B

SPEAKING PART 2

SB P73

Read through the Exam facts and tips boxes with the class. Point out that there are more questions here than the examiner will ask in the exam so that they have more chance to practise.

Pair students up with someone they don't usually work with, then draw attention to the pictures and read out the instructions in 1 to the class. Allow about two minutes for students to answer the question in pairs. Monitor while students are doing the activity and make a note of any vocabulary they have difficulty with.

Then students continue with Exercises 2, 3 and 4 asking and answering the questions in pairs. At the end of the activity feed back by highlighting any good use of vocabulary or any areas where students can improve, e.g. extra vocabulary or longer answers.

Read through the options in the *How was it?* section and elicit the meaning of each one that they learned in the first unit.

Ask students to tick the appropriate box. You might like to ask students to share how they felt about the task to get an indication of your students' confidence. Depending on your class, you might like to do this openly or allow students to give their feedback without their classmates seeing. For example, give students a piece of A4 paper each with the *How was it?* scale written in large letters. Allow students to tick the relevant box then hold up their papers at the same time so that you can see how well students think they are doing. Finally, ask students if they found it easier, harder or the same as the exam practice in previous units.

➡ **SPEAKING BANK** / Pages 241–242

REAL WORLD

SB P74

GOING ON A SIGHTSEEING TOUR IN ... BERLIN

WARMER

Ask the class if they have ever been on an organised sightseeing tour in a city. Initiate a class discussion using some questions such as, *What type of tour was it?; What type of transport did you use?; What type of tour do you think is best when visiting a new city?*

1 Draw attention to the photos and ask students to discuss their answers in pairs. Then give students a minute or two to read the text quickly to check answers.

> **A** a hop-on/hop-off bus tour
> **B** a walking tour
> **C** a bike tour
> **D** a Trabi safari

2 Go over the statements as a class, helping with vocabulary as necessary and allowing students to suggest answers before they read the text again to check. Encourage them to find the sentences in the text which say why the statements are true or false. Feed back as a class.

> **1** F You can get on and off when you want.
> **2** F You can buy tickets for more than one day.
> **3** T   **4** T   **5** F You can drive the car yourself.

3 Students work in pairs. Encourage them to underline and read around the phrases in the text and to read through all the options (a–f) before choosing the answer. As they do the exercise move around the classroom helping with vocabulary as necessary. Check answers as a class.

> **1** e   **2** b   **3** f   **4** c   **5** a   **6** d

4 🎧 050 Go over the instructions with the class. If necessary, pre-teach *hire* (to rent, to pay some money to use something for a period of time) and *book* (to reserve, to arrange to have tickets for a time in the future).

Play the three recordings, asking students to listen for words or phrases which help them choose the answer. Then ask students to discuss their answers with a partner. Play the recordings again to check answers.

> **1** d **2** c **3** a

AUDIOSCRIPT 🎧 050

1
Receptionist:	Hi. Can I help you?
Tourist:	Yes, I'd like some information about the City Circle sightseeing tour.
Receptionist:	OK. What would you like to know?
Tourist:	How long does the tour take?
Receptionist:	The whole tour takes about two hours from start to finish, but of course you can hop on and hop off as often as you like, and the ticket is valid all day, from ten till six.
Tourist:	Great. And where does it go?
Receptionist:	It takes in all the main sights – the Brandenburg Gate, Checkpoint Charlie, Potsdamer Platz, everywhere you want to see.
Tourist:	That sounds good. How much are the tickets?
Receptionist:	Tickets are €22 per person, but you save 25% with the Welcome Card. Do you have one of those?
Tourist:	Yes, I do.
Receptionist:	OK. So with a Welcome Card it's €16.50.
Tourist:	Great. I'd like to buy two tickets for that, please.

2
Tourist:	Hello. Do you sell Berlin Welcome Cards here?
Assistant:	Yes, we do.
Tourist:	Can you give me some information about the card? What do you get with it?
Assistant:	There's free admission to the most popular tourist places, like the Berlin TV Tower, and also free admission to all museums, including the Berlin Wall Museum. You get one free tour, which can be bus, bike or on foot, and up to 30% discounts in some restaurants and theatres, plus a free information leaflet about travel in the city, and a tourist map. There's also free public transport anywhere in the city. It's very popular, and most people find it really good value for money.
Tourist:	OK. How much does it cost?
Assistant:	Would you like 48 hours, 72 hours or 4 days?
Tourist:	48 hours.
Assistant:	So, for 48 hours it's €19.90.
Tourist:	OK. I'll buy one.

3
Tourist:	Hello. Can we hire some bikes here?
Receptionist:	Of course. Is it for a bike tour, or just for you?
Tourist:	No. Not a bike tour. We just want to cycle round the city on our own.
Receptionist:	That's fine. So, it's €10 per day per bike and you have to pay this before you take the bike. A helmet is included in the price if you want one. There's also a returnable deposit of €200 per bike, which must be paid straightaway and we need some formal ID.
Tourist:	OK. That's no problem.
Receptionist:	And if you decide to extend the hire, it's one euro for each additional day.
Tourist:	OK. That sounds good.
Receptionist:	Great. So, do you want to hire one?
Tourist:	Yes, please.

PHRASES YOU MIGHT USE

5 🎧 050 Direct students' attention to the phrases from the recordings and ask them to work in pairs to complete them. Play the recording to check answers.

> **1** some information **2** How long **3** How much
> **4** Do you sell **5** Can we hire

⊕ EXTENSION

The recording can be used as a model for pronunciation by asking students to listen and repeat the phrases focusing on stress patterns and intonation. Then students can work in pairs to ask the questions and invent possible answers to them, creating mini dialogues. Ask two or three pairs to repeat their dialogues to the class.

PHRASES YOU MIGHT HEAR

6 With a weaker class it may be helpful to read through the definitions together, checking understanding before students try to match the phrases to them. Students work in pairs before class feedback.

| 1 c | 2 e | 3 a | 4 f | 5 b | 6 d |

WATCH

7 ▶ Tell students they are going to watch a video about the places in Berlin which are listed. Before watching, ask if anyone knows anything about each of the places. Brainstorm information as a class.

Then play the first part of the video and ask students to listen to the information about the Berlin Wall.

After listening, students discuss ideas in pairs. Then ask four or five students to tell you what they learned.

Make brief notes of what they say on the board.

If students have missed some details, play the first part of the video again. Otherwise, point out the notes on the board and ask students to make similar notes for the other places as they watch the rest of the video.

8 ▶ After watching, students compare their notes with a partner before feedback as a class.

It may be necessary to pause the video to give students time to make notes, or to play it more than once with a weaker class.

> **the Berlin Wall:** built in 1961 to separate East Berlin from West Berlin; came down in 1989; some sections still standing, tourists visit it.
> **the Brandenburg gate:** built in 1700s, a major tourist attraction; important because it shows the city is not divided.
> **Checkpoint Charlie:** one of the official places where people could cross from East to West Berlin; now popular with tourists.
> **ghost stations:** old East German train stations under Berlin that closed because of divided Berlin; people couldn't get off at them; now tourists can visit them.
> **Potsdamer Platz:** public square that was divided by the Berlin Wall; now modern buildings and great place for shopping and eating.

VIDEOSCRIPT ▶ Berlin

Berlin is the capital of Germany. It's a great place for tourists to visit, as there are so many things to see and do. Going on a sightseeing tour is a great way to see all the sights, and learn about the history of the city.

Here you can see a sign where the Berlin Wall was in the past. The Berlin Wall was built in 1961 and separated the city into two different parts – East Berlin and West Berlin.

The wall came down in 1989. But some sections are still standing and tourists visit them and remember this important part of 20th-century history.

The Brandenburg Gate was built in the 1700s and is a major tourist attraction. But for many Berliners, it's important because it shows that the city is now whole again, not two different cities.

This is Checkpoint Charlie. It was a famous crossing for people between East and West Berlin. Now anyone can walk past it and it's a popular place for tourists to visit.

When Berlin was divided, Metro trains from West Berlin went under parts of East Berlin for short distances. People couldn't get off the train at these stations, so they were closed. They were called 'ghost stations' and tourists can now visit them.

Potsdamer Platz is a large public square in Berlin. In the past, the wall came down the middle of this square, but now there are lots of new, modern buildings and it's a great place for shopping and eating. An excellent way to end your sightseeing tour of Berlin!

LIFE COMPETENCIES
SB P75

DECISION-MAKING AND MAKING NOTES

9 Go over the instructions with the class. Encourage students to make notes while they plan their visit. Ask each group to prepare a short presentation of a minute or two about which places they want to visit and which tours they want to go on and why.

As students make their presentations to the class, ask them to keep track of the most popular type of tour and sights.

➡ **WORKBOOK** / Unit 5, page 24

PROGRESS CHECK 2
UNIT 3 TO UNIT 5

SB P76

1
1 B   2 F   3 C   4 A   5 E   6 D

2
1 brain   2 fingers   3 neck   4 toes   5 knees
6 stomach   7 heart   8 back

3
1 couldn't sleep   2 can speak   3 couldn't play
4 can't swim   5 could ride

4
1   1 matter   2 ill   3 should   4 pharmacy
2   1 get up   2 much   3 streamed   4 shouldn't
3   1 How about   2 horror   3 comedy   4 Shall
4   1 trip   2 crowded   3 should   4 relaxing
5   1 ache   2 Why don't you   3 problem   4 rest

5
1 news   2 quiz shows   3 science fiction   4 crime drama   5 comedy   6 documentaries

6
1 backpack   2 campsite   3 crossings
4 suitcase   5 journey   6 delay   7 cruise
8 tourist information centre

7
1 Last night I **went** to a disco on the beach.
2 We **enjoyed** it when the country's team won.
3 Did you **go** anywhere for your summer vacation?
4 We **played** volleyball at the lake last summer.
5 The weather **was** warm and cloudy.
6 The T-shirt only **cost** me £5.

8
1 called, didn't answer
2 was playing, hurt
3 went, was
4 didn't hear, was listening
5 were you doing, phoned
6 was, read

9
1 was
2 found
3 Did
4 called/contacted
5 have
6 went
7 could

6 TIME FOR FOOD

UNIT OBJECTIVES

Topic:	food and drink
Grammar:	countable and uncountable nouns; *a/an*, *some* and *any*; expressions of quantity
Vocabulary:	food and meals; preparing food
Listening:	Part 3: three-option multiple choice about a dinner party
Reading:	Part 1: three-option multiple choice: signs and notices
Speaking:	making suggestions: choosing where to eat
Writing:	a recipe
Pronunciation:	pronouncing -s endings
Exam focus:	Reading Part 1; Listening Part 3
Real world:	buying a coffee and a snack in Vienna

Ask your students to watch the Grammar on the Move videos on pages 80 and 82. You can use these to present or reinforce countable and uncountable nouns and expressions of quantity.

READING
SB P78

LEAD-IN

Elicit *breakfast*, *lunch*, *dinner* and *snack* by asking *What is the name of the meal you eat in the morning/at 1pm/in the evening?* and, if you eat something at mid-morning or mid-afternoon what is it called? Brainstorm as a class the different types of snacks that students eat.

1 Students work in pairs to answer the questions. Move around the classroom helping with vocabulary as necessary. Feed back by asking several students to tell you what their partner eats for one of the meals.

> **Suggested answers**
> **A** Someone is taking a photo of their meal with their phone.
> **B** Someone is watching a cookery programme on TV.
> **C** Two men are cooking together.

2 Direct students' attention to the pictures of people and food. Give students a minute or so to read the text and answer the question. Students compare with a partner before class feedback.

> taking photos of their food and posting them on social media

3 Students work in pairs to read the texts again to find the answers. Feed back as a class.

> **1** F Many people don't want to cook and they say that they don't have time to cook. **2** T **3** T **4** F 70% take photos to share online. **5** F Some chefs don't want customers to take photos in their restaurants.

4 Students discuss the questions in pairs and then report back to the class.

VOCABULARY
SB P79

FOOD AND MEALS

1 Students complete the definitions. During feedback, elicit or supply the different use of *hot* in 3 (spicy) and 7 (temperature).

> **1** Beef, chicken **2** Broccoli **3** Chillies, curry **4** yoghurt **5** cereal **6** mushroom **7** mango **8** omelette

⊕ EXTENSION

Look at the definitions in Exercise 1 again and highlight the expressions used to describe the different types of food. For example, *X is a kind of meat/fruit/vegetable … it's yellow/brown/sweet/hot … we eat it with / we get it from …* These can be written on the board.

Students work in pairs to write definitions for other types of food without saying the name. Then they change pairs and read their definitions to their new partner who has to guess the name.

2 Students work in pairs to ask and answer the questions.

PUSH YOURSELF — B1
SB P79

VOCABULARY: PREPARING FOOD

LEAD-IN

Draw attention to the pictures and elicit some vocabulary to describe what can be seen. For example, *rice, mango, potatoes, meat, bread*, etc.

1 🔊 051 Tell students the photos show three people's favourite snacks. Go over the instructions and play the recording.

> **Speaker 1:** fried potatoes (B)
> **Speaker 2:** steak sandwich (C)
> **Speaker 3:** sweet coconut rice (A)

74

AUDIOSCRIPT 🔊 051

1

Woman: First, I peel the skin off potatoes and then I use a sharp knife to chop them into small rectangular pieces. After that I put some oil in a frying pan. When the oil is very hot, I put the potatoes in the pan and fry them until they are brown. I eat them with lots of salt. I love them!

2

Man: The best way to cook the meat is to grill it. I usually cook the steak for about three to five minutes on each side. You can cook it for longer if you want to, but be careful not to burn it! When it's ready, I put the steak between two pieces of bread and then it's ready to eat. It's my favourite sandwich.

3

Woman: First, I steam the rice for 15 minutes above a saucepan of boiling water until it's soft. Then I put some coconut milk in another saucepan and add sugar or honey to make it sweet. I put the rice and the sweet coconut milk together and cook them gently for three minutes. I make sure that I stir the rice and coconut milk every few seconds. When the rice is ready, I eat it with fresh mango. Delicious!

2 🔊 **051 Point out that all the words in the boxes are verbs connected to preparing and cooking food. Play the first recording again to give students the chance to complete the spaces with the verbs. After checking answers elicit the meaning of the verbs (*peel* = remove skin, *chop* = cut into pieces, *fry* = cook in hot oil). Then repeat for the second and third descriptions.**

1 peel	2 chop	3 fry	4 grill	5 burn
6 steam	7 add	8 stir		

GRAMMAR
SB P80

COUNTABLE AND UNCOUNTABLE NOUNS

LEAD-IN

Ask students to look at the three photos of the snacks on page 79 again. Ask some questions to try to elicit the difference between countable and uncountable nouns. For example, *How many sandwiches can you see?* (one); *How many potatoes can you see?* (20?); *How much rice is there?* (we can't count the rice).

1 Go over the example sentences and ask the students to complete the rule. Elicit the answers.

one

➡ **GRAMMAR REFERENCE** / *Page 208*

2 Students do the exercise. Then feed back as a class. It may be necessary to explain that we can talk about bread rolls or pieces of bread which are countable, but *bread* is uncountable.

1 yoghurt U   2 bread U   3 apple C
4 mushroom C

3 🔊 **052 Draw attention to the example sentence and the instances where the -s is highlighted. Tell students you are going to play the recording so that they can hear the three different -s sounds.**

- Point out the words in the table and the different phonemes.
- Repeat the recording and then drill the sounds, and then individual words, chorally and individually.
- Then ask students to practise saying the sentence to their partner.
- Now turn to the rules. Go over them with the class, demonstrating how the words in the table fit with each rule.

Tell students it is most important for them to understand when to use the /ɪz/ sound.

AUDIOSCRIPT 🔊 052

Man: cakes
Woman: sandwiches
Man: bananas
Woman: pieces
Man: mangos
Woman: apples
Man: snacks
Woman: cups
Man: fridges

4 🔊 **052 Ask students to listen to the recording of the words in the box and write them into the correct column. If necessary, play the first word and then check answers before moving on.**

Students check their answers with a partner by reading the words aloud with the correct pronunciation before checking as a class.

/s/	/z/	/ɪz/
eats	eggs	slices
cakes	bananas	sandwiches
snacks	mangos	pieces
cups	apples	fridges

A/AN, SOME AND ANY

5 Direct students' attention to the first two examples and then ask students to read rules 1 and 2 below and choose the correct options. Check answers together.

Next, read the third and final sentences, and ask students to complete the rules for negative sentences and questions. Feed back as a class.

1 countable   2 some   3 any   4 any

➡ **GRAMMAR REFERENCE** / *Page 208*

UNIT 6 | TIME FOR FOOD

6 Students work in pairs to choose the correct options using the rules in the box. When checking the answers encourage students to explain why they chose the answer they did. For example, 1 is a negative sentence and *bread* is uncountable.

| 1 any | 2 Are, are | 3 some |
| 4 Is, isn't, are | 5 some | |

7 Elicit a recap of the rules of use to see if students can remember when we use each word. Then put students into pairs to do the task. Check as a class.

| 1 some | 2 any | 3 a | 4 some | 5 some |
| 6 some | 7 a | 8 any | | |

8 Draw attention to the photo on page 193 and elicit some example sentences to describe what students can or can't see. For example, *I can't see any … I can see some …* Then ask students around the class to continue the description using the appropriate word (*some, any, a, an*).

READING PART 1 TRAINING
SB P81

✓ EXAM INFORMATION

In Reading Part 1, students have to read six short emails, notices, signs or text messages. There are three sentences next to each one. Candidates have to choose which sentence matches the meaning of the email, notice, sign or text message. This part tests the students' understanding of various kinds of short texts.

In the Student's Book there are only three texts with one set of questions each. The focus in the Student's Book is to provide exam training and find the important words in the texts. The whole Reading and Writing paper has seven parts.

Parts 1–5 are reading tasks and Parts 6 and 7 are writing tasks. Students have 60 minutes in total to complete the paper, so they should spend about 15 minutes on the writing tasks and 45 minutes on the reading tasks. Students should allow about eight minutes to do Part 1 in the exam.

LEAD-IN

Ask students in pairs to describe the contents of their fridge at home. Allow two to three minutes for the pairs to discuss and then elicit ideas from the whole class. Write their suggestions on the board.

1 Ask students to discuss the questions in small groups before class feedback.

2 Ask students to read the note and check understanding of *carton*. Then read through the statements with the class. Students then discuss in pairs which statement is correct. Elicit the answer from the class.

| C |

3 Read the rubric with the students and ask one or two questions to check understanding of *sofa*, *squash* and *gardener*. Allow the students a few minutes to read the three messages and underline the important words. Encourage students to read quickly as it is not necessary to understand every word to find the answer. In the exam there may be vocabulary which is above A2 level, but students will not need to understand it in order to answer the questions. Not being put off by 'unknown' words is an important reading skill. Feed back as a class and check which words students underlined.

| 1 C | 2 B | 3 C |

GRAMMAR
SB P82

EXPRESSIONS OF QUANTITY

1 Initiate a class discussion using the questions in the book. If students can't cook, ask them if they would like to learn and what type of food they would like to cook.

2  053 Draw attention to the photos and go over the instructions with the class. Check understanding by asking some questions. For example, *Who is cooking?* (Rob); *Who is he cooking for?* (his friend Vanessa and her friends); *Where are they?* (Buenos Aires).

Encourage students to read the questions and answer options before they listen. Pre-teach *chilli* (a spicy dish with meat or vegetables cooked slowly with a little liquid). Then play the recording. Students discuss their answers with a partner before listening again. Feed back as a class.

| 1 a | 2 b | 3 a | 4 b | 5 a |

AUDIOSCRIPT 053

Vanessa: That smells delicious, Rob. What is it?
Rob: It's a vegetable chilli for tonight. For dinner with your friends.
Vanessa: What's in it?
Rob: All the vegetables I found in your fridge – onions, carrots, potatoes, mushrooms and tomatoes.
Vanessa: Is there a lot of chilli in it?
Rob: No, not much. I know you and your friends don't like hot and spicy food.
Vanessa: That's not true! I do! … I love spicy food. But some people don't. Can I taste it? Mmm, delicious … I don't like food that has a lot of salt in it, but this is just perfect! I'm going shopping now. Do you need anything?
Rob: I'm not sure. How much rice do we have in the cupboard?
Vanessa: Let's see. Not much. There's half a packet of rice.

Rob:	OK, well can you get another two packets of rice, please? And do we have any lemons? I need a lot of lemons to make the dessert with.
Vanessa:	Yes, we do, but not many. Just two.
Rob:	Can you get me six lemons and a little cream? Oh, and also a few oranges, not many, just one or two.
Vanessa:	OK, that's two packets of rice, six lemons, a little cream and a few oranges. OK, I'll get them. See you later!

3 Read the first two questions and answers with the class and try to elicit the difference between *lemons* and *rice* (countable plural and uncountable). Students complete rules 1 and 2.

Then direct attention to the other examples and ask students to work in pairs to complete rules 3, 4 and 5. Feed back as a class, highlighting that *a lot of* can be used with both countable and uncountable nouns.

1 many, much   **2** much, much   **3** few
4 little   **5** lot of

→ **GRAMMAR REFERENCE** / Page 209

4 Students work in pairs to choose the best answer, referring back to the rules in the box. Feed back as a class, asking students to explain their answers. For example, the first answer is *a little* because *sugar* is uncountable.

1 a little   **2** a few   **3** much, much   **4** How many
5 a few, a little   **6** much

5 Direct attention to the photos and go over the instructions with the class. Remind students to refer to the rules in the box. With a weaker class you could read through the nouns in the dialogues before they start the exercise and elicit whether they are countable or uncountable, singular or plural. Students work in pairs before checking as a class.

1 many   **2** any   **3** some   **4** much   **5** much
6 many   **7** an   **8** an   **9** some   **10** a little
11 many   **12** a lot of   **13** a few   **14** a few

FAST FINISHERS

Students can practise reading the two dialogues with a partner, remembering the rules for the pronunciation of *-s*.

6 Students complete the sentences individually and then tell their partner their sentences. They then discuss similarities and differences and report back to the class.

LISTENING PART 3 TRAINING
SB P83

✓ EXAM INFORMATION

In Listening Part 3 students listen to a longer dialogue and answer five three-option multiple-choice questions. Students have to listen to identify key information and opinion. They hear the recording twice. This section in the Student's Book encourages students to identify and underline the important words before listening and to learn to exclude the incorrect answers as well as selecting the correct answer. The task in the Student's Book has only four questions.

1 Initiate a class discussion to answer the questions. If necessary you could provide some models for the students by telling them your answers to the questions. For example, *Last weekend I invited some friends to my house for dinner. I cooked a vegetable curry with rice and we drank sparkling water.*

2 054 Elicit or supply information about Listening part 3, then read the instructions and ask some questions to check understanding *Who is speaking?* (Katie and Ben), *What is Katie telling Ben about?* (a dinner party). Then go over the information in the box. Play the recording to allow students to hear the three answer options and the correct answer.

AUDIOSCRIPT 054

Ben:	Hi, Katie, how are you?
Katie:	Hi, Ben. I'm fine. I went to dinner at Maria's house last night. You know, Maria, my Italian friend.
Ben:	Yes, I remember Maria. I met her once at your mum's house. She's very nice! Is she a good cook?
Katie:	I don't know. Maria's husband Dan did the cooking. It was delicious!

3 055 Give students a few minutes to read the other questions and underline the important words. Try to elicit the meaning of *course* (a part of a meal, such as the main course), *starter* (usually a small dish served as the first part of the meal) and *dessert* (something sweet at the end of a meal).

Then play the complete conversation. Students discuss their answers with a partner before listening again. Feed back as a class. Encourage students to tell you why an answer is correct or incorrect.

2 B   **3** A   **4** B

UNIT 6 TIME FOR FOOD

AUDIOSCRIPT 🔊 055

Ben: Hi, Katie, how are you?

Katie: Hi, Ben. I'm fine. I went to dinner at Maria's house last night. You know, Maria, my Italian friend.

Ben: Yes, I remember Maria. I met her once at your mum's house. She's very nice! Is she a good cook?

Katie: I don't know. Maria's husband Dan did the cooking. It was delicious!

Ben: What did you eat?

Katie: We had spicy chicken with fresh mango and rice. The rice had lots of salt in it – I couldn't eat it. But the mango was sweet and juicy and the chicken was delicious. I don't usually like spicy food but this was excellent.

Ben: What was for dessert?

Katie: Strawberries and a cake made with oranges. We didn't have coffee after the meal. We had a drink made with yoghurt instead. It was delicious after the sweet dessert.

Ben: Interesting! I made chocolate cake yesterday. Not from the book I got for my birthday – those recipes need too much chocolate – I found it online. The cake was delicious. I ate some while watching TV.

Katie: Mmmm.

SB P84

MAKING SUGGESTIONS

LEAD-IN

Ask the class, *What can you eat at your favourite type of restaurant? Why do you like that type of food best?* Allow students to contribute to the discussion helping with vocabulary, as necessary.

1 Draw attention to the photos, and ask students to work in pairs to answer the questions. If necessary, brainstorm some vocabulary for each picture before starting. For example, *sushi, pizza, curry, spicy, delicious, cheap, expensive*, etc. Feed back by finding out which restaurant in the photos is most popular with the class by asking for a show of hands.

2 Go over the instructions and draw attention to the text messages. Read text 1 together. Then allow students a three or four minutes to complete the task. Check as a class.

> 1 Hi, Izzy, would you like to meet for lunch today? I'm free after 12.00. What about you?
> 2 Hi, Henry, I'd love to. I have some things to do this morning, but I'm free at 12.30. Where shall we meet?
> 3 Shall we meet in front of the art museum? There are lots of restaurants near there.
> 4 OK. Great. I'll see you in front of the art museum at 12.30.

3 🔊 056 Tell students they are going to hear the conversation Izzy and Henry have when they meet. Read the questions and ask students to listen for the answers. Play the recording.

> 1 cheese   2 the sushi restaurant

AUDIOSCRIPT 🔊 056

Izzy: Hi, Henry. Sorry I'm late!

Henry: Hi, Izzy. That's OK. It's only just after half past 12. We've got lots of time. Are you hungry?

Izzy: Yes, I am. I didn't have any breakfast!

Henry: Let's find somewhere to eat straightaway then. Where shall we go?

Izzy: I don't mind. Do you like pizza? How about that pizza restaurant over there? My sister says it's very good.

Henry: I'm afraid I don't eat cheese. I don't like it.

Izzy: OK. How about going for an Indian meal? I know you like curry.

Henry: You're right. I love curry, but we ate it at Paul's house yesterday. Do you feel like eating fish? What about having some sushi? There's a sushi place over there.

Izzy: That's a great idea. Let's go to the sushi restaurant. Shall we sit outside?

4 🔊 056 Students do the task from memory before listening again to check answers.

> 1 Izzy   2 Henry   3 Izzy   4 Henry   5 Izzy
> 6 Henry

5 Go over the instructions and do 1 as a class. Highlight the meaning of *straightaway* (immediately). Then allow students a few minutes to do the exercise with a partner. Check as a class.

> 1 Let's   2 shall   3 mind   4 says   5 afraid
> 6 about   7 feel   8 What   9 idea   10 sit

6 Work through the exercise as a class. Make a note on the board, for students to copy, of the expressions in each category.

> **Making suggestions/asking questions:**
> 1, 2, 4, 6, 7, 8 and 10
> **Responding to suggestions:**
> 3, 5 and 9.

7 Point out the photos of different places to eat and ask some students to tell the class which place they would prefer to go to and why.

With a weaker class you could model the dialogue by playing the part of A and asking different students around the class, or the whole class, to suggest responses for B. Point out the language on the board and the phrases in Exercise 5 before asking students to have their own conversations with a partner.

8 Students change roles and, if possible, partners, to have another conversation. Ask one or two pairs to repeat their conversations to the class.

WRITING
SB P85

A RECIPE

> **LEAD-IN**
>
> Draw attention to the photo and brainstorm comments about what students can see (two friends cooking together).
>
> Tell students about your experience of cooking. For example, *I love cooking. I cook every day. I have some recipe books, but I prefer looking for new recipes online. My favourite recipe is…*, etc. If necessary, explain *recipe* (instructions for how to cook food) and model and drill the pronunciation.

1 Students work in pairs to ask and answer the questions. If students don't cook at all, suggest they talk about their favourite meal. Move around the class, helping with vocabulary as necessary. Feed back by asking some students to tell the class about their favourite recipes.

2  057 Close books. Tell students they are going to listen to Sunita describing how to make a meal. Ask them to listen and try to understand what she is making.

curry

> **AUDIOSCRIPT** 057
>
> **Sunita:** OK. So this is a really easy meal to make … and really lovely. First, peel the garlic and ginger and chop them into small pieces. Then chop the onions and other vegetables. Fry the garlic, ginger and chopped onion lightly in some oil. When they are soft, add the curry powder. After that, add the other chopped vegetables and mix everything together. Cook for 15–20 minutes until the vegetables are soft. While the curry is cooking, wash the rice and put it into a saucepan. Add water and a pinch of salt. Cook for 20 minutes. Finally, serve the curry with the rice and enjoy!

3 057 Ask students to open their books again and look at the verbs in the box. If necessary pre-teach the verbs *peel* (to take the skin off fruit or vegetables), *fry* (to cook food in hot oil or fat), *chop* (to cut something into pieces with a knife). Then encourage students to read through Sunita's instructions and complete them with the correct verb. Play the recording again to check answers.

| **1** peel, chop | **2** chop | **3** Fry, add | **4** add, mix |
| **5** Cook | **6** wash, put | **7** Add | **8** serve |

4 Encourage students to read the sentences before choosing the correct verb. Check answers with a partner before class feedback.

| **1** Peel | **2** fry | **3** serve | **4** Mix | **5** Chop |

5 Go over the instructions with the class, checking understanding. Then give students three or four minutes to think about their answer to the first question. Move around the class helping with vocabulary as they do this. Students write their recipe and then swap it with a partner.

> **FAST FINISHERS**
>
> Students could be asked to write a message to their friend after eating the meal at their house and thanking them for the food.

EXAM FOCUS
SB P86

READING PART 1

Read through the Exam facts and tips boxes carefully with the class. Answer any questions the students might have. In Reading Part 1 students read six items (an email, a text message, a web message or a notice). The focus is on overall understanding of the message and students have to choose the correct answer from three options.

The tips in the Student's Book encourage students to identify and underline the most important words and to try not to be distracted by answers which use a word from the message but which do not express the same meaning.

Remind students they have about 1.5 minutes per question in the Reading part of the exam, so allow nine minutes for students to complete the task under exam conditions, individually, without speaking.

When checking answers, ask students to justify the answer they gave.

| **1** A | **2** B | **3** C | **4** B | **5** A | **6** C |

LISTENING PART 3
SB P87

Read through the Exam facts and tips boxes with the class and answer any questions they may have. Remind students that they will have 20 seconds to read through the questions before they listen and that they should underline any important words as they read.

If you prefer not to do this exactly under exam conditions you could help students with any vocabulary they don't know before playing the recording. Otherwise, play the recording twice while students choose the correct answers and then check them. Check answers as a class.

UNIT 6 TIME FOR FOOD

Allow students a minute or so to complete the *How was it?* self-assessment box at the bottom of the page. Then hold a show of hands to see how many students ticked each box.

| 1 B | 2 C | 3 B | 4 A | 5 A |

AUDIOSCRIPT 058

Narrator: For each question, choose the correct answer. You have 20 seconds to look at Part 3. You will hear Lewis talking to his friend Laura about a cooking course. Now listen to the conversation.

Lewis: Why didn't you come to our first cooking lesson yesterday, Laura?

Laura: Sorry, Lewis! I didn't forget, but my college teacher needed to speak to me after class, so I missed the bus. But I'll come next week!

Lewis: Well, it doesn't matter. You're such a good cook already.

Laura: You only think that because I always make the same things. I make so many omelettes, I should open an omelette restaurant! I need to learn to prepare new dishes. What did you make yesterday?

Lewis: The teacher said we could make soup or a dessert. I chose ice cream. Next week it's curry. I'll send you the list of things you'll need.

Laura: So what's the teacher like?

Lewis: She's okay. She explains things quite well, and shows people how to do things. But what I didn't like was that she shouted, and wasn't very nice about what someone cooked.

Laura: Oh dear! Can we go together next week?

Lewis: Sure. The class starts at 7 pm, but I like being early. I'll come to your college at 6.30, so we can arrive at 6.45. Okay?

Laura: Yes, thanks.

Read through the options in the *How was it?* section and elicit the meaning of each one that they learnt in the first unit.

Ask students to tick the appropriate box. You might like to ask students to share how they felt about the task to get an indication of your students' confidence. Depending on your class, you might like to do this openly or allow students to give their feedback without their classmates seeing. For example, give students a piece of A4 paper each with the *How was it?* scale written in large letters. Allow student to tick the relevant box then hold up their papers at the same time so that you can see how well students think they are doing. Finally, ask students if they found it easier, harder or the same as the exam practice in previous units.

REAL WORLD

SB P88

BUYING A COFFEE AND A SNACK IN ... VIENNA

WARMER

Brainstorm what students know about Vienna. If you have a map, show students where Vienna is.

CULTURAL INFORMATION

Vienna is the capital city of Austria. It is well known for its music as many famous composers lived there, for example, Mozart, Beethoven and Johan Strauss. Viennese coffee houses are famous across the world.

1 Direct attention to photos A–D and discuss the questions as a class. Try to elicit some vocabulary which will help students when they read the text such as, *cup of coffee, cakes, glass of water, waiter*.

2 Go over the instructions with the class and give students one or two minutes to read the statements helping with vocabulary if necessary. Students read the text and do the exercise with a partner before class feedback. When checking answers encourage students to tell you why the false statements are false.

> **1** T
> **2** T
> **3** F Water is always served with the coffee.
> **4** F Guests should feel welcome and shouldn't feel that they have to leave quickly.

3 Draw attention to the reviews, and allow students two or three minutes to find the answers. Check as a class, encouraging students to tell you which parts of the texts give the answers.

> **1** Café 100 **2** Café Schokolade **3** Café 100
> **4** Café Vienna

4 Students find the phrases in the reviews and choose the correct definition. Explain that they can check their answers by substituting the phrase in the text with the answer they choose. Feedback as a class.

> **1** a **2** a **3** b **4** a **5** a **6** a

⊕ EXTENSION

Students work in pairs to write a short description of a cake or dessert they like and then read it to another pair who have to guess the name of the dessert. Before starting, highlight the useful language in the descriptions such as, *It's made from ... It's often served with ... It's a speciality of ...*

5 🔊 059 Go over the instructions with the class and ask them to suggest the differences that might help them choose the correct answer (the main difference will be what the people order to eat or drink).

Play the recording, and ask students to make a note of one or two words or phrases which tell them the answer in each case. Repeat the recordings if necessary. Check answers as a class, encouraging students to tell you the notes they made.

> **1** c **2** d **3** a

AUDIOSCRIPT 🔊 059

1
Waiter:	Hello. Are you ready to order?
Customer 1:	Yes. I'd like a Viennese coffee, please.
Customer 2:	And a black coffee for me, please.
Waiter:	Anything to eat?
Customer 1:	Yes. What's a *Kardinalschnitte*?
Waiter:	It's a traditional Viennese cake. It has layers of vanilla sponge on the outside, then a layer of strawberry jam and a fresh cream filling.
Customer 2:	Mmm. That sounds nice. Does it have nuts in it?
Waiter:	No. There are no nuts, but it does have gluten. We do also have gluten-free options if you like.
Customer 2:	That's OK. I'm allergic to nuts, but nothing else. So can we have one *Kardinalschnitte*, with two forks, please?
Waiter:	Of course. Any whipped cream with that?
Customer:	No, thank you.
Waiter:	OK. That's fine.

2
Server:	Who's next, please?
Customer:	Hi, can I have a cheeseburger, please?
Server:	Eat in or take away?
Customer:	To eat in.
Server:	Any fries with that?
Customer:	Yes, please.
Server:	And a drink?
Customer:	A cola, please.
Server:	Regular or large?
Customer:	Regular, please.
Server:	OK. One cheeseburger with fries, and a regular cola. Thank you.

3
Server:	Hi. Can I help you?
Customer:	Yes. Can I have a chicken sandwich, please?
Server:	Sorry, we're out of chicken sandwiches at the moment. I've got a chicken wrap.
Customer:	OK. Can I have a chicken wrap, please? And do you do decaf coffee?
Server:	Yes, we do.
Customer:	OK. I'd like a small decaf latte, please.
Server:	No problem. Have you seen our combos? For €10 you can have any wrap or roll, plus a coffee and a cookie or muffin.
Customer:	Oh. OK. What muffins do you have?
Server:	Chocolate, lemon, or blueberry.
Customer:	I'll have a chocolate muffin, please.
Server:	Coming up! If you take a seat, someone will bring you your food.
Customer:	Thank you.

PHRASES YOU MIGHT USE

6 🔊 059 Students work in pairs to complete the phrases before listening to the recordings to check their answers.

> **1** What's a **2** Does it have **3** allergic to
> **4** with two forks **5** Do you do **6** What muffins

PHRASES YOU MIGHT HEAR

7 Students work in pairs to choose the correct definitions before checking answers as a class.

> **1** b **2** b **3** a **4** a **5** a **6** b

WATCH

8 ▶ Go over the instructions and the list together, checking understanding as necessary. Examples of meals are *breakfast*, *lunch* and *dinner*, a *coffee house* is the same as a *café*. Play the video and ask students to take notes under the headings while they watch.

9 ▶ Then students compare their notes with a partner's. Repeat the video to allow students to check answers, pausing as necessary.

> **the city:** capital of Austria and the largest city; busy modern city, famous for old coffee shops
> **coffee shops and cafés:** great place to relax and chat with friends, often have piano music; cakes, sandwiches, salads, sausages
> **types of desserts:** *Apfelstrudel*, *Kardinalschnitte*
> **Wiener Schnitzel:** flat steak dipped in flour, eggs and breadcrumbs, fried in oil, served with chips and lemon
> **three famous cafés:** Café Central, popular with writers and artists; Café Mozart, named after the musician and composer; Café Sacher, where *Sachertorte* was first made, a chocolate cake with smooth chocolate icing

UNIT 6 TIME FOR FOOD

VIDEOSCRIPT ▶ Vienna

Vienna is the capital city of Austria, and is the country's largest city. It's a busy, modern city, but it's famous for its old coffee shops. Many of them are in old buildings, and they look amazing inside.

They are great places to go and relax, to have a cup of coffee or chat with friends. You can often hear music in coffee shops, especially piano music.

And of course you can eat delicious Austrian desserts, like *Apfelstrudel* and *Kardinalschnitte*. As well as coffee and cake, you can also have light meals, like sandwiches and salads and you could try Vienna's famous sausages or *Wiener Schnitzel*. This is a kind of flat steak, which is dipped in flour, egg and breadcrumbs and then fried in oil. It is usually served with a slice of lemon and chips.

And, of course, there's the coffee, which always comes with a glass of water. There are lots of different kinds of coffee, like *Melange*, which is made with hot milk, and is similar to cappuccino and mocha, which is made with coffee and hot chocolate together.

Famous Viennese coffee shops include Café Central, popular with writers and artists in the past and Café Mozart, named after the famous Austrian musician and composer. And, of course, the famous Café Sacher, where the *Sachertorte* was first made. One of Vienna's most famous cakes, it's a delicious chocolate cake, with smooth chocolate icing. So if you are a fan of great architecture, coffee shops and delicious snacks, then perhaps Vienna is the perfect destination for you.

LIFE COMPETENCIES
SB P89

EVALUATING OPTIONS AND COMMUNICATION

10 Go over the instructions. Students work in pairs to choose a city and then research its traditional food in the classroom or at home.

Explain to students that the objective of their presentation is to try to persuade their classmates to go to the city they have chosen and eat the food they describe.

Each pair makes a one-minute presentation to the class, explaining why they chose the city and the food, as well as the best place to eat it. They can include photos or pictures.

There could be a class vote to decide which destination (and food) is the most popular. Students cannot vote for their own destination and should be encouraged to give a reason for their choice.

➡ **WORKBOOK** / Unit 6, page 28

LIVE LIFE!

UNIT OBJECTIVES

Topic:	hobbies and leisure
Grammar:	present perfect: *Have you ever …?* present perfect with *just*
Vocabulary:	free time; the theatre; music performers; linking words
Listening:	listening for detail: interviews about hobbies and a talk about the recycled orchestra
Reading:	Part 3: three-option multiple choice about an actor
Speaking:	Part 1: questions about hobbies and weekends
Writing:	a leaflet about a festival
Pronunciation:	pronouncing *Have you ever …?*
Exam focus:	Reading Part 3; Speaking Part 1
Real world:	spending your free time in London

Ask your students to watch the Grammar on the Move video on page 92. You can use this to present or reinforce the present perfect.

VOCABULARY
SB P90

FREE TIME

WARMER

Tell students about your hobby. For example, I like going climbing in the mountains. I go every weekend in the spring. Encourage students to ask you questions about your hobby.

1 Put students in groups of three to answer the questions. Ask two or three groups to tell the class their answers.

2 Draw attention to the pictures and read text 1 as a class. Elicit the letter of the correct picture (G) and if necessary ask students if they know another word for *gigs* (*concerts*).

Then students do the rest of the exercise in pairs. Check answers as a class.

A photography	**B** doing nothing	**C** board games
D doing Massaoke	**E** baking	**F** doing exercise
G gigs	**H** going to the gym	

3 Students complete the sentences. Point out that one of the words in orange needs to be used in a different form (*gigs* is used in the singular in item 2). Feed back as a class.

1 photography	**2** gig	**3** doing nothing
4 baking	**5** board games	
6 exercise	**7** gym	**8** does Massaoke

4 Ask one or two students the first question and try to elicit different ways of talking about the last time they did one of their hobbies. For example, *yesterday, last week/month, two days/weeks ago*. Make a note of these expressions on the board to encourage students to use them when they are answering the questions. Students work in pairs to ask and answer the questions.

LISTENING
SB P91

1 🔊 060 Go over the instructions with the class, play the recording and elicit the two hobbies.

1 photography	**2** Massaoke

AUDIOSCRIPT 🔊 060

1

Interviewer: Thanks for talking to me, Declan. Can I ask how old you are and where you are from?

Declan: I'm 22 and I come from Dublin in Ireland.

Interviewer: Thank you. And your hobby is photography, isn't it? So when did you start taking photos?

Declan: I started when I was at secondary school. I was doing a project and I needed some photos for it. I borrowed my dad's camera and I haven't stopped taking photos since then.

Interviewer: Does it take a long time to learn to take good photos?

Declan: Yes, and no. A person can always take good photos and it's a very personal thing. But photography is a big subject and you can spend your whole life learning about it. In fact, I've just been on a weekend course to learn some new techniques.

Interviewer: And do you use lots of special equipment? Is photography an expensive hobby?

Declan: Yes, I've got quite a lot of different cameras. But I bought them over a long time. You don't need an expensive camera to begin with. You can start with your phone and share photos with friends online.

Interviewer: And how good are you at photography now?

Declan: I don't know. Look at my photos and you decide! The important thing is that I love it.

Interviewer: So why do you like it? How does taking photos make you feel?

Declan: Taking photos makes me forget my problems. I look at the world through my camera and I see new things I have never noticed before.

2

Interviewer: I'm talking to Kimberley from Manchester, who is 19 years old, and Kimberley has done Massaoke for a year. Thank you for talking to us Kimberley. So how did you start singing and can you explain what Massaoke is?

Kimberley: Well, I started singing because I've got two big sisters who sang a lot at home, and when my sisters started going to Massaoke clubs, I wanted to go along as well. Massaoke is a really fantastic night out. There's a brilliant live band, which plays the biggest pop or rock songs, and the crowd sings along. The words to the songs are on a big screen at the front, so everyone can join in. Have you ever been to a Massaoke club?

Interviewer: No, I haven't tried Massaoke, but it sounds great. So, how does singing Massaoke make you feel?

Kimberley: Singing along with hundreds of other people makes me feel really happy and full of energy! It's a great way to relax and have fun with my friends, so we try to do it every Saturday night if we can.

Interviewer: And where do you go to do it?

Kimberley: Well, it's becoming really popular. There are now two or three clubs in Manchester where you can do Massaoke, as a new club has just opened in the city centre.

2 060 Read through the notes in the book and ask students what type of information they need to listen for. For example, *age* will be a number, *where from* will be a city or country, *hobby* will be an activity.

Students then listen to the recording again. Check answers as a class.

> **Interview 1**
> Name: Declan
> Age: 22
> Where from: Dublin, Ireland
> Hobby: photography
>
> **Interview 2**
> Name: Kimberley
> Age: 19
> Where from: Manchester
> Hobby: Massaoke

3 060 Students read through the sentences and choose a name before listening to the recordings again to check their answers.

> 1 D   2 D   3 K   4 D   5 D   6 K

4 Elicit opinions from the class to answer the questions. If necessary, ask students one or two other questions to generate a greater response, for example, *Why do you think some people enjoy Massaoke?*

5 060 Students work in pairs to reorder the words to make sentences. Check answers as a class.

> 1 When did you start taking photos? 2 Do you use lots of special equipment? 3 How good are you at photography? 4 Why do you like it? 5 How does singing Massaoke make you feel? 6 How often do you do it?

6 Ask students if they remember your hobby and encourage them to take turns to ask you the questions in Exercise 5. Make sure they change the wording where appropriate. Answer the questions as students ask them.

Ask students to make notes about their own hobby individually before asking their partner the questions in Exercise 5.

⊕ EXTENSION

Each student writes a paragraph about their partner's hobby using the information they learned in Exercise 6.

SB P92

PRESENT PERFECT: *HAVE YOU EVER ...?*

LEAD-IN

Ask one or two questions using the present perfect with *ever* around the class. For example, *Have you ever had swimming lessons?*; *Have you ever played tennis?*; *Have you ever studied Russian?* Elicit short answers (*Yes, I have. / No, I haven't.*).

Then ask students what time period *ever* refers to. Try to elicit *their whole life / at any time / general time up to now.*

1 Draw attention to the box and read through the examples and 1 as a class. Point out that *never* means *not ever*, so the time reference is the same as *ever*. Allow students a few minutes to read the examples again and complete the rules, then check as a class.

> 2 *have*   3 *-ed*

➡ **GRAMMAR REFERENCE** / Page 210

2 Explain that irregular verbs do not follow the rules of regular verbs. Students work in pairs to match the base forms with the irregular past participles.

> **1** take/taken **2** win/won **3** be/been
> **4** eat/eaten **5** sing/sung **6** speak/spoken
> **7** swim/swum **8** get/got

LANGUAGE NOTE

The past participle *been* is used for the verb *be* and also the verb *go* with the meaning *to go and return from*.

You can explain this to students by writing the following two sentences on the board:

1 *Maria has been to London.*

2 *Maria has gone to London.*

Ask *Where is Maria now?*

(In 1, Maria is not in London (somewhere else), in 2 she's in London.)

3 Students work in pairs to complete the sentences. Check answers as a class.

> **2** Have … ever watched **3** have never been
> **4** has always enjoyed **5** Has … ever swum
> **6** have always lived

FAST FINISHERS

Students can make sentences of their own using the present perfect forms of the verbs in Exercise 3 or other verbs.

4 🔊 061 Explain to students that when we say words together in a sentence or question we link them, sometimes adding sounds that are not used when we say the separate words.

Play the first question and ask students to listen carefully to the pronunciation of *you ever*. Try to elicit the sound they hear, repeating the recording if necessary.

Then play the next two questions pointing out that the words *they ever* and *I ever* are linked by another sound.

5 🔊 061 Repeat the recording and drill chorally and individually before allowing students a few minutes to repeat the questions to their partner.

> /w/ sound before *you* (*have you/w/ever*)
> /j/ sound before *I* and *they* (*I/j/ever, they/j/ever*)

AUDIOSCRIPT 🔊 061

Man: Have you ever eaten sushi?
Woman: Yes, I have.
Man: Have they ever swum in a lake?
Woman: Yes, they have.
Man: Have I ever asked you to help me before?
Woman: No, you haven't.

PRESENT PERFECT WITH *JUST*

6 Draw attention to the box and read through the examples as a class.

Allow students a minute to read the examples again and complete the rules, then check as a class.

> **1** a short time ago **2** after, before

➡ **GRAMMAR REFERENCE** / Page 211

7 Students work in pairs to complete the sentences. Check answers as a class.

> **2** 've/have just seen **3** have just painted
> **4** 've/have just bought

8 Start by telling the class about something new, using one of the bullet prompts as the subject. Get students to ask you some questions.

Students work in pairs, using the idea prompts, to tell each other about something new. Remind them that they should use *just* and encourage them to ask their partners follow-up questions.

READING PART 3 TRAINING
SB P93

✓ EXAM INFORMATION

In Reading Part 3, students read a text and answer five three-option multiple-choice questions about it. They read for detailed understanding and main ideas. In the example here there are only three questions. The focus in the Student's Book is on encouraging students to underline the key words and find the correct answer by thinking about why the other answer options are incorrect.

The whole Reading and Writing paper has seven parts. Parts 1–5 are reading tasks and Parts 6 and 7 are writing tasks. Students have 60 minutes in total to complete the paper, so they should spend about 15 minutes on the writing tasks and 45 minutes on the reading tasks. Students should allow about eight minutes to do Part 3 in the exam.

Ask the class what they remember about Reading Part 3 and, if possible, elicit the information already seen in Unit 3.

UNIT 7 LIVE LIFE! **85**

1 Allow about one minute for students to look at the photo and scan the text, just looking at the paragraph headings, before asking them to suggest what hobby he may have.

> acting

2 Read the question with the class, and ask students to read question 1. Direct attention to the first paragraph in the text and ask students to find the sentences which correspond to the three options A, B and C.

Ask students to tell you the phrases in the text which have a similar meaning to *make new friends* (meeting some new people) and *try something new* (doing something different).

Point out that the words in the text will not usually be exactly the same as those in the answers, but they will have the same meaning. As a class read through the box which explains why B is correct and A and C are incorrect.

Students answer questions 2 and 3. Tell them you will ask them to justify the answers they choose and remind them that saying why the incorrect options are wrong is also helpful.

When checking answers, ask students to justify their answers by telling you the phrases in the text which correspond to the correct answer options, and then ask other students to explain why the other options are incorrect.

> **2** B **3** C

THE THEATRE

> **LEAD-IN**
>
> Write the title on the board and brainstorm any words students know that are connected to it. You may be able to elicit *actor, play, performance* and *audience* if students remember them from the reading text in Exercise 1. If students don't remember them move straight on to Exercise 1.

1 Students work in pairs to put the definitions in order. Check answers as a class, modelling and drilling pronunciation of the words as necessary.

> **1** The audience are the people who watch a performance.
> **2** A performance is acting, playing music or dancing in front of people.
> **3** An actor's costume is the set of clothes he or she wears during the performance.
> **4** A rehearsal is when the actors practise the play.
> **5** The stage is the place where the actors perform.

2 Students complete the sentences with the words in the box and check their answers with a partner before class feedback.

> **1** audience **2** stage **3** performance
> **4** rehearsal **5** costumes

Read through the information in the *Did you know?* box with the class.

3 Students work in pairs to ask and answer the questions. Feed back by asking three or four students to tell the class their answers.

1 Discuss the questions with the class. If students have been to a concert ask them for some more information, for example, *Where?; When did you go?; Who did you go with?* If they haven't, ask them, *Why would(n't) you like to go?*

Draw attention to the photos and the title and tell students they are going to read about a special orchestra. Ask them what they can see in the photos that looks special.

Allow students a minute to read the text quickly to find out whether their suggestions were correct.

2 Students read the text again more carefully to answer the questions.

> **Suggested answers**
> **1** They are children. They are from the city of Asunción in Paraguay.
> **2** They are made of recycled rubbish.

3 Ask students to cover the text and read the definitions. Try to elicit the words before uncovering the text to check answers.

> **1** rubbish **2** recycled

4 062 Ask students to suggest possible answers to the question. Then play the recording while students listen for the answer.

> Because he didn't have any money to buy them.

AUDIOSCRIPT 062

Woman: In 2006, Favio Chavez began working in Asunción in Paraguay on a recycling project. He was also a musician and he started to give music lessons to some of the children in the local area in his free time. The problem was that he didn't have any money to buy instruments for the children to use. So he asked Cola, a local man who was very good at making things, if he could make some instruments out of old things. Cola made some drums and flutes and then violins and guitars. They sounded great and they cost nothing! It was also better for the children to have instruments like this and not expensive 'real' instruments that people would want to steal. Chavez formed an orchestra with his students and they started to give concerts in Asunción. They made beautiful music with their recycled instruments. They played classical music – Mozart, Beethoven and Bach – and they sounded fantastic. In 2012, a Paraguayan film director made a film about the orchestra and put it online and they started to become famous all over the world. They now get invited to play in different countries. One of the first countries they went to was Brazil. The young musicians were very excited to visit Rio de Janeiro, not just because it was a famous city in a different country but because they saw the ocean for the first time.

5 Go through the questions and answer options with the class, helping with vocabulary as necessary. Play the recording again for students to choose the correct option. If necessary, the recording can be repeated or paused after each answer to check answers.

> 1 b   2 b   3 c   4 a

LEAD-IN

Close books and brainstorm names of musical instruments on the board. Help with vocabulary, in particular if students want to know the names of an instrument they play. If possible try to elicit the instruments listed in the Student's Book.

6 Open books and ask students to work in pairs to ask and answer the questions.

VOCABULARY

SB P95

MUSIC PERFORMERS

LEAD-IN

Write *types of music* on the board. Ask students to brainstorm as many types of music as they can think of and write them on the board. After a minute, elicit singers and groups that fit each type of music. Then tell students about your favourite piece of music and why you like it.

1 Ask students to discuss the questions in small groups before class feedback.

2 Ask students to describe the photos and elicit any guesses about what the people in the photos do. Then ask students to read the interviews. Set a time limit of two minutes and remind students that they don't have to understand every word in the texts. Students then discuss their answers. Elicit the answer from the class.

> **1** Valeria and Diego perform music; Alex listens to music.
> **2** Valeria plays the guitar and the drums.

3 Allow the students a few minutes to read the interviews and underline the answers. Feed back as a class and check which words students underlined.

> **1** a mix of pop and soul
> **2** They both write it.
> **3** female solo artists
> **4** the drums

4 Students work in pairs to complete the definitions. Check answers as a class, modelling and drilling pronunciation of the words as necessary.

> **1** guitarist   **2** solo artist   **3** Songwriters
> **4** drummer   **5** lead singer   **6** musician

5 Students complete the text with words from Exercise 4 and check their answers with a partner before class feedback. Then ask the class if they like the type of music *Clean Bandit* make (electronic music).

> **1** lead singer   **2** drummer   **3** guitarist
> **4** songwriters   **5** musicians   **6** solo artists

6 Students work in pairs to discuss the questions. Feed back by asking three or four students to tell the class their answers.

UNIT 7   LIVE LIFE!   87

WRITING
SB P96

A LEAFLET

LEAD-IN

Tell students about a festival you have been to, e.g. *I went to the Edinburgh International Festival in Scotland last August. I saw dance performances and music concerts as well as theatre and comedy. I stayed in an apartment with some friends.*

1 Draw students' attention to the questions and elicit the names of some festivals they have been to. If there are a significant number of students who have been to a festival, encourage them to discuss the questions in groups of two or three. If only a few students have been to a festival, ask them to tell the class about their experience.

2 Draw attention to the leaflet and allow students one or two minutes to look through the information to answer a question; *What type of accommodation is there at this festival?* (a campsite/camping).

Then read through the questions, as a class, checking understanding as necessary before students work in pairs to answer the questions. Check answers as a class.

> 1 26–29 July, Charlsbury Park, Kent
> 2 an international music festival
> 3 four days
> 4 £185
> 5 yes, £70
> 6 £40 per tent
> 7 You can watch music and dance performances, buy things to eat and drink, do art and painting, and learn dance and music styles.

3 Remind students they are looking for adjectives only. Do the first one together and point out that sometimes more than one adjective can be used. Students continue the task individually before checking answers with a partner.

> 1 international/favourite
> 2 amazing/world-famous
> 3 pleasant
> 4 excellent
> 5 fun
> 6 international
> 7 delicious

4 Read the rubric together. Point out that the ideas listed are suggestions, but students can use other ideas if they prefer. Students work in groups of three to plan their leaflet using the one in Exercise 1 as a model. Encourage students to make notes at this stage rather than writing complete sentences.

As students are preparing, move around the classroom to help with vocabulary and answer questions about their ideas.

5 Point out that the leaflet should be a type of advert for the festival and so students should try to make it as attractive as possible, with pictures or photos and different colours and fonts if they wish.

If you have facilities, students can do this on a computer in class or they can do it by hand.

When they have finished, you can display the leaflets around the room so that the class can decide which festival they would prefer to go to and why.

SPEAKING PART 1 TRAINING
SB P97

✓ EXAM INFORMATION

Students take the Speaking test in pairs or a group of three. There will only be a group of three at the end of a session if there is an odd number of candidates. Students cannot take the Speaking test on their own. There is one examiner who asks the candidates questions and another examiner who listens to them. In Speaking Part 1 there are two phases. In the first, students have to answer personal questions about themselves. In the second, they answer two short-answer questions and one longer, 'tell me something about…' question about their daily life, interests, preferences, etc. Part 1 lasts three to four minutes for each pair of candidates.

1 🔊 063 Elicit any information students know about Part 1 of the Speaking test, supplying the information from the Exam information box above if students do not know.

Then go over the instructions and tell students they will hear the first phase of Speaking Part 1. Play the recording, asking students to complete the information required. Check answers as a class.

	Yannis	Carmen
Work or studies	student	works as a shop assistant
Age	17	19
Nationality	Greek	Spanish
City	Athens	Madrid

AUDIOSCRIPT 063

Examiner: Good morning. What's your name?
Carmen: I'm Carmen.
Examiner: And what's your name?
Yannis: Yannis.
Examiner: Yannis, do you work or are you a student?
Yannis: Erm, erm … Student.
Examiner: How old are you?
Yannis: 17.
Examiner: Where do you come from?
Yannis: Greece.
Examiner: Where do you live?
Yannis: What?
Examiner: Do you live in Athens?
Yannis: Yes, near the centre of Athens.
Examiner: Thank you. Carmen, do you work or are you a student?
Carmen: I'm working at the moment. I have a job as a shop assistant. But after the summer, I'm planning to go to university.
Examiner: How old are you?
Carmen: I'm 19 years old.
Examiner: Where do you come from?
Carmen: I'm from Spain.
Examiner: Where do you live?
Carmen: I live in Madrid.
Examiner: Thank you.

2 Elicit answers to the questions pointing out that students should try to extend their answers in the Speaking test rather than using just one or two words.

> Carmen gives better answers because they are longer and have more information in them.

3 064 Now students will listen to the second phase of Speaking Part 1.

In this example, the questions are about hobbies and weekends, but make sure students understand that the topics are always different.

Play the recording and ask students to make notes about Yannis and Carmen's hobbies and weekends.

Point out that both Yannis and Carmen are giving good, longer answers in this part of the test. Then ask students to compare their notes with a partner before checking answers as a class. It may be necessary to repeat the recording for a weaker group.

> **1** Yannis: he plays sports in the evenings; he enjoys going to the cinema and sailing with his father at weekends.
> **2** Carmen: she likes watching and playing tennis; she'd like to try painting; she had a birthday party last weekend.

AUDIOSCRIPT 064

Examiner: Now, let's talk about hobbies. Carmen, what's your favourite hobby?
Carmen: I love tennis. I like watching it, I like reading about tennis players, and best of all I love playing it.
Examiner: Yannis, how much time do you have for doing hobbies?
Yannis: Quite a lot of time. After school I play different sports, usually for one or two hours in the evening.
Examiner: Now, Carmen, please tell us something about a new hobby you would like to try.
Carmen: I'd like to try painting. I don't know if I could do it very well. But I'd like to paint some pictures, for example, of my city. I could give them to my friends.
Examiner: Now, let's talk about weekends. Yannis, where do you enjoy going at weekends?
Yannis: I enjoy going to the cinema with my friends, and I enjoy going sailing with my father.
Examiner: Carmen, what was the best thing about last weekend?
Carmen: Oh, that's easy! It was my birthday, and I had a party on Saturday night.
Examiner: Now, Yannis, please tell me something about your plans for next weekend.
Yannis: I don't have any plans at the moment. I might have to do some homework, but I hope there's time to see my friends. I'll probably watch TV as well.

4 064 Encourage students to read through the questions in pairs and write in any words they remember. Then play the recording again for them to complete their answers. Feed back as a class. Point out that questions 3 and 6 are similar and that students will always be asked the 'tell me something about …' question in phase 2 of Speaking Part 1. They should know that a longer answer is expected to that question.

> **1** favourite **2** much time **3** something about
> **4** enjoy going **5** was, best **6** Please tell me

5 A weaker group can use the questions in Exercise 4 to find out some information about their partner. Otherwise, ask students to work in pairs to write some questions similar to those in Exercise 4 using the different question words in the book. Then, ask them to write another question about something in the past or future, similar to questions 5 and 6 in Exercise 4.

Students work with a different partner to ask their questions and try to remember the answers given. Ask four or five students to tell the class some information about their partner.

FAST FINISHERS

Students can ask their partner some more questions about their home town or country.

PUSH YOURSELF / B1

SB P97

VOCABULARY: LINKING WORDS

LEAD-IN

Ask one or two students to tell you why they started doing their hobby. Elicit some reasons such as, *because my friends do it*, *because I like keeping fit*, etc. and write them on the board to use later in Exercise 2.

1 Go over the instructions with the class and check understanding of the two reasons listed for starting a hobby. Students read the texts and match the reason with each person. Check answers as a class, asking students to tell you which phrase from each text told them the answer. For example, *time to myself = be alone*; *help friends = it was impossible to find somebody else*.

> **1** Lotti   **2** Michael

LANGUAGE NOTE

In both questions in Exercise 1 *they* is used to refer to an individual. This happens when we don't know whether the person we are referring to is male or female, so to avoid the rather long-winded *he or she* we use *they*.

2 Read the rubric together and explain that the words in bold are used to explain and give reasons. Refer students back to the reasons written on the board and point out the use of *because*.

Then read the first rule together and ask students if they can change the phrases on the board to use *because of* instead of *because*. For example, *because of my friends*, *because of my fitness*.

Then go through the other rules with the class and ask them to find the correct word for the gaps by looking at the way they are used in the texts.

> **1** because   **2** so that   **3** so

3 Students complete the sentences using the rules in Exercise 2 to help. Check answers as a class.

> **1** so that   **2** because of   **3** so   **4** Because

FAST FINISHERS

Students can write a sentence about themselves using each linking word or phrase (*so, so that, because, because of*).

EXAM FOCUS

SB P98

READING PART 3

1 Brainstorm any information students can remember about Reading Part 3. Then ask them to complete the Exam check text by choosing the correct answer option. They can look at the model question in 2 to help them if necessary. Check answers as a class.

> **1** one long text   **2** five   **3** three
> **4** choose   **5** title of the text

2 Draw attention to the photo and ask students to say what they think the text might be about. Point out that the photo is there to help them understand the general topic before they start reading.

Remind students that it is a good idea to underline the key words in the questions and to think about why answer options are incorrect as well as which one is the correct answer.

It can be helpful to read the questions before reading through the text as the time available in the exam is limited and students need to learn to look for the answers to the questions without worrying about understanding every word of the text.

Allow students eight minutes to complete the task under exam conditions, i.e. without conferring.

When checking answers encourage students to say why the other options are incorrect.

> **1** A   **2** B   **3** B   **4** A   **5** C

SPEAKING PART 1

SB P99

With books closed, brainstorm what students remember about the Speaking test and Speaking Part 1 in particular. Then open books and ask students to read through the Exam facts box to see if there is any more information that they did not remember.

Go over the exam tips with the class and reassure students that they do not need any special knowledge as they will be asked to talk about themselves and their everyday life.

Remind students to give long answers where possible and not to use just one or two words.

1 Ask two or three students to answer the questions, encouraging them to give more than one-word answers, e.g. *My name's Rita Lopez, I live in a small town near Valencia in Spain*. Then give students a minute to ask and answer the questions with a partner.

2 Students can work in pairs and take it in turns to be the examiner, or in a group of three with two 'candidates' and one 'examiner'. Remind students that in the exam, they will only be asked three questions in this part, with the third question being a longer answer, 'tell me something about…' question. Move around the class while students answer the questions, helping with vocabulary and making sure they are giving answers of more than one or two words.

At the end of the task allow students a minute or so to answer the *How was it?* question, then hold a show of hands to see how many students chose each option.

> **Suggested answers**
> I usually see my friends at school and sometimes we go out on Saturday afternoon.
> I have known my best friend for nine years. We went to primary school together.
> My best friend is Charlie. He is tall with blond hair and blue eyes. He likes football and rugby. I like him because he is very funny.

Read through the options in the *How was it?* section and elicit the meaning of each one that they learned in the first unit.

Ask students to tick the appropriate box. You might like to ask students to share how they felt about the task to get an indication of your students' confidence. Depending on your class, you might like to do this openly or allow students to give their feedback without their classmates seeing. For example, give students a piece of A4 paper each with the *How was it?* scale written in large letters. Allow students to tick the relevant box then hold up their papers at the same time so that you can see how well students think they are doing. Finally, ask students if they found it easier, harder or the same as the exam practice in previous units.

↳ *SPEAKING BANK / Page 240*

REAL WORLD

SB P100

SPENDING YOUR FREE TIME IN … LONDON

1 Read the instructions and the phrases in the box together, asking questions to check understanding as necessary, for example, *Where do you go to watch a play?* (The theatre).

Students discuss the question in pairs for two or three minutes. Then ask three or four pairs to tell the class their ideas.

2 Draw attention to the photos and ask students what they can see. Elicit *street art, market, food*. Then students read the texts and match each one with a photo before telling their partner which activity they would prefer and why. If necessary, ask some questions to elicit more information, such as *What would you like to buy at Camden Market? Which food would you like to eat?*

Ask three or four students to tell the class which activity they chose.

> **A** Street Art Tour
> **B** Camden Market
> **C** East End Food Tour

3 Read the statements as a class and help with vocabulary as necessary. Then students work in pairs to find the answers in the texts. Feed back as a class. Encourage students to correct the false statements.

> **1** F The tours change all the time.
> **2** F It started as an arts and crafts market.
> **3** T

4 Students find the phrases in the texts and choose the correct definition. Explain that they can check their answers by substituting the phrase in the text with the answer they choose. Feed back as a class.

> **1** a **2** a **3** b **4** a **5** b **6** b

5 🔊 065 Go over the instructions with the class and ask them to suggest what the people might talk about in the different situations, e.g. a: clothes, prices; b: information, questions; c: art, artists; d: food. Play the recordings and ask students to make a note of one or two words or phrases which tell them the answer in each case. Repeat the recordings if necessary.

Check answers, as a class, encouraging students to tell you the notes they made.

> **1** d **2** a **3** c

AUDIOSCRIPT 🔊 065

1
Woman: Ooh, this is nice. I love cooking, and I love spicy things! Do you like it?
Man: Yes, it's really nice. It's very different. I didn't know that London had all these different kinds of food.
Woman: Oh, yes. London's a city with people from all over the world. I love it!
Man: Are you from London?
Woman: No, I'm from Cornwall, in the south west, but I've just moved up to London for my job. How about you?
Man: Oh, I'm a tourist. I'm here for two weeks.
Woman: Cool. Where are you from?
Man: I'm from Sevilla, in Spain. Spanish food is quite different.
Woman: Yeah. I love Spanish food, too.
Man: I really like this tour. You see a different side of the city when you think about its food.
Woman: Yes, that's true.
Man: Oh, it looks like we're on the move again!
Guide: Right, everyone, are you ready to go and …?

2

Man: I'm sorry I haven't got the colour you wanted. You could try again next week? Are you local?

Woman: No, I'm a tourist. I'm only here for one week.

Man: Oh, that's a shame. Is this your first time at the market?

Woman: Yes. I really like it. I collect vintage clothes and there are some really interesting clothes here. But it's very busy.

Man: Yeah. It's crazy some days! It's best to get here early. It's OK till lunchtime, then it goes mad!

Woman: Yes, there are so many visitors. It's my first time in London, but I hope I'll be back next year.

Man: Well, if you are, nip down here again, and we'll see if we've got anything you like.

Woman: OK. Thank you.

Man: See you. Bye.

3

Man: Wow! That's amazing!

Woman: I know. I can't believe the city has so many artists!

Man: Where are you from?

Woman: I'm from the US.

Man: Really? Is street art a big thing where you come from?

Woman: In the big cities, yes. I'm from New York, and there's a lot of street art. But I've never seen a tour like this in my city. Are you from London?

Man: No. I'm from Manchester, and we don't have anything like this. I think it's great. I mean, you can always walk around and just look at the works yourself, but it's worth the few pounds to get the tour. You learn so much, and they know where the best pieces are. It'd be difficult to find them on your own.

Woman: That's true. And they take you to some really interesting places.

Man: Yeah. You get off the tourist track, that's for sure.

PHRASES YOU MIGHT USE

6 🔊 065 Students complete the phrases before listening to the recordings again to check their answers.

1 Are you   2 I'm here   3 very busy   4 first time
5 never seen   6 true (Use this to agree with someone.)

PHRASES YOU MIGHT HEAR

7 Students work in pairs to choose the correct definitions before checking answers as a class.

1 b   2 a   3 a   4 b

WATCH

8 ▶ Go through the questions with the class, checking understanding. With a weaker group play the first part of the video and ask students to listen for questions 1 and 2 only. Pause and check answers. Then play the rest of the video and encourage students to take notes.

1 a big wheel
2 30 minutes
3 a hop-on, hop-off ticket
4 Big Ben
5 to take photos on the famous crossing from a *Beatles* album
6 1,000 years, traditional British food and food from many different countries

VIDEOSCRIPT ▶ London

London is a great city to visit. If you're interested in history, London is full of interesting historical sites, and there are also lots of fun things to do.

The London Eye is a big wheel that you can ride on. You get an amazing view of the whole city at the top. A trip on the London Eye takes 30 minutes, so you get plenty of time to look around.

A boat trip is another way to enjoy the city. It's best to buy a hop-on, hop-off ticket, which means you can get on and off the boat in different places, to look around. If you're interested in politics, one place to get off is the Palace of Westminster, where the British parliament meets. Here, you can see and hear Big Ben, the famous clock.

Fans of Harry Potter will also love visiting London. As well as seeing the Harry Potter play in the theatre, you could go on a Harry Potter tour and visit some of the locations from the films, such as King's Cross station, or do the Warner Brothers film studio tour.

Or take a cab and go on a rock tour of London and learn about famous groups and singers that performed here. For example, this is Abbey Road, where you will find the crossing that the *Beatles* used on one of their album covers. Tourists love to take photos of themselves on it.

Borough Market is a food market that has existed for over 1,000 years and lots of people visit it every day to buy delicious things to eat. There's traditional British food and also food from all around the world, such as fruit and vegetables, and all kinds of fish. It's also a great place to grab a sandwich. Enjoy!

9 ▶ Students compare their notes with a partner before watching the video again to check. Feedback as a class.

LIFE COMPETENCIES
SB P101

DECISION-MAKING AND EMOTIONAL SKILLS

10 Students work in groups of three or four. Go over the instructions as a class, checking understanding.

First, students choose a city as a group, then they select some exciting activities to do there. Encourage them to say why they prefer one activity to another.

Explain it is important for each group member to participate in the decision and discussion.

Each group tells the rest of the class about their choices and should talk about at least one of the activities the group has chosen.

➡ **WORKBOOK** / Unit 7, page 32

8 FEELS LIKE HOME

UNIT OBJECTIVES	
Topic:	house and home
Grammar:	present perfect with *for* and *since*, *yet* and *already*; present perfect vs past simple
Vocabulary:	houses; kitchen items; prepositions
Listening:	listening for gist and specific information: a report about a celebrity home
Reading:	Part 5: completing gaps in an email
Speaking:	describing where you live; describing a picture
Writing:	Part 6: writing an email
Pronunciation:	pronouncing prepositions
Exam focus:	Reading Part 5; Writing Part 6
Real world:	living and learning in Malta

Ask your students to watch the Grammar on the Move videos on pages 105 and 107. You can use these to present or reinforce the present perfect with *for* and *since* and the present perfect with *yet* and *already*.

READING
SB P102

WHERE I LIVE

LEAD-IN

Draw attention to the photos and go over the questions. Give an example answer for yourself, for example, *My house is like photo A because it's a flat but it is not very modern. I would like to have a swimming pool like photo E because I love swimming and the house looks fantastic. I would not like to live in the house in photo D because I don't want to live in the countryside.*

1 Allow two or three minutes for students to discuss the questions in pairs.

2 Encourage students to read the descriptions before choosing the word from the box and the photo. When checking answers, elicit or point out that *apartment* is American English while *flat* is more common in British English. A *studio flat* usually has one space for living and not separate rooms.

| 1 villa E   2 houseboat C   3 cottage D |
| 4 townhouse B   5 studio apartment/flat A |

3  066 Go through the instructions with the class. Play the recording once and check answers.

| Shanghai, China |

AUDIOSCRIPT 066

Ling: My name is Ling. I'm 43 years old and I live in Shanghai, a big city in China. I live with my sister in a small house in an old part of the city. It's in the centre of Shanghai, near the river. The house is 100 years old. My sister and I were born in it and we've lived there all our lives!

Huan: My name is Huan and I'm 25 years old. I live in an apartment in Shanghai in China. My apartment is very new. I moved into it four weeks ago! The building is modern and my apartment is on the 23rd floor, so I have a great view across the whole of the city. It's not near the city centre but that's OK.

4 066 Ask students to read through the questions and the answer options. Ask questions to check understanding as necessary, e.g. *If something is expensive do I pay a lot or a little for it?* Check pronunciation of the numbers in 3 and 5 by asking students to read out all the options.

Repeat the recording. Students compare answers in pairs before checking answers as a class. The recording can be repeated if required.

| 1 c   2 b   3 c   4 b   5 a   6 a |

5 Point out the city of Shanghai in the photo and ask students to guess which home belongs to Ling and which to Huan.

| Ling: Photo B   Huan: Photo A |

6 Allow students a couple of minutes to read the texts to check their answers.

7 Students work in pairs to find the answers to questions in the texts. Check answers as a class.

| 1 because it's modern and has a balcony |
| 2 the fantastic view |
| 3 in the garage under the apartment building |
| 4 three |
| 5 on the roof |
| 6 pay rent |

VOCABULARY
SB P103

HOUSES

1 Point out the words in purple in the text and remind students that reading the sentence around the word in the text will help them understand the meaning. Students complete the sentences. Check answers as a class.

> **1** rent   **2** roof   **3** garage   **4** view   **5** building
> **6** balcony   **7** furniture   **8** ground floor
> **9** neighbours   **10** basement

FAST FINISHERS

Students can write some sentences about their own homes using the words in purple in the texts.

2 Read through the *Did you know?* box with the class. Ask students if they use the same system as the UK or the USA in their countries.

Allow students two minutes to put the words in order and then check as a class. Put each question to a different student to elicit example answers and other language which may be useful to answer or extend answers, e.g. *I don't know; I think it's about 20 years old; My favourite room is the kitchen because …*

Students work in pairs to ask and answer the questions. Encourage them to extend answers where possible and then ask three or four students to tell their answers to the class.

> **1** How old is your home?   **2** How many floors does it have?   **3** What's your favourite room?   **4** Do you have a garden or a balcony?

LISTENING
SB P104

LEAD-IN

Draw attention to the photo, covering the text and ask students where they think the house might be, what type of person they think lives there and whether they would like to live there. At this stage accept all answers students suggest and note any new vocabulary on the board.

1 Allow students two minutes to read the text to find the answers. Feed back as a class, commenting on whether anyone had correctly predicted the answers.

> **1** The house is in Beverly Hills, Los Angeles. A actress/singer lives there.   **2** eight years   **3** $9.5 million

2 🎧 067 Go over the instructions with the class and then play the recording. Students check answers with a partner before class feedback.

> indoor swimming pool, gym, kitchen

AUDIOSCRIPT  067

Reporter: Hello and welcome to *Homes of the Rich and Famous*. So, here I am standing in the hall of this amazing home. In front of me are the stairs. Let's go up … There are ten bedrooms in this house and five bathrooms, but the room I want to visit is the famous swimming pool … Yes, here it is. A big, indoor swimming pool on the first floor. Wow! Next to the swimming pool is the gym. Let's go inside. Well, this gym has everything, so it's the perfect house for fitness fans.

OK, let's go downstairs now. I'd like to visit the kitchen … Yes, here it is, between the dining room and the hall. It's so big and everything is white … and gold. Just look at that big sink with gold taps. And is that really a fridge opposite the window? It's as big as a bus. I love it! There are loads of cupboards and the cooker and the oven are twice as big as normal ones! People who love cooking will be very happy here.

I think if we look out of the window, we can see the recording studio behind the house. Lots of famous musicians have recorded there. Let's see if we can look inside! There's a small cinema in the basement, under the recording studio, and there's also an amazing games rooms for adults and children.

3 🎧 067 Encourage students to read through the questions and answer options before listening to the recording again. Feed back as a class.

> **1** b   **2** a   **3** a   **4** b   **5** b

VOCABULARY
SB P104

KITCHEN ITEMS

1 Students match the words to the definitions. Check answers as a class.

⊕ EXTENSION

Ask students to underline the expressions used in the definitions to describe things, e.g. *a piece of furniture/equipment … the part above … which is used for/to …-ing*. Then ask students to work in pairs to write definitions for things in the classroom or in another room in the house. Students swap their list with another pair and write the names of the things described.

> **1** f   **2** d   **3** a   **4** e   **5** b   **6** c

PREPOSITIONS

2 Students match the correct word with each picture.

> **A** in front of   **B** between   **C** opposite   **D** under
> **E** behind   **F** next to

3 Initiate a class discussion to answer the question. Elicit some of the things students do in their kitchens by asking questions if necessary, e.g. *Do you eat in the kitchen?; Do you study in the kitchen?*

4 You could first describe your kitchen to the whole class so they can draw the plan as you describe it. Then students compare their plans to check understanding. After that, students do the task in pairs, taking turns to describe their kitchen.

5 068 Play the recording and repeat the phrases chorally.

> **AUDIOSCRIPT** 068
>
> Under the sink
> Opposite the fridge
> Behind the oven
> Next to the tap
> Between the cooker and the fridge
> In front of the oven

GRAMMAR
SB P105

PRESENT PERFECT WITH *FOR* AND *SINCE*

> **LEAD-IN**
>
> Write a sentence about yourself on the board using the present perfect, e.g. *I have worked at this school for six years.* Ask students, *Do I work at this school now?* (yes); *When did I start working at this school* (six years ago, in… add year). Then write a second sentence: *I have worked at this school since* (add the appropriate year). Ask students if there is any difference in meaning in the two sentences (there isn't).

1 Open books and draw attention to the example sentences and questions 1–2. Work through the questions with the class, if possible, asking students who seemed less confident with the first questions (about you) first.

> **1** eight years ago, yes **2** last year, yes

2 Students read through the box and complete the rules. Check answers as a class.

Then read through the example questions and answers in the box, pointing out the question form *How long* + present perfect and highlighting that either *for* or *since* can be used in the answers.

> **1** for **2** since

➡ **GRAMMAR REFERENCE** / Page 212

3 Students work in pairs to choose the correct answers. Check answers as a class.

> **1** for **2** since **3** for **4** since **5** since **6** for

> **FAST FINISHERS**
>
> Students can rewrite all the sentences using *for* or *since* (the option which is not used in the original sentence).

4 Ask students how to form the present perfect (*have/has* + past participle) and elicit the past participles of the verbs in the phrases (*lived, known, had, known, liked*).

To do the task it may be necessary for students to ask questions in the present before they can ask the ones in the book, e.g. *Have you got a car?; How long have you had your car?; Do you know how to ski?; How long have you known how to ski?* Ask one or two students these questions to demonstrate.

With a weaker class it may be helpful for students to write the questions before they ask them.

Students then take turns to ask and answer questions using *for* or *since* in their answers.

DESCRIBING WHERE YOU LIVE

1 069 Draw attention to the photo and ask students which town or country they think it shows. Accept all answers. Go over the questions and play the recording. Check answers as a class.

> **1** Portugal **2** an apartment

> **AUDIOSCRIPT** 069
>
> **Woman:** OK, Luzia, so where do you live?
> **Luzia:** I live in Porto. It's a large city in the north-west of Portugal. It's on the Atlantic Ocean. It's a very old city and it's very beautiful.
> **Woman:** And where do you live in the city? Who do you live with?
> **Luzia:** I live in the centre, near the cathedral. I live in a big apartment with my parents, my sister, and my two brothers. It's on the third floor and it's old and big. There are eight rooms.
> **Woman:** How long have you lived there?
> **Luzia:** I've lived there all my life. I was born there.
> **Woman:** Do you like your apartment? What's your favourite room?
> **Luzia:** Yes, I like my apartment very much. The apartment building is old and the lift is broken, so we often have to climb lots of stairs, but it's still beautiful. My favourite room is the kitchen because it's where we eat and where the family spends time together.
> **Woman:** Is there anything you don't like about your apartment?
> **Luzia:** Yes, it's a bit noisy. I can often hear the noise from the street.
> **Woman:** Do you have your own room?

UNIT 8 **FEELS LIKE HOME**

Luzia:	No, I don't. I share a room with my sister.
Woman:	Can you describe your room?
Luzia:	Yes, it's quite big. The walls are white. There isn't a carpet on the floor; there are wooden floorboards. The curtains are blue and in front of the window is a big desk where we do our homework. On the wall next to the door there are shelves with some books in them.

2 069 Students order the questions, then listen to the recording again to check their answers.

> 1 And where do you live in the city?
> 2 Who do you live with?
> 3 How long have you lived there?
> 4 Do you like your apartment?
> 5 What's your favourite room?
> 6 Is there anything you don't like about your apartment?
> 7 Can you describe your room?

3 With a weaker class it may be necessary to pick out five adjectives (*noisy, old, ugly, big, cheap*) and ask students to find the opposites from the list. Otherwise students work in pairs to choose opposites from the complete list.

> noisy – quiet, old – modern, ugly – beautiful, big – small, cheap – expensive

4 Weaker students can use the sentences in the book and underline the answers which are appropriate for them before adding any other information.

Otherwise, go through the suggested answers and then ask students to close their books and make a few notes to talk about the three points (where you live / what your house/apartment is like / what your room is like) using the language they remember. Encourage them to use adjectives where possible.

5 In pairs students ask the questions in Exercise 2 and use the notes they made in Exercise 4 to answer them.

PUSH YOURSELF / B1

SB P106

SPEAKING: DESCRIBING A PICTURE

LEAD-IN

Draw attention to the photo and elicit some information about what students can see. Start them off by saying, *There's a picture on the wall*. Then ask students, in turn, to say something about the photo.

1 070 Encourage students to read the description and complete it with the phrases in the box. Then play the recording again to check answers.

> 1 At the back of   2 In front of   3 In the middle of
> 4 On the left   5 on the wall

AUDIOSCRIPT 070

Man: This is a photo of a living room. The walls are white and there's a grey rug on the floor. At the back of the room there are three big windows, but there aren't any curtains. In front of the window there's a round table with a white chair on each side of it. The part of the chair that we sit on – I don't know the name in English – is red. In the middle of the room there's a big glass table and on the table there are some pink flowers in … I don't know what it's called in English, but it's a kind of pot for flowers. On the left there's a grey sofa and above the sofa, on the wall, there's a big picture. On the right of the table there are two black chairs and there's a dog standing in front of them.

2 Go over the instructions together and elicit answers from the class.

> The part of the chair that we sit on – I don't know the name in English …
> I don't know what it's called in English, but it's a kind of …

3 Encourage students to read through the five descriptions before they choose the correct answers from the box. Check answers as a class.

> 1 seat   2 vase   3 rug   4 lamp   5 bookshelf

⊕ EXTENSION

Students work in pairs. One person from each pair describes a room in their house using the man's description as a model. Allow a few minutes for students to choose and think about vocabulary.

Then students take it in turns to describe their room while their partner listens and identifies which room they are talking about.

SB P107

PRESENT PERFECT WITH *YET* AND *ALREADY*

1 Direct attention to the photo and elicit or supply the phrase *to move house*. Ask the students one or two questions to check understanding and then initiate a class discussion to ask and answer the questions.

2 🔊 071 Go over the instructions and then play the recording. Check answers as a class.

> **1** because he's got a new job   **2** on the internet

AUDIOSCRIPT 🔊 071

Anthony: Hi, Laura, it's Anthony. You know that job in Helsinki I told you about? Well, I got it! And I'm moving to Finland in ten days.

Laura: Wow! Congratulations about the job, but that doesn't give you much time to do everything! Have you found anywhere to live yet?

Anthony: Yes, I have actually. I've already found my new apartment.

Laura: That was quick! How did you do it?

Anthony: I found it online. I looked on the internet for apartments in Helsinki and I found it there.

Laura: So you've only seen photos of it online then? You haven't actually visited it yet?

Anthony: Yes, I have. I went to Helsinki last week to see it and I really like it. It's quite old but it's big – well, big for me. It's got two bedrooms! It's near the centre and I've already paid the first month's rent and bought a new sofa. You must come and visit me. Helsinki is a great city.

Laura: I'd love to … But tell me about the job. Have you met your new boss yet?

Anthony: Yes, I've already met my boss. He offered me the job! I haven't visited the office yet. I haven't had time! Anyway, I must go now. There are some other people I need to phone. But come and visit me soon!

3 🔊 071 Encourage students to read the phrases before listening to the recording again and completing them. Students check answers in pairs before class feedback.

> **1** found, yet   **2** already found   **3** visited, yet
> **4** already paid   **5** yet   **6** already met

Read through the rules in the box with the class and then ask students to work in pairs to look at the sentences in Exercise 3 and complete the gaps. If necessary, provide some other examples to confirm the meaning and use of the two words, e.g. *We haven't finished Unit 8 yet, but we've already done Units 1 to 7.*

> **1** already   **2** yet

> **1** Have you phoned your parents yet?
> **2** He's already done his homework.
> **3** I've visited lots of cities, but I haven't visited New York yet.
> **4** I think you've already met my friends.
> **5** They haven't finished breakfast yet.

➡ **GRAMMAR REFERENCE** / Page 213

4 Direct the students' attention to Anthony's list and check understanding of the vocabulary. Then ask a question, *Has Anthony finished packing yet?* (Yes, he has.)

Allow students three or four minutes to read and complete the gaps in the conversation using the information on the list. Check answers as a class.

> **1** Have you finished packing yet?
> **2** already said goodbye
> **3** have you texted your friends
> **4** haven't booked a taxi yet

5 Point out that the questions all use *yet* and that students can use *not yet* or *already* in their answers. Elicit an example question, e.g. *Have you had a cup of coffee yet?* And some answers from the students (e.g. *Yes, I've already had two./ No, I haven't yet.*, etc.).

Students work in pairs to ask and answer the other questions. Encourage them to extend their answers where possible. For example, *I had a cup of coffee at home with my breakfast; I haven't had lunch yet because it's only 11 am!*

GRAMMAR

SB P108

PRESENT PERFECT OR PAST SIMPLE

1 Read the questions and elicit suggestions from the class. If necessary, encourage students with some questions such as, *Is it important to invite people to visit your new home? Why? Is it a good idea to try to start conversations with new colleagues?* etc. Ask students how important they think it is to make new friends and meet people in these new situations.

2 Draw attention to the photo of Paula and read the instructions together. Allow students a minute or so to read the text quickly to answer the question. Then ask students where Paula met the new people.

> Yes, she's met her neighbours and some girls from her exercise class.

3 Go through the example sentences and ask some questions to check understanding. For example, *Was Paula in her apartment two months ago?* (no); *Is she there now?* (yes). If necessary, provide one or two more examples, e.g. *My sister lived in Manchester for two years.* Ask, *Does she live in Manchester now?* (No, she doesn't.); *Angelica has lived in London for six months. Does she live in London now?* (Yes, she does.).

Students work through the rules, completing the gaps with the words in the box. Feedback as a class.

> **1** unfinished   **2** for   **3** finished   **4** ago

UNIT 8 FEELS LIKE HOME

4 Students complete the sentences using the correct tense. Encourage them to check their answers with a partner. If they don't agree with their partner encourage them to explain why they think their answer is correct using the rules in the box. Check answers as a class asking for explanations of their choices as necessary.

> **1** moved **2** 's/has lived **3** haven't finished
> **4** bought **5** has been **6** put **7** found
> **8** has … been

5 Point out that the prompts use the tense that students need to use in their responses. Ask one or two students to suggest answers before putting students into pairs to continue.

With a stronger group, encourage the listening partner to ask follow-up questions to elicit more information. For example, *Where did you go on holiday?; When did you go there?; Who cooked the food you ate?; What was it made from?*

Feed back by asking some students to tell you something about their partner.

READING PART 5 TRAINING
SB P108

✓ EXAM INFORMATION

In Reading Part 5 students read a short message or email and complete six gaps with one word each. The focus is on grammar.

The task in the Student's Book is simplified with four questions instead of six. This section teaches students that they should read the words before and after the gaps to help them decide which type of word is missing from the sentence and then which word fits best.

Students should allow about nine minutes to complete Part 5.

Direct attention to the email to Lucy from Ben and ask students what they think they have to do (complete each gap with one word).

Read through the instructions and the explanation of the example sentence with the class. Point out that it is important to read the words before and after the gap in order to choose the correct answer.

Encourage students to continue the task by first identifying the type of word that is missing and then deciding which word it is. Explain that if they don't know the answer but they know it is a preposition, for example, it can be helpful to think of a list of prepositions and then decide which one fits best. There is only one correct answer.

When checking answers ask students to tell you the first type of word and then the word.

> **1** on **2** is **3** the **4** go

WRITING PART 6 TRAINING
SB P109

✓ EXAM INFORMATION

In Writing Part 6, students have to write a short message in response to a short text or instruction. There are always three pieces of information to include, or three questions to answer. Students should write 25 words or more.

The whole Reading and Writing paper lasts 60 minutes and has 30 reading questions (Parts 1–5) and two writing questions (Parts 6 and 7). Students should spend about five minutes on Part 6.

1 Try to elicit what students have to do in Writing Part 6. If students don't remember you can direct them to Unit 2 to check.

Read the instructions as a class and allow students a minute or so to read the text to help with the answer.

> It's a party you have when you have just moved into / bought a new place to live.

CULTURAL INFORMATION

A housewarming party is often held when someone moves into a new home. Traditionally the party would be organised a few weeks after moving in and friends and relatives as well as any new neighbours are invited. Most guests bring a present for the new home such as a houseplant or something useful or attractive.

2 Encourage students to read through the questions before they read the email again to find the answers. Students compare answers in pairs, explaining where they found their answers, if they are different. Then feed back as a class.

> **1** They go to the same language school.
> **2** She has just moved house.
> **3** 7.30 pm on Saturday at 21, Lake Street
> **4** It's on the ground floor, is large, and has a beautiful modern kitchen and a garden. It's near the station on Lake Street.
> **5** other students from the language school and her brother Harry

3 Students identify the phrases before checking as a class.

> **1** Hi + (name) **2** How are you?
> **3** I'm writing to … **4** Best wishes

4 Explain that the phrases listed are alternative expressions for the functions in Exercise 3. Students work in pairs to match them.

Remind students that they will have to write a short message in the exam, so it is a good idea to learn some of these useful phrases. Check answers as a class.

1 Dear + (name); Hello + (name)
2 How are things?; I hope you are well.
3 I wanted to ask you; So, I wanted to know if …
4 See you soon!; All the best

5 Go through the instructions and remind students that they will have to include three pieces of information in their message in the exam. Elicit what those are in this question (questions about the transport Harry is using, if they can go to the party together and a place to meet).

Students work in pairs to write the three questions. There could be more than one correct answer.

Suggested answers
How are you getting to the party? Can we go together? Where shall/can we meet? What about the bus stop?

6 Give students a few minutes to look back at the example email and the other useful language to choose the phrases. Students can use any appropriate phrases.

7 The email can be written at home after the preparation tasks above or in class.

When they have finished students exchange their email with a partner for peer feedback. The partner should check that the three questions have been included and that some appropriate phrases are used at the start and end and in the first line. They should also check spelling and the number of words (more than 25).

Model answer
Hello Harry
How are things?
Are you going to Rose's party? How are you getting to the party? Can we go together? Why don't we meet at the bus stop?
See you soon
Fran
(34 words)

EXAM FOCUS   SB P110
READING PART 5

EXAM INFORMATION

In Reading Part 5 students read a short message or email and complete six gaps with one word each. The focus is on grammar.

They should allow about nine minutes to complete Part 5.

Elicit what students remember about Reading Part 5 before reading through the Exam facts box to check. Then go through the Exam tips box to remind students how to approach the task.

Allow students nine minutes to complete the task under exam conditions, i.e without conferring before checking answers.

1 it   2 of   3 Do / Would   4 to
5 your / the   6 the

EXAM FOCUS   SB P111
WRITING PART 6

EXAM INFORMATION

In Writing Part 6, students have to write a short message in response to a short text or instruction. There are always three pieces of information to include or three questions to answer. Students should write 25 words or more. The whole Reading and Writing paper lasts 60 minutes and has 30 reading questions (Parts 1–5) and two writing questions (Parts 6 and 7). Students should spend about five minutes on Part 6.

1 Read the question as a class and ssk some questions to check understanding, e.g. *Who are your writing to?* (Jamie); *Why?* (you want him to stay at your house); *What information should you include?* (the three bullet points); *How many words should you write?* (more than 25).

1 D   2 A   3 E   4 B   5 C

2 Allow students five to six minutes to write their messages and check them through using the checklist above. Remind them to check spelling too.

When students have finished, allow them a few minutes to complete the *How was it?* chart.

Suggested answer
Dear Jamie, would you like to come and stay at my house next weekend? We can watch films and you can meet some of my friends. Bring some computer games too. Andres. (32 words)

Read through the options in the *How was it?* section and elicit the meaning of each one that they learned in the first unit.

Ask students to tick the appropriate box. You might like to ask students to share how they felt about the task to get an indication of your students' confidence. Depending on your class, you might like to do this openly or allow students to give their feedback without their classmates seeing. For example, give students a piece of A4 paper each with the *How was it?* scale written in large letters. Allow students to tick the relevant box then hold up their papers at the same time so that you can see how well students think they are doing. Finally, ask students if they found it easier, harder or the same as the exam practice in previous units.

➜ **WRITING BANK** / pages 233–234

REAL WORLD

SB P112

LIVING AND LEARNING IN … MALTA

LEAD-IN

Brainstorm any information students know about Malta. If necessary, use the information below to help.

BACKGROUND INFORMATION

Malta is an island country in the Mediterranean Sea between Sicily and the coast of North Africa. It is a popular tourist destination and the sights include everything from prehistoric temples and wonderful beaches. The official languages are Maltese and English.

1 Go through the instructions and brainstorm answers to the question.

2 Direct students' attention to the headings in the text and check understanding of *accommodation* (a place to stay) and *self-catering* (accommodation which includes facilities so that you can cook for yourself). Then read through the statements with the class, helping with vocabulary as necessary.

Students read the text and decide whether the statements are true or false. When checking answers, encourage them to correct the false statements.

> 1 F They can come all year round.   2 T
> 3 F Adult classes are for all levels.   4 T
> 5 T   6 F There are different prices for the self-catering apartments.

3 Students work in pairs to find the phrases in the text and choose the correct definition. Explain that they can check their answers by substituting the phrase in the text with the answer they choose. Feed back as a class.

> 1 a   2 a   3 b   4 b   5 b   6 a

4 072 Go over the instructions with the class and ask them to suggest what the people might talk about in the different situations.

For example, a: personal questions and information; b: information about the house; c: questions and information about the school and courses; d: information about the course.

Play the recording, and ask students to make a note of one or two words or phrases which help them choose the answer in each case. Repeat the recording if necessary. Check answers as a class, encouraging students to tell you the notes they made.

> 1 c   2 d   3 b

AUDIOSCRIPT 072

1
Receptionist: Hello. International English College.
Rafael: Hello. My name's Rafael Lopez. I'm coming to your school in the summer with my family, and I'd like to book some accommodation.
Receptionist: OK. What was your name again?
Rafael: Rafael Lopez.
Receptionist: OK. Yes, I've got you here. Can you just give me the dates, please?
Rafael: We're arriving on the twenty fifth of July, and we're leaving on the eighth of August.
Receptionist: Well, there are a couple of options available – you can go for a hotel or a self-catering apartment.
Rafael: We'd like an apartment, please.
Receptionist: That's fine. And how many of you are there?
Rafael: There are four people in my family.
Receptionist: That's great. So, I've got a really nice apartment here. It's quite new, so it's nice and fresh. Shall I send you the details? I've got your email address. And then if you want to go ahead, just send me an email and I can book it for you. Or we can have another look if this one's no good.
Rafael: Yes, thank you. That's perfect.

2
Teacher: Hi. Come in. You're a bit early, but that's OK. Are you Maria?
Maria: Yes.
Teacher: Well, welcome to Malta. When did you get here?
Maria: I arrived last night.
Teacher: And where are you from?
Maria: I'm from Slovakia.
Teacher: Lovely. I think you're with a host family, aren't you? Have you settled in OK?
Maria: Yes, thank you. I've met my host family; they're really nice.
Teacher: Oh, that's good. Are you here with friends, or just on your own?
Maria: I've come with two friends from Slovakia, but they're in different classes.
Teacher: OK. Well, you'll see this is a really friendly class and there are plenty of other students your age, so you'll soon feel at home. Have you dealt with all the formalities?
Maria: Yes. I filled in all the forms and I've got my student card. And they told me to come to this class.
Teacher: That's perfect. Ah, here come the others. I'll introduce you, and then we can get started. Come in, everyone! This is Maria, …

3

Woman: Hello. You must be Jakob. Come on in. Here, let me take your bag.
Jakob: Thank you.
Woman: How was your flight?
Jakob: Yes, it was fine. The plane was on time.
Woman: Well, I'm Anna, and you'll be staying with us while you're here. You'll meet the rest of the family later when they get back. Shall I show you to your room first and we can get rid of these bags?
Jakob: OK. Thanks.
Woman: So, this is you in here. I'm sure you'll want to use the internet, so I've left the code for the wi-fi on the desk for you, so you can get that up and running.
Jakob: OK. Thanks.
Woman: So, just let me know if there's anything you need. Now, with food, do you have any allergies?
Jakob: No. I don't have any allergies. I eat everything.
Woman: Well, that's nice and easy. And is there anything you don't like? Any particular preferences?
Jakob: I'm not very keen on spicy food. And I don't like fish very much. But I love pasta and pizza.
Woman: OK. That's fine. I'm sure we can find things you'll like.

PHRASES YOU MIGHT USE

5 072 Students complete the phrases before listening to the recordings to check their answers.

> 1 like to book   2 There are   3 I've met
> 4 I've got   5 don't have   6 not very keen

PHRASES YOU MIGHT HEAR

6 Students work in pairs to choose the correct definitions before checking answers as a class.

> 1 c   2 f   3 d   4 a   5 e   6 b

WATCH

7 Go through the instructions with the class. With a weaker group play the first part of the video and ask students to listen for the information about towns and cities only. Pause at the end of the first part of the video and check answers. Then play the rest of the video and encourage students to take notes.

> **towns and cities:** largest city is Valletta, the capital, small streets and lovely buildings; Mdina is over 2,500 years old with narrow streets; St Julian's is a more modern town, with lots of shops and restaurants and a great beach
> **history and culture:** English is one of the official languages; many examples of British culture, such as telephone boxes and post boxes, double-decker buses
> **language schools:** more than 40 language schools on the island
> **free-time activities:** boat trips, sailing, scuba diving and horse riding, relaxing on the beach.

VIDEOSCRIPT ▶ Malta

Malta is a small island in the Mediterranean Sea. It is to the south of Italy and to the north of Libya in North Africa. It's a great place to visit, and a great place to live and study. Because it's an island, it has lots of beaches and Malta has a long and fascinating history, so there are lots of lovely places to see.

The largest city on the island is Valletta. Valletta is also the capital of Malta. It has lots of small streets and lovely old buildings. Another place to visit is the old city of Mdina. It was first built over 2,500 years ago and has beautiful narrow streets. St Julian's is a more modern town, with lots of shops and restaurants, and a great beach!

English is one of Malta's official languages, and some of its culture is like British culture, so you can find British phone boxes and post boxes, and double-decker buses.

There are more than 40 English language schools on the island, so it's a good place to study. There are also plenty of fun things to do in your free time, like boat trips, sailing, scuba diving, horse riding, or just relaxing on the beach. So Malta is a great place to live, to learn, and to have fun!

8 Students compare their notes with a partner before watching the video again to check. Feed back as a class.

9 Go over the instructions with the class. Encourage students to look back at the text on page 112 about courses and accommodation in Malta to help generate some ideas. Then students work in pairs to make notes.

LIFE COMPETENCIES
SB P113

CREATIVITY, INNOVATION AND DECISION-MAKING

10 When planning the leaflet remind students it will be an advertisement for their course, so it should be persuasive and attractive to the reader. Encourage students to think about design and layout and to add some pictures.

The leaflets can be displayed on the wall or desks so that all the students can read them and make their choice about which course to do and why.

Feed back by asking students to tell the class one positive thing from each of the leaflets and then why they chose the course they did.

➡ **WORKBOOK** / Unit 8, page 36

PROGRESS CHECK 3
UNIT 6 TO UNIT 8

SB P114

1

1 in
2 between
3 in front of
4 behind
5 under
6 next to

2

1 solo artist
2 drummer
3 musicians
4 band

3

1 broccoli
2 beef
3 chicken
4 omelette
5 mushroom
6 mango/melon
7 yoghurt

4

1 some
2 a little
3 much
4 some
5 many
6 a few
7 a

5

1 going to the gym
2 baking, photography
3 going to gigs
4 playing board games
5 doing nothing, doing exercise

6

1 **A:** Have you **ever** travelled somewhere by plane?
   B: Actually, I've **just** come back from New York. It was fantastic!
2 **A:** Have you finished that book **yet**?
   B: Of course! In fact, I've **already** started a new one.
3 **A:** What game is that you're playing? I have **never** seen it before.
   B: Oh, we've had this **for** years. My dad bought it in China.

7

1 I bought **some** jeans and **some** beautiful trainers.
2 It was good weather.
3 My favourite meal is pasta.
4 At the park no-one sells **any** food.
5 Don't forget to buy **some** juice.
6 We took **many** photos.

8

1 bought
2 Has … had
3 left
4 haven't seen
5 haven't put
6 met

9

1 A
2 B
3 C
4 C
5 A
6 B
7 A

9 GETTING ALONG

UNIT OBJECTIVES

Topic:	personal feelings, opinions and experiences
Grammar:	verbs/adjectives + *to* + infinitive; verbs + *-ing*; more expressions with *-ing* and *to*
Vocabulary:	feelings and emotions
Listening:	Part 4: identifying the main idea in short dialogues
Reading:	reading for gist: different kinds of friends; Part 2: three-option multiple-choice texts about life changes
Speaking:	giving advice
Writing:	an email giving advice
Pronunciation:	unstressed *to*
Exam focus:	Reading Part 2; Listening Part 4
Real world:	meeting people in Melbourne

Ask your students to watch the Grammar on the Move videos on pages 118 and 120. You can use these to present or reinforce verbs and adjectives + *to* + infinitive and verbs + *-ing*.

READING
SB P116

LEAD-IN
Tell the class about one of your friends to provide a model answer for the questions, e.g. *I met my best friend at university and I have known her for ten years. We like to go to the cinema and concerts together because we enjoy the same type of films and music.*

1 Students work in pairs to read through the questions and tell their partner about one of their friends.

2 Draw attention to the photos and the texts and allow students two or three minutes to match them. Encourage them to scan the texts quickly at this stage without worrying about understanding every word.
Check answers as a class.

> **1** E **2** A **3** D **4** B **5** C

3 Point out the words in blue and ask students to complete the definitions. When checking answers, ask students if they have friends who they can describe with these adjectives and why. For example, *Do you have any friends who are busy? Yes, Alice is busy because she works and she is a student.*

> **1** busy **2** confident **3** shy **4** friendly
> **5** generous **6** reliable

4 🎧 073 Go over the instructions and point out that students will hear the first person in each pair talking about their best friend, the second person.

Play the recording while students listen to complete 1–4. Check answers together. With a weaker group you can play the recording again.

> **1** at art school, 20 years ago
> **2** at a birthday party, 25 years ago
> **3** at a tennis club, (about) ten years ago
> **4** at a restaurant, last year

AUDIOSCRIPT 🎧 073

Chris: I met my best friend John when we were students at art school. That's 20 years ago now! We were both 18 and both very bad artists! I liked him immediately because he was so friendly, but he's also generous with his time. He's always willing to help people.

Emma: My best friend's Sonia. I've known her all my life. That's 25 years now! We lived in the same street. We met at a friend's birthday party and we played together when we were small. She's like my sister. I love her because she's so reliable. I know she will always be there for me.

Enrique: Juan is probably my best friend. He's my tennis partner. We're professional tennis players, so it's an important relationship. I met him at the tennis club about ten years ago. I get on so well with Juan because he's clever and funny. He makes me laugh and he's always telling me about something new he's read about. We spend a lot of time together, but I'm never bored when I'm with him.

Helena: I met Jasmine last year in the restaurant where we both work after school. We haven't known each other very long, but she's my best friend and I'm hers. I think she's the most generous person I've ever met. She's always giving people things and helping them.

5 🎧 073 Repeat the recording to allow students to listen for the answers to the question.

> **1** Chris and John: He's friendly and generous with his time.
> **2** Emma and Sonia: She's reliable and always there for her.
> **3** Enrique and Juan: He's clever, funny, makes him laugh, and he's never bored with him.
> **4** Helena and Jasmine: She's generous, gives people things, and helps people.

UNIT 9 GETTING ALONG 103

6 Students work in twos or threes to discuss the question. Encourage them to use the vocabulary from Exercises 1 and 2.

7 Draw attention to the photos and go over the instructions. Elicit suggested answers from the class. If necessary you could ask some questions such as, *How old do you think they are?; What kind of person do you think they are?; What job do you think they do?* etc. Accept all suggestions at this stage.

8 Give students three or four minutes to read the text quickly to find out if their answers in Exercise 7 were right and say where they work. It may be helpful for students to underline the parts of the texts where they find the answers. Students compare answers with a partner, pointing out the answers in the text, before class feed back.

> They met in Grace's restaurant in London when Matteo asked for a job ten years ago.
> Grace is friendly and generous. She never gets angry with Matteo.
> Matteo is always calm. He's a quiet person, but people never argue with him. They work in Grace's restaurant.

9 Students read the questions and find the answers in the text. Feed back as a class.

> **1** her smile   **2** ten years   **3** Because she thought he was too young.   **4** Because he's very calm. He's a quiet person, but people listen to him and do what he says.

VOCABULARY
SB P117

FEELINGS AND EMOTIONS

1 With a stronger class, point out the words in red in the text and ask students if they can describe the meanings of the words and expressions. You can help them with language by asking questions such as, *What do you get worried about?; When do you get stressed?*

Then give students a few minutes to match the two parts of the definitions. Check answers as a class.

> **1** b   **2** f   **3** e   **4** a   **5** d   **6** c

2 Students complete the sentences before checking answers.

> ### FAST FINISHERS
> Students can write some sentences of their own using the words in the box.

> **1** get on well   **2** worried   **3** bad mood
> **4** argue   **5** stressed   **6** angry

3 Read the *Did you know?* box together and ask if anyone knows what a British person means when they say *mad* (usually with mental health issues or out of control, or very silly or crazy). Students discuss the questions in pairs. Encourage them to ask follow-up questions and give extended answers of one or two sentences if possible. Then get feedback from some pairs and compare ideas in the class for what to do when you are in a bad mood, or whether people get stressed by similar situations.

SB P118

VERBS / ADJECTIVES + TO + INFINITIVE

1 Read through the example sentences with the class and elicit the correct answer to complete the rule.

It may be necessary to point out that the verbs and adjectives listed can also be followed by other structures, e.g. *I'm happy because…/I learn maths at school,* etc. but that if they are followed by a verb then it will be in the infinitive.

> infinitive

➡ **GRAMMAR REFERENCE** / Page 214

FAST FINISHERS

Students can work in pairs to write the first part of a sentence using a verb or adjective from the box, then they exchange phrases with a partner and each person finishes the other's sentences.

2 Students work in pairs to put the sentences in order. Feed back as a class.

> **1** It was interesting to find out about life in a different country.
> **2** We were excited to hear that there's a trip to America next year.
> **3** They were sad to say goodbye to their friends.
> **4** She promised to help him in the evening.
> **5** I tried to learn how to ski, but it was too difficult.

3 Point out that the missing word may be an adjective or a verb followed by *to*. Then students do the task individually before checking answers with a partner.

> **1** easy to   **2** learned to   **3** want to   **4** decided to
> **5** happy to   **6** exciting to

4 🔊 074 Point out the syllables marked in bold which are stressed.

Then play the recording, asking students to try to focus on the pronunciation of *to* as well as the stress.

> /tə/

104

AUDIOSCRIPT 074

It's easy to get stressed.
I needed to get a job.
I didn't really want to give Matteo a job.
He's happy to pay for the drinks.

5 074 Play the recording again and listen while students repeat the sentences. If necessary, do some individual drilling too. The sound of the *to* when unstressed is very common in English and it is important for students to begin to use it in order to use natural rhythm patterns when speaking.

6 Give students a few minutes to complete the sentences individually and then listen while they tell their partner the sentences, focusing on the stress patterns and the sound of the unstressed *to*.

READING PART 2 TRAINING
SB P119

✓ EXAM INFORMATION

Part 2 of the Reading paper is a matching task. Students have to read three short texts on the same topic and answer seven questions by choosing the correct option. The task in the Student's Book is simplified with five questions instead of seven. This section encourages students to underline key words in the questions before reading the texts.

They should allow about ten minutes to do Part 2.

1 Read the question and elicit some suggestions from the class. With a weaker class you can write some sentence starters on the board to help, e.g. *You can feel … / because … / It is difficult to …*

2 Go through the first question with the class and ask students to find the part of the text about Tom which gives the answer. Go over the information in the box to reinforce the answer. Then ask students to find the sentences in the other two texts which tell us they are not the correct answer (Michael: *Our family moved … /* Eric: *I was 20 and then I went away.*).

Read through the other questions, checking understanding as necessary, encouraging students to underline the key words and then ask students to find the answers. Encourage them to underline the words in the texts which tell them the answer.

Feed back as a class, eliciting the explanation as well as the answers.

| 2 C | 3 A | 4 C | 5 A |

3 Students discuss the questions with a partner. Feed back by asking two or three students to tell the class about their experience.

GRAMMAR
SB P120

VERBS + -ING

1 075 Draw attention to the photos and go through the instructions. Ask the class what they think the people in the photos are doing and help with any vocabulary as necessary.

Then play the recording and ask students to number the photos. Students compare answers with a partner before checking as a class.

| 1 Paola | 2 Tima | 3 Monica | 4 Fahad |

AUDIOSCRIPT 075

1
Paola: When I'm sad, I try to find something that will make me laugh. I love watching funny films, so I stream some of my favourite comedies – and before sitting down on the sofa to watch, I make some hot chocolate. This always cheers me up.

2
Tima: If I feel stressed, I try to find some friends to play a game of football with. I always enjoy running around, and thinking about the game helps me to forget my problems.

3
Monica: When I want to cheer myself up, I phone a friend. I soon stop thinking about sad things when we're talking and laughing. I have two or three good friends I can always call and I always feel better after talking to them.

4
Fahad: I clean my apartment when I'm feeling stressed. It always cheers me up! I hate being in a dirty, untidy place, so washing up and making everything clean and tidy makes me happy.

2 075 Encourage students to read through the sentences before listening again and suggest answers if they can. Then repeat the recording for them to check or complete the answers. Feed back as a class.

| 1 watching, sitting | 2 running | 3 thinking, talking |
| 4 being |

3 Students work in pairs to ask and answer the questions. Ask one or two students to tell the class what they do.

4 Read through the example sentences and the rules with the class and elicit answers.

| 1 After | 2 prepositions |

UNIT 9 GETTING ALONG

LANGUAGE NOTE

Remind students that they have already looked at verbs followed by the infinitive and now they can see other verbs which are followed by verb + -ing.

Students need to learn which verbs follow which rule.

It may be helpful for students to make a list of verbs under the headings *followed by infintive / followed by verb + -ing* in their notebooks, which they can add to as they find new verbs.

It is usually easier to remember the meanings if the verbs are in a sentence, so students could write an example sentence using each verb under the list.

➡ **GRAMMAR REFERENCE** / Page 214

5 A stronger class can start the exercise without looking at the verbs in the box. Ask students to try to think of a suitable verb for each space, then allow them to look at the box to complete or check their work. Feed back as a class.

> 1 visiting 2 being 3 reading 4 going
> 5 playing 6 revising

6 Students need to focus on the form of the verbs in this exercise as well as the meaning. Allow a few minutes for students to work through the exercise and then check answers as a class.

> 1 going, watching 2 to learn, taking
> 3 to help, to carry

7 Go through the questions with the class, eliciting an example answer for each question to check understanding if necessary. Then put students into pairs to ask and answer the questions.

LISTENING PART 4 TRAINING
SB P121

✓ EXAM INFORMATION

In Part 4 of the Listening paper, students listen to five short monologues or dialogues. They have to choose the correct answer from three multiple-choice options by listening for the main idea/gist/topic. In the exam students hear the recording twice.

This section in the Student's Book teaches students to focus on and underline important information in the question and answer options before they listen. They are also encouraged to listen for why the other options are wrong.

1 076 Go through the instructions and check understanding of the adjectives by asking students to tell you a situation when they feel sad/excited/worried/angry.

Play conversation 1 with Lisa and ask students to identify the correct feeling. Check answers and then play the other conversations. Feed back as a class.

> **Conversation 1:** angry
> **Conversation 2:** worried
> **Conversation 3:** excited
> **Conversation 4:** sad

AUDIOSCRIPT 076

Narrator: One. You will hear two friends talking. Why is Lisa angry with Alfie?
Alfie: What's the matter, Lisa?
Lisa: Don't you know, Alfie?
Alfie: I know I lost your tablet, but I got you a new one.
Lisa: It's not the tablet. You didn't come to my birthday party. I don't care about not getting a present, but how could you forget my party?! I'm so disappointed.
Narrator: Two. You will hear a mum and a dad talking about their daughter, Alison. Where's Alison now?
Dad: It's late. Why isn't Alison home?
Mum: She's with her friends. They went for a pizza. I expect she'll be back soon.
Dad: It's almost 10 o'clock. I rang her mobile just now and she didn't answer. I'm afraid something's happened.
Mum: Oh, they were planning to see a crime film called *The Party* after the pizza. She'll be at the cinema. That's why she didn't answer.
Narrator: Three. You will hear Jill and Lenny talking about Jill's holiday. What has Jill never done before?
Lenny: Are you ready for your holiday, Jill?
Jill: Yes, my suitcase is packed. I can't wait to get on the plane tomorrow.
Lenny: Is it your first holiday abroad?
Jill: No, I've been to Spain and France a couple of times, but I've never flown anywhere. My cousins are coming too, so there'll be five of us, including my parents.
Lenny: Have fun.
Narrator: Four. You will hear Lara saying goodbye to her friend Tom. What's Tom going to do?
Lara: Bye, Tom, I'm so sorry you're leaving the company.
Tom: I'm not going far, Lara. I'm not leaving town! You know where I live. I'm staying in the same house. We'll still be friends. There'll be lots of chances to keep in touch.
Lara: But we won't see you so much, now you're moving to a different place of work. It won't be the same here.

2 🔊 076 Draw attention to the questions and ask what is different about this task and Listening Part 4 in the exam (there are five questions in the exam).

Read through question 1 with the class and then repeat the first conversation for students to listen to the answers. You could ask them to put their hands up when they hear Lisa saying that Alfie didn't come to her party.

Now allow two or three minutes for reading through the other questions and underlining key words before playing the recording.

Students compare their answers with a partner.

If possible, they should try to explain why they chose the answer they did.

Feed back as a class.

> **2** A **3** C **4** B

PUSH YOURSELF B1

SB P121

GRAMMAR: MORE EXPRESSIONS WITH -ING AND TO

1 Tell students they are going to read some more conversations which include expressions followed by a verb in the infinitive or -ing form.

Go through the expressions in the box and check understanding.

Go through the first extract and elicit or supply the meaning of *don't mind* (don't have a preference) and *can't stand* (hate).

Students complete the gaps with words from the box. Feed back as a class.

> **1** going to the park, getting wet and cold
> **2** coming to the beach, move
> **3** study computing, getting a good job
> **4** visiting Paris, go up the Eiffel Tower

2 While answering the questions students can copy the new vocabulary into the list they made earlier.

> *to* + infinitive: can't be bothered to, plan to, hope to
> *-ing* form: don't mind, can't stand, feel like, be keen on, excited about

3 Students match the phrases to the definitions. Check answers as a class.

> **1** d **2** f **3** g **4** c **5** b **6** h **7** a **8** e

4 Students work individually to complete the sentences and then tell their partner their answers. Ask one or two students to tell the class what they wrote.

SPEAKING
SB P122

GIVING ADVICE

1 Elicit or supply the meaning of *advice* (an opinion someone gives you about what you should do). Ask students what they do and who they speak to when they need advice. Initiate a class discussion about the advantages and disadvantages of talking to the different people suggested.

Then, ask the second question in the book. Follow up with *Why? / Why not?*

2 🔊 077 Go over the instructions and play the recording. Students compare answers with a partner before checking as a class.

> **1** Sara **2** Tom **3** Mike

AUDIOSCRIPT 🔊 077

1
Man: What's the matter, Sara?
Sara: My friend isn't speaking to me and I don't know why. It started a week ago. She doesn't say 'hello' to me when I arrive in the morning and she doesn't wait for me after classes, but she won't say why she's angry with me. She says I should know, but I don't! I'm really stressed about it.

2
Woman: You look tired, Mike. Are you OK?
Mike: Not really. I just can't sleep at the moment. I'm worried about my exams and my future and I can't get to sleep. Every night, I study until very late and I feel very tired, but when I go to bed I can't stop thinking. In the morning, I'm even more tired.

3
Man: You seem worried, Tom. Do you want to talk about it?
Tom: I'm having a bad time at work. My problem is that I don't get on with my boss – she's not a nice person. She never says 'good morning' or 'please' or 'thank you' and she often gets angry and talks to me in a rude way. When she does this, I feel really stressed! I like my job and the other people I work with, but I can't stand her! Should I leave my job?

3 🔊 077 Encourage students to read the three questions before listening to the recording again for the answers. With a weaker group answers can be checked after each conversation.

> **1** She isn't speaking to her. She doesn't say 'hello' to her in the morning or wait for her after classes.
> **2** Because he's worried about his exams and his future and he can't sleep.
> **3** His boss. When she gets angry and speaks to him in a rude way.

UNIT 9 GETTING ALONG

4 078 Read through the options with the class before listening to the recording. Students compare answers with a partner.

> 1 B 2 C 3 A

AUDIOSCRIPT 078

A
Man: If this girl is really a friend, she should tell you why she's angry with you. Tell her that you're sorry that you upset her but there's nothing more you can do. Then stop worrying about it. A person like this is not a good friend. Try to spend time with other friends and forget about her.

B
Woman: You should stop studying so much and take some time to relax before you go to bed. It's not a good idea to work on a computer just before you sleep; try to do something different. Take a bath or read an interesting book. If you are worried about the future, why don't you talk to a friend about it? Talking about a problem makes most people feel better.

C
Man: You shouldn't leave your job if you enjoy it! Why don't you ask some other people if they feel the same? What about asking your boss very politely to change the way she speaks to you? If you're polite to her, it's more difficult for her to be rude to you.

5 078 Draw attention to the expressions in the box and ask students to listen again to the advice and complete the gaps in the speech bubbles with the expressions. Feed back as a class.

> **A** Tell her, stop worrying
> **B** You should, It's not a good idea to, try to, Why don't you
> **C** You shouldn't, Why don't you, What about

6 Students discuss the questions in pairs before a class discussion.

7 Read the first speech bubble as a class and ask students to give some advice using the expressions in Exercise 5 and the ideas in the box. Check that students are using the expressions in the right way. Then students work in pairs to give advice for the problems in the other speech bubbles.

Feed back by asking one or two students to give their advice for each problem.

⊕ EXTENSION

Students make brief notes to describe one or two problems, similar to the speech bubbles in the book. Then they tell their partner their problems and the partner gives them some advice using the expressions in Exercise 5.

WRITING
SB P123

GIVING ADVICE

1 Read through the questions with the class and elicit some answers from one or two students. If necessary, ask students where and when they went and what language or other skill they learned. Then ask if they had or if they think they could have problems with accommodation, food, travel, language, friends, etc. Then put students in pairs to discuss the questions. Monitor the conversations, helping with vocabulary as necessary. Feed back by asking students to tell you some of the problems they discussed.

2 Allow students one or two minutes to read the email quickly to answer the question. Check answers as a class. Encourage students to give as much detail as they can about Felix's problems.

> He wants some advice because he has a problem.

3 If necessary, students read the email again to answer the questions.

> **1** His English course is very difficult. The teachers talk very fast. He doesn't understand when people speak to him.
> **2** He doesn't want to spend time with students from his own country because they don't speak English. He is shy and not confident about his English.

4 Ask students to read Alice's reply and underline the advice that she gives Felix. Then elicit the advice from the class (ask teachers to speak more slowly, start a study group, join a club or start doing a sport, find a language-exchange partner). Encourage students to express their opinions about which piece of advice is best and why. It could be helpful for you to model an example such as, *I think it's a very good idea to start a study group because he can practise his English and make friends with other students at the same time.*

5 Encourage students to look back at both emails and find the expressions that each writer uses for the four functions listed. Check answers as a class.

> **1** say thank you for an email: Thanks very much for your email; Thanks for getting in touch
> **2** say they are happy about receiving an email: It was great to hear from you; Good to hear from you.
> **3** ask for advice (Felix): I'd like to ask you for some; What do you think I should do?
> agree to give advice (Alice): Here's what I'd do
> **4** end an email: Hope to hear from you soon; Write soon and good luck!

6 Go over the instructions and ask some questions to check understanding, e.g. *Who are you writing to? What does he want advice about? Why?*

Students work in pairs to make notes about the advice they can give.

Help with vocabulary as necessary.

7 Students write their email, remembering to use the expressions from Exercise 5. Then they exchange emails with a partner (not the same person they made the notes with) who offers feedback using the checklist in the book.

> **Suggested answer**
> Hi Pete,
> Thanks for getting in touch. It was great to hear from you.
> Here's what I'd do. Why don't you join a football club? You can meet other people who like football and make friends. Also, you could start a study group with other students on your course.
> Another idea is to invite other students to your flat to eat, or watch a film together.
> I hope this helps!
> Write soon,
> Lucy

EXAM FOCUS — SB P124
READING PART 2

> **EXAM INFORMATION**
>
> Part 2 of the Reading paper is a matching task. Students have to read three short texts on the same topic and answer seven questions by choosing the correct person.
>
> They should allow about ten minutes to do Part 2.

EXAM CHECK

1 Students work in pairs to do the task before class feedback.

> **1** T
> **2** F You answer seven questions.
> **3** T
> **4** F The questions come before the texts.
> **5** T

LEAD-IN

Draw attention to the title above the texts and point out that it provides a context. Suggest that it is a good idea to read the questions before reading the texts (that is why the questions are printed before the texts).

2 Allow students ten minutes to do the task under exam conditions, i.e. without conferring.

When checking answers encourage students to tell you which words in the texts told them the answers.

> **1** B **2** A **3** B **4** C **5** B **6** A **7** C

LISTENING PART 4
SB P125

> **EXAM INFORMATION**
>
> In Part 4 of the Listening paper, students listen to five short monologues or dialogues. They have to choose the correct answer from three multiple-choice options by listening for the main idea/gist/topic. Students hear the recording twice.

EXAM CHECK

1 Tell students they are going to read a short summary about Listening Part 4. Point out that the answers here are all a number between 1 and 5. Allow students two or three minutes to do the task before checking answers as a class.

> **1** 5 **2** 2 **3** 1 **4** 1 **5** 3

2 079 Allow students a minute to read through the questions and answer options before playing the recording.

Check answers together.

Remind students to complete the *How was it?* chart at the bottom of the page and hold a show of hands to see how many students chose each option.

> **1** B **2** C **3** A **4** C **5** B

AUDIOSCRIPT 079

Narrator: For each question, choose the correct answer. One. You will hear two friends talking about a restaurant they've been to. What did they like about it?

Woman: What did you think of that restaurant? My steak wasn't really cooked enough.

Man: A bit raw, was it? Well you don't pay much there, so you can't expect the best food in town.

Woman: Yeah. The waiters did a good job, but they weren't very friendly. But you're right about the bill – it wasn't much at all.

Man: And that made the evening better!

Narrator: Two. You will hear a woman telling a friend about her new colleague. What's her new colleague like?

UNIT 9 GETTING ALONG 109

Man:	What's your new colleague like?
Woman:	Well, the important thing for me is that he does everything I ask – not like some of the others who do almost nothing! And he's happy to talk to anyone. His jokes are terrible though! I'm sure he'll be promoted soon!
Narrator:	Three. You will hear a woman leaving a message for her husband. What does she want him to do?
Woman:	Leo, on my way home from work I'm going to stop at the supermarket and do some shopping, so I'll be a little late. We can have roast chicken for dinner. Can you start getting it ready when you get in? You won't have to go to the shops – everything you need is in the fridge. Thanks!
Narrator:	Four. You will hear two friends talking about an exhibition. How does the man know about it?
Man:	There's an interesting art exhibition on at the moment.
Woman:	Is that the one with paintings of flowers? There are posters all over town.
Man:	Are there? I haven't noticed any posters. But yes, it is the flower paintings, at the museum near the station. My brother's a guide there, and he keeps talking about the artist. He knows her quite well.
Woman:	Wow!
Narrator:	Five. You will hear a man giving a message to passengers at a train station. Why is he giving them the message?
Man:	This is a message for all passengers. Because of the bad weather, I'm afraid there were delays to some journeys at the weekend. If you experienced problems, please visit our website and click on 'refunds'. If your delay was more than 30 minutes, Central Trains will return the price that you paid for your ticket. Have a good journey!

Read through the options in the *How was it?* section and elicit the meaning of each one that they learned in the first unit.

Ask students to tick the appropriate box. You might like to ask students to share how they felt about the task to get an indication of your students' confidence. Depending on your class, you might like to do this openly or allow students to give their feedback without their classmates seeing. For example, give students a piece of A4 paper each with the *How was it?* scale written in large letters. Allow students to tick the relevant box then hold up their papers at the same time so that you can see how well students think they are doing. Finally, ask students if they found it easier, harder or the same as the exam practice in previous units.

REAL WORLD

SB P126

MEETING PEOPLE IN ... MELBOURNE

LEAD-IN

Brainstorm what the class knows about Australia and Melbourne, supplementing this with the cultural information below, if necessary.

1 Then ask students to work in pairs to look at the photos and answer the other question.

Feed back answers from the class before students read the text to find other ideas.

CULTURAL INFORMATION

Melbourne is the second most populated city in Australia with almost 5 million inhabitants. It is the state capital of Victoria which is located on the south eastern coast.

2 Read the statements as a class and help with vocabulary as necessary. Then students work in pairs to find the answers in the texts.

Feedback as a class. Encourage students to correct the false statements.

> 1 F You should only accept invitations from people you know.
> 2 T
> 3 F It's often easier because people who are travelling are more interested in meeting new people.
> 4 F It takes time to meet people and become friends.

3 Students work in pairs to complete the sentences with the words from the box. Feed back as a class.

> 1 make   2 enrol   3 have a lot   4 take up
> 5 get to   6 get on well

4 080 Go over the instructions with the class. Play the recording and ask students to make a note of one or two words or phrases which tell them the answer in each case.

Repeat the recording if necessary.

Check answers as a class, encouraging students to tell you the notes they made.

> 1 b   2 d   3 a

AUDIOSCRIPT 080

1
Receptionist: Hello, Melbourne Animal Rescue. How can I help you?
Student: Hello. My name's Maria and I've just moved to Melbourne. I love working with animals and I'd like to do some volunteering work. Is it possible to work here as a volunteer?
Receptionist: Yes, we do run a volunteer programme. I should warn you that our volunteers don't usually work with the animals. But we do use volunteers to help with collecting money. We have teams out on the streets most weekends, collecting money and giving out leaflets.
Student: That's great. Can I become a volunteer, please?
Receptionist: Yeah sure. You need to drop in here and fill out some forms, and you can meet the other members of our team. Then we can take it from there.
Student: OK. Thank you. Is it OK if I come to the centre this afternoon?
Receptionist: This afternoon would be great. We're open till six.
Student: OK. See you later. Bye.
Receptionist: Bye.

2
Receptionist: Hi. Can I help you?
Student: Yes. I'm interested in the photography course. Can you give me some information about it, please?
Receptionist: Sure. What would you like to know?
Student: Do I need an expensive camera to do the course?
Receptionist: No, not at all. As long as you have your own camera, that's fine, but it doesn't need to be a top-of-the-range one and you can also use some of the cameras we have here at the college.
Student: That's great. And how many people will be on the course?
Receptionist: There are about ten people, so you'll get to know all the other students quite well.
Student: That's good. OK. I'd like to enrol on the course, please.
Receptionist: Sure. Have you done any courses here before?
Student: No. It's my first time.
Receptionist: OK. So, I'll just have to take some details from you, and I'll need to see your visa.
Student: Yes, I have my visa here.
Receptionist: OK, that's all in order. So, can you tell me your name and your date of birth?

3
Receptionist: Hi, there. How can I help you?
Student: Hi. Is it possible to hire tennis courts here?
Receptionist: It certainly is.
Student: Oh, good. And do you have to be a member of the club, or can anyone use the courts?
Receptionist: Anyone can hire a court, but there are different rates for members and non-members. So, in the evenings, it's $24 per hour for non-members, and $12 an hour for members. If you think you'll play more than twice a week, you'd be better off joining, but if you're only going to play once a week, it's probably better just to pay each time you play.
Student: OK. I think I'll play maybe once a week.
Receptionist: OK, so it probably doesn't make sense for you to pay to become a member.
Student: So, how can I book a court?
Receptionist: You can call us, or you can do it online on the club website.
Student: OK. Thank you for your help.
Receptionist: You're welcome. Have a nice day!

PHRASES YOU MIGHT USE

5 080 Students work in pairs to complete the phrases before listening to the recording to check their answers.

1 as a volunteer	**2** OK if	**3** interested in, give me
4 to enrol	**5** have to be	**6** book

PHRASES YOU MIGHT HEAR

6 Students choose the correct definitions before checking answers as a class.

1 f **2** a **3** b **4** e **5** d **6** c

WATCH

7 ▶ Go through the instructions with the class. Then play the video all the way through and ask students to take notes under the headings.

the city: it's the capital of Victoria; on south-east coast of Australia; vibrant modern city; a good way to see the city is on a sightseeing bus, or a boat on the river.
beaches and surfing: some amazing beaches near the city; Brighton Beach is famous for its beach huts used for changing; surfing is popular; there are lifeguards on most beaches to keep people safe; sport: cricket is popular; Australia has one of the best cricket teams in the world; important games played at Melbourne Stadium.
Phillip Island: close to Melbourne; you can get there by boat; can see koalas and kangaroos, and in the evening you can watch the penguin parade, when penguins come out of the sea and walk along the beach to sleep in their burrows.

UNIT 9 GETTING ALONG

> **VIDEOSCRIPT** ▶ Melbourne
>
> Melbourne is the capital of the state of Victoria in Australia. It's on the south-east coast and is a vibrant modern city with some lovely areas to explore.
>
> A good way to see the city is on a sightseeing bus, or a tourist boat on the river.
>
> Melbourne is by the sea, and it has some amazing beaches. This is Brighton Beach, with its famous beach huts. They date back to the 19th century and are used as changing rooms by swimmers.
>
> Surfing is extremely popular on the beaches around Melbourne, and there are lifeguards on most beaches, to keep swimmers and surfers safe.
>
> Sport is very important to a lot of people in Australia, and cricket is a popular sport. Australia has one of the best national cricket teams in the world.
>
> Important games are played at the Melbourne Cricket Stadium and the stadium is usually full of cricket fans when there's a big game.
>
> Phillip Island is close to Melbourne. You can get there by boat, and it's a great place to see animals, such as koalas and kangaroos, and even a baby kangaroo if you're lucky. Or if you stay for the evening, you might catch the penguin parade, when hundreds of penguins come out of the sea and walk along the beach ready to spend the night in their burrows. Sleep well, my friend!

8 ▶ Students compare their notes with a partner before watching the video again to add to their notes. Feed back as a class.

LIFE COMPETENCIES
SB P127

EMOTIONAL SKILLS AND DESCRIBING YOUR OWN CULTURE

9 Go over the instructions together checking understanding.

Students work in groups of three or four to make notes about their ideas, then write them out in an information pack.

This can be in the form of a leaflet or just a list of information and suggestions under headings.

Students work with another group to share and compare their ideas.

➡ **WORKBOOK** / Unit 9, page 40

10 OUT AND ABOUT

UNIT OBJECTIVES

Topic:	places and buildings
Grammar:	will/may/might; will/shall for offers and promises
Vocabulary:	places in a town; directions; city words
Listening:	Part 1: choosing the correct picture with short dialogues
Reading:	reading for gist and detailed understanding: two parks in New York
Speaking:	Part 1: talking about where you live
Writing:	a thank you email
Pronunciation:	intonation
Exam focus:	Listening Part 1; Speaking Part 1
Real world:	visiting tourist sites in Rome

Ask your students to watch the Grammar on the Move videos on page 131 and page 134. You can use these to present or reinforce will/may/might and will/shall for offers and promises.

VOCABULARY
SB P128

PLACES IN A TOWN

> **WARMER**
>
> Read the heading of the section with the class and elicit or supply that *place* can refer to any area, town or building (in some languages it is a false friend for a square or piazza). Ask students if they can name some buildings to check understanding of the word (*house, university, theatre*, etc).

1 Put students into pairs to discuss the questions. Move around the room to help with vocabulary they may need. Feed back by asking two or three students to tell the class about an interesting building they've visited.

2 Draw attention to the photos and ask if anyone recognises the places or knows the names of them. Then allow students one or two minutes to read the texts and match them with the photos and see if the names they suggested were correct. Check answers as a class.

| 1 C | 2 A | 3 B | 4 F | 5 D | 6 E |

> **FAST FINISHERS**
>
> Students can write one or two sentences about some of the places in their town or country.

3 Students discuss the questions in pairs. Elicit ideas in feedback.

⊕ EXTENSION

Redirect students' attention to Exercise 2 and ask students if they have ever been to any of the places. For example, *Have you ever been to a castle?* Then ask one or two follow up questions if anyone says yes. For example, *Where was the castle?; When/why did you go there?; How did you feel when you went there?; What did you do there?* Then, encourage students to ask questions starting with *Have you ever been to …?* and some follow up questions in pairs about the other places. Feed back by asking some students to tell the class where their partner has been.

LISTENING PART 1 TRAINING
SB P129

✓ EXAM INFORMATION

In Part 1 of the Listening paper students hear five short dialogues. Students have to choose the correct answer A, B or C from the three visual options which are provided. Students also hear an example. Students need to listen to identify key information. In the exam they hear each recording twice.

This section in the Student's Book teaches students to focus on and underline important information in the question before they listen and to try to understand why the other answer options are wrong. The task in the Student's Book is simplified with only four questions.

1  081 Ask students if they remember what they need to do in Listening Part 1 in the exam.

Go through the instructions and question 1, but ask students to cover the explanation. Tell them they will hear all three times in the answer options in the recording, but need to decide which time is when the play begins.

Play the recording, encouraging students to try to identify what the different times refer to. If necessary play the recording twice and then read the explanation in the book to check answers.

Explain to students that it is important for them to try to understand the conversation and not just listen for the information in the pictures as they will often hear all three pictures mentioned as in this example.

UNIT 10 OUT AND ABOUT 113

AUDIOSCRIPT 081

Narrator: One. What time does the play begin tonight?
Anna: What time's the play tonight, Emma?
Emma: 7.00, I think. I'll look at the ticket. I'm wrong, it starts at 7.30, but we should get there early.
Anna: Shall we meet in front of the theatre at 7.15 – that gives us 15 minutes before the play begins.
Emma: I think we need more time, Anna. Shall we say 7 o'clock?
Anna: OK.

2 082 Play the recording for the other three conversations before allowing students a few minutes to discuss the answers with their partner and then the class. A stronger group can be asked to explain what the other two pictures refer to in each case.

> **2** A **3** C **4** C

AUDIOSCRIPT 082

Narrator: Two. How far away is the best sports centre?
Man: Is there a sports centre near here?
Woman: Well there's a really good one in Yorkton. That's got everything. But that's 20 km away.
Man: Isn't there one nearer?
Woman: Well, Barton, which is 15 km from here has one, but it's not very good. There is a small one in Linton, but that doesn't have a swimming pool. It's only 5 km away, so it depends what you want to do there I suppose.
Man: OK, thanks.
Narrator: Three. What are Carl and Jack going to see at the stadium?
Jack: Are you coming to rugby practice on Saturday, Carl?
Carl: No, I can't. I've got tickets for a big hockey match. The Rovers are playing! Do you want to come with me, Jack?
Jack: Thanks, I'd love to. Where's the match?
Carl: It's at the football stadium.
Narrator: Four. Where will the friends meet?
Man: So where shall we meet this evening? How about the bridge, as usual?
Woman: Oh, my bus doesn't go that way anymore. What about meeting at the statue?
Man: It'll take me a long time to get there. The town square is better for me.
Woman: No problem, I'll see you there at seven.

⊕ EXTENSION

Brainstorm some suggestions for each of the places with the class and then select one suggestion and elicit answers to questions 2, 3 and 4 about that place. Then allow students three or four minutes to talk about other places in pairs. Monitor the conversations as they talk, supplying vocabulary as necessary.

Students can then write a short paragraph about one of the places they discussed, giving information for a visitor.

READING
SB P130

1 Students discuss the questions for a few minutes. If there are no parks in the students' country, they can talk about other parks they have visited or heard about. Feed back as a class by asking three or four students to tell you about a park.

2 Draw attention to the two photos and ask students what they think is special or unusual about these two parks. Accept all suggestions without saying whether an answer is right or wrong at this stage.

Read the questions and then put students into pairs and ask one person in each pair to read about the High Line and the other to read about the Lowline. Allow about a minute for students to read and then ask them to tell their partner the answers to the two questions. Compare answers as a class.

> **1** Manhattan
> **2** The High Line is a park. It is above the city. The Lowline is a project for a future park. It will be underground.

3 Pairs now read the two texts together to find the answers to the questions. Check answers as a class.

> **1** It was a railway line.
> **2** The line closed.
> **3** It's 2.33 kilometres long.
> **4** a great view of the city.
> **5** a big, empty space under the city.
> **6** They will use special technology to bring sunlight underground.

4 Draw attention to the words in pink in the text and explain to students that if they read the phrases before and after those words it can help to fully understand the meaning. Students complete the sentences.

FAST FINISHERS

Students can write their own sentences using the words in the box.

> **1** railway line   **2** benches   **3** district   **4** fresh air
> **5** path   **6** middle   **7** space   **8** sunlight

5 Draw attention to the *Did you know?* box and ask students if they know any other examples of differences between American and British English (they may know about *soccer* and *football* for example). Explain that students can use either of the two types of English, but that it is not usually a good idea to mix them up as that can cause confusion. Most native speakers will understand both words even if they don't use them.

Initiate a class discussion using the questions.

⊕ EXTENSION

Following on from the ideas in the discussion, students work in groups of three or four to design a new park. They should think about the facilities and services, whether there might be events held there, what the park would look like, and where it would be, etc. After discussing and deciding, each group can produce a picture/diagram or a leaflet to show the other groups what their park would be like.

WILL/MAY/MIGHT

LEAD-IN

Draw a clock on the board showing a university start time, e.g. 9 am.

Then draw (or describe) two students:

Antonio is in bed and Alex is running to the university.

Write on the board:

*Antonio **will** be late for university. Alex **might** be late for university.*

Then describe a second situation:

Draw a dark cloud on the board and write, *I think it **will** rain.* Then draw a few white clouds and write, *It **may** rain later.*

Elicit or supply the difference between each pair of sentences:

Will is used when we are sure about something in the future and *may/might* are used when we are not sure.

1 Open books and allow students two or three minutes, working in pairs, to read the examples and complete the rules.

Go through the answers with the class, highlighting the form by using the Grammar box. You can explain to students that these verbs are called *modal verbs* and are used to talk about *certainty*, *probability* and *possibility*.

| **1** the future | **2** sure | **3** not sure | **4** infinitive |

➡ **GRAMMAR REFERENCE** / Pages 216–217

2 Explain that in this exercise students have to decide if the thing being described by the verb is certain or not and choose the modal verb accordingly. Students compare their answers with a partner, explaining why they put the answer they did.

When checking answers with the class, ask students to justify their choice by telling you the part of the sentence which tells them how certain the action is.

| **1** might | **2** will | **3** may | **4** won't |

3 Students work in pairs to complete the gaps in the sentences before feedback as a class. Remind students that they can use *may* or *might* to talk about possibility.

| **1** might/may come | **2** won't grow |
| **3** might/may turn | **4** might/may not be |

4 Draw attention to the photo and ask students what they think they can see. Ask if they think the building is old or new. Then read the questions together. Allow students one minute to read the article to find the answers to the first two questions and then ask students for suggestions for question 3.

| **1** It was a shoe factory. |
| **2** It's a green space. |
| **3** Student's own answer. |

5 Read the two descriptions about the two people and allow students a few minutes to discuss ideas. Then feed back as a class, making notes on the board of the students' ideas.

6 🎧 083 Play the recording, pausing after Mr Jones speaks, and ask students if any of the ideas on the board were accurate.

Then repeat that part of the recording to give students the chance to write the sentences.

Check answers as a class before playing the second speaker. Repeat as necessary.

Students check answers together.

| **1** Mr Jones will offer the city €1 million for the land / to try to buy the land. He might turn the land into a car park. He may build some apartments.
| **2** Mrs Greene says the city won't sell the land because it's a great space in the middle of the city. They might make it into a public park. / They may build a new swimming pool. |

AUDIOSCRIPT 083

Mr Jones: I'll offer the city €1 million for the old factory and I might build a car park on the land. There's a lot of traffic in the city centre and not enough parking. I'll make a LOT of money from a car park without having to spend very much. I may also build some expensive apartments there to sell.

Mrs Greene: The city won't sell the land. We'll definitely keep it because it's a great space in the middle of the city. I think we might make it into a public park. We may also build a new swimming pool on it, if that's what the community wants.

7 Students work in pairs to discuss the questions and then feed back all their ideas to the class. Hold a vote to decide on the most popular ideas.

VOCABULARY
SB P132

DIRECTIONS

1 Draw attention to the map and encourage students to work in pairs to match the letters on the map with the words in bold by reading the information in the sentences. Check answers as a class.

| 1 E | 2 A | 3 G | 4 D | 5 B | 6 H | 7 C | 8 F |

2  084 Go over the instructions and give students some time to read through the sentences. Then play the recording while they complete the numbers. Students compare answers in pairs before listening again, if necessary, and class feedback.

1 Come out of the library and turn right.
2 Go straight on down the main street.
3 Turn right at the traffic lights into Chester Road.
4 Go over the bridge and go straight on.
5 Take the first turning on the right into New Road.
6 You'll see it on your left.

AUDIOSCRIPT 084

Woman: Come out of the library and turn right. Go straight on down the main street. Turn right at the traffic lights into Chester Road. Go over the bridge and go straight on. Take the first turning on the right into New Road. You'll see it on your left.

3 084 Ask students to listen again and follow the directions on the map. Elicit the answer.

the cinema

4 085 Students find the railway station. Then they follow the directions as they listen to the recording and compare the end point with a partner after each set of instructions.

| 1 supermarket | 2 theatre |

AUDIOSCRIPT 085

1
Man: Excuse me. Do you know where the [beep] is?
Woman: Yes. Come out of the station and turn left. Then turn left into Main Street. Then take the first left and go straight over the roundabout. You'll see it on the right.

2
Man: Excuse me, where's the [beep]?
Woman: Come out of the station and turn left. Then turn left into Main Street. Go straight on and turn left at the traffic lights into Chester Road. It's on the right.

5 086 Students work in pairs to match the parts of the questions. Then listen to the recording to check answers.

| 1 c | 2 d | 3 b | 4 a |

AUDIOSCRIPT 086

1 Excuse me. Do you know where the station is?
2 Can you tell me how to get to the library?
3 Excuse me. Could you give me directions to the town square?
4 Could you tell me where the museum is?

⊕ EXTENSION

Ask one or two questions around the class using *can* or *could*, focusing on using appropriate intonation for example:

Jill, can you close your book, please? (rising ↗ then falling ↘)
Barbara, could you pass me a pen? (falling ↘)
Carlo, can you tell me the time, please? (rising ↗ then falling ↘)

Ask students what they can tell you about the intonation you are using. They may say it changes as it should go up and down.

Generally, in English, if you don't use intonation appropriately or use flat intonation, which doesn't rise and fall, you can sound impolite or rude.

Point out to students that intonation is an important part of the communication.

6 🔊 086 Play the recording and ask students to complete the exercise.

> 1 Excuse me. Do you know where the station is? ↗↘
> 2 Can you tell me how to get to the library? ↘
> 3 Excuse me. Could you give me directions to the town square? ↗↘
> 4 Could you tell me where the museum is? ↘

7 🔊 086 Play the recording again and use the recorded sentences as models to drill. Sometimes students may feel uncomfortable imitating the correct intonation, so make sure they have plenty of opportunity to drill chorally with the rest of the class before individual practice.

8 Elicit one or two example questions that students can use to ask for directions.

If necessary, encourage students to look back at Exercise 5 using, for example:

Could you tell me … Do you know where … Can you give me …, etc.

Encourage students to try to exaggerate the intonation in these dialogues in order to help them remember to use it.

⊕ EXTENSION

If appropriate, students can take it in turns to give directions from the school to another place. The listening partner has to say where the destination is each time.

SPEAKING PART 1 TRAINING
SB P133

✓ EXAM INFORMATION

In Speaking Part 1 there are two phases. In the first, students have to answer personal questions about themselves. In the second, they answer two short-answer questions and one longer question about their daily life, interests, preferences, etc. Part 1 lasts three to four minutes for each pair of candidates.

1 Elicit from students what they have to do in Speaking Part 1 (answer questions about themselves and their preferences, interests or daily life as well as one longer 'tell me something about…' question) and how much time they have (three to four minutes for two candidates). Then direct attention to the questions.

2 Students match the questions and answers. Check as a class, helping with vocabulary as necessary.

> **1** d   **2** f   **3** a   **4** e   **5** b   **6** c

3 If possible, pair students up with someone who comes from a different town. If students are from the same town ask the class the first question, eliciting as many suggestions as possible, e.g. *It's in a (country/region), near (city, mountain, coast), in the north/south, etc.*

Then students ask and answer the other questions in pairs. Feed back by asking one or two students to tell the class their answers.

4 🔊 087 Read through the questions with the class and remind students that they should say two or three sentences in response to this type of question in the exam. Play the recording and ask students to put the answers in the correct order.

Students compare answers with a partner and listen to the recording again, if necessary, to check answers.

> **1** B   **2** C   **3** A

AUDIOSCRIPT 🔊 087

Narrator: A
Student: One week ago I met two of my classmates at the bus station. We went to the cinema and afterwards we bought burgers and ate them in the park. It was good fun.

Narrator: B
Student: I don't want to stay in my home town because it's quite boring. I'd like to move to a big city because I could go shopping and go to restaurants and the theatre in the evenings.

Narrator: C
Student: There are houses and an apartment building, but there aren't many cars. The houses have nice gardens and it's quiet. I've always lived there, and I like it very much.

5 Allow students a minute or two to make notes about their answers to the questions in Exercise 4 and then ask and answer the questions in pairs. Make sure students know that in the exam they will not be able to make notes and will not have any extra time to prepare their answers.

UNIT 10 OUT AND ABOUT

PUSH YOURSELF B1

SB P133

VOCABULARY: CITY WORDS

1 Ask the class if they know anything about Hong Kong or Los Angeles. Accept all suggestions. Then tell students to read the two texts and decide which city they would prefer to live in and why.

BACKGROUND INFORMATION

Hong Kong is a well-known commercial centre but also has a vast cultural heritage. Its cuisine is world-famous and its food markets attract many visitors.

Los Angeles is a city in southern California in the USA. It is famous for being the home of Hollywood and the American film industry and also for its beaches in Santa Monica and Malibu.

2 Give students one or two minutes to complete the sentences with the words in purple in the text. Check as a class.

FAST FINISHERS

Students can write a short paragraph about another world city. When they finish they can read them to the rest of the class who guess the name of the city.

1 public transport	2 polluted	3 traffic free
4 skyscraper	5 traffic jam	6 pedestrian
7 pavement	8 historic	

GRAMMAR

SB P134

WILL/SHALL FOR OFFERS AND PROMISES

1 Draw attention to the photos and ask students to label them.

Explain that they are going to hear a conversation in each situation. Brainstorm ideas for why people go to the places and what they might be talking about in each situation and note any new vocabulary on the board. For example, *money, cash, change, stamp, send, letter, food, order, report crime, loss*, etc.

| A bank | B restaurant | C police station |
| D post office | | |

2 088 Explain that students need to match the conversations with the four photos. After listening, students compare their answers with a partner's and try to remember which words they heard to help them identify the answers.

| 1 bank | 2 restaurant | 3 post office |

AUDIOSCRIPT 088

1
Woman: Hello, I'd like to change some money, please. Can I change €150 into American dollars?
Man: Yes. No problem. I'll check how much that will be in dollars. One euro is 1.17 American dollars. So €150 will give 174 American dollars. Is that OK?
Woman: Yes, that's fine.
Man: Shall I put the money in an envelope for you?
Woman: Thank you.

2
Man: Have you finished?
Woman: Yes, thank you. It was delicious.
Man: OK, I'll take your plates. … Would you like anything else? Shall I bring the dessert menu?
Woman: No, thank you. No dessert. But could I have a cup of coffee, please? Black, no sugar.

3
Man: I'd like to send this letter to France.
Woman: Certainly. That will be €1.75 for an ordinary letter or €2.50 if you send it express.
Man: How long will it take for an ordinary letter to arrive?
Woman: Two to three days.
Man: No, that's too long … I need it to get there as soon as possible.
Woman: Shall I send the letter express then?
Man: Yes, please.
Woman: OK. Can you sign here and I'll put the letter straight in the post bag.

3 088 Encourage students to read through the questions before listening to the conversations again. Check answers as a class.

| 1 €150 | 2 no, coffee | 3 France |

4 Read through the examples with the class, eliciting what the 'll stands for (*will*) and explaining that it shows a different use of *will* to the one seen earlier (when it was used to talk about probability).

Allow students a minute to choose the correct answers to complete the rules and then check answers as a class before going through the information in the box.

| 1 will | 2 shall |

➡ **GRAMMAR REFERENCE** / Page 216

5 Students do the task individually, checking the detail in the box in Exercise 4 if necessary. Then check answers as a class.

> 1 Shall I   2 'll   3 Shall   4 'll

6 Students work in pairs to complete the sentences. Check answers as a class, asking students to say whether each sentence is an offer, a suggestion, a promise or a prediction.

> 1 shall we have   2 'll tell   3 Shall … give?
> 4 'll phone

⊕ EXTENSION

Elicit possible responses to the first sentence in Exercise 6, e.g. *Yes, that's a good idea! Yes, I'm hungry. Yes, what can we eat?*, etc. Then ask students to work in pairs to think of suitable responses to the other sentences in Exercise 6.

7 Go through the instructions and elicit suggestions for the first situation, e.g. *Shall I carry your bags?*

Ask students to suggest an appropriate response, e.g. *Thank you! / Yes, please.*

Students then work through the rest of the exercise in pairs, making offers and responding. Ask two or three pairs to say their mini dialogues in front of the class.

A THANK YOU EMAIL

1 Draw attention to the photos and initiate a brief class discussion using the questions.

> ### BACKGROUND INFORMATION
>
> Paris is the capital city of France. It has many iconic landmarks such as the world-famous art museum, the Louvre, the Arc de Triomphe and the Eiffel Tower. It is known around the world for its gastronomy, fashion and ancient and contemporary art.

2 Ask students to scan the email and answer one or two questions quickly, without worrying about understanding every detail at this stage, e.g. *Who wrote the email?* (Aylin); *Who did she write to?* (Julie); *What did she write about?* (her visit to Paris).

Then read through the questions with the class, explaining vocabulary if necessary. Elicit or supply the meaning of *looking forward to* (feeling happy about something that is going to happen).

Then students read the email more carefully to find the answers. When they check answers in pairs, encourage them to show their partner where in the email they found the answer. Feed back as a class.

> 1 To thank her for taking her to visit Paris.
> 2 She visited the Louvre, went up the Eiffel Tower and went on a boat trip on the Seine.
> 3 Her favourite moment was when they went up the Eiffel Tower because she has wanted to visit it for so long.
> 4 She hopes Julie will visit her in Istanbul soon.
> 5 She is looking forward to showing Julie her favourite places.
> 6 She says 'hello' to Julie's friends, Marie and Lilou.

3 Students underline the example phrase in the email and then read again to find other positive phrases. Check answers as a class.

> I had a great time!, I loved visiting …, it's the biggest …, I've ever visited, I also really enjoyed …, my favourite moment was …, I'll never forget seeing …, It was great to meet them.

4 A stronger class can do this exercise with the phrases in Exercise 3 covered up initially. They can then check with a partner and by looking at the phrases.

> 1 great to meet
> 2 also really enjoyed
> 3 favourite moment
> 4 I've ever visited
> 5 never forget
> 6 had a great time
> 7 loved visiting

5 Go through the instructions with the class. With a weaker group look back at the email in Exercise 2 together, and ask students to find the examples of each of the points mentioned.

Then allow students three or four minutes to think of some ideas and make notes about their own email.

Explain that the content does not have to be true. As students are planning, move around the classroom to help with vocabulary as necessary.

6 Students can do the writing task in class or at home. Remind them to include all the information and to check their work when they finish before exchanging emails with a partner who uses the checklist in the book to provide feedback.

EXAM FOCUS
LISTENING PART 1

SB P136

✓ EXAM INFORMATION

In Part 1 of the Listening paper students hear five short dialogues. They have to choose the correct answer A, B or C from the three visual options which are provided. There is also an example. Students need to listen to identify key information. In the exam they hear each recording twice.

EXAM CHECK

1. Students work together to do the task before checking as a class.

   1 F You hear five short recordings.
   2 F You choose from 3 options.
   3 T
   4 T
   5 F they're all dialogues.

2. 089 Allow students 30 seconds to read through the questions and look at the answer options before playing the recording. Encourage them to do the task under exam conditions, i.e. without conferring, and remind them that each dialogue is repeated, so they should listen the second time to check their answers.

   Feed back as a class. With a stronger class students might be able to explain why the other options are incorrect.

   1 A   2 B   3 A   4 B   5 C

AUDIOSCRIPT 089

Narrator: For each question, choose the correct answer. Now we are ready to start. Look at question one. One. Where did Chris go yesterday?
Woman: Did you have a good day with your cousin yesterday, Chris?
Man: Yes, thanks.
Woman: What did you do?
Man: Well, he really wanted to go to the theatre, but we couldn't get tickets. So we thought about the castle or the museum. We chose the castle because my cousin always goes to museums and he liked the idea of doing something different.
Narrator: Two. What is the woman looking for?
Man: Are you lost?
Woman: Yes! A man in the supermarket told me the station was around this corner, but I think he gave me the wrong information.
Man: Mm. Maybe you turned the wrong way when you came out. Just go back up this street, and turn right at the top. It's opposite the bank.
Woman: Turn right, opposite the bank. Thanks!

Narrator: Three. What is broken in the woman's house?
Man: Good afternoon, Mrs Philips. I hope your cooker isn't broken again!
Woman: Hello. Come in. Don't worry, the cooker's worked well since you repaired it! It's something else I want you to look at – a door. It doesn't open very easily.
Man: No problem. Can you move that lamp before I start? I don't want to break it.
Woman: Yes, of course.
Narrator: Four. Why will the man stay at home this evening?
Woman: Why can't you come out this evening? Are you still ill with that cold?
Man: It's better now, thanks. I'm really upset I can't come.
Woman: Yes, it's such a shame.
Man: And I even finished work early, but then my sister called to say she can't come round to look after the children, so I have to stay at home. Helen will come without me.
Narrator: Five. How did the woman find out about the job?
Man: Your new job sounds great. Did you read about it in a magazine?
Woman: I don't think most companies do that type of advertising anymore. They just use the internet.
Man: So is that how you found your job?
Woman: Actually, my friend told me about it when I was out with her last week. That was before the company did any online advertising.

SPEAKING PART 1
SB P137

✓ EXAM INFORMATION

In Speaking Part 1 there are two phases. In the first, students have to answer personal questions about themselves. In the second, they answer two short-answer questions and one longer, 'tell me something about…' question about their daily life, interests, preferences etc. Part 1 lasts three to four minutes for each pair of candidates.

EXAM CHECK

1. Students choose the correct word to complete the text and then compare answers with a partner.

   1 live   2 two   3 tell   4 understand   5 three

Before starting the exam practice tasks (Exercises 2 to 5), remind students to answer using full sentences, not just one or two words. It could be helpful to elicit some phrases they can use if they don't understand the question, e.g. *Can you repeat that please?*; *I'm sorry, I didn't understand, can you say that again?*

2 Students work in pairs and one person in each pair closes their book. The other person asks the questions.

3 Now the students exchange roles and the other student asks the questions.

4 Students exchange roles again.

5 Remind students that Exercise 5 is the 'tell me something about …' questions, so they should try to answer with two or three sentences. Students can take it in turns to talk about the street where they live.

> ### FAST FINISHERS
> Students can ask their partner another 'tell me something about … ' question. For example, tell me about your school/job, tell me about your town.
>
> When students have finished, allow a minute or so for them to complete the *How was it?* box.

Read through the options in the *How was it?* section and elicit the meaning of each one that they learned in the first unit.

Ask students to tick the appropriate box. You might like to ask students to share how they felt about the task to get an indication of your students' confidence. Depending on your class, you might like to do this openly or allow students to give their feedback without their classmates seeing. For example, give students a piece of A4 paper each with the *How was it?* scale written in large letters. Allow students to tick the relevant box then hold up their papers at the same time so that you can see how well students think they are doing. Finally, ask students if they found it easier, harder or the same as the exam practice in previous units.

➡ **SPEAKING BANK** / *Page 240*

REAL WORLD

SB P138

VISITING TOURIST SITES IN … ROME

> ### LEAD-IN
> Tell students about your favourite city. For example, *I love Berlin. It is a lively city with lots of art and music. The people are friendly and there are plenty of great restaurants.*

1 Students work in pairs to answer the questions. Feed back by asking three or four students to tell you about their favourite city and a city they would like to visit and why.

2 Go over the instructions and brainstorm what students know about Rome. Then students answer the questions in pairs before reading the text to check answers.

> **1** People fought wild animals or other fighters in front of crowds.
> **2** money
> **3** flying machines

CULTURAL INFORMATION

Rome is the capital of Italy. It is a city with a huge artistic and cultural heritage which dates back to the Roman Empire. It is also famous for its food. Pasta is an important part of Roman cuisine and typical dishes include *carbonara*, with egg, cheese and *guanciale* (cured meat), as well as *cacio e pepe*, with cheese and black pepper.

3 Students find the phrases in the texts and choose the correct definition. Explain that they can check their answers by substituting the phrase in the text with the answer they choose. Feed back as a class.

> **1** b **2** a **3** b **4** a

4 Draw attention to the reviews of the Colosseum, then read the statements as a class and help with vocabulary as necessary.

Students work in pairs to decide whether they think the statements are true or false, then read the reviews to check answers. When checking answers, encourage students to say why the false statements are false.

> **1** T **2** T **3** F It's often hot.
> **4** F It's also open at night. **5** T

5 Students try to complete the phrases before checking answers by finding them in the reviews.

> **1** your tickets **2** early **3** queues **4** video guide
> **5** Take **6** Visit

6 🔊 090 Go over the instructions with the class and ask them to suggest what the people might say or hear in the different situations.

Play the recording and ask students to make a note of one or two words or phrases which tell them the answer in each case.

Check answers as a class, encouraging students to tell you the notes they made.

> **1** c **2** d **3** a

UNIT 10 OUT AND ABOUT

AUDIOSCRIPT 🔊 090

1

Guide: So, now you can see how big the building really was and you can imagine what it was like for people to come here to watch the plays and fights. Are there any questions?
Tourist: Yes. How old is it?
Guide: It's nearly 2,000 years old.
Tourist: Wow! It's really big. How many seats were there?
Guide: We don't know for sure, but they reckon between 50,000 and 80,000. That's a lot of people!
Tourist: Yes. Wow!
Guide: Anything else?
Tourist: Yes. How long did it take to build?
Guide: It was actually quite fast. It took less than ten years to build, which is pretty amazing when you think that they had no machines and everything was done by hand.
Tourist: Yes. Oh, what's that hole in the ground?
Guide: That was one of the entrances they used to send gladiators and animals into the arena. There was a wooden door over the hole. The door opened, and animals or gladiators appeared. And in fact, that's where we're going now, so shall we move on?

2

Boy: This is lovely, isn't it?
Girl: Yes. It's so peaceful. I see you have a backpack. Are you travelling?
Boy: Yes. I'm travelling around Europe.
Girl: Me too! Have you been to any other cities in Italy?
Boy: Yes. I was in Florence last week. That was amazing!
Girl: Yes, everyone says it's beautiful. Maybe I'll go there next.
Boy: What other countries have you been to?
Girl: Lots! I was in Spain last week, and before that I was in France. But I love Italy!
Boy: Yes. Rome is an amazing city. But it's very hot. It's nice to be here, next to the water.
Girl: I agree. And the fountain's beautiful, isn't it?
Boy: Yes. Shall we throw some money in? They say that if you throw money in the Trevi Fountain, you'll come back to Rome one day.
Girl: Yes, good idea. Here we go.

3

Official: Next, please.
Tourist: Hello. Can I have two tickets, please? Is there a discount for students?
Official: Yes, there is. Do you have your student cards?
Tourist: Yes, here you are.
Official: OK. Thank you. That's €30, please.
Tourist: Thank you. Is it OK to take photos in the museum?
Official: Normal photos are fine, but there's no flash photography. And we also ask you not to spend too long taking photos, if you're holding other people up.
Tourist: OK. And what time does the museum close?
Official: It closes at 6.30 this evening. There'll be a bell 20 minutes before closing time, and we ask you to leave promptly.
Tourist: OK. And is there a gift shop?
Official: Yes. If you follow the audio guide tour through the museum, you'll end up in the gift shop. You can't miss it.
Tourist: Thank you.
Official: You're welcome. Enjoy your visit.

PHRASES YOU MIGHT USE

7 🔊 090 Students work in pairs to complete the phrases before listening to the recording to check answers.

1 Are you
2 Everyone says
3 Is there
4 Is it OK
5 What time

PHRASES YOU MIGHT HEAR

8 Students work in pairs to choose the correct definitions before checking answers as a class.

1 a   2 a   3 b   4 a   5 b

WATCH

9 ▶ Go over the instructions and brainstorm any information the students already know about the places listed.

Then play the video and encourage students to make notes under the headings as they watch.

> **the Colosseum:** theatre and gladiator fights during the Roman Empire
> **the Circus Maximus:** horse and chariot races; up to 250,000 people watching; can't see much these days
> **the Trevi Fountain:** 26m high; biggest fountain in Rome; statues of horses and people; built from same stone as the Colosseum
> **the Piazza Navona:** large square; three fountains; live music and art

---

VIDEOSCRIPT ▶ Rome

Rome is the capital of Italy, and is a popular place for tourists to visit. Rome has a long history dating back thousands of years, so it has lots of important historical sites.

In the times of the Roman Empire, the Colosseum was a place for theatre plays and Gladiator fights. You can still see the parts under the Colosseum where people and animals stayed before they came out to perform or fight.

Just outside the city is the Circus Maximus. In the past, up to 250,000 people per day came here to see horse and chariot races. You can't see much here now, but you can still imagine what it was like to race along, with people cheering and shouting.

This is the Trevi Fountain. It's 26 metres high, and is the biggest fountain in Rome.

It has wonderful stone statues of people and horses, and it was actually made of the same stone that was used to build the Colosseum. Tourists throw coins into the water because they believe it means they will come back to Rome one day.

The Piazza Navona is a large square in the centre of the city. It has three fountains, and it's a great place to see people playing music, or selling art.

There are so many places to visit and things to do in Rome. Whatever you choose to do, you are sure to have a great time. Ciao!

---

10 ▶ Students compare their notes with a partner before watching the video again to check their answers.

LIFE COMPETENCIES
SB P139

STUDY SKILLS AND LEARNING TO LEARN

11 Go over the instructions with the class and then divide students into small groups.

Encourage students to research information and reviews online before making notes about their chosen site and any advice for visitors.

Refer students back to the reviews of the Colosseum to find some useful language for advice. For example, imperatives such as, *buy your tickets online, arrive early, visit out of season.* Also *if* clauses, such as, *If you go in summer, remember to wear comfortable clothes.*

Each group then creates a tourist information booklet about the historical site.

Display the booklets around the classroom so that students can read the other groups' work.

Ask students to decide which site they would like to visit and why.

➡ **WORKBOOK** / Unit 10, page 44

11 SAVING AND SPENDING

UNIT OBJECTIVES	
Topic:	services and shopping
Grammar:	present continuous for fixed plans; present simple for schedules and timetables; *going to*
Vocabulary:	spending and saving; shopping; money and shopping
Listening:	Part 5: matching information about shops and clothes
Reading:	Part 1: three-option multiple choice: signs and notices
Speaking:	talking about shopping habits
Writing:	review of a department store
Pronunciation:	unstressed *to* in *going to*
Exam focus:	Reading Part 1; Listening Part 5
Real world:	dealing with money in Stockholm

Ask your students to watch the Grammar on the Move videos on pages 143 and 144. You can use these to present or reinforce the present continuous for future plans, the present continuous for schedules and timetables, and *going to*.

READING
SB P140

MONEY AND ME

LEAD-IN

Draw attention to the photos and ask students to say what they think is happening in each situation. Elicit or supply vocabulary as necessary, (*spend money, buy something, save, lend/borrow, waste money*). The photo C can be used to explain the difference between *lend* (give something for a period of time) and *borrow* (take something for a period of time). Encourage students to use the present continuous to describe what is happening.

1 Allow about 30 seconds to read the questions and match each one to a photo.

After checking, students work in pairs to ask and answer the questions about themselves.

Feed back by asking three or four students to tell the class their answers.

> **1** B   **2** A   **3** C   **4** D

2 Briefly discuss the people in the pictures with the class. Ask questions about where they are and what they are doing. Do the students think they are spending, saving or wasting their money?

2 Ask students if they remember the answers to the questions. Read the texts as a class to check their answers. It may be necessary to check understanding of *earn* (to receive money for work that you do) and *freecycling* (reusing things that other people don't want).

> **1** Carola   **2** Rani   **3** David

⊕ EXTENSION

After checking answers, you could ask students to tell you something about things they recycle or upcycle. Use questions such as, *Do you have to recycle waste? Which materials are recycled? Have you ever upcycled anything? What did you use? Would you like to try upcycling?* Then write *freecycle* on the board. Ask students what they think this is. (Freecycling refers to people reusing things that other people don't want. So, people give (and receive) things without exchanging money.) Ask students if they have any experience of freecycling. If they don't, ask them what type of thing they would like to receive or give away.

3 Students work in pairs to find the answers to the questions in the texts.

> **1** Rani saves money by buying reduced items and items with a discount when she is shopping and never borrowing or lending money.
> **2** Carola likes upcycling things from fleamarkets.
> **3** He never keeps receipts.

VOCABULARY
SB P141

SPENDING AND SAVING

1 Draw attention to the words in blue in the text and tell students that reading the sentences around the words helps to understand the meanings. Students match the words and definitions before class feedback. Check and drill pronunciation of receipt (/rɪˈsiːt/).

> **1** salary   **2** discount   **3** receipt   **4** sales
> **5** bill   **6** reduced items

2 This exercise revises the meanings of all the verbs about money that students have seen so far in the unit. Allow a few minutes for students to do the exercise on their own and then check answers with a partner. Encourage them to explain why the other verb is wrong in each case.

Check answers as a class.

> **1** costs   **2** saving   **3** waste   **4** spent
> **5** lend   **6** earn

124

FAST FINISHERS

Students can write six sentences with the verb they chose as the correct answer in each of the sentences in Exercise 2.

3 Students complete the dialogues with words from Exercises 1 and 2. Check answers as a class.

| 1 borrow 2 sales 3 discount 4 lend 5 cost |
| 6 bill 7 paid 8 earn 9 salary 10 save |

4 Read through the *Did you know?* box with the class and ask students if they can remember any other differences between American and British English. They could read back through their book to find some and make a list in their notebooks.

Read through the questions as a class and draw attention to the example answer in the speech bubble. Tell students it's a good idea for them to give answers which are one or two sentences long, like the example, rather than just a few words.

Allow students two or three minutes to ask and answer the questions in pairs.

SB P142

MAKING PLANS

1 Briefly discuss the questions with the class. Ask how they remember things they need to do and elicit other ways of organising time such as, *a diary, online calendars* or *apps* (a diary is usually a book while a calendar is often on the wall or on a desk).

2 Draw attention to the two calendars and go through the questions with the class. Then allow two minutes for students to answer the questions. Check answers as a class.

| 1 Marta – department store, garden centre |
| Josh – supermarket, music shop |
| 2 Marta – summer clothes, birthday present for mum |
| Josh – food and drink for a party |
| 3 Marta plans to go for dinner in a restaurant. |
| Josh plans to go to a party. |

3 091 Tell students they are going to hear first Marta and then Josh speaking about their plans for Saturday. They will talk about their plans. With a weaker class you could pause the recording after Marta speaks and check answers to the first question before playing Josh.

| 1 to find something for her mum's birthday present. Her mum loves plants. |
| 2 a surprise party |

AUDIOSCRIPT 091

Marta: I'm going shopping with my sister this Saturday. We're meeting in front of Darby's, the big department store, at 11.30 and we're going to go shopping for summer clothes. I saw a dress online that I liked and I'm going to try it on in the shop if they have it in my size. I hope so! I don't like the changing room there because it's always busy, but the shop assistants are really helpful. We're also going to look for a birthday present for my mum. She loves plants, so we're going to go to the garden centre to see if we can find something. In the evening, we're having dinner at a new restaurant called Milo's by the river. It opens at 7.00 pm and we've booked a table. I'm really looking forward to it!

Josh: Jez and I are going shopping for the food and drink for Alfie's surprise party on Saturday afternoon. The bus to town leaves at 2.00 pm and we're meeting outside the supermarket at 2.30. I'm going to pay for everything by card and I mustn't forget to ask for a receipt at the till. Alfie's friends want to share the cost of the food and drink, so we need to have something to show how much we spend. After the food shopping, we're going to the music shop. Alfie's parents have bought him some drums as a birthday present and they asked us to collect them. Alfie's dad gave me £50 in cash to pay for a taxi, but it's not going to cost that much, so I must remember to give him the change. The party is starting at 7.00, so we're going to take everything straight to Alfie's house by taxi.

4 091 This exercise can be done as a memory game. Ask students to cover up the rest of the page and try to answer the questions. Then they listen to the recording again to check their answers.

| 1 b 2 b 3 a 4 a 5 b 6 a |

SB P142

SHOPPING

1 091 Point out that the sentences are from the recording. Give students some time to try to complete the sentences individually before listening to the recording again to check answers.

After checking, you could ask students some questions to check understanding, e.g. *I don't have a credit card. How can I pay for things?* (in cash); *Where can I go to try something on in a shop?* (the changing room); *Where can I go to pay for something in a shop?* (the till); *Who can help me in a shop?* (the shop assistant).

| 1 try it on, size   2 changing rooms, shop assistants |
| 3 by card, till   4 in cash   5 change |

UNIT 11   SAVING AND SPENDING   125

2 Students complete the two texts with the words from Exercise 1 before checking answers.

> **1** try on **2** size **3** changing room
> **4** shop assistant **5** by card **6** in cash
> **7** change **8** till

BACKGROUND INFORMATION

Contactless payments are made with a credit or debit card or a smartphone or other smart device. The user waves their card or device near a card reader to make a payment. It is the fastest way of paying for something. In the UK, Canada and Australia, this is a very popular way of paying for things as people don't have to carry much cash with them.

3 Students work in pairs to ask and answer the questions. Encourage them to give answers of one or two sentences.

FAST FINISHERS

Students can ask their partner about other aspects of shopping. For example, *Do you prefer shopping online or in physical shops?*; *Do you usually go to small shops or big shopping centres?*; *Why do some people dislike going shopping?*

SB P143

THE PRESENT CONTINUOUS FOR FIXED PLANS

LEAD-IN

Refer students back to the photos on page 142, Exercise 1. Ask students what the people are doing. Elicit and write on the board some example sentences such as, *She is shopping with a friend. He is shopping in the supermarket.* Ask students the name of the tense and elicit the present continuous. Ask why we used it to describe the photos and elicit that it is used to talk about something that is happening when we are speaking.

1 Explain that the present continuous can also be used to talk about other situations and direct attention to the two example sentences. Answer the question as a class (the sentences are talking about the future).

Read the information in the box as a class and ask students to choose the correct answer. Then focus on the form of the present continuous, using the two example sentences in the book and those on the board.

> the future   Rule: fixed plans

➔ **GRAMMAR REFERENCE** / Page 219

2 Tell students that all the verbs are in the present continuous and they are all being used to talk about future plans. Point out also that as this is a conversation they should use contracted forms where possible, e.g. *he's* rather than *he is*, which are more common when speaking.

Students work individually to complete the text before checking answers with a partner. Feed back as a class.

> **1** are going **2** 're visiting **3** 're travelling
> **4** 're staying **5** are, leaving **6** 're flying
> **7** 're coming **8** 're not/aren't staying
> **9** 's/is meeting **10** 're going **11** 're taking

3 Draw attention to Ben's diary and go through the example with the class. Then ask one or two students to give the class a further sentence about Ben's plans for next week, using the information in the diary.

Students write some more sentences about Ben's plans. Check answers as a class.

> **Suggested answers**
> **1** On Tuesday, he's playing football at the leisure centre at 7.00 pm.
> **2** On Wednesday, he's going to the dentist's at 9.00am.
> **3** On Thursday, he's having a guitar lesson at 6.30 pm.
> **4** On Friday, he isn't working / going to work. He's going running in the park with Liz in the morning.
> **5** On Saturday afternoon, he's going shopping with Pete.

4 With a weaker class it may be helpful for students to make some notes about their plans before they start speaking. Stronger students can ask their partner questions as well as give information. For example, *What are you doing next weekend? I'm going to the cinema on Saturday afternoon. Who are you going with?*, etc.

THE PRESENT SIMPLE FOR SCHEDULES AND TIMETABLES

LEAD-IN

Ask one or two questions using the present simple. For example, *What time does the lesson finish?*; *When does the cinema open on Saturdays?* Explain to students that we can also use the present simple to talk about the future in specific situations.

5 Read through the example sentences with the class and complete the rule together. Remind students that we can only use the present simple to talk about fixed events or schedules for the future.

> a schedule or timetable

➔ **GRAMMAR REFERENCE** / Page 219

6 Ask students if they can remember the difference in use between the present continuous and the present simple for the future. Refer them back to the two sets of rules if necessary.

Then allow students a few minutes to do the exercise individually before checking answers as a class. When checking, ask students if they can explain why they used the tense they did (fixed time or schedule for present simple and future plans for present continuous).

> 1 closes   2 is having   3 leaves   4 is visiting
> 5 're meeting, starts

⊕ EXTENSION

Ask students to write three or four sentences about their plans for next week, using both the tenses. For example, *I'm seeing my best friend on Monday evening; My swimming lesson is at 6 pm on Tuesday.*

7 Students complete the sentences using the present simple or present continuous. Check answers as a class.

> 1 leaves   2 're/are going   3 ends
> 4 's/is meeting

LISTENING PART 5 TRAINING
SB P144

✓ EXAM INFORMATION

In Part 5 of the Listening paper students listen to an informal conversation between two people about an everyday topic such as travel, free-time activities or daily life. Students listen to identify specific information such as objects, places, feelings, etc. and have to match five items with a choice of eight options. In the example task in the Student's Book students have to match the clothes that people should buy in the different places listed. In the exam there is always an example and students hear the recording twice.

In this section in the Student's Book there are four places and seven options. Students are encouraged to focus on listening for information which tells them why each answer is correct.

LEAD-IN

With books closed, ask students where they go to buy their clothes and if they can name any other places that sell clothes. Elicit the names of different types of shops such as, *supermarket, market, department store, second-hand shop, chain store, boutique*. Then draw attention to the photo in the book and ask students what type of shop they think it is.

1 Elicit a brief class discussion and help with vocabulary as necessary. Students may want to use adjectives, such as *fashionable, cheap, expensive, second-hand, smart, casual*.

2 🔊 092 Draw attention to the question and ask some questions to check that students remember what they have to do in Listening Part 5, for example, *How many people do you hear speaking?* (two); *How many questions are there?* (five in the exam, but only four here); *How many answer options are there?* (eight in the exam, but only seven here – there are some extra options you don't need); *How many times do you hear the recording?* (twice).

AUDIOSCRIPT 🔊 092

Paula: Maria, I'm going to buy some new clothes for my holiday. Has the supermarket got lots of summer clothes at the moment?

Maria: Not lots, Paula. I looked for a sun hat there last week. They didn't have any. You could get a swimsuit there – they've got a lot of them. I'm going to get one for myself.

Then ask students some questions about this task, for example, *Who is speaking?* (Paula and Maria); *What are they speaking about?* (advice about clothes shopping).

Remind students that they may hear more than one answer from the list, but they have to understand which one is correct. Read the example and then play the recording, checking that students understand the task and the answer.

3 🔊 093 Play the recording and allow students a minute to compare their answers with a partner before listening again to check their answers. With a weaker class it may be helpful to pause the recording after each answer.

> 1 F   2 G   3 C   4 D

AUDIOSCRIPT 🔊 093

Paula: Maria, I'm going to buy some new clothes for my holiday. Has the supermarket got lots of summer clothes at the moment?

Maria: Not lots, Paula. I looked for a sun hat there last week. They didn't have any. You could get a swimsuit there – they've got a lot of them. I'm going to get one for myself.

Paula: Great. … I could try the clothes shop near your college.

Maria: They've got some T-shirts you'd love – there's one that's perfect for you – but the dresses are expensive!

Paula: OK. What about the department store?

Maria: I think that's good for buying trainers, but not shirts and dresses. They have so many pairs to choose from.

Paula: Do you go shopping at the market?

Maria: I bought a sun hat there last year, but it didn't last long. The market's a good place for buying socks – you can get six pairs for a pound.

Paula: And I suppose I could get things online.

Maria: But you need to see swimsuits and shorts before buying them. I've just remembered. There are half-price sun hats on the Love-Clothes site.

Paula: Great.

UNIT 11 | SAVING AND SPENDING

GRAMMAR
SB P144

GOING TO

1 Write the first example sentence on the board (*I'm going to buy some new clothes for my holiday.*) and then ask some questions to check understanding, e.g. *Has she already bought the clothes?* (no); *Is she buying the clothes now?* (no); *Is she buying the clothes in the future?* (yes).

Then go through the rules as a class.

> the future   Rule: our intentions

LANGUAGE NOTE

Students may have difficulty understanding the difference between present continuous for future plans and *going to* for future intentions. Sometimes we can use either form, but generally the present continuous is used for something which is <u>already</u> arranged, so, for example, if we have an appointment (*I'm meeting Julie at the restaurant at 7 pm*), and *going to* for something we <u>intend</u> to do (*I'm going to look for a new job.*).

➡ **GRAMMAR REFERENCE** / Page 218

2 Point out the form of *going to* using the information and example sentences and elicit one or two examples from students about things they are going to do later today. For example, *I'm going to do my homework; I'm going to have lunch with my friends.*

Then students complete the sentences using *going to* and the verb given. Check answers as a class.

> **1** is/'s going to go shopping   **2** is she going to learn
> **3** are … going to get   **4** 'm/am not going to walk
> **5** Are … going to buy

3 Students write five sentences. To make this more fun, you could suggest they include one or two sentences which are not true. When they read their sentences to their partner they have to try to identify the false sentence(s).

4 094 Before playing the dialogue, ask students to look at how the stress is marked on the words in bold and to think about different aspects of the pronunciation to listen for. For example, *Is every letter pronounced? Which syllables are stressed?*

Play the recording and try to elicit the answers. It may be necessary to repeat the recording for students to listen out for the sounds once you have gone over the answers together.

> /gəʊntə/ The 'g' at the end of *going to* is not pronounced and *to* is pronounced with the weak form /tə/.

AUDIOSCRIPT 094

Man: What are you going to do this weekend? Do you have any plans?
Woman: Not really. I'm going to stay at home and watch TV this evening.
Man: Yes, so am I! And I'm going to go to bed early for once.

5 094 Use the recording as a model and drill chorally, focusing on the rhythm the stress pattern produces, before giving students a few minutes to practise reading the dialogue in pairs. Encourage them to exchange roles so that they all have a chance to read both parts.

6 Go over the three forms used to talk about the future (present simple and continuous and *going to*) and elicit some examples of each. Refer students back to the three sections in the unit if they cannot explain the differences between them.

> **1** 'm working   **2** 's going   **3** starts   **4** 're going to watch   **5** leaves   **6** 's taking

FAST FINISHERS

Students can read their answers out to a partner, remembering to use the pronunciation rules.

READING PART 1 TRAINING
SB P145

✓ EXAM INFORMATION

In Reading Part 1 students read six items (an email, a text message, a web message or a notice). The focus is on overall understanding of the message and students have to choose the correct answer from three options.

In the Student's Book here there are three questions and an example and students are encouraged to think about why the other options are wrong in order to check they have chosen the right answer.

Ask students some questions to check how much they remember about Reading Part 1. E.g. *How many questions do you have to answer?* (six in the Exam but there are only three here); *What type of text do you have to read?* (short emails, messages and notices); *What do you have to do?* (choose the answer from three options which is most similar to the meaning of the message). Go through the example together.

Students work through the exercise individually and then check answers in pairs, explaining why they chose that particular answer each time. Feed back as a class.

> **2** B   **3** C   **4** A

PUSH YOURSELF / B1

SB P145

VOCABULARY: MONEY AND SHOPPING

1 Draw attention to the photo and ask students to predict what the text might be about. Accept all suggestions and then allow a minute for students to read the text quickly to answer your question. (It's about Shona Evans, a songwriter, and how she spends her money.)

Encourage students to re-read the text and focus on the words around those in bold before they do the exercise. Check answers as a class.

> **1** d **2** e **3** f **4** b **5** c **6** h **7** g **8** a

2 Go through the questions, giving some examples from your own experience to help students understand the meaning and the task. For example, *I opened my first bank account just before I went to university. I didn't have much money, but I wanted to have a bank card.* Students work in pairs to discuss the questions. Encourage them to give longer answers of two or three sentences if possible. Feed back by asking different students to tell the class about each topic. Encourage interaction from the class to say if they have had similar experiences or if they agree or disagree with what each student says.

SB P146

REVIEW OF A DEPARTMENT STORE

1 Draw attention to the photos and ask students to describe what they can see. Elicit vocabulary related to the photos.

Then have a brief class discussion to answer the questions. Ask students if they have visited any famous department stores in other countries.

> **BACKGROUND INFORMATION**
>
> The first department stores opened in the 19th century following the increase in the size of cities, better transportation and electric lighting. Some of the most famous stores are Harrods and Selfridges in London, Macy's and Bloomingdale's in New York, Le Bon Marché in Paris and La Rinascente in Rome. In spite of competition in recent years from big shopping malls and online retail, they continue to be popular destinations for visitors and residents of cities across the world.

2 Tell the class they are going to read a review of a department store. Read through the questions and ask students to suggest what type of answers they might find, e.g. they liked the café or a particular department, the sales assistants were polite, rude, helpful, they didn't like the service, the queues at the tills, etc.

Allow students a few minutes to look for the answers and compare their ideas with a partner. Then check answers as a class.

> **1** the clothes department because of the on-trend clothes and the stylish changing rooms
> **2** They were friendly but there weren't many of them.
> **3** The reviewer had to wait a long time to pay and prices were high.
> **4** Good – the reviewer says, 'I would recommend Bryson's'.

3 Explain that there are certain fixed phrases that can be useful to remember when writing a review. Ask students to find the first example phrase in the box in the text and underline it. Then ask them to underline other expressions to talk about good points, before using different colours to underline the other categories of expression in the box. Feed back as a class.

> **Talking about good points:**
> One of the best things about it is …
> For me, the high point of Bryson's is …
> **Talking about bad points:**
> The worst thing about Bryson's is …
> Another negative point for me is …
> Don't go there if …
> **Giving a final opinion:**
> Overall …

4 Read through the instructions and the points with the class. Students can invent a department store if they have never visited one.

With a weaker class you could work with them to elicit or supply some adjective, or descriptive phrases for the different points. For example, you could ask them to tell you how the building is described in the model text in Exercise 2 (*200 years old, in the centre of the city …*) and ask how they could you describe the building (*modern, old, historic,* etc.) or the places to eat (*café, restaurant, bistro, coffee bar, quiet, busy, serves tasty food,* etc.).

Allow students a few minutes to make notes on each of the points and move around the classroom helping with vocabulary as they work.

5 Again it is helpful to point out that the model text follows this plan in paragraphing. Encourage students to look back at the review in Exercise 2 to confirm that and remind them of the other language they looked at in Exercise 3. Students decide which information they are going to include in each paragraph and make their own plan with notes, but not complete sentences.

6 Students use their plans to write the review. When they are finished, encourage them to check their own work through for spelling and grammar mistakes before exchanging their work with a partner. If possible, ask students to say one good thing about the review as well as one way it could be improved.

SPEAKING
SB P147

SHOPPING HABITS

LEAD-IN

Look at the photo with the class and elicit what they can see (the two people are window shopping). With a stronger class you could teach *shopaholic* (someone who loves shopping and spends a lot of time doing it) and *fashionista* (a person who loves fashionable clothes and accessories).

1 Students work in pairs to put the words in order.

> 1 Do you enjoy shopping?
> 2 What sort of things do you like buying?
> 3 Where do you go shopping?
> 4 What's your favourite shop?
> 5 Have you bought anything recently?
> 6 Where and when did you buy them?

2 095 Tell students the two people are being interviewed about their shopping habits. First they will hear Ines and then Luca. Play the recording and allow a few seconds at the end for students to make or complete their notes. If necessary, you could pause the recording when Ines has finished speaking to allow them some extra time.

Students compare their answers before checking as a class.

	Ines	Luca
Enjoy shopping?	no	yes
Where shop?	supermarket, online	shopping centre
Favourite shop?	doesn't have a favourite shop	*Place* – a clothes shop
Bought recently?	a new road bike	black boots
When and where?	bought in a sports shop last month	bought in a department store in London at the weekend

AUDIOSCRIPT 095

1

Woman: So today I'm on the streets of London, interviewing people about their shopping habits. The first person I'm talking to is Ines. Hello, Ines! So, can you tell me – do you enjoy shopping?

Ines: No, I don't.

Woman: OK, but when you have to go shopping where do you go?

Ines: The supermarket near my house and online.

Woman: What's your favourite shop?

Ines: Well, I really don't have a favourite shop.

Woman: And other than food – have you bought anything recently? Something like new clothes or a new computer?

Ines: Yes, last month I bought a new bike.

Woman: OK! So tell me about it. Where did you buy it? What kind of bike is it?

Ines: I bought it in a sports shop. It's a road bike and it's very good. But I still don't like shopping.

2

Woman: And next up is Luca. So what about you, Luca? Do you enjoy shopping?

Luca: Yes, I do. I like shopping a lot. I especially like clothes shopping. That's why I love going to cities on holiday.

Woman: And what sort of things do you like buying? Where do you go shopping?

Luca: I really like wearing fashionable things, so when I have money, I like buying clothes and shoes a lot. There's a big shopping centre in my town and I go there. It's very crowded, but I really like it because it has a lot of shops!

Woman: And what's your favourite shop?

Luca: I don't know, there are so many. There's a clothes shop called *Place* that I like a lot. That's probably my favourite shop as the shop assistants are really helpful and I always see things I want to buy.

Woman: Have you bought anything recently?

Luca: Umm … Yes, I bought some boots – some really nice black boots – from a department store in London last weekend. Unfortunately, they weren't in the sale, so they were quite expensive, but they look great.

3 Read the questions with the class and discuss the answers together.

> **Suggested answers**
> Luca gives better answers than Ines because he gives more detail, including giving examples.

4 096 Direct students' attention to the text and give them a few minutes to read through it. Ask students to try to complete the gaps and then play the recording of Luca again to check answers.

> 1 That's why 2 so 3 because 4 as 5 so

AUDIOSCRIPT 096

Woman: And next up is Luca. So what about you, Luca? Do you enjoy shopping?

Luca: Yes, I do. I like shopping a lot. I especially like clothes shopping. That's why I love going to cities on holiday.

Woman: And what sort of things do you like buying? Where do you go shopping?

Luca: I really like wearing fashionable things, so when I have money, I like buying clothes and shoes a lot. There's a big shopping centre in my town and I go there. It's very crowded, but I really like it because it has a lot of shops!

Woman: And what's your favourite shop?

Luca: I don't know, there are so many. There's a clothes shop called *Place* that I like a lot. That's probably my favourite shop as the shop assistants are really helpful and I always see things I want to buy.

Woman: Have you bought anything recently?

Luca: Umm … Yes, I bought some boots – some really nice black boots – from a department store in London last weekend. Unfortunately, they weren't in the sale, so they were quite expensive, but they look great.

5 Students discuss the question. Feed back as a class.

A

6 Refer students back to the questions in Exercise 1, and ask them to make some notes for their answers to the questions. A weaker group can re-read Luca's replies in Exercise 4 to help with ideas. Help students with vocabulary while they are making their notes.

7 Allow students a few minutes to ask and answer the questions. Remind them to give longer answers where possible and to use adjectives and reasons for their answers. Stronger students can be encouraged to make up their own follow-up questions.

When asking for feedback, ask two or three students to tell the class as much as they can remember about their partner's answers.

⊕ EXTENSION

Following the feedback to Exercise 7, note down on the board the names of some of the most popular shops and shopping websites that were suggested by students. Put students into small groups and allocate a shop or website to each group. Then allow them a few minutes to prepare a short description of their shop/website to present to the class. This could include information about what is sold, prices, etc. After the presentations, hold a class vote to establish the favourite shop/website.

EXAM FOCUS
READING PART 1

⊘ EXAM INFORMATION

In Reading Part 1 students read six items (an email, a text message, a web message or a notice). The focus is on overall understanding of the message and students have to choose the correct answer from three options.

The whole Reading and Writing paper has seven parts. Parts 1–5 are reading tasks and Parts 6 and 7 are writing tasks. Students have 60 minutes in total to complete the paper, so they should spend about 15 minutes on the writing tasks and 45 minutes on the reading tasks. Students should allow about nine minutes to do Part 1.

EXAM CHECK

1 Ask students if they can remember any of the advice for doing Reading Part 1. Elicit the fact that it can be helpful to think about why answer options are wrong as well as why one is right. Students do the Exam check task before checking answers as a class.

Shorter texts – label on a product, sign on a wall, shop notice
Longer texts – email, text message, post-it note, web message, notice on a work/school/club noticeboard

2 Remind students they have about 1.5 minutes per question in the Reading part of the exam, so allow nine minutes for students to complete the task under exam conditions, individually, without speaking. When checking answers encourage students to explain why they think the answer options are right or wrong.

LISTENING PART 5
SB P149

⊘ EXAM INFORMATION

In Listening Part 5 students listen to an informal conversation between two people about an everyday topic such as travel, free-time activities or daily life. Students have to identify specific information such as objects, places, feelings, etc. and match five items with a choice of eight options. There is an example and students hear the recording twice.

EXAM CHECK

1 Draw attention to the exam-style question in Exercise 2 and ask students to use the information there to complete the sentences in the Exam check task. When they have finished, they can compare answers with a partner. Elicit the answers around the class.

> **1** a conversation between two people **2** five
> **3** You hear these in the order you read them. **4** eight
> **5** will not

2 097 Allow students 30 seconds to read the question and the answer options. Then remind them they will hear the recording twice, so it is important to continue listening even if they miss one of the answers.

Tell students to complete the task under exam conditions, i.e. without discussing answers with other students. Play the recording, allowing students a few seconds to think about their answers before listening again. Check answers as a class. With a stronger class try to elicit the reasons why the students chose the answers they did.

> **1** A **2** H **3** G **4** B **5** D

AUDIOSCRIPT 097

Narrator: For each question, choose the correct answer. You will hear Alicia talking to a friend about her party. What job will Alicia do each day?
Man: Hi, Alicia. Are you ready for your party?
Alicia: Nearly. I've decided to do one job each day, starting on Monday, when I'm going to get some new plates and glasses. I haven't got enough.
Man: Right. And what about Tuesday? Don't you have an appointment at the hairdresser's?
Alicia: I decided I don't need to do that. I'm going shopping for a new dress that day instead.
Man: And on Wednesday?
Alicia: I don't know yet.
Man: Have you remembered to ask everyone to the party? The people who live near you, for example?
Alicia: I forgot about them! I'll do that on Wednesday. And on Thursday I'm planning to clean the house.
Man: It'll get dirty again before the party!
Alicia: You're right. I'll download the music that day, instead.
Man: Good idea. What are you going to do on Friday?
Alicia: Get the snacks. I'm not going to cook anything. It's too much work.
Man: And on Saturday?
Alicia: In the morning I'll clean the house. So I'll have lots of time to put my dress on and do my make-up before the party.
Man: Great! See you there!

Read through the options in the *How was it?* section and elicit the meaning of each one that they learned in the first unit.

Ask students to tick the appropriate box. You might like to ask students to share how they felt about the task to get an indication of your students' confidence. Depending on your class, you might like to do this openly or allow students to give their feedback without their classmates seeing. For example, give students a piece of A4 paper each with the *How was it?* scale written in large letters. Allow students to tick the relevant box then hold up their papers at the same time so that you can see how well students think they are doing. Finally, ask students if they found it easier, harder or the same as the exam practice in Unit 1.

REAL WORLD

SB P150

DEALING WITH MONEY IN … STOCKHOLM

> **WARMER**
> Ask students if they know where Stockholm is (the capital of Sweden in northern Europe).

1 Draw attention to the photos and ask students to match the photos with the ways of paying. Check answers as a class.

> **1** A **2** C **3** D **4** B

2 Draw attention to the Fact box about currencies and give students a few seconds to look at it. Then ask them to close their books. Call out a currency or a country and ask students to tell you the corresponding country or currency. Elicit any other currencies students know.

Then ask students to read the text quickly to answer the question.

Students compare answers in pairs.

> They use cards or smartphones.

3 Read the statements as a class and help with vocabulary as necessary. Ask students to predict the answers before working in pairs to find the answers in the blog. Feed back as a class.

> **1** F Most stores only accept kronor.
> **2** T **3** F You can pay by credit card for most things.
> **4** T **5** F There are cash machines all over the city.
> **6** F You need to use your pin.

4 Students match the words from the blog with the correct definition. Feed back as a class.

> **1** b **2** h **3** e **4** d **5** f **6** g **7** a **8** c

5 🔊 **098** Go over the instructions with the class and ask them to suggest a question the people might ask in the different situations. For example, *Where is the cash machine?*; *How many kronor are there to one euro?*; *How much does this cost?*; *Can I have two tickets please?*

Play the recordings and ask students to make a note of one or two words or phrases which tell them the answer in each case. Repeat the recordings if necessary.

Check answers as a class, encouraging students to tell you the notes they made.

| **1** d | **2** a | **3** c |

AUDIOSCRIPT 🔊 098

1
Tourist: Hello. Can I have two tickets, please?
Official: Certainly. Full price?
Tourist: Is there a student discount?
Official: Yes, there is. The full price is 130 kronor, but it's 110 kronor with the student discount. Do you have your student ID card?
Tourist: Yes, here it is.
Official: That's fine. So two tickets will be 220 kronor, please.
Tourist: Here you are.
Official: Oh, I'm sorry. We don't take cash. Only cards and smartphone payments.
Tourist: Oh, OK. I've got my card. Can I use contactless?
Official: Yes, of course. There you go.
Official: Yes, that's gone through. So, here are your tickets. Enjoy your visit.
Tourist: Thank you.

2
Tourist: Excuse me. Is there a cash machine near here?
Man: A Bankomat? Yes, let me think. There's one near the Royal Palace. I'm just trying to think of the best way for you to get there. It's quicker to use the back streets, but you might get lost. So, I think maybe it's best to go straight along this road until you see the Nobel Museum on your right. Then take a right turn, any one will do, and you'll see the Royal Palace. There's a Bankomat just on the right there, opposite the palace. You can't miss it.
Tourist: OK. Thanks. How far is it?
Man: Oh, it's only a five-minute walk. Not too far.
Tourist: OK. Thank you.

3
Tourist: Hello. Can I have these things, please?
Shopkeeper: Of course. That's 175 kronor, please.
Tourist: Do you take cards?
Shopkeeper: Oh, no. I'm sorry. We don't take credit cards. We're only a small shop and it's expensive for us to process the payments.
Tourist: Oh. This isn't a credit card. It's a debit card.
Shopkeeper: Oh, OK. Problem solved. Is it contactless?
Tourist: No. I need to use my PIN number.
Shopkeeper: OK, no problem.
That's ready for you now. No. The other way round. Thank you. Now, if you can just put in your PIN number. That's fine. If you could take your card? And here's your receipt. Thank you. Have a nice day.
Tourist: Thank you. Bye.

PHRASES YOU MIGHT USE

6 🔊 **098** Students work in pairs to complete the phrases before listening to the recording to check their answers.

| **1** discount | **2** use | **3** cash machine | **4** far |
| **5** take | **6** PIN number |

PHRASES YOU MIGHT HEAR

7 Students work in pairs to choose the correct definitions before checking answers as a class.

| **1** b | **2** a | **3** a | **4** b | **5** a |

WATCH

8 ▶ Go through the questions with the class, checking understanding. With a weaker group play the first part of the video and ask students to listen for the information about the old town. Pause the video and check answers. Then play the rest of the video and encourage students to take notes.

9 ▶ Students compare their notes with a partner before watching the video again to check. Feed back as a class.

> **old town:** called Gamla Stan; it's on an island, you have to cross a bridge to get there; Royal Palace, home of the Swedish Royal Family; Nobel Museum has information about the Nobel Prize.
>
> **currency:** the krona, most common banknotes are 20, 50, 100, 200, 500; there are 1, 2, 5 and 10 kronor coins; Bankomats all over the city, always the same colour.
>
> **paying for things:** use your credit or debit card to take out money; some small shops don't accept credit cards; some shops still have chip and PIN machines, but many now accept contactless and smartphones; new ways of paying for things are becoming popular, e.g. using your eyes to recognise you and using fingerprints.

UNIT 11 SAVING AND SPENDING

VIDEOSCRIPT ▶ Stockholm

Stockholm is the capital city of Sweden, in the north of Europe. It's a busy city, with a mix of old and modern buildings. In the summer, the days are long, but in the winter they are short and it gets cold, often with snow.

The old town of Stockholm is called Gamla Stan. It's on an island, so you have to cross a bridge to get to it. The Royal Palace is in Gamla Stan. It's the home of Sweden's Royal Family. The Nobel Museum is also here on the island. This has lots of information about the Nobel Prizes, and people who have won them, like Nelson Mandela.

The Swedish currency is the krona, with banknotes of 20, 50, 100, 200 and 500 krona. And there are 1, 2, 5 and 10 krona coins. To get money out of your bank, you can use one of the Bankomats that are all over the city. They are always the same colour, so you'll see them easily.

But most people prefer to pay for things in other ways. You can use a credit card or a debit card. It's important to know the difference, because some small shops only accept debit cards. To pay using a card, some shops still have machines where you need to use your PIN number, but many shops now use contactless machines for your card or phone, so you don't have to remember your PIN number for these.

Some new ways of paying for things are also becoming popular. In some places you can use your eye to show who you are and it's also possible to use your fingerprint to pay for things in some places. So you'll always have your money with you, even if you forget your bank cards and your wallet!

LIFE COMPETENCIES
SB P151

CRITICAL THINKING AND UNDERSTANDING YOUR OWN CULTURE

10 Go through the list of points with the class, checking understanding.

11 Students work in pairs to present their ideas in a visually attractive way for visitors to their town or city.

Two pairs work together to show their information pack to each other.

➡ **WORKBOOK** / *Unit 11, page 48*

PROGRESS CHECK 4
UNIT 9 TO UNIT 11

SB P152

1
1 D
2 F
3 B
4 C
5 A
6 E

2
1 earn
2 lend
3 cost
4 save
5 pay
6 waste

3
1 h
2 e
3 f
4 a
5 b
6 g
7 d
8 c

4
1 happy to
2 learned to
3 prefer to
4 ask

5
1 size, changing room
2 by card, change
3 receipt, till

6
1 corner
2 roundabout
3 main square
4 district

7
1 … because I don't like **cooking**.
2 I want **to invite** you …
3 You need **to buy** some food …
4 … it stopped **raining** …
5 … have **to study** hard …
6 I'd like **to know** which …

8
1 I'm going
2 leaves
3 I have
4 will be
5 I'm going to buy
6 Are you going
7 might
8 may

9
1 Are
2 'll / will / might
3 can / shall
4 Do
5 am / 'm
6 be / get

12 THROUGH LIFE

UNIT OBJECTIVES

Topic:	education, work and social interaction
Vocabulary:	school subjects; jobs and work
Pronunciation:	intonation in questions
Listening:	Part 3: three-option multiple choice about a new job
Grammar:	zero conditional; first conditional; the passive
Speaking:	a job interview
Reading:	reading for gist and detail: three texts about education; Part 4: 3-option multiple-choice cloze about an actor
Writing:	a job application
Exam focus:	reading Part 4; Listening Part 3
Real world:	planning to study in Geneva

Ask your students to watch the Grammar on the Move videos on page 156 and page 158. You can use these to present or reinforce the zero and first conditionals and the passive.

SB P154

SCHOOL SUBJECTS

LEAD-IN

With books closed, brainstorm the names of school subjects students already know on the board with the class.

1 Read through the questions with the class and allow students a few minutes to discuss the answers.

During feedback, extend the discussion by asking students, *Do you think the stages in 1 happen at the right age?*; *Why do think in some countries students start school or university earlier or later?*; *Is there a right age?*; *Does a student's favourite subject depend on the teacher?*; *If you like a teacher are you more likely to like their subject?*; *Do many people do their perfect job? Why (not)?*

2 Open books and allow students a minute or two to match the subjects with the texts. Check answers as a class.

FAST FINISHERS

Students can write a similar sentence for any other school subjects which they can think, or which were mentioned in the initial class brainstorm. When checking answers, they can read the sentence and the rest of the class says the name of the subject.

> 1 maths   2 modern languages   3 history
> 4 biology   5 geography   6 chemistry
> 7 physics   8 drama

3 Refer students back to the expressions in bold in Exercise 2 and point out that they may have to change the form of the verbs when using them to complete the sentences. Check answers as a class. After checking answers ask students if they can tell you which of the expressions includes a noun which is uncountable, so has no plural form (*research*).

> 1 write (an) essay   2 do (some) research
> 3 do equations   4 do (an) experiment
> 5 take part (in a) performance   6 find out

4 Students work in pairs to ask and answer the questions. Encourage them to try to use some of the expressions in Exercise 3 and to extend their answers where possible.

SB P155

MY EDUCATION

LEAD-IN

Remind students of their answer to the question at the start of the lesson, *What's your perfect job?* Ask them what they would have / had to do to get that type of job. Would it be / Was it easy or difficult?

1 Go over the instructions with the class and allow them two or three minutes to scan the texts quickly to find the answers. Explain that it is not important to understand every word of the text; they should just look for the answers to the questions. Students compare answers with a partner before checking as a class.

> Fung – wants to go to university. We don't know what job she wants to do.
> Angeles – wants to be an engineer.
> Massimo – wants to be an accountant.
> Massimo already has a job.

2 Read through the questions with the class and try to elicit the meaning of *revise* (to study or read again in preparation for an exam). Students read the texts again more carefully to find the answers to the questions. Check answers as a class.

> 1 so she could study in the city
> 2 the *gaokao*. She hopes that she will get a place at university
> 3 because it's one of the best universities for studying her subject
> 4 a physics exam
> 5 to become an accountant
> 6 when he has a qualification and can change jobs

136

3 If necessary, encourage students to find the words in bold in the texts and try to understand them in context, before matching the parts of the definitions.

After checking answers, read through the *Did you know?* box with the class and ask students whether secondary school in their country is separated into two levels or not. You may want to point out that university in the US is often referred to as *college*.

| 1 f   2 e   3 b   4 c   5 d   6 a |

FAST FINISHERS

Students can write a sentence about themselves using each of the words or phrases in bold.

4 Explain to students that there are different verbs which collocate (often go together) with *an exam*. Ask them if they can think of any before looking back at the texts to find the five examples.

When checking answers, ask students if they can explain the differences between *take* and *pass* (to do an exam / to be successful in one) and *to study for* and *revise for* (they have similar meanings, but *revise* suggests studying something not for the first time).

Students may want to know the difference between an *exam* and a *test* (again, they have similar meanings, but *exam* is usually used for a more formal, perhaps longer test at the end of a course or period of study).

| revise for, take, pass, study for, fail |

5 Students work in pairs to complete the sentences with the correct form of the verbs. Check answers as a class.

| 1 revised for   2 fail   3 pass   4 studying for   5 taken |

6 Students discuss the questions in pairs.

GRAMMAR
SB P156

ZERO CONDITIONAL

LEAD-IN

Write on the board, *Some people think it is important to get good qualifications if you want to get a good job.*

Underline the verbs in the sentence and elicit the tense they are in (present simple).

Circle *if* and explain that using *if* in a sentence tells us about a condition. The action in the main clause (getting a good job) can only happen if the action in the *if* clause (getting good qualifications) is fulfilled.

1 Draw attention to the example sentences in the book and point out that the *if* clause can go before or after the main clause. Tell students the name of this type of sentence is the *zero conditional*.

Note that we use a comma after the *if* clause when it comes first.

Students complete the rules before checking as a class.

| 1 facts that are generally true   2 present |

➔ **GRAMMAR REFERENCE** / *Page 220*

2 Allow students a few minutes to complete the sentences before checking as a class.

| 2 doesn't understand, asks   3 feel, is   4 take, fail |

FAST FINISHERS

Students can write four more sentences of their own using the zero conditional.

FIRST CONDITIONAL

3 Explain to students that there are other types of conditionals and read through the example sentences of the first conditional in the book.

Point out that here too the two clauses can go in any order. Elicit, *I'll be happy if I pass it* as an alternative to the first example.

Try to elicit the meaning of the two sentences before looking at the rules together. (We use the first conditional to talk about the possibility (*if* clause) of something happening in the future and the consequence (main clause) of that.)

Check through the rules as a class and look at the form presented in the box.

| 1 in the future   2 present, future |

➔ **GRAMMAR REFERENCE** / *Page 220*

4 Elicit that in the first conditional we use the simple present after *if* even when it refers to something in the future. We use the *will* form of the verb in the other clause.

Go through the example sentence.

Students complete the sentences in pairs before checking as a class. When checking, make sure that students know how to pronounce the short form of *will* ('ll).

| 2 will be, don't pass   3 get, won't give   4 'll fail, doesn't work |

5 Weaker students may need extra support to do this task. Students have to decide whether the sentence is zero or first conditional, so first try to elicit the difference (zero conditional for something which is always or generally true, and first conditional for something which may happen in the future).

UNIT 12   THROUGH LIFE   137

Then students need to remember that after the *if* clause we use the present tense even when referring to the future.

Finally, they will need to remember question forms.

Work through 1 with the class, pointing out that it is a question and underlining the verbs. Ask students if it is zero or first (first) and why (it refers to a possible condition in the future). Then elicit the verb forms (*will happen / don't pass*).

Then, with a weaker group, you could ask the class to think about the verb forms they would use in the second sentence. Allow a few seconds thinking time before eliciting suggested answers from three or four students. Make sure all the students understand before asking them to complete the last two sentences individually.

When checking answers, ask students to say which type of conditional they are using and which tense they think is correct so that you can identify whether mistakes are due to form or misunderstanding.

> **1** What will happen if I don't pass the exam?
> **2** If students arrive late for the class, the teacher never lets them in.
> **3** If he studies late tonight, he'll be tired in the morning.
> **4** What will you give me if I help you with your essay tomorrow?

⊕ EXTENSION

Write some prompts on the board from the following list:

If you want to pass all your exams, …
If students go to university, they …
If I have time this evening, I …
If you are good at maths, …
If I go out with my friends this weekend, we …

Check understanding as necessary and then allow students three or four minutes to complete the sentences with their own ideas. Remind them to think about whether they need to use the zero or first conditional and the correct tenses for each option. Then ask students to compare their answers with a partner.

PUSH YOURSELF / B1

SB P156

GRAMMAR: *UNLESS* AND *WHEN*

1 Read through examples *a* and *b* in the first set of speech bubbles with the class and discuss the difference between the two (*if I see him,* means I may or may not see him, *when I see him,* means I will definitely see him).

Then look at the second set of speech bubbles and ask students if they can think of another way to say *unless* (*if* + not).

Ask students to read through the rules and complete the sentences.

Then ask students which tense is used after *when* and *unless* (they are followed by the simple present tense when referring to the future in a first conditional sentence, just like *if*).

Remind students that these are more examples of first conditionals, so the *if/when/unless* clause can go before or after the main clause.

> **1** not sure **2** sure **3** unless

2 Give students a few seconds to read the first sentence and think about the answer individually. Some students may find the negative meaning of *unless* a little challenging at first. Check the answer with the class before allowing students to work through the rest of the exercise in pairs. Then check answers as a class.

> **1** unless **2** If **3** unless **4** when **5** unless **6** If

FAST FINISHERS

Students can write three first conditional sentences about themselves starting *If I … / When I … / Unless I …*

⊕ EXTENSION

Students write some sentences about themselves using *when* and *unless* and then read them to their partner.

READING PART 4 TRAINING

SB P157

✓ EXAM INFORMATION

In Reading Part 4, students read a text from which six words have been removed. Students choose the appropriate words to fill the gaps from six three-option multiple-choice options. The main focus is on vocabulary, but there may be one or two questions which test grammar. In the example in the Student's Book there is one example and four other questions. Students are encouraged to think about why each answer option is right or wrong.

LEAD-IN

Draw attention to the photos and elicit descriptions of them from the class. Help with vocabulary as necessary, e.g. *driving test, driving licence, start school, graduate/ graduation, degree ceremony, have a baby.*

Then ask students to match the photos with some of the phrases below the photos.

1 Read the instructions and the examples in the speech bubbles with the class and then allow students three or four minutes to talk to a partner about their experiences. Encourage students to give as much information as possible and move around the classroom monitoring and helping with vocabulary as they do so.

CULTURAL INFORMATION

In the UK you can learn to drive when you are 17, in the US it depends on the state, but in many states you can drive at 16, whereas in Europe the minimum age is usually 18.

Most bachelor's degrees in the US are four years, whereas in the UK they are usually three years long.

Some young people in the UK move away from home when they go to university or get their first job, but others stay at home until they earn enough money to live alone.

2 Direct attention to the photo and ask students if they know Rebel Wilson. If most of the class recognise her, allow a few minutes for students to talk to a partner about what they know about her before feeding back to the class. If she is less familiar, this could be a class discussion or students could try to predict information using the photo. Accept all suggestions the students make.

3 Elicit what students have to do in Reading Part 4. (Choose the correct word from three options to complete a text. In the exam there are six questions.)

Tell students it is a good idea to read the whole text quickly to understand a little about the topic before thinking about the answers. Ask the class to read the text through and find out any other information about Rebel Wilson which was not mentioned in the class discussion.

After eliciting comments, draw attention to the example (1). After reading the sentence, look at the explanation with the class and make sure they understand why C is the correct answer. Explain that it can be helpful to try to exclude the wrong options while identifying the correct answer.

Allow students a few minutes to choose the other answers and when comparing their answers with a partner ask them to explain why the other options are wrong. Then feed back as a class.

| **2** B | **3** C | **4** A | **5** B |

THE PASSIVE

LEAD-IN

Write on the board:

They clean the classroom every morning.

Then elicit or supply:

The classroom is cleaned every morning.

Ask students if they know the name of the forms used (active and passive) and why we use the passive form (because we don't know or are not interested in who does the action).

1 Open books and ask students to work in pairs to read the example sentences and complete the rules.

Check answers as a class. When checking, ask students some more questions about the example on the board, e.g. *Which word is the past participle?* (cleaned); *Can you extend the passive sentence using by?* (... *by the cleaner*).

Then ask students if it is necessary to use this extension to the sentence (No, because we are more interested in the cleaning than the person who does it.).

No, No, Yes
Rule: 1 don't know / not important   **2** to be   **3** by

➔ **GRAMMAR REFERENCE** / Page 221

2 Go through the examples of present and past passive in the box and point out that the verb *to be* changes tense but we always use the past participle of the other verb.

With a weaker class, ask students to look at the past participles of each of the sentences ending (a–e), and say the infinitive of the verb (*teach, write, speak, eat, take*). Then allow a few minutes for students to match the sentences. Check answers as a class.

| **1** c | **2** e | **3** a | **4** d | **5** b |

3 Point out that students need to decide whether the sentence is in the present or past and that they must then use the correct passive form. Students do the exercise in pairs.

⊕ EXTENSION

Students work in pairs to use the passive form to describe a simple process from their everyday life. You can get them started with some suggestions, e.g. making a cup of tea or coffee. If necessary, do the first sentence together with the class, e.g. *First the water is boiled.*

If pairs choose to describe different processes they could read them to another pair when they finish and ask them to guess the process they have described.

| **1** was asked | **2** isn't taught | **3** was taken |
| **4** are collected | **5** was given | |

LISTENING
SB P158

1 Read through the questions and prompts with the class and check understanding.

You may want to elicit or explain the vocabulary first, for example:

- the difference between *job* and *work* (*work* can be a verb or a noun and *job* is a noun. Job usually refers to your role, e.g. *She's got a new job, she's a police officer.* Work is more general, e.g. *She works in the city centre.*)
- *salary* is the money you receive for the work you do, *pay* can be used with a similar meaning.
- a *boss* can also be called a *manager*.

UNIT 12   THROUGH LIFE   139

Allow students two or three minutes to discuss the questions and encourage them to extend and give reasons for their answers.

Feed back by asking students to rate from 1–5 the most and least important criteria when considering a job. What are the most and least important features for the class in general?

2 099 Draw attention to the photos and check that students understand the names of the different jobs. Tell them they are going to hear each person talking about their job and that they have to number them in order. With a weaker class you could pause after the first person speaks and check that students have understood. Otherwise, play the recording through and allow students time to check answers with a partner before class feedback.

> **1** farmer   **2** receptionist   **3** dentist   **4** engineer
> **5** businesswoman   **6** journalist

AUDIOSCRIPT 099

1
Farmer: Everyone knows that farmers don't earn much money, but that's not the most important thing to me. I really enjoy my work. I love being outside all day in the fresh air. The problem is that I never have any holidays or days off – it's too difficult to find someone to look after the animals.

2
Receptionist: I enjoy my work because I like talking to people and helping them. The receptionist knows everything that's happening in the hotel. It's a very interesting job! The only problem is that there are only two receptionists, so we don't get many breaks during the day. One of us has to be at the front desk all the time.

3
Dentist: In my country it takes eight years to study to be a dentist. I have a couple of degrees and diplomas! I earn a good salary, but I don't really enjoy my work. Nobody likes coming to the dentist and I often work with people who think I am going to hurt them.

4
Engineer: The good thing about my job as an engineer is that it is always interesting. I love working on big international projects with people from all over the world. The only difficult thing is that I often need to give instructions to people in English, so I really need to improve it.

5
Businesswoman: I have my own company with a staff of 500 people. I work long hours and my diary is full every week. I'm in the office by 7.00 in the morning every day and I often don't get home before 9 pm. But I love my job. It's very exciting to have your own business.

6
Journalist: I love doing research and finding exciting new stories. I always try to give true information – as a journalist that's my job. The only thing I don't like about my job is my boss. I hate people telling me what to do! Luckily, we don't see each other very much.

3 099 Allow students some time to read through the questions and answer options before playing the recording again. Check answers as a class.

Finish by asking students to talk to their partner about which of the jobs they would find most interesting to do and why.

> **1** a   **2** a   **3** a   **4** a   **5** b   **6** b

SB P159

JOBS AND WORK

1 Allow students a few minutes to do the task before checking answers with a partner.

> **1** e   **2** b   **3** d   **4** a   **5** c   **6** f

2 Students work in pairs to complete the sentences. Then check as a class.

FAST FINISHERS

Students can write their own sentences using the words in bold from Exercise 1.

> **1** time off   **2** breaks   **3** diplomas   **4** staff
> **5** long hours   **6** boss

3 Students work in small groups to answer the questions and then discuss the ideas as a class. If necessary, you could write some words on the board to help get the discussions started, e.g. *flexibility, freedom, salary, risk-taking, routine, colleagues, security*. Help with vocabulary as necessary.

LISTENING PART 3 TRAINING
SB P159

> ### ✓ EXAM INFORMATION
>
> In Listening Part 3 students listen to a longer dialogue and answer five three-option multiple-choice questions. Students have to listen to identify key information and opinion. They hear the recording twice. This section in the Student's Book encourages students to identify and underline the important words before listening and to learn to exclude the incorrect answers as well as selecting the correct answer. The task in the Student's Book has only four questions.

Elicit what students have to do in Listening Part 3. (Listen to a dialogue and answer five three-option multiple-choice questions about it. In this example there are only four questions.)

 100 Read the instructions and ask, *Who is speaking?* (Annie and Mick); *What are they speaking about?* (Annie's new job).

Encourage students to read through the questions before listening and then play the recording, pausing at the end of Annie's first speech.

Read through the explanation with the class, making sure students understand why B is the correct answer.

Play the rest of the recording and tell students to choose the correct answers. Allow a few minutes for them to compare their answers with a partner before playing the whole recording again. Check answers as a class. If possible, elicit reasons for the correct answers.

| 2 C | 3 C | 4 A |

AUDIOSCRIPT 🎧 100

Mick: Hi, Annie. I hear you left your computer programming job.
Annie: Yes, Mick. I had to spend so much time away from home. Staying in hotels every week was lonely and boring. So I decided to change my life completely. I've started my own business and I'm working at home.
Mick: How exciting! So what's your new business?
Annie: I was never very interested in computer programming and I wanted to do something completely different. I'm making and selling cakes.
Mick: Wow! That's amazing. I mean, I knew you didn't enjoy computer programming, but I didn't know that you liked baking! It's great you can work at home.
Annie: Exactly.
Mick: How do you sell the cakes? Where do your customers come from?
Annie: I have several customers who order cakes through my website and I sell a few in the baker's shop in town, but nearly all of my cakes are sold at the market.
Mick: And do you like having your own business?
Annie: Well, I earned a lot more in my old job and was always going on holiday, but I don't really care about money. The hardest thing now is I have to decide everything by myself. When I had a job, I could talk to the people I worked with.

WRITING
SB P160

A JOB APPLICATION

1 As a class look at the photos and brainstorm answers to the questions. Elicit suggestions for what they can see in the photos and help with vocabulary as necessary, e.g. *diver, shark, trapeze artist, circus ring*.

2 Then allow students time to read the job adverts and talk about the good and bad points of each job. Feed back by comparing ideas with the whole class.

| A 1 | B 2 |

3 Read through the questions as a class, checking understanding. Students work in pairs to complete the information. Check answers as a class.

Place of work	
Job 1	with a circus which will travel in Europe
Job 2	at the Sea World Aquarium
Tasks	
Job 1	perform as a trapeze artist in a new show
Job 2	clean the shark tank
Salary	
Job 1	€25–€35,000 per year
Job 2	€40–€45,000 per year
Hours	
Job 1	6–8 performances a week
Job 2	35 hours a week
Qualifications	
Job 1	no formal qualifications
Job 2	degree in marine biology
Things to send	
Job 1	photos and videos of performances
Job 2	CV and letter

4 Draw attention to the application email and ask the class to identify who wrote it (Talia Jones). Then ask, *Who did she write to?* (Billy Cain, Cain's Circus) and, *What did she write about?* (the trapeze artist job).

Explain that the language used in this type of email is different from the language used in an email to a friend because it is more formal and polite. The writer is trying to make a good impression when he/she applies for a job. Tell students there are some fixed phrases they can learn (e.g. the ones in bold) to use in a formal email.

Then read through the email with the class before asking them to find the phrase which matches *a*.

Students match the rest of the expressions before checking answers as a class.

| a 2 | b 5 | c 4 | d 3 | e 6 | f 1 | g 8 | h 7 |

5 Students work in pairs to put the sentences in the correct order before checking as a class.

> **1** I am writing to apply for the job of English teacher as advertised on your website.
> **2** I am attaching my CV and a copy of my teaching diploma.
> **3** I am a patient, friendly teacher.
> **4** As you will see from my CV, I have worked for several schools in Grenada.
> **5** I look forward to hearing from you.

6 Go through the instructions with the class, checking understanding of the vocabulary in the notes. Then refer students back to the job advert before they start writing their email. Encourage students to include some of the expressions from Exercise 4.

When they finish writing, encourage them to check their work for spelling and grammar mistakes as well as the correct use of the new phrases and expressions.

✚ EXTENSION

Encourage students to think about the differences between an informal email to a friend and a formal email for a job application. Elicit from the class the different ways they can start and finish an email to a friend, e.g. *Dear, Hi, Hello, How are you?*, etc. and *Write soon, Best wishes, All the best, Love*, etc. Then tell students they are going to write an email to a friend telling them about the job application email they wrote.

Students work in pairs to make notes and then write an email to a friend telling them about the email in Exercise 4 or the one they wrote in Exercise 6. Encourage them to think about alternative words and expressions they can use, e.g. *I sent my CV.* (instead of *attached*); *I saw the advert …* (instead of *as advertised*).

When they have finished, students exchange emails with another pair for peer feedback.

SB P161

JOB INTERVIEW

1 Try to elicit *job interview* by asking students, *What usually happens after you send a job application?* Then read through the questions with the class. Allow a few minutes for students to discuss their answers in pairs before class feedback about the questions people ask and the questions students would ask potential employers in an interview.

2 🔊 101 Draw attention to the photo and ask students who it is to elicit, *Talia, the trapeze artist* (from page 160, Exercise 4). Tell students they are going to listen to her interview for the job. Students listen to complete the information.

| **1** 21 | **2** Circus Arts | **3** a year and a half |

AUDIOSCRIPT 🔊 101

Billy: Hello, Talia. I'm Billy Cain. Please take a seat.
Talia: Thank you.
Billy: So, you're 21 years old, is that right?
Talia: Yes, I am.
Billy: We liked your videos of your performances. Can you tell us about your qualifications and experience? It says on your CV that you have a Diploma in Circus Arts.
Talia: Yes, I studied for two years at the National Centre for Circus Arts in London and at the end of the course I got a diploma.
Billy: OK, that's interesting, but for us, experience of performing is more important, so how many years' experience of trapeze work do you have?
Talia: I started when I was 16, but I didn't perform all the time. I have a year's experience at the Melodia Variety Theatre and six months with Smith's Circus – so in total I have a year and a half's experience.
Billy: Can you tell us something about your other skills? Can you drive?
Talia: Yes, I can. I've got my driving licence.
Billy: Good. And we'll be travelling through a lot of different European countries. Which other languages do you speak?
Talia: Well my mother is Russian, so I speak Russian, English and a little Italian.

3 🔊 101 Students work in pairs to try to match the question parts before listening to the recording again to check answers. Feed back as a class.

| **1** e | **2** d | **3** a | **4** b | **5** c |

4 Go over the instructions to explain that these are the questions Talia asks. Students order the questions before class feedback.

> 1 What salary are you offering?
> 2 Are the costumes provided?
> 3 Will I get my own hotel room?
> 4 Am I going to perform with other people?
> 5 Who will be my boss?
> 6 How many hours will we practise?
> 7 How much time off will I get per week?

5 Students match the answers a–g with the questions in Exercise 4.

FAST FINISHERS

Students can invent different answers to the questions in Exercise 4.

> 1 b   2 g   3 f   4 a   5 c   6 d   7 e

6 102 Explain that we use different intonation when we are asking questions, depending on the type of question. Point out the different question types in the examples and then play the two *wh-* questions, asking students to listen to the intonation pattern. Play the recording again, if necessary, before playing the second two questions and asking students if they can hear the difference.

> 1 c   2 a

AUDIOSCRIPT 102

Man: What time do we start in the mornings?
Woman: Where is the photocopier?
Man: Can I park here?
Woman: Is this my chair?

7 102 Use the recording as a model for choral and then individual drilling.

⊕ EXTENSION

Refer students back to the questions in Exercise 4 and ask them to decide whether they are *wh-* questions or *yes/no* questions. Then ask them to practise the intonation patterns by reading them to a partner.

8 Go over the instructions as a class and ask students to work in pairs to write some questions. Stronger students can write other questions which are not included in the prompts. Students also need to think about the possible answer the interviewer might give.

9 Students work together to ask and answer the questions. Remind them to use the correct intonation in the questions and to make up appropriate answers to the questions. Then students change partners to play the other role.

EXAM FOCUS   SB P162
READING PART 4

✓ EXAM INFORMATION

In Reading Part 4, students read a text from which six words have been removed. Students choose the appropriate words to fill the gaps from six three-option multiple-choice questions. The main focus is on vocabulary, but there may be one or two questions which test grammar.

The whole Reading and Writing paper has seven parts. Parts 1–5 are reading tasks and Parts 6 and 7 are writing tasks. Students have 60 minutes in total to complete the paper, so they should spend about 15 minutes on the writing tasks and 45 minutes on the reading tasks. Students should allow about nine minutes to do Part 4 in the exam.

EXAM CHECK

1 Encourage students to look at the exam-style question in Exercise 2 and then work in pairs to match the sentence parts before checking as a class.

> 1 e   2 d   3 c   4 a   5 b

2 Allow students about nine minutes to complete the task under exam conditions, i.e. without conferring. Then check answers as a class. A stronger group can be encouraged to explain why they chose the answers they did.

> 1 C   2 B   3 A   4 A   5 C   6 B

UNIT 12 THROUGH LIFE **143**

LISTENING PART 3

SB P163

✓ EXAM INFORMATION

In Listening Part 3 students listen to a longer dialogue and answer five three-option multiple-choice questions. Students have to listen to identify key information and opinion. They hear the recording twice.

EXAM CHECK

1 Students complete the task by looking at the Exam task in Exercise 2 before checking answers as a class.

> **1** two   **2** five   **3** no   **4** three   **5** yes

2  103 Elicit ideas about how to approach Listening Part 3. (Read the situation and the questions carefully before listening. Keep listening even if you miss an answer as the recording will be repeated. Use the second listening to check your answers, etc.).

Tell students to quickly read through the questions and then play the recording twice before checking answers as a class. If possible, elicit explanations for why the other answers are wrong.

> **1** A   **2** B   **3** C   **4** A   **5** B

AUDIOSCRIPT 🎧 103

Narrator: For each question, choose the correct answer. You will hear Lena and Max talking about a course which Max has done. Now listen to the conversation.

Lena: Max, that course on working in a team – is it good?

Max: It's not bad. When my boss sent me I was worried – I thought he was angry with me for being bad at working in a team!

Lena: What's the teacher like?

Max: Some people thought she needed to help them more – she often seemed to explain things to only a few students. But she included lots of good examples. And it was interesting. We did lots of different things.

Lena: Was there anything that you didn't like?

Max: Getting to that college in the morning is hard – there's so much traffic. One day, most students didn't arrive until the coffee break! They should start later. Why, are you going to do the course?

Lena: Well, my job's different now from when I first got it. Before, I worked alone – now I'm part of a group. It's like having a completely new job – but without any extra money!

Max: So are you going to do it soon?

Lena: Well, next week's course is full. And so was next month's. But then someone decided not to go next month, so I can do it then. Better than waiting until next year!

Max: Enjoy it!

Read through the options in the *How was it?* section and elicit the meaning of each one that they learned in the first unit.

Ask students to tick the appropriate box. You might like to ask students to share how they felt about the task to get an indication of your students' confidence. Depending on your class, you might like to do this openly or allow students to give their feedback without their classmates seeing. For example, give students a piece of A4 paper each with the *How was it?* scale written in large letters. Allow students to tick the relevant box then hold up their papers at the same time so that you can see how well students think they are doing. Finally, ask students if they found it easier, harder or the same as the exam practice in previous units.

REAL WORLD

SB P164

PLANNING TO STUDY IN … GENEVA

1 Brainstorm students' ideas about the question. Talk about the good and bad things about studying in another country. Help students with vocabulary as necessary. Encourage the discussion by asking students to think about some of the following: keeping in touch with friends and family, language, food, accommodation.

2 Ask students if they know where Geneva is (Switzerland). Then give them three or four minutes to match the photos with the paragraphs and compare their answers with a partner. Check answers as a class.

> **1** C   **2** D   **3** A   **4** B

3 Read the statements as a class and help with vocabulary as necessary. Students work in pairs to decide whether the statements are true or false before checking answers in the texts.

Feed back as a class. Encourage students to correct the false statements.

> **1** T
> **2** F You can study any subject.
> **3** F You can go skiing in the winter.
> **4** F it's quite small.

4 Students work in pairs to match the words and phrases with the correct definition. Feed back as a class.

| 1 d | 2 c | 3 e | 4 a | 5 f | 6 b |

5 🔊 104 Go over the instructions with the class and ask them to suggest what the differences might be in the different situations. For example:

a   arranging a time and place to meet
b   talking about preparations and organization
c   personal questions and answers
d   questions and answers.

Play the recordings and ask students to make a note of one or two words or phrases which tell them the answer in each case. Repeat the recordings if necessary. Check answers as a class, encouraging students to tell you the notes they made.

| 1 d | 2 a | 3 c |

AUDIOSCRIPT 🔊 104

1

Receptionist: Hello. Can I help you?
Student: Yes. I'm a new student. Can you give me some information about the welcome event, please?
Receptionist: Of course. What would you like to know?
Student: What time does it start?
Receptionist: It starts at 7 o'clock this evening. You might want to get there nice and early. It can get quite crowded.
Student: OK, thanks. And which room is it in?
Receptionist: It's in the main hall. That's just by the main entrance to the building. You can't miss it. There are signs up all over the place.
Student: Thank you. Do I need to take anything with me?
Receptionist: Just your student card. I think that's it.
Student: Is there food at the event?
Receptionist: There are a few snacks, but not a full meal. And drinks, of course.
Student: OK. Thank you. Bye.
Receptionist: Bye. Enjoy the event.

2

Woman: Oh, hi, Xavier. How are things?
Man: Hi. I'm OK, thanks. There's a lot to do when you first arrive in a new place.
Woman: That's true. And it's quite hard to find your way around, too.
Man: Yes. And you don't want to ask for help all the time!
Woman: Yeah. Are you going to the welcome event later today?
Man: Yes, I want to go. How about you?
Woman: Yeah, I'm definitely going. It should be good, and hopefully we'll meet lots of people, too.
Man: Shall we go together?
Woman: That's a good idea. Where shall we meet?
Man: Let's meet in the student café near the main entrance at 6.30. We can have a coffee, then go to the event.
Woman: That sounds great. See you later.
Man: See you.

3

Man: Hi. Are you a new student?
Woman: Yes. My name's Maria.
Man: Nice to meet you. I'm Bartek.
Woman: Where are you from?
Man: I'm from Poland. And you?
Woman: From Italy.
Man: Oh, nice. I went to Rome last year. I really liked it. When did you arrive?
Woman: Last week, on Wednesday.
Man: Oh. I just arrived yesterday. What are you studying?
Woman: International Business. It's a one-year course, and I hope I can get some work experience in the holidays. What about you?
Man: I'm studying Biology.
Woman: Oh, that's interesting. Shall we go and find some food? I think there's some over there.
Man: Good idea. I think there are some …

PHRASES YOU MIGHT USE

6 🔊 104 Students complete the phrases before listening to the recordings to check their answers.

> 1 Can you give me   2 What time   3 Which room
> 4 Do I need to   5 Is there   6 about you

PHRASES YOU MIGHT HEAR

7 Students work in pairs to choose the correct definitions before checking answers as a class.

> 1 a   2 b   3 a   4 b

WATCH

8 ▶ Go over the instructions and then play the video. Then students talk to a partner about what they learned about the different prompts and take notes.

9 ▶ Students watch the video again to complete their notes and check their answers.

> **the city:** Switzerland, close to the Alps, high mountains all around it, old and modern and lots of young people study there. One of the most famous sights in the city is the Water Jet, the water goes up to 140 metres into the air.
> **organisations in the city:** a lot of well-known organisations have their main buildings in Geneva, such as the United Nations and the Red Cross. Also a lot of big companies have offices there, so a great place to study and get work experience.
> **the university:** one of the best universities in the world, attracts students from all over the world, nearly 40% of the students from other countries; has a lot of modern scientific equipment, great place to study science; halls of residence all over the city, and most students choose to live in these, but some choose to live in apartments.
> **life in the city:** quite expensive, but clean and safe; good public transport, lots of cafés and restaurants, and in the winter you can try skiing

VIDEOSCRIPT ▶ Geneva

> Geneva is in Switzerland, close to the Alps. There are high mountains all around it, which make it a beautiful place to live. The city centre has a mix of old and modern buildings, and lots of young people study there.
> One of its most famous sights is this tall fountain. It's called the Water Jet, and the water goes up to 140 metres into the air.
> Many famous organisations have their main buildings here, like the United Nations and the Red Cross, which helps people all over the world when there are natural disasters.
> A lot of big international companies also have offices in Geneva, so it's a great place to study and get work experience.
> The University of Geneva is one of the best universities in the world, and it attracts students from all over the world. In fact, nearly 40% of students who come here are from other countries, so it's very international. The university has a lot of modern scientific equipment, so it's a great place to study science. There are halls of residence all over the city, and most students choose to live in these, but some live in apartments in the centre.
> Life in Geneva is quite expensive, but the city is clean and safe, so the quality of life is good. There's good public transport, so you can travel around the city easily. And there are lots of cafés and restaurants. And, of course, it's in the mountains, so in the winter you can go skiing.

LIFE COMPETENCIES
SB P165

SOCIAL RESPONSIBILITIES

10 Go over the instructions as a class, then divide the students into groups of three or four.

Encourage students to make notes for each prompt to plan their event.

11 Each group makes a two-minute presentation of their plan to the rest of the class.

At the end, the class decide together on one plan bringing together the best ideas from the different presentations.

➡ **WORKBOOK** / Unit 12, page 52

13 ABOUT ME

UNIT OBJECTIVES

Topic:	clothes and people
Grammar:	comparative and superlative adjectives; equal comparisons with (*not*) as ... as
Vocabulary:	personality adjectives; *look like* and *be like*
Listening:	Part 2: gap-fill: a monologue about a new shop
Reading:	Part 5: completing gaps in an email
Speaking:	describing appearance and personality
Writing:	a product review
Pronunciation:	pronouncing *-est* endings
Exam focus:	Reading Part 5; Listening Part 2
Real world:	shopping for clothes in Dubai

Ask your students to watch the Grammar on the Move videos on pages 168 and 171. You can use these to present or reinforce comparative adjectives and superlative adjectives.

READING
SB P166

FAMILY RELATIONSHIPS

1 If you have any students with sensitive family situations you may wish to avoid some of the questions in this unit. Introduce the topic by telling the class about your own family, then ask students to discuss the questions in pairs. Feed back by finding out if most of the class prefer big or small families.

2 Draw attention to the photos and allow a minute for students to quickly scan the texts to answer the question.

> **A:** Aidan
> **B:** Jasmine

3 Read through the questions with the class and ask students to find the answers in the texts before comparing with a partner. Then feed back as a class.

> **1** She hasn't got any.
> **2** how to draw and paint
> **3** She's getting married.
> **4** six
> **5** younger
> **6** move to/get his own flat

4 Draw attention to the words in blue in the text and remind students that reading around the words will help them understand their meaning. Encourage students to read the complete sentence before choosing the words to fill the gaps. Check answers as a class.

FAST FINISHERS

Students can write additional sentences of their own using the words in colour.

> **1** only child **2** single **3** engaged, fiancé
> **4** stepfather **5** stepsister **6** relatives
> **7** important person in my life

5 Read through the prompts with the whole class, checking understanding.

With a weaker group, provide one or two examples of answers from your own experience.

Then ask students to work in pairs, encouraging them to ask questions for more information and give extended answers rather than using just one or two words.

Feed back by asking one or two students to tell the class about their partner's answers.

VOCABULARY
SB P167

PERSONALITY ADJECTIVES

1 Direct students' attention to the photos and elicit a description of the person in the first photo by asking four or five students to each say a sentence. With a weaker class make a note on the board of some useful vocabulary such as *tall, thin, slim, straight, dark, glasses*, etc.

Put students in pairs to take turns to make sentences to describe the other photo.

2 🎧 105 Read the instructions and then play the recording for students to label the photos. Check answers as a class.

> **A** Harry **B** Leo

AUDIOSCRIPT 🔊 105

Jane: Oh, let me see that photo … are those little girls your stepsisters?

Aidan: Yes, that's Minnie on the right and Lulu on the left. Aren't they sweet?

Jane: Yes, they are! I wish I had little sisters like that. But what about your brothers? They aren't in the photo? What do they look like?

Aidan: Well Harry is the oldest and he's very tall already. He's taller than me – and thinner. He goes running and to the gym a lot, so he's quite thin and very fit. He's got straight brown hair and brown eyes and he wears glasses. He looks a lot like me – you can see that we're brothers. However, he's much cleverer than I am – he's really brilliant! He's studying maths at university and he's really good at it – he gets great marks in all his exams. Leo's the youngest. He's got very fair, curly hair and blue eyes. He's not very tall, but he's quite good-looking – much better-looking than me and Harry! And he's funnier. He's always making people laugh. All the girls like him. But Leo and I don't get on very well. He's not my favourite brother.

Jane: Really, why's that? What's he like?

Aidan: He's just very annoying! To start with he's a bit lazy. He doesn't help around the house and I often do his jobs for him. And he's also not very kind to Harry. Leo's younger than Harry, but he's much more confident and sociable. He has lots of friends and goes out a lot, but Harry is quiet and shy. Leo makes jokes about Harry and laughs at him in front of his friends.

Jane: No, that isn't very kind – poor Harry! Does he get upset?

Aidan: No, I don't think he notices. He's thinking about other things, but I notice – and I don't like it.

3 🔊 105 Encourage students to read the sentences before they listen to the recording again to complete the gaps. Check answers as a class.

1 sweet	**2** brilliant	**3** annoying, lazy	**4** kind
5 confident, sociable		**6** quiet	

4 Students complete the definitions before class feedback.

1 brilliant	**2** sweet	**3** Sociable	**4** quiet

5 Students work in pairs to answer the question.

⊕ EXTENSION

Students talk to a partner and describe a person they know, or a famous person, who they think fits each adjective and say why.

LOOK LIKE AND BE LIKE

6 Read the two questions and answers, A and B, with the class. Then look at the questions together. Give students a minute or so to answer the questions with a partner before checking answers as a class.

Explain to students that *look like* is an ordinary verb (so uses *do/does* in the question form) while question B uses the expression *to be like* and the verb *to be* does not use *do* or *does*. Elicit that A asks about a person's physical appearance while B asks about their character or personality.

1 A	**2** B	**3** A	**4** B

➡ **GRAMMAR REFERENCE** / Page 223

7 Students do the task individually before checking answers with a partner. Ask them to explain the answer they gave if it is different from their partner's.

1 B	**2** B	**3** A	**4** B	**5** A

8 Read through the instructions and if necessary choose a famous person to use as an example. Ask the class to take turns telling you a sentence about what the person looks like and then what the person is like.

Then students continue in pairs describing another person they both know. Finally, students describe someone, as in the example sentences, while their partner listens and then guesses who is being described.

⊕ EXTENSION

Students take turns to ask their partner two questions about someone in their family. For example, *What does your brother look like?*; *What is he like?*

GRAMMAR
SB P168

COMPARATIVE ADJECTIVES

1 Read through the example sentences with the class and ask them to underline all the adjectives.

Tell students that all the adjectives in these sentences are being used to compare people.

Work through the questions as a class or in pairs before checking together.

> **1** -er **2** more **3** than **4** better

Read through the box with the class looking at the examples.

⊕ EXTENSION

Write a list of adjectives the students know on the board. Ask the class to call out which adjective each word on the board is similar to when making the comparative form.

For example, *happy* follows the same rule as *funny* when making a comparison. Other adjectives could be, *intelligent* (expensive), *small* (thin), *sad* (big), *difficult* (expensive), *easy* (funny).

➡ **GRAMMAR REFERENCE** / Page 222

2 Ask the class if they know the names Alistair and Jonny Brownlee. If they do, elicit any information they know about them. If not, ask them to look at the title and the picture (of a trophy) and brainstorm suggestions for what they might be famous for. Accept all answers and then allow students two minutes to read the text to find out if any of the suggestions were correct. Tell students not to worry about the gaps at this stage.

Then students read the text again and fill the gaps with the comparative forms of the adjectives. Feed back as a class.

> **1** older **2** taller **3** more successful **4** stronger **5** faster **6** quicker

3 With a weaker class work through an example together, encouraging different students to make sentences using the adjectives in the list. Then students continue to do the rest of the exercise in pairs. Feedback by asking one or two students to say a sentence.

PUSH YOURSELF B1
SB P168

GRAMMAR: EQUAL COMPARISONS WITH (NOT) AS ... AS

LEAD-IN

With books closed, explain that there are other ways of comparing two things or people. Then give a few examples using students in the class. For example, *Rachele is as fair as Pablo; Jan is not as tall as Cristina.* Elicit the meanings, e.g. *Is Rachele fairer than Pablo?* (no); *Is Pablo fairer than Rachele?* (no); *Are they the same?* (yes); *Is Jan taller than Cristina?* (no).

1 Then open books and draw attention to the speech bubbles. Students read the rules and complete them. When checking answers, point out that we are comparing, but we don't use the comparative form of the adjectives here. We use this structure to say if two people or things are the same or not.

> **a** the same **b** different

2 Students complete the sentences before class feedback.

> **1** not as shy as **2** as good as **3** not as expensive as
> **4** not as dangerous as **5** as boring as **6** as long as

➡ **GRAMMAR REFERENCE** / Page 223

LISTENING PART 2 TRAINING
SB P169

✓ EXAM INFORMATION

In Part 2 of the Listening paper students listen to a longer monologue. They have to fill five gaps with one word, number, date or time. One word is always dictated and the spelling of that word has to be correct. Students listen for names, places, numbers, dates or times. In the exam the recording is played twice.

1 Encourage students to discuss the questions and give reasons for their answers. If necessary, ask them to think about why some people like to have a lot of clothes and shoes and whether you can understand anything about a person's personality from the colours or style of their clothes.

2 Turn to page 195 and draw attention to the photos and the adjectives describing each one. Then allow students two minutes to match the texts with the photos. Ask students to answer the question in pairs and say why they are most similar to that photo, e.g. *I'm sporty because I like wearing trainers and tracksuits.*

Ask students if they know any other names for any of the words in bold in the texts and, if possible, elicit *sneakers* for *trainers*. If students do not know the difference, read through the *Did you know?* box at the bottom of page 169 as a class. You can also point out that *wallet* is used in British English to refer to where a man usually keeps his money.

> **1** D casual **2** C sporty **3** B smart
> **4** E fashionable **5** A cool

3 🎧 106 Read through the instructions with the class. Ask students to work in pairs to decide what type of word they are listening for in each gap: 1 a date; 2 an activity / a type of person / a season / an event; 3 a time; 4 a name. Remind students that in the exam it is a good idea to think about what type of word they are listening for before listening. Point out that in the exam there will be five gaps but here there are only four. Then play the recording. Students compare answers with a partner before listening to the recording again to check answers.

> **1** 1st October **2** teenagers **3** 7.30 **4** Derrick

AUDIOSCRIPT 🎧 106

Woman: A fantastic new shop is opening in town. It's called Lily's Fashion Boutique and it's going to open in the town centre. You'll need to know the address; it's 149 High Street. There will be an opening party on September 30th and the store will open on the first of October. As you know, there are already many shops here selling ladies' and men's clothes, but Lily's Fashion Boutique will be the only store where you can buy things for teenagers to wear.

The store will open at 9.30 in the morning and shut at 7.30 in the evening. This is later than most shops in town, which close at 7 o'clock. If you're looking for work in the new shop, contact the manager. His name's Mr Derrick. I'll spell that for you – D-E-double-R-I-C-K. He'll be happy to give more information.

READING PART 5 TRAINING
SB P169

✓ EXAM INFORMATION

In Reading Part 5, students read a short message or email and complete six gaps with one word each.

The task in the Student's Book is simplified with five questions instead of six. This section teaches students that they should read the words before and after the gaps to help them decide which type of word is missing from the sentence and then which grammar word fits best.

Elicit what students have to do in Reading Part 5 (read a text with six gaps and choose the correct word to fill the gap).

After reading through the example as a class, ask students to work in pairs to decide which type of word goes in each gap, e.g. past tense verb, part of comparative adjective, preposition, part of fixed expression, part of superlative adjective.

Then students complete the text using one correct word for each gap. Check answers as a class.

> **1** went / was **2** than **3** to **4** lot **5** more

READING
SB P170

1 Ask the class if there are any famous people they know who dress well. Hold a brief class discussion using the questions in the book and encourage students to tell you what they think *dressing well* means. If necessary, prompt with vocabulary such as, *expensive clothes, smart clothes, original style, famous brands,* etc.

2 Draw attention to the photos and ask students to describe what the people are wearing. Help with vocabulary as necessary. Then students scan the texts quickly to match each one with a photo. Tell them it is not necessary to understand the whole text at this stage.

> **1** B **2** C **3** A

3 Read through the questions with the class, checking understanding, e.g. *Where can you buy a designer dress?* (*Armani, Stella McCartney,* etc.); *Is 'excited' a positive emotion?* (yes), etc.

Then students read the texts again and answer the questions. Check answers as a class.

> **1** Rihanna **2** Eddie Redmayne **3** Lupita Nyong'o
> **4** Rihanna **5** Eddie Redmayne

4 Point out the words in red in the texts and allow students two or three minutes to complete the sentences with those words. Note that sometimes the words in the text have to change from singular to plural, or vice versa. Check answers as a class.

| 1 jewellery | 2 brands | 3 suits, ties | 4 fashions |
| 5 trainers | 6 handbag | 7 sunglasses | 8 sandals |

FAST FINISHERS

Students can write one or two sentences about themselves using the words in red in the text.

5 Students work in pairs to discuss the questions. You could extend the discussion to talk about the worst dressed celebrities, too. Then students could discuss their own personal style, if appropriate.

SB P171

SUPERLATIVE ADJECTIVES

1 Ask if students know when we use the superlative form (to compare three or more things or people).

Allow students a few minutes to read the rules and answer the questions using the examples in the text and the rules to help them. Check answers as a class and use the information in the box to add detail and examples. It may be helpful to ask students to compare the form of superlative adjectives with that of comparative adjectives (-er/-est, more / the most, etc.).

| 1 -est | 2 most | 3 the | 4 best |

➡ **GRAMMAR REFERENCE** / Page 222

2 Students complete the sentences using superlative adjectives. Check answers as a class.

| 1 the most boring | 2 the cheapest | 3 the ugliest |
| 4 the most famous | 5 the best, the most expensive |
| 6 the hottest |

3 Read the title of the article and give students a minute to scan the text to find out what is *new* (recycled clothes). Then students work in pairs to complete the gaps with the correct form of the adjective provided. Check answers as a class, focusing on spelling as well as form.

| 1 more important | 2 the most interesting | 3 more difficult | 4 more expensive | 5 happier |

4 🔊 107 Ask student to focus on the pronunciation of *-est* in the adjectives on the recording. Play the recording and ask students to repeat the sound.

/ɪst/

AUDIOSCRIPT 🔊 107

hottest, biggest, thinnest, prettiest, funniest, ugliest

5 🔊 107 Play the recording again and ask students to repeat the words with the correct pronunciation of the *-est* ending.

6 Read through the prompts, checking understanding, and if necessary ask one or two students to answer the first prompt in front of the class. Encourage students to use superlative adjectives and the correct pronunciation. Ask one or two questions, as appropriate, to elicit more information, e.g. *Where did you buy the dress? How much did it cost? What colour was it? Did you enjoy wearing it?* etc.

Then students work in pairs to continue the exercise. Tell students to ask their partner one or two questions to find out more.

Feed back by asking one or two students to tell the class their answers and allow the class to ask follow-up questions.

7 Elicit a brief class discussion to answer the questions.

BACKGROUND INFORMATION

Recycled clothes could refer to the clothes made from other materials such as plastic, as described in the text, or clothes made from textiles or old clothes which have been reused. Second-hand or vintage clothing is also popular in some places. Generally the term *vintage* is used for clothes which are at least 20 years old.

SB P172

A PRODUCT REVIEW

LEAD-IN

With books closed try to elicit *review* by asking questions such as, *Where can you find information about something new before you buy it?*

1 Then open books and allow students time to discuss the questions with a partner.

Feed back as a class by comparing ideas and asking one or two follow-up questions such as, *Why is it (not) a good idea to read/watch reviews?*

2 Read through the instructions and the questions as a class. Then ask students to read the text and answer the questions. When checking answers, encourage students to use complete sentences.

> **1** People can buy the trainers now, online and in sports shops.
> **2** He likes the colours; they are light and comfortable to wear; they are so cool they will make all your other clothes look good.
> **3** They are expensive, not good value for money, not strong or practical; his feet got wet when he went out in the rain.
> **4** You shouldn't buy them if you want trainers to wear every day. You should buy them if you want trainers that look great.

3 Draw attention to the phrases in bold and point out that there is more than one answer to some of the questions. Students work in pairs to complete questions 1–3 with phrases from the text before checking as a class.

> **1** I fell in love with … They are the best-looking trainers I've seen for a long time. … For me, the best thing about them is …
> **2** On the less positive side …
> **3** So do I recommend … It depends on what you want … (aren't) a good buy …

4 Ask students why they think the writer uses exclamation marks in the first and last sentences (they show enthusiasm and make the words sound more exciting). Encourage students to offer suggestions to answer the question, before confirming the correct meaning. Point out that *on sale* in the first sentence comes from the same verb as *sell out* in the last sentence.

It may be helpful to elicit or explain the difference in meaning between *on sale* and *sales*, which students may have seen online or in the shops (*on sale* means you can buy something, it is available to buy; *sales* are when products are sold at a lower price than usual or with a discount for a limited period of time).

> *Sell out* means that the shops/websites will sell all the trainers and none will be left to buy.

5 Students work in pairs to match the paragraphs to the topics.

> **Paragraph 1** d introduction: where/when you can buy the product
> **Paragraph 2** c the good things about the product
> **Paragraph 3** a the bad things about the product
> **Paragraph 4** b conclusion: overall opinion of the product and recommendation

6 Ask students to discuss in which part of the review they could use the phrases, before checking as a class.

> **1** Paragraph 2
> **2** Paragraph 4
> **3** Paragraph 3
> **4** Paragraph 2
> **5** Paragraph 4
> **6** Paragraph 3

7 Students can work in pairs or individually to plan their writing. Encourage them to make notes for the points listed and help with vocabulary as necessary. Then tell them to separate their ideas into paragraphs as in Exercise 5 before starting to write.

8 Before starting to write, remind students to use the expressions in Exercise 6, as well as the adjectives and other vocabulary from their notes. Students check their own work before exchanging with a partner.

During peer feedback, encourage students to say at least one good thing that their partner did, as well as pointing out any mistakes.

SB P173

APPEARANCE AND PERSONALITY

1 Draw attention to the photos and read through the questions as a class. Then students work in pairs to ask and answer the questions. As you monitor the activity, make sure students are using the present simple and continuous appropriately, e.g. *I think they're at a café. They are talking and drinking.*

2 Read the instructions and ask individual students to complete the sentence starters about a person in one of the photos as an example for the task. Make sure that students remember the difference between sentences with *look, is, has got* and *wear*:

He looks happy. / He is tall. / She's got long blonde hair. / She's wearing sunglasses.

Students continue to describe the other people in the photos to a partner, taking it in turns to listen and describe.

3 Read through the phrases in the speech bubbles as a class and ask students to comment on them by answering the questions.

> **1** A **2** A & B **3** A & B **4** B **5** B **6** B

4 108 Go through the instructions and then play the recording. If necessary, repeat the recording before checking answers as a class. Ask students to tell you which words or phrases helped them decide.

> **1** B **2** A

AUDIOSCRIPT 🔊 108

1
Man: Well, I think the people in the middle of the photo are friends. I'm sure they're having a really good time because they look very happy. They are wearing casual clothes, like jeans and shirts, and the tall man with the dark hair is wearing sunglasses, too. One of the young women has got long, red hair and she's got something on her face – it might be face paint. Perhaps they are at a music festival or gig. The women are holding some fruity drinks, but the men haven't got any. It's a sunny day, but I don't think it's very hot because I can see some people with jackets in the background. There are trees with lots of green, so I think it's probably summer. It could be in Britain.

2
Woman: So, I can see a little café in a street. It's really quiet there because there are only two people walking along the street. I think it's probably in a town or city because there are lots of parked cars, but maybe it's early in the morning. In the middle of the photo I can see two people sitting at a small round table. There are some coffee or tea cups, so maybe they're having breakfast. The people are young, maybe 25 to 30 years old and I think they are going to work because they are wearing smart clothes. They look quite serious – maybe they're thinking about work. The woman has got red hair and is wearing a dark jacket and skirt and the man has got short, dark hair and is wearing jeans and a jacket. The woman is holding something, but I can't see what it is. I think one of them goes to work by bike because I can see a bike and a bike helmet behind them.

5 🔊 108 Students work in pairs to complete the sentences before listening to the recording to check answers. It may be helpful to stop the recording after each phrase.

Point out that there is no difference in meaning or use between *maybe* and *perhaps*, or between *it could be* and *it might be*. These two expressions are used when we are talking about a possibility or something we are not sure about, so have a similar meaning to *I think* in this context. *Probably* is used to talk about something we have a little more certainty about, and *I'm sure* is used when we are certain.

After going through the answers, try to elicit some sentences from the class about the same photos using the expressions in the box to check understanding of the similarities and differences in meaning.

| 1 I think | 2 I'm sure | 3 it might be | 4 Perhaps |
| 5 I don't think | 6 probably | 7 could be | 8 maybe |

6 Students use the language on the page to talk about the photo on page 194. Elicit one or two examples to check understanding of the task before allowing students a few minutes to continue in pairs.

EXAM FOCUS
SB P174

READING PART 5

✓ EXAM INFORMATION

In Reading Part 5, students read a short message or email and complete six gaps with one word each.

The whole Reading and Writing paper has seven parts. Parts 1–5 are reading tasks and Parts 6 and 7 are writing tasks. Students have 60 minutes in total to complete the exam, so they should spend about 15 minutes on the writing tasks and 45 minutes on the reading tasks. They should allow about nine minutes to complete Part 5.

EXAM CHECK

1 Students look at the exam-style task in Exercise 2 and work through the task in pairs before checking answers as a class.

1 F It tests your grammar.
2 F There are no options.
3 F There may be two shorter texts.
4 T
5 T

2 Remind students of the exam training task they did on page 169 and tell them they are now going to do a full-length exam-style question. Encourage students to read the instructions and the whole text before trying to complete the gaps. Allow about nine minutes for students to complete the task under exam conditions (without conferring with a partner).

When they have finished, students can check their answers with a partner, explaining why they chose the word they did if possible before class feedback.

| 1 than | 2 of | 3 Did | 4 Was | 5 there |
| 6 Would |

LISTENING PART 2
SB P175

✓ EXAM INFORMATION

In Part 2 of the Listening paper students listen to a longer monologue. They have to fill five gaps with one word, number, date or time. One word is always dictated and the spelling of that word has to be correct. Students listen for names, places, numbers, dates or times. In the exam the recording is played twice.

UNIT 13 ABOUT ME

EXAM CHECK

1 Encourage students to look at the exam-style question in Exercise 2 to help them answer the questions. Check answers as a class.

> **1** c **2** d **3** e **4** b **5** a

2 🔊 109 Allow students a minute to read through the instructions and the questions before playing the recording twice. Check answers as a class.

> **1** 9.15 / quarter past nine **2** Tuesday **3** Wralstone
> **4** smartphone **5** dress

AUDIOSCRIPT 🔊 109

Narrator: For each question, write the correct answer in the gap. Write one word or a number or a date or a time. You will hear a woman talking at the start of a course on fashion.

Woman: Welcome to this short summer course on fashion. When I've finished speaking, your teacher will take you to the North room for your classes. Thank you for being here at quarter to eight. The early start was because there's so much information to give you. Classes begin at 9.15 today, and every other day. There's been a change to the timetable: on the one we sent you, it says Wednesday for the lesson on drawing, but it's actually going to be on Tuesday. Then on Thursday a famous fashion photographer is coming to talk to you. His name is Peter Wralstone – you spell that W-R-A-L-S-T-O-N-E. We'll give you most of the things you need for the course – a pen, notepad, etc., but please make sure you have your smartphone to take photos – you'll use that every day. On the last day, you'll make something. I'm sure you've all made a skirt at least once already, so it'll be a dress. That's a little more difficult!

Read through the options in the *How was it?* section and elicit the meaning of each one that they learned in the first unit.

Ask students to tick the appropriate box. You might like to ask students to share how they felt about the task to get an indication of your students' confidence. Depending on your class, you might like to do this openly or allow students to give their feedback without their classmates seeing. For example, give students a piece of A4 paper each with the *How was it?* scale written in large letters. Allow students to tick the relevant box then hold up their papers at the same time so that you can see how well students think they are doing. Finally, ask students if they found it easier, harder or the same as the exam practice in Unit 1.

REAL WORLD

SB P176

SHOPPING FOR CLOTHES IN ... DUBAI

LEAD-IN

Draw attention to the three photos and ask what students can see. Try to elicit *market, shopping mall, stalls, big wheel, festival*.

1 Then students work in pairs to answer the question. Feed back by asking four or five students to tell the class about their preference.

2 Give students time to read the introduction and answer the question.

> Prices are lower.

3 Students scan the three texts, without worrying about understanding every word, and match each one to photos A–C. Feed back as a class.

> **1** B **2** A **3** C

4 Read the statements as a class and help with vocabulary as necessary. Then students work in pairs to find the answers in the texts.

Feed back as a class. Encourage students to correct the false statements.

> **1** F There are lots of malls. **2** F Mornings are a good time because it's quieter. **3** T **4** F The prices aren't fixed, so they can change. **5** T **6** T

5 Students find the words and phrases in the texts and choose the correct definition. Explain that they can check their answers by substituting the phrase in the text with the answer they choose. Feed back as a class.

> **1** a **2** a **3** a **4** b **5** b **6** a

6 🔊 110 Go over the instructions with the class.

Play the recordings and ask students to make a note of one or two words or phrases which tell them the answer in each case. Repeat the recordings if necessary. Check answers as a class, encouraging students to tell you the notes they made.

> **1** d **2** c **3** b

AUDIOSCRIPT 🔊 110

1
Assistant: Hello. Can I help you?
Customer: Yes. I really like this dress, but it's too small. Do you have a bigger size? I'm not sure what size this one is.
Assistant: Let me see. This is a size 36. With designer clothes like this, the sizes are all international, so we use the same sizes here as in most countries in Europe. We usually have all sizes in stock, so let me see if we've got a size 38. Do you want the same colour?
Customer: Yes, I like this colour. But do you have it in other colours? Maybe I could see those, too?
Assistant: No problem. Ah, yes. Here we are. This is a 38. We've got it in red or green. Would you like to try it on?
Customer: Yes, please. Can I try them both?
Assistant: Of course. There you go. The changing rooms are just over there, on your left.
Customer: Thank you.

2
Assistant: Hello. Can I help you?
Customer: Yes, please. Are these shoes in the sale?
Assistant: I'm afraid not. They're full price.
Customer: Oh. So, how much are they?
Assistant: They're 450 Dirham.
Customer: Oh, OK. Is there a discount for students?
Assistant: No, I'm sorry, we don't offer any discounts. But there are plenty of other shoes in the sales. If you come this way, I can show you our special offers. Here you are. These are all the sale items. There are some very good price reductions at the moment. Everything on this shelf is half price, so it's worth taking a look.
Customer: OK, thanks for your help.

3
Customer 1: So, what do you think? How do they look?
Customer 2: They're lovely jeans and they look great on you. That colour really suits you. Do you like them?
Customer 1: I'm not sure about them. They're a bit loose. What do you think?
Customer 2: Hmm. I can see what you mean. What about these jeans?
Customer 1: I'll go and try them on. Back in a minute!
Customer 1: Right. How do they look?
Customer 2: Wow! They look amazing! Do you like them?
Customer 1: Yes, I really like these ones. They fit me perfectly and they're really comfortable to wear, too.
Customer 2: Yes. And the colour's nicer than the other one. How much are they?
Customer 1: That's the other good thing about them. They're on special offer for the shopping festival, so they've got 30% off.
Customer 2: A bargain!
Customer 1: Yeah. I think I'll get them!

PHRASES YOU MIGHT USE

7 🔊 110 Students work in pairs to complete the phrases before listening to the recording again to check their answers.

1 bigger	**2** colours	**3** sale	**4** How much
5 discount	**6** look	**7** suits	**8** fit

PHRASES YOU MIGHT HEAR

8 Students work in pairs to choose the correct definitions before checking answers as a class.

1 b **2** a **3** b **4** a

WATCH

9 ▶ Go through the instructions with the class and check understanding. Play the video and encourage students to take notes for each of the prompts. Allow a few minutes for students to compare their notes with a partner.

the city: in the United Arab Emirates; a big, modern city important for business; lots of interesting modern buildings and some of the tallest buildings in the world; on the coast, popular with tourists, lots of beaches, some on islands built especially for tourism; gets very hot in summer, sometimes 50 degrees.

shopping malls: more than 70 shopping malls; Dubai Mall is the biggest shopping mall in the world; designer clothes are often cheaper than in other countries; malls also have other interesting things, like an aquarium and an indoor ski slope!

the souks: the place to go if you want cheaper clothes, colourful scarves, carpets, gold jewellery, tasty spices for cooking with, and foods grown in the country, like dates.

the shopping festival: started in 1995, now takes place for one month every year; entertainment in the streets, people come all over the world to find cheap designer clothes; Dubai Global Village has stalls selling clothes and other things from over 40 different countries; there are fireworks at night.

VIDEOSCRIPT ▶ Dubai

Dubai is in the United Arab Emirates. It's a big, modern city that is important for business.

It has a lot of interesting modern buildings, including some of the tallest buildings in the world.

It's also on the coast, and is a popular place for tourists. There are lots of beaches, like the ones on these islands, which were specially built for tourism.

Be warned though, in summer it gets very hot, sometimes up to 50 degrees, so make sure you use sun cream and drink plenty of water.

Many tourists come to Dubai for the shopping. The city has more than 70 shopping malls. The Dubai Mall is the biggest shopping mall in the world.

Dubai is popular for shopping because things such as designer clothes are often cheaper than in other countries. As well as the shops, the malls also have other interesting things, like this aquarium, and one even has an indoor ski slope!

The *souks* are the place to go if you want cheaper clothes, or colourful scarves. You can also buy carpets, gold jewellery, tasty spices for cooking with, and foods that are grown in the country, like dates. The Dubai Shopping Festival started in 1995, and now takes place for one month every year.

There's entertainment in the streets, and people come from all over the world to buy their cheaper clothes. The Dubai Global Village has stalls selling clothes and other things from over 40 different countries. And there are fireworks at night, to make shopping for clothes a really amazing experience!

LIFE COMPETENCIES
SB P177

CREATIVTY AND INNOVATION

10 ▶ Play the video again and ask students to check their answers in pairs. Go over the instructions, checking understanding. Brainstorm some ideas for what to write into a search engine in order to find the necessary information. For example, *currency exchange rate*, *shopping in Dubai*, etc. It may be helpful to suggest one half of the class 'shops' in a shop and the other half in a *souk* to be able to compare what they are able to buy with that amount of money. Students can research the information in class if you have internet access. Otherwise, they can do the research at home and present their ideas and choices to the class in the next lesson.

➡ **WORKBOOK** / *Unit 13, page 56*

14 PLAY IT, WATCH IT, LOVE IT

UNIT OBJECTIVES

Topic:	sport
Grammar:	can, must, have to, need to; tenses review
Vocabulary:	sports; do, play and go with sports; adverbs
Listening:	listening for gist and detail: an interview about Kenyan runners
Reading:	reading for gist and specific information: a text about football
Speaking:	Part 2: discussing pictures about sports
Writing:	Part 7: a story with picture prompts
Pronunciation:	the /ɔː/ sound
Exam focus:	Writing Part 7; Speaking Part 2
Real world:	going to a sports event in Madrid

Ask your students to watch the Grammar on the Move video on page 180. You can use this to present or reinforce *can, must, have to,* and *need to.*

VOCABULARY
SB P178

SPORTS

1 Brainstorm the names of sports students do, watch or know on the board. Then students work in pairs to ask and answer the questions. If students are not interested in sports, ask them to say why not. Feed back with the class, finding out how many different sports the students enjoy doing or watching.

2 Students work in pairs to match the photos with the sports. Then they continue to do the quiz as a race. Check answers as a class.

> **Photos: A** basketball **B** rugby **C** cricket
> **D** athletics **E** tennis **F** football
> **Quiz: 1** tennis **2** football **3** athletics **4** rugby
> **5** cricket **6** basketball

3 🎧 111 Remind students that these are the most popular sports in the world and ask them to work in pairs to put them in order of popularity. Play the recording so that students can check their answers.

> Most popular to least popular:
> **1** football **2** basketball **3** cricket **4** tennis
> **5** athletics **6** rugby

4 Have students make a note of what they think are the six most popular sports in their country and compare ideas with a partner and then the class. Elicit ideas to explain the differences between the most popular sports in their country and the world.

AUDIOSCRIPT 🎧 111

Man: Football is the most popular sport in the world. People play and watch football in every country and on every continent in the world. The second most popular sport is basketball. The game comes from the USA and is very popular in North and South America, but there are also lots of basketball fans in China and Europe. Cricket is the world's third most popular sport. This might be a surprise for some people because cricket is not well known in many countries. But you will find a lot of cricket fans in countries like India, Pakistan, the UK, Australia and New Zealand. Tennis is the world's fourth most popular sport. Both men and women play and enjoy tennis all over the world on indoor or outdoor courts. One of the most popular sports in the summer Olympic Games is athletics and it's the fifth most popular sport in the world. In sixth place is rugby. People mostly play rugby in Europe and English-speaking countries like Australia and New Zealand, but it's also very popular in Argentina.

5 Draw attention to the words in bold in the quiz and ask students to choose the correct answer in the sentences by reading the words in context in the quiz. Check answers as a class.

⊕ EXTENSION

Ask students if they can name any other sports which use a bat, e.g. *table tennis, baseball*; a racket, e.g. *squash, badminton*; or a net, e.g. *volleyball, badminton, netball*. Then ask which other sports have goals, e.g. *hockey, water polo*; and in which sports you throw something, e.g. *discus, shot put, hammer, javelin*.

If students do other sports, they may be interested in the specific vocabulary for their sport, e.g. *golf club, hockey stick, ice hockey puck, gymnastics,* etc.

> **1** kick **2** throw, team **3** winning, scored
> **4** racket **5** races **6** net **7** bat, match

UNIT 14 PLAY IT, WATCH IT, LOVE IT

READING
SB P179

1 Ask students to remember the most popular sport in the world (football). Read the quotation from Fernando Torres (a Spanish professional footballer) and:

- encourage the class to suggest what they think the quote means.
- ask students to work in pairs and decide if they think this idea of being a team is true for other team sports.
- ask students to talk to their partner about whether they are football fans and why (not). Ask some students to tell the class how they feel.

⊕ EXTENSION

The discussion could be opened out to talk about whether students think team sports are better than individual sports and why some people prefer one or the other. What about the team behind individual professional sports people, e.g. his/her trainer, physio, psychologist, manager, etc. Does this mean they can also be considered team sports?

2 Ask students if they know another name for *football* and if possible elicit *soccer*. Ask if students know the difference before drawing attention to the *Did you know?* box.

Read the title of the text and the questions with the class. It may be necessary to pre-teach or check understanding of *ordinary* (not special, usual), *rules* (instructions which tell you what you can and cannot do), *referee* (the person in charge, who decides if the rules are being respected) and *upset* (unhappy). Then allow time for students to find answers and compare their ideas with a partner before discussing as a class.

3 Read through the statements, checking understanding as necessary. Encourage students to work in pairs to say if the statements are true or false before reading the text again to check their answers. Ask students to say why the false statements are incorrect using information from the text.

Check answers as a class, asking students to justify their answers each time.

> **1** T
> **2** F It was called football because you played it on foot and not riding on a horse.
> **3** F You couldn't play football in the street or in public places.
> **4** F Women used the same pitches as men before 1921 and then again after 1971.
> **5** F It's becoming more popular.

4 With a stronger class, to make this exercise more challenging: students can cover the words in the box and try to do the task without looking at them. After comparing answers with a partner, they can uncover the words and check their answers again. Feed back as a class.

> **1** teams **2** pitch **3** goal **4** score **5** loses
> **6** match **7** rules **8** referee **9** red card
> **10** send **11** off

FAST FINISHERS

Students can write their own definitions/explanations for some of the words in the box and then read them to a partner or the rest of the class who have to say the correct word.

GRAMMAR
SB P180

CAN, MUST, HAVE TO, NEED TO

LEAD-IN

The verbs can be introduced by writing on the board or eliciting some rules which may already be familiar or used in the school or classroom. For example, *Students **must** listen when the teacher or other students are speaking; Students **can** use online or paper dictionaries; Students **don't have to** stand up when the teachers enter the classroom.* Ask the class if they can explain the difference in meaning between the verbs used in the examples on the board. You may be able to elicit, *it's possible / it's not possible / it's necessary*, etc.

1 Allow students a few minutes to read through the example sentences in the book and complete the rules. Then go through answers as a class using the information in the box to highlight the form of the modals, pointing out that *can('t)* and *must(n't)* are followed by the verb without *to*. This is also a good moment to model and practise pronunciation, in particular, of *mustn't* with its silent *t*.

> **1** can **2** mustn't **3** have to **4** don't need to

➡ **GRAMMAR REFERENCE** / Pages 224–225

2 If necessary, check or pre-teach the meaning of *hurry* (move or do something quickly), *improve* (get better) and *proper* (suitable, correct) before students work in pairs to match the sentence parts. Check answers as a class.

> **1** c **2** f **3** e **4** b **5** d **6** a

3 Point out that students need to think about the meaning and the form when choosing the correct verb. Remind students to refer to the information in the box if necessary. Students complete the sentences. A stronger class can be asked to say all the options where there is more than one correct answer. Encourage pairs to justify their answers during class feedback.

> 1 have to/need to, can't
> 2 don't have to/don't need to, can
> 3 Can, can't
> 4 must/have to/need to
> 5 don't have to/don't need to
> 6 must/need to/have to
> 7 must/need to/have to, must/needs to/has to
> 8 Do … have to/need to

4 With a weaker class, ask for one suggestion to complete each sentence from the class as an example before allowing students a few minutes to finish the sentences with one or more ideas of their own. Then ask them to compare and discuss their ideas with a partner, explaining their opinions if necessary.

LISTENING
SB P181

1 Read through the questions with the class before allowing students a few minutes to discuss them with a partner. Feed back by asking why students like or dislike running.

2 Encourage students to read through the questions before finding the answers in the text. Students then check answers with a partner before class feedback.

> 1 long-distance races
> 2 the mountains above the Rift Valley

3  112 Read through the instructions and ask students to make suggestions about what her answer may be. Point out that there is not one specific answer but two or three reasons that contribute. Then play the recording and ask students to listen for the answers.

> Because they run all the time as they are poor and don't have transport.
> For example, they have to run to school every day because their families don't have cars and there aren't any buses.
> Because they live in the mountains, they often have to run up and down hills. This makes their legs strong and is good for their breathing.

AUDIOSCRIPT 112

Interviewer: I'm here in the Rift Valley in Kenya, at a school which specialises in training local children to become long-distance runners. With me is Florence Kipoge, a teacher at the school. Florence, I've just watched some of the students from the school running and they all look like future champions to me. What do you think are the reasons there are so many amazing runners here?

Florence: Well, the children you saw today don't come from rich families. This means that all their lives they have to walk – and run – everywhere. For example, they have to run to school every day because their families don't have cars and there aren't any buses. When I was a teenager, I lived five kilometres from school and I ran there and back every day.

Interviewer: So people here need to be good at running because there's very little transport?

Florence: Yes. Also, because we live in the mountains, we often have to run up and down hills. This makes our legs strong and is good for our breathing.

Interviewer: Lots of the children run barefoot, without shoes, don't they? Do you think that helps?

Florence: Yes, it's very good for your whole body to run and walk without shoes. It makes your feet strong and you have to use your legs and body in a different way. It gives you a good running style.

Interviewer: But doesn't it hurt your feet?

Florence: You mustn't run long distances on hard, flat roads without shoes – that would hurt your feet. But the roads here are not like city roads. When students from our school start winning competitions and get some money, they often buy running shoes, but sometimes they don't like wearing them!

Interviewer: All the students I see seem very serious and they train very hard. Is this another reason why they do so well?

Florence: Absolutely. This part of Kenya is beautiful but there aren't many jobs. For the young people here, becoming a professional runner or getting a sports scholarship is a dream. It can change their lives and the lives of their families. So they work very, very hard.

4 🔊 112 Encourage students to read the questions through and try to remember the answers. Help students with vocabulary as necessary before listening to the recording again to check.

| 1 b | 2 a | 3 b | 4 a | 5 b | 6 a | 7 b |

5 If necessary, demonstrate the task by asking the first question to a few students and then asking a follow-up question using the past simple. Remind students that the present perfect is used to ask about experiences at any time in your life, but the past simple is then used to talk about a specific time when you did something, e.g. *Have you ever run barefoot? Yes, I have. Where were you? I was at the beach.* Students work in pairs to answer the questions and then feed back to the class.

VOCABULARY
SB P181

DO, PLAY AND GO WITH SPORTS

LEAD-IN

With books closed write three sentences on the board:
I play football every weekend. My best friend does judo. I'd like to go swimming more often.

Point out the verbs and ask students how we decide which verb to use for the different sports. Try to elicit the rule from the box if possible.

1 Open books and encourage students to read the three example sentences before completing the rules in the box.

| 1 do | 2 play | 3 go |

2 If necessary, check understanding of some of the activities before students start the exercise, e.g. *Where can you do rock climbing?* (In the mountains). Students work in pairs to choose the correct verb for each sport or activity.

do	play	go
gymnastics	baseball	horse riding
aerobics	handball	cycling
yoga	volleyball	fishing
judo		snowboarding
		surfing
		rock climbing
		skiing
		sailing
		windsurfing

3 If necessary, demonstrate or elicit the questions students can ask, e.g. *How often do you do yoga?; When do you play baseball?; Where do you go horse riding?; How does it make you feel?* and read through the example answers in the speech bubble, before allowing a few minutes for students to ask and answer. Feed back by asking students to tell the class something about a sport or activity their partner does.

WRITING PART 7 TRAINING
SB P182

✓ EXAM INFORMATION

In Reading and Writing Part 7, students have to write a short story based on three pictures. They should write 35 words or more.

The focus in the Student's Book is on verb tenses and using adjectives to make the story more interesting.

Tell students that in the exam, if they want to change or add a word after they finish writing, they do not have to re-write the whole text. It is sufficient to make sure any changes are clear and legible.

1 Ask students if they can remember what they have to do in Reading and Writing Part 7 (write a story describing three pictures using 35 words or more).

Draw attention to the pictures and the sets of words. Allow a few minutes for students to match the pictures with the sets of words and talk to their partner about what is happening in each picture.

Elicit some suggestions about each picture from the class, making sure to check understanding of the words in the lists by asking questions.

| 1 B | 2 C | 3 A |

2 Elicit the tense students should use to describe what is happening in a picture (usually present continuous but when writing the story for the exam students can use the present or the past tense). With a weaker class, work together to write one or two example sentences about the first picture on the board. Then students continue to write sentences about the other pictures with a partner. Remind them to use some of the words in the list.

3 Allow a few minutes for students to read the text in the book and compare it with the story they wrote. Discuss similarities and differences with the class. Make sure students know there is more than one correct answer and if their text is different that doesn't mean it's wrong.

| Tenses used: past continuous and past simple |

4 Students read the longer version of the story and answer the questions in pairs. Elicit answers from the class and discuss why adjectives make a story more interesting.

1 It's longer because some words have been added. It's more interesting because of the adjectives used.
2 adjectives – they give you more information to help you imagine and 'see' what is happening in the story.

5 If necessary, check the meanings and pronunciation of the adjectives in the box by asking students in turn to read the adjective and a noun that it can describe. For example, *an angry man*, *a beautiful house*, etc.

Then students work in pairs to add adjectives to the sentences. When checking, accept all answers that could fit. You can use the various answers students give to point out how much difference the adjectives can make to a story or description. For example, *a crowded café, an expensive bag, the shiny table, a quiet café, a small bag, the round table*, etc.

> **Suggested answers**
> **1** One day I was sitting in a busy/quiet **café** when I noticed that there was a big/colourful **bag** on the round **table** next to me.
> **2** A beautiful **woman** was walking through the quiet/big **park** when suddenly she saw a shiny/strange/big/colourful **object** on the small **path** in front of her.
> **3** One afternoon, as I was crossing the busy **road** to my house, a/an expensive/new/big **car** stopped in the street next to me and a/an strange/angry **man** put his big **head** out of the window to speak to me.

FAST FINISHERS

Students can add adjectives to the sentences in Exercise 4 and then compare their suggestions with a partner.

6 Ask students to look at the pictures on page 194. With a weaker class you could brainstorm some useful vocabulary with the whole class and write it on the board before they start writing, e.g. *basketball team, windy, throw, roof*, etc.

Encourage the class to make a checklist of points to think about before they start writing and then that they can check after writing. This list could be elicited by asking questions such as, *Which tenses can I use?* (past simple / past continuous) and could also include a reminder to use adjectives, names for the people if appropriate, connecting words such as *while* and *as*, correct spelling, correct grammar, etc.

Students can do the writing in the class or at home. Encourage them to check their writing after they finish, to see if they can improve it or correct any mistakes.

> **Model answer**
> Charlotte was playing basketball with her friends. When she threw the ball, the wind carried it away. It landed on a roof. 'Why did you do that, Charlotte?' shouted her friend. Charlotte was upset because everyone was angry. She climbed up and got the ball. Everyone was happy because they could play again. (53 words)

SB P183

TENSES REVIEW

> ### LEAD-IN
> Brainstorm the names of tenses and verb forms on the board and, if possible, elicit an example for each one, e.g. present perfect: *I've never been to London.* Alternatively, write or say some sentences and ask students to tell you the name of the tense or verb form, e.g. *I went to the cinema last night.* (past simple).

1 Brainstorm what the class knows about the Paralympics. Encourage students to read the text through without worrying about the gaps in order to find out who it is about and why she is famous. Then students re-read the text and complete the text with the verbs.

> **1** was born   **2** began   **3** was, studying
> **4** won   **5** has taken part   **6** has won
> **7** stopped   **8** works   **9** is working

> ### BACKGROUND INFORMATION
> The first sports competitions for athletes in wheelchairs were held in the 1940s to help with rehabilitation after the second world war. Since then the Paralympic Games have grown into a huge international event for people with many different impairments. Since 1988 they have been held in the same year and venue as the Olympic Games.

2 Ask students to work together to name the tenses used in each gap and explain why that particular tense is used. Check answers as a class.

> Past simple is used in gaps 1, 2, 4 and 7 as they are referring to finished actions or events in the past.
> Past continuous is used in gap 3 as it describes a background event.
> Present perfect is used in gaps 5 and 6 as they are referring to experiences in Trischa's life.
> Present simple is used in gap 8 as it refers to a present routine.
> Present continuous is used in gap 9 because it refers to a temporary action.

3 🔊 113 Draw attention to the words and ask students what type of words they are (irregular past tense verbs). Ask students if they can tell you the present of each verb (*buy, think, teach, see*).

Then play the recording of the words and ask students what they notice about the sounds.

> ### AUDIOSCRIPT 🔊 113
> **Woman:** bought, thought, taught, saw

UNIT 14   PLAY IT, WATCH IT, LOVE IT

Then repeat the recording and drill chorally and then individually as necessary to give students an opportunity to practise saying them.

> All the words have the same vowel sound.

PUSH YOURSELF B1

SB P183

VOCABULARY: ADVERBS

LEAD-IN

Elicit some adverbs from the class. They may be able to suggest words such as, *quickly, suddenly, finally*. Then ask what each of the adverbs they have suggested tells us information about. It may be possible to elicit *when* and *how* for time and manner adverbs (e.g. *quickly, suddenly – how* something happened, *finally – when* something happened).

1 Read through the information and complete the gaps as a class. Ask if anyone can add any other adverbs to any of the lists.

> 1 when something happened
> 2 how something happened
> 3 how the speaker or writer feels about something

2 Read through the example sentences with the class and allow students two or three minutes to match them with the different types of adverb.

> Adverbs of time: Afterwards
> Adverbs of manner: slowly, carefully, quickly
> Sentence adverbs: Surprisingly, Luckily

3 Students work individually to choose the best options to complete the sentences before comparing with a partner. Feed back as a class.

> 1 afterwards 2 fortunately 3 suddenly
> 4 before 5 Unfortunately

LISTENING

SB P184

1 With books closed, elicit the meaning of *fan* (a person who admires a sports team, player, musician, etc.). Then draw attention to the photos and initiate a class discussion using the questions in the book. Encourage students to tell you everything they know about the sports and say why they think the people are fans.

> A Arno   B Loli   C Sandra

CULTURAL INFORMATION

Cardiff is the capital city of Wales and rugby is the most popular sport in Wales. The Welsh rugby team has always been one of the top ten teams in the world.

Motor racing is very popular in Italy and the Italian Grand Prix is one of the oldest events on the Formula 1 calendar.

Fuerza Regia are a pro basketball team based in Monterrey, Mexico. The top professional basketball league in Mexico was established in 2000 but is now one of the most important in Latin America.

2 114 Read the instructions with the class and tell them to listen and order the speakers. Check answers as a class.

> 1 Sandra   2 Arno   3 Loli

AUDIOSCRIPT 114

1
Sandra: I went to my first rugby match when I was living in Cardiff. I was about 18 years old and I wasn't interested in sport at all. I only went because my friends were going, but I loved it! It was cold and raining, but the game was very exciting. The other great thing was the way the fans in the stadium never stopped singing. It was fantastic! Now I'm a serious fan and I have a season ticket to watch the Cardiff Blues, the team I support. I go to all the Blues' home matches and I sometimes follow them to the away matches, too.

2
Arno: I started going to race tracks with my father when I was six. He was a big fan all his life so I became one too. Some people can't understand why I like it. They ask things like: 'Why do you want to watch cars go round and round on a race track? Doesn't it get boring?' The answer is 'No, never!' It's easier to follow what is happening in a race if you watch it on TV, but, for me, that isn't as exciting. I prefer to be there. I love the atmosphere, the smell of the petrol and the noise.

3
Loli: I got interested in basketball out of love! I started going to matches at college when I was about 20 because my college boyfriend was a basketball player. For a long time, I was bored. Basketball rules are very complicated, so I didn't know what was happening. But then, slowly, I started to understand the game. Now I like it and find it interesting because it's complicated and because it's a team game. I love watching how the team play together on the court – this is very important in basketball and it changes all the time.

3 🔊 **114** Go through the information in the table with the class and read the two example answers. Then play the recording again for students to complete the table. With a weaker class it may be helpful to stop the recording after each speaker to allow students time to complete their notes and check answers. Feed back as a class.

	Sandra	Arno	Loli
Age when he/she started watching the sport	18	6	20
Why he/she started watching the sport	because her friends were going	because his father was a fan – he started going to races as a child	because her boyfriend was a basketball player
Where the sport is played/practised	stadium	race track	(basketball) court
What the person likes about the sport / feels when watching a match	It's exciting – she likes the singing during matches.	He loves the atmosphere, the smell of the petrol and the noise.	It's a complicated, interesting game. She loves watching the team play together.

4 Students work in pairs to match the words with the definitions before class feedback.

> **1** c **2** a **3** d **4** b

5 Encourage students to read the text and try to guess the answers before using the words in the box to complete the gaps.

> **1** season ticket **2** home matches
> **3** away matches **4** live

6 Students work in pairs to discuss the questions. Then ask for class feedback.

⊕ EXTENSION

Students could write a short text about their own experience of being a fan using the ideas in the table in Exercise 3 and some of the vocabulary in Exercises 4 and 5.

SPEAKING PART 2 TRAINING
SB P185

✓ EXAM INFORMATION

In Speaking Part 2, phase 1, candidates talk to their partner about some pictures of activities, places or objects for one to two minutes, then answer one or two short questions about the pictures asked by the examiner. In phase 2, the examiner takes the pictures away and candidates answer two further questions on the same topic and give longer answers. The total time allowed for Part 2 is five to six minutes.

1 Hold a brief class discussion to answer the questions.

2 🔊 **115** Go through the instructions with the class and play the recording. Allow a few minutes for students to compare their notes with a partner before checking as a class. With a weaker class it may be necessary to repeat the recording before checking answers as a class.

	Mei	Luca
basketball	✗ played a little at school She's not very good very fast game	✓ game popular in his country *Olimipia Milano* is a good team played in basketball team in college
running	✓ likes running alone it's good to keep fit was in running competitions	✗ doesn't like running a long way
swimming	✓ lives near the beach – goes often	✓ swims a lot in summer when he goes to visit grandfather
tennis	✗ learned at school difficult to hit the ball makes her arms hurt	✓ goes to a tennis club likes watching tennis

AUDIOSCRIPT 🔊 115

Examiner: Now, in this part of the test you are going to talk together. Here are some pictures that show different sports. Do you like these different sports? Say why or why not. I'll say that again. Do you like these different sports? Say why or why not? All right? Now, talk together.

Luca: This is basketball, isn't it? This game is very popular in my country. I like it. I come from Milan and *Olimpia Milano* is a good team. Do you play basketball?

Mei: I played a little at school, but I don't like it very much. I'm not very good. … It's a very fast game. What about you? Do you play basketball?

Luca:	Yes, I play basketball sometimes with my friends, when we have time. And I played in the basketball team in my college, but not this year.
Mei:	And this one is running. I like running alone. It's good for exercise and to keep fit. In the past I was in running competitions – races. What about you? Do you like running?
Luca:	No, not very much. I don't like running a long way. I like this sport – swimming. In the summer, I go to stay with my grandfather. His house is near a lake and I swim a lot.
Mei:	I live near the beach so I go swimming very often. It's great.
Luca:	And this sport is tennis. I enjoy playing tennis. In the summer I go to a tennis club – and I like watching it, too. Do you play tennis?
Mei:	I learned tennis at school, but I think it's difficult. I'm often too slow to hit the ball and it makes my arms hurt.

3 Hold a brief class discussion to elicit students' ideas. Point out that Mei and Luca do the task well by asking each other questions and giving extended answers saying why they like or don't like each activity, as well as adding some extra information.

> Students' own answers.

4 116 Elicit what happens at the end of phase 1 (the examiner asks each candidate one or two questions on the same topic). Students listen to the recording and make a note of the questions that the examiner asks.

> Do you think playing basketball is difficult?
> Do you think swimming is fun?
> Which of these sports do you like best?

AUDIOSCRIPT 116

Examiner:	Do you think playing basketball is difficult, Luca?
Luca:	I suppose it's not easy to score goals. You have to be very tall to be a good basketball player.
Examiner:	Do you think swimming is fun, Mei?
Mei:	In my opinion, swimming is fun, but I don't like swimming in cold water. Also, it's a cheap sport to do.
Examiner:	So, Luca, which of these sports do you like best?
Luca:	Definitely tennis. I think it's fun to play and exciting to watch.
Examiner:	And you, Mei, which of these sports do you like best?
Mei:	From these sports, I like running best. But actually, my favourite sport is football.
Examiner:	Thank you.

5 Direct students to the pictures on page 195 and allow them a few minutes to think about what they can say about each one using the ideas in the box next to the pictures. Help with vocabulary as necessary. In the exam, students do not have any thinking time before they speak. Remind students to talk about all the pictures and not just the one which shows an activity they are more familiar with or have experience of. Then point out the questions in the other box and tell students it is important they try to include their partner in the conversation.

Students discuss the pictures with their partner. Monitor by moving round the classroom as students do the task.

Students take it in turns to ask and answer the examiner's questions. (In the exam students will have to answer one or two questions and they may be the same questions as their partner. It is important that both students listen to all the examiner's questions. This is because the examiner may follow up with, *What do you think?*).

6 117 Try to elicit what happens in phase 2 of Part 2 (students have to answer two more questions with longer answers). Play the recording after reading through the questions. Check answers as a class.

> Luca would like to try snowboarding.
> Mei prefers watching sports.

AUDIOSCRIPT 117

Examiner:	Now, which new sport would you like to learn, Mei?
Mei:	I'm interested in learning how to water ski.
Examiner:	Why?
Mei:	Because it looks awesome. Some people say it's a dangerous sport, but I think it's amazing.
Examiner:	And what about you, Luca?
Luca:	I'd like to try snowboarding. My cousins are very good snowboarders and I'd like to go snowboarding with them. I think you need a lot of lessons to stay safe, and they're quite expensive.
Examiner:	Which do you prefer, watching sports or playing sports, Luca?
Luca:	I don't know really. It's different for different sports. But probably playing sports, because it's fun and it's good for you.
Examiner:	And you, Mei?
Mei:	Definitely watching sports. My favourite thing is to go to a football match to watch my team.
Examiner:	Thank you. That is the end of the test.

7 117 Encourage students to read through the sentences in pairs and complete the gaps before listening to the recording again to check.

> **1** it looks awesome; I think it's amazing **2** I'd like to go
> **3** it's good for you   **4** My favourite thing is

8 Encourage students to use some of the expressions in Exercise 7 in their answers to the questions.

EXAM FOCUS

SB P186

WRITING PART 7

> **✓ EXAM INFORMATION**
>
> In Reading and Writing Part 7, students have to write a short story based on three pictures. They should write 35 words or more.
>
> The whole Reading and Writing paper lasts 60 minutes and has 30 reading questions (Parts 1–5) and two writing questions (Parts 6 and 7). Students should spend nine to ten minutes on Part 7.

EXAM CHECK

1 Students complete the gaps. Tell students to use the exam-style question below to help them, before comparing answers with a partner.

> **1** pictures **2** tell **3** decide **4** write **5** words

2 Students can look back at the checklist they prepared in Exercise 7, page 182, or the same ideas can be elicited in a ten minutes to write their story individually under exam conditions, i.e. without using a dictionary or comparing ideas with a partner. They can exchange finished texts with a partner for peer feedback, using the checklist, when they finish.

> **Model answer**
> The women were playing football in the park. One player kicked the ball into the lake. The players were sad because they couldn't play anymore, but the people in the boat picked up the ball and returned it to the players. The players were happy. (45 words)

➡ **WRITING BANK** / Pages 235–236

SPEAKING PART 2

SB P187

> **✓ EXAM INFORMATION**
>
> In Speaking Part 2, phase 1, candidates talk to their partner about some pictures of activities, places or objects for one to two minutes, then answer one or two short questions about the pictures asked by the examiner. In phase 2, the examiner takes the pictures away and candidates answer two further questions on the same topic and should try to give longer answers. The total time allowed for Part 2 is five to six minutes.

EXAM CHECK

1 Students match the sentences individually before checking answers with a partner.

> **1** b **2** e **3** d **4** a **5** c

2 The instructions in the book are those that the examiner gives in the exam, so students could work in groups of three with one student reading the examiner's words while the other two discuss the pictures and answer the questions.

Students can then exchange roles so that everybody has a chance to play the part of a candidate.

3 **4** and **5** In these tasks students work in pairs to ask and answer the questions, taking turns to be the examiner and a candidate. Remind them to extend their answers using two or three sentences where possible. Monitor the activity as students work through the tasks.

Read through the options in the *How was it?* section and elicit the meaning of each one that they learned in the first unit.

Ask students to tick the appropriate box. You might like to ask students to share how they felt about the task to get an indication of your students' confidence. Depending on your class, you might like to do this openly or allow students to give their feedback without their classmates seeing. For example, give students a piece of A4 paper each with the *How was it?* scale written in large letters. Allow students to tick the relevant box then hold up their papers at the same time so that you can see how well students think they are doing. Finally, ask students if they found it easier, harder or the same as the exam practice in previous units.

➡ **SPEAKING BANK** / Pages 241–242

REAL WORLD

SB P188

GOING TO A SPORTS EVENT IN ... MADRID

> **WARMER**
>
> Ask students if they know the names of any Spanish football clubs.

1 Draw attention to the photos and elicit vocabulary, such as *stadium*, *football scarf*, *museum*. Then students work in pairs to answer the questions.

2 Ask students if they know the names of any football stadiums in Madrid. Go over the instructions and give students one or two minutes to read the web page and answer the question.

3 Students find the words and phrases in the web page and match them with the definitions. Explain that they can check their answers by substituting the phrase in the text with the answer they choose. Feed back as a class.

> **1** a **2** f **3** d **4** b **5** e **6** c

4 Allow students time to read the three reviews and find the person who didn't enjoy the tour.

> KizziGrand

UNIT 14 PLAY IT, WATCH IT, LOVE IT

5 Students work in pairs to find answers to the questions by reading the reviews again. Feed back as a class.

1 KizziGrand	2 ClareM	3 TomR44
4 KizziGrand	5 TomR44	6 ClareM

6 🔊 118 Go over the instructions with the class. Play the recordings and ask students to make a note of one or two key words or phrases which tell them the answer in each case. Repeat the recording if necessary.

Check answers as a class, encouraging students to tell you the notes they made.

1 b	2 c	3 d

AUDIOSCRIPT 🔊 118

1
Customer: Hello. I'd like to buy two tickets for the match next Saturday.
Official: OK. Let's see what we've got. Yes, I've got tickets available at most prices. Which part of the stadium did you have in mind?
Customer: Well, where are the cheapest seats?
Official: They're at both ends, behind the goals. There are a few seats in the North Stand for €40 each. They're right at the top.
Customer: Will I get a good view of the game?
Official: Well, it's hard to say. It depends how the game goes. If the action's all at your end, you'll be fine. If the action's all at the other end of the pitch, you won't see so well. There are some tickets in the side stands for €55. You should get a better view from there.
Customer: Oh, OK. I'll take those ones.
Official: OK. No problem.
Customer: And what time do the gates open?
Official: They open 45 minutes before the game starts. And next Saturday, the game starts at 7.30, so it will be 6.45.
Customer: OK. Thanks.

2
Guide: So, this is where the players come out onto the pitch. Can you imagine coming out and seeing the stadium full of people, all cheering for you?
Male: Wow! The stadium's amazing, isn't it?
Female: Yeah. It's so big!
Male: I can't imagine playing in front of a big crowd like this!
Female: No! I'd be really scared! But I don't play football. I only watch it.
Male: Which team do you support?
Female: Well, I'm from Paris, so I support Paris Saint-Germain. They're doing quite well this season. What about you?
Male: I support Arsenal. I go and watch them play quite a lot, with my uncle.
Female: Cool.
Guide: Right, if you'd like to come this way, we'll go and see the changing rooms.

3
Girl: That was a great game – so exciting!
Boy: Yeah. I'm so glad Real Madrid won.
Girl: Me too. They played well. And their first goal was amazing.
Boy: Yeah, a brilliant shot. The goalkeeper had no chance!
Girl: They were lucky to get a penalty in the second half.
Boy: Yeah. I don't think it was really a penalty. I think the referee got that wrong.
Girl: Yes, but that's football.

PHRASES YOU MIGHT USE

7 🔊 118 Students work in pairs to complete the phrases before listening to the recording to check their answers.

1 support	2 What	3 great	4 too
5 chance	6 referee		

PHRASES YOU MIGHT HEAR

8 Students choose the correct definitions before checking answers as a class.

1 a	2 b	3 b	4 a	5 b

WATCH

9 ▶ Go through the prompts with the class, checking understanding. Then play the video and encourage students to take notes about the different prompts.

VIDEOSCRIPT ⬢ Madrid

Madrid is the capital city of Spain, and it's also Spain's largest city. It is home to the Spanish Royal Family and many important government buildings.

This is the Plaza Mayor, or Main Square, and it's over 400 years old. The beautiful buildings on all sides of the square are flats where people live, but they're very expensive, of course.

Football is very important here. There are two big teams in the city, Real Madrid and Atlético Madrid.

Both teams have thousands of fans who support them every week. Both teams are also good at winning matches and trophies. Real Madrid have won 64 trophies in Spain and 24 trophies in European and world competitions. It's one of the most successful clubs in the world. Atlético Madrid aren't quite as successful, but in the last ten years, they have won the Spanish League and the UEFA Europa League. Atlético Madrid used to play at the Vicente Calderón Stadium, but now play at the Wanda Metropolitano, and Real Madrid play at the Bernabéu Stadium. Both stadiums are usually full on match days, as fans go along to support and cheer for their teams.

This is the Bernabéu Stadium, which first opened in 1947 and can hold 81,000 fans. You can go on a tour of both stadiums in Madrid. People love the fact that they can walk out onto the pitch where so many famous players have played. Sometimes when you go on a stadium tour, you can see the players practising on the pitch before a game. Ticket prices can vary from about 40 to over 400 euros! If you want to see a match, make sure you book a few weeks in advance. Then you can go along and enjoy the match, and cheer for your favourite team! Don't forget to take your flags and scarves!

Madrid: the capital city of Spain, also the country's biggest city, home to the Spanish royal family; important government buildings; Plaza Mayor, or Main Square, 400 years old, buildings on the square are expensive flats.

football teams in the city: two big teams – Real Madrid and Atlético Madrid, both teams have thousands of fans and are good at winning; Real Madrid has won 64 trophies in Spain and 24 trophies in European and world competitions; one of the most successful clubs in the world; Atlético Madrid has won the Spanish League and Europa League Cup recently, used to play at the Vicente Calderón Stadium but now Wanda Metropolitano; Real Madrid plays at the Bernabéu Stadium.

stadium tours: can go on a tour of stadiums in Madrid; the Bernabéu Stadium first opened in 1947 and can hold 81,000 fans; can sometimes see the players practising on the pitch before a game.

buying tickets for matches: cheapest tickets are about 40 euros, most expensive are over 400 euros; best to book your tickets in advance.

10 ▶ Students compare their notes with a partner before watching the video again to check. Feed back as a class.

LIFE COMPETENCIES
SB P189

SHARING IDEAS AND RESPECTING OTHERS' CONTRIBUTIONS

11 Go over the instructions with the class, checking understanding.

Students work in pairs to research a sports event and find some information about tickets and tours. They could choose a stadium tour, a trip to a championship match or tournament, or an international sporting event.

Then two or three pairs work together to share the information they have found.

As a group, students decide which event would be most popular.

➙ **WORKBOOK** / *Unit 14, page 60*

PROGRESS CHECK 5
UNIT 12 TO UNIT 14

SB P190

1
1 D
2 A
3 C
4 B

2
1 sociable
2 funny
3 quiet
4 kind
5 lazy
6 clever

3
1 relatives
2 small family
3 only child
4 married
5 important person in my life
6 fiancé

4
1 have to
2 need to
3 don't have to
4 can
5 must
6 mustn't

5
1 going, train, competition
2 played, catch, bat
3 play, red card, matches
4 team, do, races
5 went, do, rules

6
1 bigger
2 more interesting
3 best
4 friendliest
5 worse
6 busier

7
1 ~~better~~ best
2 ~~more fast~~ faster
3 ~~sport more popular~~ most popular sport
4 one of my ~~most~~ favourite games
5 ~~more~~ safer

8
1 f
2 d
3 a
4 b
5 c
6 e

9
1 B
2 A
3 C
4 C
5 A
6 B

10
1 doing – maths
2 taking – drama
3 do – chemistry
4 revising – history
5 doing – journalist
6 qualifications – farmer

11
1 The dentist pulled my tooth out. / The dentist pulled out my tooth.
2 A really famous engineer built that bridge.
3 Our geography teacher asked us to find out about rivers.
4 My modern languages teacher gave me really good marks.

GRAMMAR REFERENCE

Page 196
STARTER UNIT
BE
Exercise 1
1 You're
2 isn't
3 I'm not
4 aren't, We're
5 She's

Exercise 2
1 is/'s
2 am/'m
3 are
4 Is, isn't, is/'s
5 Are, am

HAVE GOT
Exercise 3
1 hasn't
2 have
3 have
4 Have, haven't
5 have

Exercise 4
1 've got
2 haven't got
3 has got
4 Have … got, haven't
5 haven't got

CAN/CAN'T/LIKE/DON'T LIKE
Exercise 5
1 She can't paint very well.
2 We don't like dogs.
3 Correct
4 Correct
5 I like watching films on TV.
6 Correct

WH- QUESTION WORDS
Exercise 6
1 Where
2 Who
3 How
4 When
5 Whose

Exercise 7
1 What
2 Where
3 How
4 Whose
5 When

THE APOSTROPHE 'S
Exercise 8
1 This is my best friend's car.
2 Steve Brown's in my class.
3 The children's books are on the teacher's desk.
4 The new pilots' uniforms are dark blue.
5 It's very noisy here.
6 Peter's so friendly, he's always helping me.

3RD PERSON S IN THE PRESENT SIMPLE
Exercise 9
1 like
2 eats
3 loves
4 come
5 walks

Page 198
UNIT 1
PRESENT SIMPLE
Exercise 1
1 plays
2 get up
3 likes
4 live
5 goes

Exercise 2
1 Paul doesn't play the piano every evening.
2 I don't get up at 6 o'clock every day.
3 My brother doesn't like football.
4 My friends don't live near me.
5 Hannah doesn't go to school by bus.

Exercise 3
1 My brother **works** in Moscow.
2 Tom **doesn't** play the piano.
3 I **play** football every weekend.
4 Does she **start** work at 9 o'clock every morning?
5 My parents **don't** watch TV in the afternoon.

ADVERBS OF FREQUENCY
Exercise 4
1 I never go to work in the evening.
2 I sometimes help my brother with his homework.
3 My sister and I walk to college every day.
4 I am sometimes late for work.
5 I always work hard at college.

Exercise 5
Students' own answers.

Exercise 6
1 He doesn't like to go camping.
2 They don't like getting up early.
3 He loves to drink iced coffee.
4 We don't want to go shopping this morning.
6 She wants to wear her new top to the party.

Page 200
UNIT 2
PRESENT CONTINUOUS
Exercise 1
1 are not/aren't watching, are/'re listening
2 am/'m writing
3 Are you doing?, 'm not, am/'m playing
4 is/'s running
5 isn't washing

Exercise 2
1 reading
2 putting
3 cooking
4 sitting
5 dancing

PRESENT SIMPLE OR PRESENT CONTINUOUS?
Exercise 3
1 go
2 's doing
3 love
4 's starting
5 play
6 have

Exercise 4
1 ~~we are usually getting~~ we usually get
2 ~~I isten~~ I'm listening
3 ~~my family is hating~~ my family hates
4 ~~Mateo is having~~ Mateo has
5 ~~Jon has~~ Jon is having
6 ~~Are you understanding~~ Do you understand

Page 202
UNIT 3
PAST SIMPLE
Exercise 1
1 were, broke, walked
2 did … have, ate, drank
3 did … get, got, gave
4 Did … go, did, went
5 Did … watch, didn't, took, was
6 came, weren't, was

Exercise 2
1 left
2 won, felt
3 made
4 met, bought
5 began

ANSWER KEY AND AUDIOSCRIPTS

Page 204

UNIT 4
CAN/CAN'T, COULD/COULDN'T + INFINITIVE WITHOUT TO

Exercise 1
1 can't
2 can, can
3 can't
4 couldn't, could
5 Can, can't

Exercise 2
2 Could you swim when you were three?
Yes, I could. / No, I couldn't.
3 Can you speak more than two languages?
Yes, I can. / No, I can't.
4 Can you skateboard?
Yes, I can. / No, I can't.
5 Can both of your parents drive?
Yes, they can. / No, they can't.

SHOULD/SHOULDN'T

Exercise 3
You should: go to bed early, ask parents or friends to help you.
You shouldn't: work late the day before, spend too much time alone, worry

Exercise 4
1 should drink
2 should wear
3 shouldn't eat
4 shouldn't ride
5 should get
6 shouldn't arrive

Page 206

UNIT 5
PAST CONTINUOUS

Exercise 1
1 were listening/listened, were having
2 was sleeping, phoned
3 was doing
4 woke up, was raining
5 were you doing

Exercise 2
1 were driving
2 were travelling
3 were reading
4 were listening
5 saw
6 was standing
7 was telling
8 passed
9 was coming
10 was

PAST CONTINUOUS AND PAST SIMPLE

Exercise 3
1 was watching
2 often phoned
3 realised
4 was shining, were singing
5 won

Exercise 4
1 was tidying, found
2 was leaving, realised
3 was watching, cooked/was cooking
4 heard, stopped, were doing, walked
5 crashed, was updating

Page 208

UNIT 6
COUNTABLE AND UNCOUNTABLE NOUNS

Exercise 1
Countable nouns: baby, box, child, knife, man, person, school, strawberry, student, teacher
Uncountable nouns: bread, coffee, juice, milk, money, rice, tea, water

Exercise 2
babies, boxes, children, knives, men, people, schools, strawberries, students, teachers

Exercise 3
1 an
2 any
3 Some
4 some
5 any
6 a

Exercise 4
1 How much
2 How many
3 A lot of
4 a few
5 a lot of
6 no
7 a little
8 a few

IMPERATIVES

Exercise 5
1 Don't use
2 Don't shout, Talk
3 Don't run, Walk
4 Don't come, Use

Exercise 6
2 Wash them.
3 Don't forget to buy her a present.
4 Turn it off.
5 Go to bed.

Page 210

UNIT 7
PRESENT PERFECT

Exercise 1
1 has met
2 have/'ve never been
3 Have … travelled
4 has/'s won
5 has never swum

Exercise 2
1 didn't see
2 Have you ever been
3 haven't
4 have been
5 have been

PRESENT PERFECT WITH JUST

Exercise 3
1 I'm really hot. I've just run home from college.
2 We've just finished eating.
3 I've just texted my brother.
4 He's just told me he passed his exam.
5 They've just arrived back from India.

Page 212

UNIT 8
PRESENT PERFECT WITH FOR AND SINCE

Exercise 1
for	since
24 hours	6 o'clock
400 years	last November
ten minutes	my birthday
three weeks	October 12th
12 months	the end of May
	yesterday

Exercise 2
1 two weeks
2 25 years
3 last weekend
4 January
5 23 years
6 the age of nine

PRESENT PERFECT WITH YET AND ALREADY

Exercise 3
1 Have you tidied your bedroom yet?
2 They've already finished their college project.
3 I don't want to watch that programme. I've already seen it twice.
4 Tania doesn't want to go to bed yet. She isn't tired.

Exercise 4
1 I haven't worn my new shoes yet.
2 We've already finished eating.

3 I've already texted all my friends. / I've texted my friends already.
4 Have you finished reading that book yet?
5 I've already phoned my older sister.

Page 214

UNIT 9
–ING OR TO INFINITIVE AFTER VERBS, ADJECTIVES AND PREPOSITIONS

Exercise 1
1 to tell
2 to help
3 playing
4 watching
5 playing
6 helping

Exercise 2
1 My friends and always enjoy **meeting** in town on Saturdays.
2 I hope **to visit** Brazil one day.
3 I'm sorry **to hear** you're ill.
4 All my friends enjoy **watching** football.
5 Do you mind **waiting** a little longer?

Exercise 3
1 to visit
2 playing
3 having
4 to finish
5 to spend
6 to pass
7 being
8 going

Page 216

UNIT 10
THE FUTURE WITH WILL

Exercise 1
1 won't have
2 will go
3 Will … be, won't
4 won't pass, will be
5 will meet

Exercise 2
1 We'll probably go to Spain for our holiday next year.
2 I think it will be colder tomorrow.
3 Perhaps we'll have a new teacher next term.
4 Are you sure you'll be OK?
5 He probably won't come to our party.

Exercise 3
1 Shall
2 I'll
3 Will

4 won't
5 will
6 I'll

Exercise 4
1 b   3 e   5 f
2 c   4 a   6 d

MAY/MIGHT

Exercise 5
Tom and Julie are going. The others are not sure.

Exercise 6
1 e   3 a   5 c
2 f   4 b   6 d

Page 218

UNIT 11
BE GOING TO

Exercise 1
1 're going to miss
2 're going to ride
3 'm going to do
4 aren't going to need
5 are going to visit

Exercise 2
2 **A:** What are you going to do this evening?
   B: I'm going to play a video game.
3 **A:** Is it going to rain tomorrow?
   B: No, Look at the red sky. It's going to be sunny all day.
4 **A:** What are you going to do when you leave college?
   B: I'm going to look for a good job.
5 **A:** Is your team going to win the match?
   B: No, the other team is much better. We're going to lose.

PRESENT CONTINUOUS FOR THE FUTURE

Exercise 3
1 going to eat
2 catching
3 seeing
4 going to do, going to phone
5 having

PRESENT SIMPLE TO TALK ABOUT THE FUTURE

Exercise 4
1 leaves
2 's having
3 is coming
4 starts
5 finish

Page 220

UNIT 12
ZERO AND FIRST CONDITIONAL

Exercise 1
1 d   3 b   5 c
2 a   4 e   6 f

Exercise 2
1 see, 'll/will tell
2 'll/will hurt, fall
3 don't catch, 'll/will have
4 'll/will be, don't leave
5 is, 'll/will wake

Exercise 3
1 If I get a new job, I'll earn more money.
2 I'll buy a car if I have enough money.
3 If I buy a car, I'll use it to go to work.
4 I'll get fit if I ride my bike to work.
5 I won't get fit if I go to work by bus.

CONJUNCTIONS: WHEN, IF, UNLESS + PRESENT , FUTURE

Exercise 4
1 Unless
2 unless
3 If
4 if
5 unless
6 When/If
7 If
8 when

THE PASSIVE

Exercise 5
1 is grown
2 are sold
3 are shown
4 is made
5 is closed

Exercise 6
1 was built
2 were told
3 was closed
4 was given
5 were taken
6 was sent

Page 222

UNIT 13
COMPARATIVES AND SUPERLATIVES

Exercise 1
1 bigger
2 more interesting
3 heavier
4 warmer
5 worse
6 larger

Exercise 2
1 I am the **best** footballer at my college.
2 Anna is **happier** than she was this morning.
3 I want to be **fitter** so I do lots of exercise.
4 What is the **most expensive** thing you have?
5 Ben's apartment is **larger** than mine.
6 Tom is **taller than** his father.

TO BE LIKE AND TO LOOK LIKE
Exercise 3
1 What does he look like?
2 What are your new neighbours like?
3 What is their new baby like?
4 What does she look like?

AS... AS, NOT AS... AS
Exercise 4
1 He is **as tall as** his father now.
2 The climate in England is **as pleasant as** the climate in Ireland.
3 You must play **as hard as** you can, if you want to win the match.
4 This ice cream's not **as tasty as** the one we bought yesterday.
5 I'm making **as many mistakes as** I did yesterday.

Page 224
UNIT 14
MUST/MUSTN'T
Exercise 1
1 mustn't be
2 must wear
3 mustn't run
4 mustn't talk
5 mustn't use
6 must finish

Exercise 2
1 You must visit / go to
2 You mustn't use
3 You must try
4 You mustn't lose
5 You must see / visit

HAVE TO
Exercise 3
1 have to help
2 do you have to do
3 have to tidy
4 Does she have to tidy
5 she does
6 has to wash
7 don't have to do

Exercise 4
1 have to
2 don't have to
3 don't have to
4 have to
5 have to

NEED TO/DON'T NEED TO
Exercise 5
1 You don't need to finish the project by Friday.
2 I need to phone home to check that everything is OK.
3 I really need to work harder or I won't get very good marks.
4 She needs to buy some food for dinner tonight.

CAN/CAN'T
Exercise 6
1 Anyone can become rich and famous.
2 Learning a foreign language can be very hard.
3 A room in a small hotel can't cost more than fifty pounds.
4 When you have small children, you can't leave objects around the house.

PHRASAL VERB BANK

Page 227
GETTING ABOUT
Exercise 1
get back = return
take off = leave the ground (a plane)
come round = visit someone's house
come in = enter a place
pick (someone) up = collect someone from somewhere

Exercise 2
1 takes off
2 get back
3 picked me up
4 come in
5 came round

Exercise 3
Students' own answers.

IN THE MORNING
Exercise 1
take something off = stop wearing
wake up = stop sleeping
get up = get out of bed
go out = leave
put something on = start wearing

Exercise 2
1 wake up
2 get up
3 take off
4 put (my school uniform) on
5 go out

Exercise 3
Students' own answers.

PEOPLE AND COMMUNICATION
Exercise 1
grow up = become an adult
call someone back = return a phone call
find out = get information about
look after = take care of
get on with someone = be friendly with someone

Exercise 2
1 look after
2 get on
3 find out
4 call (you) back
5 grew up

Exercise 3
Students' own answers.

OTHER PHRASAL VERBS
Exercise 1
lie down = usually something you do before you go to sleep
turn off = stop a machine or light from working
fill in = write information on a form
give back = give something to the person who gave it to you
try on = put on clothes to see if they fit

Exercise 2
1 lie down
2 turn off
3 try (shoes) on
4 fill in
5 give back

Exercise 3
Students' own answers.

WRITING BANK

Page 229
HOW TO MAKE YOUR WRITING BETTER: ADJECTIVES
Exercise 1
2b We had lunch in a <u>small</u>, <u>friendly</u> restaurant.
3b A <u>kind</u> woman showed me the way home.
4b I knew I had made a <u>big</u> mistake.

Exercise 2
1 true
2 false
3 true

Exercise 3
1 heavy
2 important
3 modern/lovely
4 lovely
5 expensive

Exercise 4
1 exciting, funny
2 beautiful, lovely
3 brilliant, great
4 friendly, kind
5 sunny, pleasant
6 great, excellent

Exercise 5
1 wonderful
2 terrible
3 amazing
4 horrible
5 awful
6 fantastic

very good	very bad
wonderful	terrible
amazing	horrible
fantastic	awful

HOW TO MAKE YOUR WRITING BETTER: ADVERBS AND INTERESTING VERBS
Exercise 1
2b The children were playing <u>happily</u> in the garden.
3b I read the invitation <u>carefully</u>.
4b She opened the letter <u>slowly</u>.
5b I couldn't see <u>well</u> because it was cloudy.

Exercise 2
1 true
2 true
3 false
4 true

Exercise 3
1 loudly
2 hungrily
3 clearly
4 fast
5 carefully
6 easily
7 well
8 beautifully

Exercise 4
2 I quickly read the letter.
3 She closed the door quietly.
4 He carefully carried the hot drinks into the sitting room.
5 We walked slowly through the park.
6 Mark didn't sleep well last night.

Exercise 5
1 hurried
2 shouting
3 relaxing
4 jumped
5 threw
6 cried

Exercise 6
1 ran
2 shouted
3 relaxed
4 jumped
5 threw

USE VERB FORMS CORRECTLY TO TALK ABOUT THE PAST, PRESENT AND FUTURE
Exercise 1
Hi Jo,
I <u>go</u> swimming next Saturday. My cousin <u>are</u> here at the moment, and he <u>love</u> films. <u>Are you want</u> to come too? There's a new cinema on Wood Road. We can <u>to</u> get the bus. I <u>meet</u> you at the bus stop.
Sam

Exercise 2
Hi Jo,
<u>I'm going</u> swimming next Saturday. My cousin <u>is</u> here at the moment, and he <u>loves</u> films. <u>Do you want</u> to come too? There's a new cinema on Wood Road. We <u>can get</u> the bus. I <u>can/will meet</u> you at the bus stop.
Sam

Exercise 3
1 'm going
2 is
3 loves
4 Do you want
5 've never been
6 went
7 get
8 can meet

Exercise 4
1 'm going
2 went
3 've never been
4 can get, can meet

Exercise 5
1 'm going
2 bought
3 starts
4 to come
5 have met
6 go

Exercise 6
Model answer
Hi Max,
I'm going to a water park next Saturday. Would you like to come? My friend Paul is coming too. He went there last month and loved it. We can get there by train. I think it will be amazing!
Stan

USE LINKING WORDS AND RELATIVE PRONOUNS TO MAKE SENTENCES LONGER
Exercise 1
10 sentences

Exercise 2
Dan woke up <u>and</u> got out of bed. He didn't look at his clock. He opened the fridge, <u>but</u> it was almost empty. He was hungry, <u>so</u> he decided to go out for some food. He went to a café, <u>but</u> it was closed <u>because</u> it was only 6.30 in the morning!

Exercise 3
1 but
2 and
3 so
4 because
5 but
6 so

Exercise 4
1 which
2 who
3 who
4 that

Exercise 5
1 who
2 which

Exercise 6
1 who
2 which
3 which
4 who

Page 233
WRITING PART 6: A SHORT MESSAGE
Exercise 1
Write about three things. Write 25 words or more.

Exercise 2
1 don't
2 could
3 Shall
4 Let's
5 Why

Exercise 3
1 c   3 d   5 b
2 a   4 e

Exercise 4
2 I'm afraid I can't come to your party.
3 I'm sorry, but I'll be a bit late.
4 Guess what! I won the competition!

Exercise 5

Hi Joe,

My cousin <u>Beth is</u> (Beth's) coming to visit on Saturday, and I <u>am</u> (I'm) really excited. <u>She is</u> (She's) very good at computer games <u>I have</u> (I've) got a new game and <u>we are</u> (we're) going to play some games together. Do you want to come too? <u>I will</u> (I'll) call you later.

Sam

Exercise 6

You should say that you can't go to the concert, give a reason why you can't go and suggest another day when you can go.

Exercise 8
Model answer

Hi Laura,

I'm sorry, but I can't go to the concert on Saturday. I have to stay at home because my grandparents are coming to visit. Why don't we meet on Sunday and go to the cinema?

See you soon,
Ana

Page 234
WRITING PART 7: A STORY

Exercise 1
35 words or more

Exercise 2
1 was feeling
2 was raining
3 arrived
4 was carrying
5 ate
6 played

Exercise 3
1 First
2 Next
3 Finally
4 Suddenly
5 Then
6 Finally

Exercise 4
1 tall
2 empty
3 pleased
4 quick
5 high
6 ready

Exercise 5
Students' own answers.

Exercise 6
Model answer

Alice wanted to watch TV, but her TV was broken. She told her sister. They looked on their computer and quickly found a big, new TV online. It wasn't expensive, so Alice's sister bought it. The next day, the new TV arrived, and Alice felt really happy.

Exercise 7
Students' own answers.

SPEAKING BANK

Page 237
GIVING PERSONAL INFORMATION

Exercise 1

	Pablo	Lucia
Age	17	18
From	Madrid	Milan

Exercise 2
1 b 2 c 3 d 4 a

🎧 Track 119

Pablo: Hello. My name's Pablo and I'm 17 years old. I'm Spanish and I come from Madrid.
Lucia: Hi. My name's Lucia. I'm 18 years old, and I'm Italian. I live in Milan.

TALKING ABOUT HABITS, LIKES AND DISLIKES

Exercise 1
doing homework, meeting friends, playing tennis, watching TV

Exercise 2
1 always get up
2 am never
3 usually do
4 often watch
5 on Saturdays
6 sometimes meet

🎧 Track 120

Girl: I always get up early on school days, and I'm never late for school. I usually do my homework when I get home from school. I don't often watch TV. I usually play tennis on Saturdays, and I sometimes meet my friends at the weekend too.

Exercise 3
basketball

Exercise 4
1 like
2 don't
3 listening
4 prefer
5 favourite

🎧 Track 121

Boy: I like maths and science, but I don't like art. I enjoy listening to music, but I don't like singing because I'm not a very good singer. I love sport! I like tennis, but I prefer football to tennis. Basketball is my favourite sport because it's very exciting.

GIVING OPINIONS AND REASONS

Exercise 1
cycling

Exercise 2
1 Do
2 do
3 about
4 don't
5 think
6 going
7 What
8 prefer
9 fun
10 love

🎧 Track 122

Girl: Do you like swimming?
Boy: Yes, I do. It's fun. What about you?
Girl: No, I don't like swimming. I think it's boring. But I love going to the cinema. It's really interesting. What do you think?
Boy: No, I think going to the cinema is expensive. I prefer to watch films at home. My favourite activity is cycling. Do you think cycling is fun?
Girl: Yes, I do. I love cycling!

Exercise 3
1 b 2 a 3 a

🎧 Track 123

Narrator: One
Boy: I often travel to other countries with my family. I like travelling because you visit interesting places and you learn about different countries.
Narrator: Two
Girl: My brother loves skateboarding, but I don't like it because I think it's dangerous. You can fall down and hurt yourself.
Narrator: Three
Boy: This is my new computer game. I play it a lot. I'm not very good at it, but I love it because it's exciting. Oh, no!

Exercise 4
Students' own answers.

🎧 Track 124

Narrator: One
Girl: I like reading because it's relaxing and you can learn about a lot of different things.

Narrator: Two
Boy: I love football because it's an exciting game, and you feel really good when you win.
Narrator: Three
Boy: I don't like shopping because there aren't any good shops here.

AGREEING AND DISAGREEING
Exercise 1
1

Exercise 2
1 not sure about
2 That's true
3 agree with you
4 Yes, but

Track 125
Girl: Do you play any musical instruments?
Boy: Yes, I'm learning to play the guitar. What about you?
Girl: I'm learning the piano. I think it's very difficult to learn an instrument.
Boy: I'm not sure about that. The guitar isn't very difficult, but it's important to practise every day.
Girl: That's true. I agree with you that it's important to practise so that you can get better. I think that lessons are very expensive, too.
Boy: Yes, but you can watch lessons online and teach yourself. That isn't expensive.

DEALING WITH PROBLEMS
Exercise 1
1 Could you repeat
2 Can you repeat
3 say that again

Exercise 2
1 Could you repeat ~~again~~ that <u>again</u>, please?
2 Can you repeat ~~me~~ the question, please?
3 Could you say <u>that</u> again, please?

Track 126
Narrator: One
Teacher: Don't forget the trip to the museum tomorrow. We're meeting at 9.45.
Girl: Could you repeat that, please?
Teacher: Yes. It's 9.45 tomorrow morning.
Girl: Thank you.
Narrator: Two
Teacher: Do you think swimming in the sea is dangerous?
Boy: Can you repeat the question, please?
Teacher: Of course. Do you think swimming in the sea is dangerous?
Boy: Yes, I think that sometimes it can be dangerous, especially in bad weather.

Narrator: Three
Girl: I'm glad you can come to my party. It's at my house. I live at 29, West Street.
Boy: Could you say that again, please? I need to write it down.
Girl: Sure. It's 29, West Street. It isn't far from here.

Exercise 3
1 c 2 a 3 b

Exercise 4
1 not, word
2 what, called
3 know, is

Track 127
Man: I'm not sure what the word is, but you often play this on the beach, with your friends. You have a ball, and you hit the ball with your hand.
Woman: I'm not sure what this is called, but it's something you wear around your neck in winter, when it's very cold.
Man: I don't know what the word is, but it's something you eat. It's sweet, and very cold, and you often eat it in the summer.

Page 240
SPEAKING PART 1
Exercise 1
Yes, she does.

Exercise 3
1 or
2 because
3 because

Track 128
Examiner: Now, let's talk about weekends. What do you do at weekends?
Ana: I often go shopping, or I sometimes go to the cinema.
Examiner: And who do you like spending your weekends with?
Ana: I like spending my weekends with friends, because we laugh and have fun together.
Examiner: Now, let's talk about shopping. Where do you like going shopping?
Ana: I like going shopping in London because there are lots of good shops.
Examiner: And what do you like buying?
Ana: I like buying clothes and shoes because I'm interested in fashion.

Exercise 4
1 love
2 buy
3 bought
4 liked
5 'm going to take

Track 129
Examiner: Now, please tell me something about presents that you buy for other people.
Ana: Well, I love buying presents for people. I usually buy presents for people when it's their birthday. For example, last month I bought a T-shirt for my brother and he really liked it. It's my friend's birthday next week, and I'm going to take her to the cinema as a present.

Exercise 5
1 b 3 b 5 b
2 a 4 a 6 b

Exercise 6
1 have – present
2 'm going to meet – future
3 watch – present
4 cooked – past
5 'm going to play – future
6 bought – past

Exercise 7
1 c 3 e 5 a
2 d 4 b

Track 130
Examiner: Tell me something about what you like doing at home.
Ana: I like watching films, and I enjoy playing video games. I've just got a new game, so I'm quite excited about that.
Examiner: Tell me something about what you like to eat with friends.
Ana: I sometimes go to restaurants with my friends, and I prefer Italian food. We went to a pizza restaurant last weekend, and it was very nice.
Examiner: Tell me something about the clothes you like to buy.
Ana: I love buying new clothes, and my favourite thing to buy is jeans, because I like wearing them. I bought some really nice jeans last week, so I was happy.
Examiner: Tell me something about the places you like to visit.
Ana: I don't like going to big cities because there's too much traffic. I like visiting places that are near the sea. I love swimming when the weather's hot.
Examiner: Tell me something about the sports you like to do.
Ana: I like playing football. I play for a team, and we have a game every Saturday. My team doesn't often win, but it's still fun.

Exercise 8
Students' own answers.

Page 241
SPEAKING PART 2
Exercise 1
Yes, they do.

🎧 **Track 131**
Girl: So, do you like playing video games?
Boy: Yes, I do. I've got a lot of video games, and I often play with my friends. I think they're exciting. What do you think?
Girl: I'm not sure about that. I sometimes play video games, but I think they're a bit boring.
Boy: What about taking photos? Do you like taking photos?
Girl: I often take photos when I'm with my friends, but I don't have a camera. I take photos on my phone. What about you?
Boy: I like taking photos, too. I have got a camera, and I love taking photos of animals and the countryside.
Girl: What about cycling? I love cycling because it's fun, and it's healthy. I always go cycling at weekends. What do you think about it?
Boy: I agree with you that it's fun and it's also good exercise. What about music? Do you play any instruments?
Girl: No, I don't. But I enjoy listening to music. What about you? Do you play an instrument?
Boy: I'm learning to play the drums. I'd like to be in a band one day.
Girl: And what about reading books? Do you like reading?
Boy: Yes, I like reading books, for example adventure books. But I prefer films to books.
Girl: Yes, I agree with you. I think films are more exciting than books.

Exercise 2
Yes, she does.

🎧 **Track 132**
Examiner: So, which of these hobbies do you like best?
Girl: I like cycling the best because I enjoy being active and I like spending time outside, and I think that cycling keeps you fit and healthy.

Exercise 3
1 think
2 sure
3 like
4 about
5 do
6 agree

🎧 **Track 133**
Boy: I think video games are exciting. What do you think?
Girl: I'm not sure about that.
Boy: What about taking photos? Do you like taking photos?
Girl: I often take photos when I'm with my friends.
Girl: I take photos on my phone. What about you?
Boy: I like taking photos, too. I've got a camera.
Girl: I always go cycling at weekends. What do you think about it?
Boy: I agree with you that it's fun.

Exercise 4
1 d   3 e   5 c
2 a   4 b

Exercise 5
Students' own answers.

🎧 **Track 134**
Boy: Well, I love music festivals because I'm a music fan. I think they're great. What about you?
Girl: I agree with you. I like going to music festivals with my friends. And do you like going to the beach?
Boy: Yes, I do. I like swimming in the sea and playing with a ball on the beach. What about you?
Girl: Yes, I agree. Going to the beach is fun when the weather's hot. And what about walking in the mountains? I don't like that because it's really difficult. What do you think?
Boy: I'm not sure. I like it because you can see the beautiful countryside. I like camping, too because it's fun and you're outside. Do you agree?
Girl: No, I don't agree. I hate camping because I prefer to sleep in a comfortable bed! But I like picnics. I often go for picnics with my friends in the summer. Do you like picnics?
Boy: Yes, I do. When it's sunny, it's lovely to eat outside in a nice place, for example near a river.

Exercise 6
Students' own answers.

🎧 **Track 135**
Examiner: Which of these activities do you like the best?
Boy: I like going to music festivals because you can listen to some exciting bands and also spend time with your friends and have fun.
Examiner: Do you prefer to go on holiday to the beach or the countryside?
Boy: I prefer to go to the beach because in the countryside it's sometimes a bit boring, because there aren't many people and there are no restaurants or cafés. At the beach there are lots of people, so it's more exciting.
Examiner: Do you prefer swimming in the sea or in a swimming pool?
Boy: I prefer swimming in the sea. It's more interesting because you can see different things around you, but in the swimming pool you just have to go up and down all the time, so I think it's a bit boring.

WORKBOOK ANSWER KEY

STARTER
VOCABULARY
Exercise 1
1. grandfather
2. niece
3. husband
4. daughter
5. uncle
6. cousin
7. child
8. sister
9. grandparent
10. grandma/granny
11. dad/father
12. granddaughter

Exercise 2
1. (north) American
2. Mexico
3. Portuguese
4. France, Canadian
5. China
6. Italian
7. Spain

Exercise 3
1. 076953221
2. 25th July 2002
3. 21
4. 2024
5. 290
6. SW14 8GM

Exercise 4
1. driving licence
2. passport
3. identity card
4. first name, surname
5. DOB

GRAMMAR
Exercise 1
A. am, 'm/am, Are, 's/is
   Correct order: 4,2,3,1
B. aren't/are not, 're/are, are, 'm/am, Are
   Correct order: 2,3,1
C. 's/is, isn't/'s not/is not, 's/is, 're/are, 's/is, Is
   Correct order: 4 2 3 1

Exercise 2
1. Tanya's
2. Mike's
3. Nihal's
4. name's/is
5. Nick's car's/car is

Exercise 3
1. Dean has got/'s got a/one brother.
2. Dean's parents have got two sons.
3. Dean's parents haven't got a big house.
4. Dean has got/'s got a motorbike.
5. Dean hasn't got a car.

Exercise 4
1. Carla can swim one kilometre.
2. Roberto can't swim one kilometre.
3. Roberto and Carla can speak Spanish.
4. Carla can't cook paella.
5. Roberto can cook paella.
6. Roberto and Carla can write computer programs.

Exercise 5
1. does, come
2. doesn't live
3. lives
4. Does he work
5. does
6. works
7. doesn't
8. Does he speak
9. loves

LISTENING
Exercise 1
1. T, R, K, S, H, I, U
2. H, S, I, N, C, E, E

Exercise 2
1. Turkish
2. Chinese

Exercise 3
1. 1st May 2018
2. 31st August 1992
3. 20th September 2004
4. 15th March 2025

Exercise 4
1. Chinese
2. Lucy
3. Mansfield
4. 2nd June
5. American
6. 58 Charnwood
7. 0795301244

READING
Exercise 1
1. B
2. D
3. A
4. C

Exercise 2
1. Mexico
2. Italian
3. USA
4. 20 years old
5. fish
6. art

SPEAKING
Exercise 1
1. C
2. C
3. A
4. B
5. B
6. C

Exercise 2
1.
Q: What's your first name?
A: Patricia.
2.
Q: How old are you?
A: I'm twenty.
3.
Q: What's your job?
A: I'm an actor.
4.
Q: Where do you come from?
A: I'm Italian.
5.
Q: How many brothers and sisters have you got?
A: One of each.
6.
Q: Where do you live?
A: In Paris, France.

WRITING
1. is/'s
2. has got/'s got
3. 's/is
4. doesn't live
5. speaks/can speak
6. 's/is
7. 's got/has got

UNIT 1
VOCABULARY
Exercise 1
1. wake up
2. stay
3. get up
4. have
5. get dressed
6. have
7. get on
8. take off
9. put on

Exercise 2
1. after
2. before
3. before
4. after
5. after
6. before

Exercise 3
1. (a) quarter to five
2. (a) quarter past six
3. 11 o'clock
4. half past one

Exercise 4
a. 6
b. 3
c. 2
d. 4
e. 1
f. 5

GRAMMAR
Exercise 1
1. are
2. works
3. am
4. start
5. don't get up
6. get up
7. doesn't like
8. have
9. doesn't eat
10. has

Exercise 2
1. Does Natalie work
2. Do the sisters/they get up
3. Does Mischa like
4. Does Mischa stay
5. Do the sisters/they have
6. Does Natalie have

Exercise 3
1. C
2. A
3. C
4. B
5. A
6. C

Exercise 4
1. do, want to do, want to go
2. does. want to be, wants to travel
3. does, want to do, doesn't want to get, wants to win
4. do, want to work, want to work

Exercise 5

1. Stefi likes going out dancing on Friday evenings.
2. Louis doesn't like staying in bed after he wakes up.
3. Leo and Tom like playing computer games together.
4. My mum and I love swimming in the sea.
5. Johnnie hates going shopping at the supermarket.
6. My English teacher doesn't like working in hot weather.

LISTENING
Exercise 1

	Kenny	Zadie
A	4	6
B	3	1
C	1	2
D	2	4
E	5	5
F	6	3

Exercise 2

1. Kenny
2. Zadie
3. Kenny
4. Zadie
5. Zadie

READING PART 2

1. C
2. B
3. A
4. C
5. B
6. C
7. A

PUSH YOURSELF B1

1. ✗
2. ✗
3. ✓
4. ✗
5. ✓

SPEAKING
[Suggested answers]

1. Where do you work? I work at a newspaper office.
2. How do you go/get/travel to work? I go to work by bus.
3. When do you get to work? I get to work at 8.00 am.
4. Why do you like your job? I like my job because I like meeting interesting people.
5. Who do you live with? I live with three friends.

WRITING

1. Dear
2. wishes
3. Hi
4. Love from
5. the best

UNIT 2
VOCABULARY
Exercise 1

1. January
2. September
3. July
4. March
5. June
6. October
7. December

Exercise 2

1. summer
2. autumn
3. winter
4. spring

Exercise 3

1. ice
2. stormy, lightning
3. temperature
4. cloud, rain
5. sunny
6. foggy
7. snowy

Exercise 4

A. a lake
B. a mountain
C. a coast
D. a valley
E. a waterfall
F. an island
G. a desert
H. a forest

GRAMMAR
Exercise 1

1. 'm/am wearing
2. 's/is snowing
3. 're not/aren't studying
4. 're/are talking
5. 're/are leaving
6. aren't going

Exercise 2

1. What are you doing there?
2. We're working here this week.
3. Are you staying in a hotel?
4. I am having a great week!
5. So I'm not working.
6. Where are you staying?
7. Some friends are visiting us at the moment.

Exercise 3

1. 'm/am having, have
2. enjoys, 's/is enjoying
3. lives, 's/is living
4. are playing, play
5. drives, 's/is driving
6. rains, 's/is raining

READING
Exercise 1

B

Exercise 2

1. conservation officer
2. south
3. South America, Africa
4. smaller islands
5. visitors
6. the weather/temperature/climate

PUSH YOURSELF B1

1. heavy
2. strong
3. thick
4. bright, clear
5. hard

LISTENING PART 1

1. C
2. A
3. C
4. B
5. C

SPEAKING
Exercise 1

1. there's
2. Maybe
3. sitting
4. in the middle
5. it's
6. are enjoying
7. aren't wearing
8. see
9. below

Exercise 2

What is there in the photo?
Sentence number: 1

Describing details
Sentence number: 7, 8

What is happening in the photo?
Sentence number: 3

The weather in the photo
Sentence number: 5

Where are things in the photo?
Sentence number: 4, 9

What do you think?
Sentence number: 2, 6

WRITING
Exercise 1

Do you want to come with us?
how about staying at our house tonight?
would you like to bring a friend with you?

Exercise 2

1. I'd love to come but I'm afraid I've got football practice from 4 pm–6.30 pm.
2. That would be wonderful.
3. Thanks for asking but all my friends are busy tomorrow.

UNIT 3
VOCABULARY
Exercise 1

1. blogger
2. upload
3. social media
4. comments
5. series
6. episode
7. download
8. stream

Exercise 2

1. news
2. documentary
3. crime drama
4. comedy
5. quiz show
6. action film

Exercise 3

1. a
2. e
3. c
4. b
5. d

It's a science-fiction film.

GRAMMAR
Exercise 1

1. were
2. wasn't
3. Were, were
4. was
5. weren't
6. were

Exercise 2

1. Did … watch, played
2. did … decide, loved
3. did … finish, didn't work
4. helped, Did … enjoy

Exercise 3
1 spoke to her uncle
2 went shopping
3 got up at 10 o'clock
4 had breakfast in/at a café

READING PART 3
1 C   4 A
2 C   5 C
3 B

PUSH YOURSELF B1
Exercise 1
1 enjoyable, amusing
2 amusing, silly
3 awful, disappointing
4 dull, uninteresting

Exercise 2
1 true   4 false
2 false   5 true
3 false

LISTENING
Exercise 1
1 the weather on Saturday
2 different kinds of TV
3 doing something with family members
4 an outside activity

Exercise 2
1 Anna   4 Ryan
2 Anna   5 Anna
3 Ryan   6 Ryan

SPEAKING
Exercise 1
1 How was your weekend?
2 What did you get up to last night?
3 Did you have a good weekend?
4 What do you do on Friday afternoons?
5 Do you usually go shopping on Saturdays?

Exercise 2
A 4   D 1
B 5   E 2
C 3

Exercise 3
1 d   4 c
2 b
3 a

WRITING
1 The setting is
2 The story is about
3 The plot is
4 My favourite character is
5 My favourite moment is
6 The best things about the film are

UNIT 4
VOCABULARY
Exercise 1
1 false – five toes
2 true
3 true
4 true
5 true
6 false – in the middle of your legs
7 true
8 false – part of your hand(s)

Exercise 2
1 brain   4 back
2 neck   5 knees
3 fingers

Exercise 3
1 dentist, toothache
2 medicine, pharmacy
3 sick, fine
4 hospital, leg

GRAMMAR
Exercise 1
1 can   4 can't
2 couldn't 5 couldn't
3 could   6 could

Exercise 2
1 Can Leah ride a motorbike?
2 Can Leah swim 1,000 metres / drive a car
3 Could Leah ride a horse
4 Could Leah swim 1,000 metres / drive a car

Exercise 3
1 shouldn't 5 should
2 should   6 shouldn't
3 shouldn't 7 should
4 should   8 Should

PUSH YOURSELF B1
1 (on your) wrist
2 (your) lungs
3 (the) ankle
4 (the) hips
5 (your) elbow
6 (your) muscles

LISTENING PART 2
1 Tuesday(s)
2 7.00
3 6/six
4 forest
5 picnic

READING
Exercise 1
D, E

Exercise 2
1 fly   5 field
2 foot   6 leg
3 office   7 towel
4 finger   8 wrist

SPEAKING
Exercise 1
1 Are you OK?
2 better
3 how's
4 How are you?
5 sorry to hear that
6 What's the matter

Exercise 2
1 d   4 a
2 b   5 e
3 f   6 c

WRITING
1 One day
2 suddenly
3 then
4 After that

UNIT 5
VOCABULARY
Exercise 1
1 a flight
2 a traveller
3 street food
4 catch a train
5 go to work
6 a national park

Exercise 2
1 backpacks, luggage
2 miss, delay
3 accommodation, tent
4 tour guide, tourist information centre

Exercise 3
1 journey
2 flight
3 trip
4 travel
5 cruise
6 crossing

GRAMMAR
Exercise 1
1 was reading
2 wasn't listening
3 were watching
4 Were … camping
5 Was … raining
6 weren't looking
7 Were … winning

Exercise 2
1 was reading, was sitting
2 booked
3 was packing, called
4 was packing, found
5 asked, was looking
6 was looking, found

READING PART 4
Exercise 1
1 Paragraph 2
2 Paragraph 1
3 Paragraph 2
4 Paragraph 2
5 Paragraph 1
6 Paragraph 1

Exercise 2
1 C   4 B
2 B   5 A
3 A   6 C

LISTENING
Exercise 1
A 4
B 5
C 1
D 3
E 2

Exercise 2
1 B   4 C
2 B   5 A
3 A

PUSH YOURSELF B1

1. C
2. D
3. F
4. B
5. A
6. E

SPEAKING

Exercise 1

a 5
b 4
c 6
d 2
e 1
f 3

Exercise 2

1. enjoy
2. had
3. fantastic
4. terrible
5. for me
6. think

WRITING

1. This morning
2. Right now
3. while
4. Yesterday
5. after that
6. the evening

UNIT 6
VOCABULARY

Exercise 1

A an omelette
B a chicken
C some cereal
D a beef curry
E some broccoli
F a mango
G some mushrooms
H some yoghurt

Exercise 2

1. Starters
2. Main courses
3. Desserts
4. Lunch
5. Dinner

Exercise 3

1. yoghurt, ice cream
2. chocolate
3. soup, cereal
4. eggs

GRAMMAR

Exercise 1

1. some
2. some
3. any
4. an
5. any
6. any
7. a
8. a

Exercise 2

how many: apple, biscuit, burger
how much: rice, salt, bread
a little: rice, salt, bread
a few: apple, biscuit, burger
not much: rice, salt, bread
not many: apple, biscuit, burger
a lot of: apple, rice, biscuit, burger, salt, bread

Exercise 3

1. How many (packets of) crisps does Nadya eat? A lot.
2. How much meat does Nadya eat? Not much.
3. How much chocolate does Martin eat? / How many bars of chocolate does Martin eat? Not much. / Not many.
4. How many eggs does Nadya eat? Not many.

Exercise 4

1. doesn't drink much
2. eats a lot of
3. doesn't eat much
4. eats a lot of
5. doesn't eat many

LISTENING PART 5

1. G
2. C
3. B
4. A
5. H

PUSH YOURSELF B1

1. peel
2. Chop
3. Peel
4. Fry
5. stir
6. add
7. add
8. burn
9. Grill
10. Steam

READING

Exercise 1

B

Exercise 2

1. F
2. T
3. T
4. F
5. T
6. F
7. F
8. F

SPEAKING

Exercise 1

1. go
2. having
3. eating
4. ask
5. paying

Exercise 2

1. shall
2. How about
3. I'm afraid
4. Let's
5. That's a good idea
6. I don't mind
7. Shall

WRITING

1. First
2. Then
3. After
4. when
5. until
6. While
7. Next
8. Finally

UNIT 7
VOCABULARY

Exercise 1

1. baking
2. doing photography
3. going to the gym
4. hanging out with friends
5. playing board games
6. going to gigs
7. doing Massaoke
8. doing exercise

Exercise 2

1. e
2. b
3. c
4. a
5. d

Exercise 3

1. flute
2. drums
3. violin
4. piano
5. keyboard
6. trumpets

Exercise 4

1. songwriter
2. musician
3. solo artist
4. drummer
5. singer
6. guitarist

(answers in any order) Ed is a songwriter, a musician, a solo artist, a singer and a guitarist.

GRAMMAR

Exercise 1

1. Has Joe ever won a game of chess?
   Yes, he has.
2. Have Max and Joe ever lived near a desert?
   No, they haven't.
3. Have Max and Joe ever visited a country in Africa?
   Yes, they have.
4. Has Joe ever spoken to a famous person?
   Yes, he has.
5. Have Max and Joe ever been to a gig together?
   No, they haven't.

Exercise 2

1. has won
2. have never lived
3. have visited
4. has never spoken
5. have never been

Exercise 3

1. He's just driven into the garage.
2. Because she's just run up some stairs.
3. I've just found it on the desk.
4. They've just left their flat!

LISTENING

Exercise 1

1. C
2. B

Exercise 2

1. C
2. A
3. C
4. A
5. B
6. C

READING PART 1

1. A
2. B
3. B
4. B
5. C
6. A

PUSH YOURSELF B1

1. A
2. B
3. A
4. B
5. B
6. B
7. A
8. A

SPEAKING
Exercise 1
1. Because it makes me feel fantastic!
2. I think it's important to learn new things.
3. It helps to relax me/me to relax after a busy day at work.
4. It makes me feel like a rock star!
5. I think it helps me to be a stronger person.

Exercise 2
1. e 3. c 5. d
2. f 4. a 6. b

WRITING
Exercise 1
1. isn't
2. know
3. is
4. doesn't mean
5. is something
6. isn't
7. is
8. isn't
9. enjoyed
10. was

Exercise 2
1. delicious
2. Special
3. world-famous
4. traditional
5. amazing
6. excellent

UNIT 8
VOCABULARY
Exercise 1
1. villa
2. cottage
3. townhouse
4. houseboat
5. studio flat
6. apartment

Exercise 2
1. ground
2. building
3. balcony
4. furniture
5. roof
6. neighbours
7. views
8. garage
9. basement
10. rent

Exercise 3
1. fridge
2. oven
3. cooker
4. cupboard
5. tap
6. sink

Exercise 4
1. a rug
2. stairs
3. a shelf
4. curtains
5. a lamp
6. a sofa

GRAMMAR
Exercise 1
1. 's/has already had a shower.
2. haven't/have not arrived at work yet.
3. haven't/have not left the house yet.
4. 've/have already eaten.
5. hasn't/has not finished the exam yet.
6. 've/have already met him.
7. 's/has already bought three.
8. haven't found one they like yet.

Exercise 2
since: June, this morning, 12 o'clock
for: 10 years, five minutes, a few hours

Exercise 3
1. finished, hasn't been
2. found, has/'s rented
3. have … had, bought
4. did … go, didn't go
5. have known, met
6. has/'s been, have/'ve lived

PUSH YOURSELF B1
Exercise 1
1. forgotten, kind of
2. how to, keep
3. it's called but, use it for
4. the English word, part of

Exercise 2
1. sofa/bench
2. cupboard/fridge
3. oven/cooker
4. basement/cellar

LISTENING PART 4
1. C   4. A
2. B   5. B
3. B

READING
Exercise 1
A, C, D, E, F

Exercise 2
Paragraph 1 B
Paragraph 2 A
Paragraph 3 C
Paragraph 4 B
Paragraph 5 C
Paragraph 6 A

SPEAKING
Exercise 1
1. home
2. part
3. anything
4. best
5. describe

Exercise 2
a. south   d. cafés
b. floor   e. tiles
c. noisy

Exercise 3
1. b   4. d
2. a   5. e
3. c

WRITING
Exercise 1
1. e   4. b
2. f   5. a
3. d   6. c

Exercise 2
1. My new apartment
2. Hello
3. How are you?
4. I'm writing to tell you
5. near
6. at
7. I wanted to ask you
8. All the best

UNIT 9
VOCABULARY
Exercise 1
1. b   4. e   7. f
2. c   5. a
3. g   6. d

Exercise 2
1. good mood
2. worried
3. angry
4. bad mood
5. get on well
6. argue
7. get on badly

Exercise 3
1. happy
2. exciting
3. easy
4. decide
5. ask
6. agree
7. prefer
8. teach
9. want

GRAMMAR
Exercise 1
1. hated/hates working
2. enjoys riding
3. before eating
4. started playing
5. after watching
6. at writing
7. without paying

Exercise 2
1. to play
2. playing
3. to play
4. to play
5. having
6. to go
7. playing
8. to book
9. not to forget

PUSH YOURSELF B1
1. don't mind
2. be bothered
3. feel like
4. excited about
5. hoping
6. am planning

LISTENING PART 3
1 B 3 C 5 A
2 A 4 B

READING PART 5
Exercise 1
1 at   4 What
2 an   5 all
3 am/'m 6 to

Exercise 2
1 T 4 T 7 F
2 F 5 F
3 T 6 F

SPEAKING
1 don't you write
2 should/could look on
3 turning it off / turning off your phone
4 shouldn't go to
5 about preparing
6 him to listen to
7 idea to cycle

WRITING
1 for your email
2 It was great
3 How about joining
4 It's not expensive
5 I'd like to ask you
6 Could you tell me
7 hear from you soon
8 Best wishes

UNIT 10
VOCABULARY
Exercise 1
1 fountains
2 library
3 theatre
4 castle
5 department store
6 statue
7 stadium

Exercise 2
1 don't go   5 aren't
2 are   6 shouldn't
3 aren't   7 can
4 need

Exercise 3
1 roundabout
2 crossing
3 underground station
4 traffic light
5 bus stop
6 corner

Exercise 4
1 Excuse   6 Take
2 know   7 go
3 walk   8 tell
4 turn   9 get
5 give   10 see

GRAMMAR
Exercise 1
1 won't   6 won't
2 may   7 might not
3 won't   8 might
4 'll/will 9 'll/will
5 may not   10 might

Exercise 2
1 'll be
2 'll chop
3 Shall ... make
4 'll look
5 Shall ... go
6 'll stay
7 'll drive
8 Shall ... get
9 'll see

PUSH YOURSELF B1
1 Public transport
2 skyscraper
3 historic
4 traffic-free
5 polluted
6 pavements
7 pedestrians
8 traffic jams

LISTENING PART 2
1 station   4 4th/fourth
2 15th   5 pen
3 8.30

READING
Exercise 1
A, C, D, E

Exercise 2
1 C   4 E
2 B   5 A
3 F

SPEAKING
1 B, C   5 B, C
2 B, C   6 A, B
3 A, C   7 B, C
4 A, B

WRITING
a I'll never forget seeing that fantastic view of the city.
b It was great to meet him.
c I had a wonderful day.
d It's the most amazing market I've ever been to.
e My favourite moment was when we arrived at the top.
f I'm looking forward to showing you the city.

1 c
2 d
3 e
4 a
5 f
6 b

UNIT 11
VOCABULARY
Exercise 1
1 reduced items
2 receipt
3 sale
4 bill
5 salary
6 discounts

Exercise 2
1 borrowed 5 earn
2 cost   6 wasted
3 saved   7 paid
4 spent   8 lent

Exercise 3
1 b 3 e 5 g 7 d
2 f 4 c 6 a

GRAMMAR
Exercise 1
1 leaves
2 does ... close
3 starts
4 do ... arrive

Exercise 2
1 are taking
2 is not/isn't/'s not going
3 am/'m working
4 does ... stop
5 are ... meeting
6 start

Exercise 3
1 doing/going to do
2 is getting married
3 is playing
4 are/'re staying/going to stay
5 are you going to spend
6 'm/am going to save
7 'm/am going to buy

READING
Exercise 1
B, C

Exercise 2
1 (boxes of) strawberries
2 strawberries, tomatoes
3 angry (and stupid)
4 (some) blogs
5 more often
6 in the fridge
7 world

PUSH YOURSELF B1
1 bank account
2 afford
3 owes
4 on credit
5 second-hand
6 bargains
7 worth
8 value for money

LISTENING PART 1
1 C   4 A
2 B   5 C
3 B

SPEAKING
Exercise 1
1 as/because, old and dirty
2 because/as, really boring
3 lovely little, That's why
4 delicious, so

Exercise 2
1 c
2 d
3 a
4 b

WRITING
1 near
2 building
3 One of the best
4 Another good
5 high point
6 bargains
7 One bad
8 Another negative
9 the worst thing
10 All in all
11 wouldn't recommend
12 go back

UNIT 12
VOCABULARY

Exercise 1
1. biology
2. geography
3. physics
4. history
5. drama
6. maths
7. chemistry

Exercise 2
[Suggested answers]
1. history, geography, modern languages
2. maths, physics
3. geography, physics
4. physics
5. drama
6. history, modern languages
7. history, geography, physics

Exercise 3
1. secondary school
2. a qualification
3. graduate
4. get good marks
5. a degree
6. primary school

Exercise 4
1. Are … revising/studying
2. revising/studying
3. pass
4. fail
5. take

Exercise 5
1. diploma
2. long hours
3. break
4. boss
5. day off
6. staff

GRAMMAR

Exercise 1
1. If I eat fish, I feel ill.
2. Plants die if they don't have water.
3. The room is too hot if you close the windows.
4. Phones sometimes break if you drop them.
5. If we go to Rome, we can visit my family there.
6. Cars get very dirty if you don't clean them.

Exercise 2
1. e If the train arrives late at the airport, we'll miss our flight.
2. f You won't have enough money for the video game if I don't lend you some.
3. b If you have any questions during the tour, the guide will try to answer them.
4. d If the mangoes in the supermarket are very small, I won't buy any.
5. a We'll go to the cinema if it rains on holiday.
6. c Bernardo will win the whole competition if he wins another game.

Exercise 3
1. was built
2. are made
3. were told
4. was enjoyed by
5. is visited by
6. are taken

LISTENING PART 4
1. B
2. A
3. B
4. A
5. C

PUSH YOURSELF B1
1. unless
2. When
3. unless
4. if
5. Unless
6. If
7. When

READING

Exercise 1
C

Exercise 2
1. e
2. g
3. d
4. c
5. a
6. i

SPEAKING

Exercise 1
1. Person applying for job
2. Interviewer
3. Person applying for job
4. Person applying for job
5. Person applying for job
6. Interviewer
7. Person applying for job
8. Interviewer
9. Person applying for job
10. Person applying for job

Exercise 2
a 4 e 10 i 2
b 6 f 8   j 3
c 7 g 9
d 5 h 1

WRITING
1. I am writing to apply for the job of waiter as advertised in your café.
2. I am attaching/attach/ have attached my CV with my qualifications and experience.
3. As you will see/As you can see from my CV, I have worked/worked in another café for a year and I have a diploma in business studies.
4. I am always very friendly and polite.
5. I look forward to hearing from you.

UNIT 13
VOCABULARY

Exercise 1
1. c
2. b
3. a
4. e
5. d

Exercise 2
1. brilliant
2. confident
3. annoying
4. sweet
5. quiet
6. Sociable
7. lazy
8. kind

Exercise 3
1. sporty
2. cool
3. fashionable
4. smart
5. casual

Exercise 4
1. handbag
2. sandals
3. tie
4. jewellery
5. sunglasses
6. suits
7. trainers

GRAMMAR

Exercise 1
1. What does he look like?
2. What's/is she like?
3. What are they like?
4. What does she look like?

Exercise 2
1. shorter than
2. thinner than
3. better looking / more good looking than
4. happier than
5. worse than
6. more boring than

Exercise 3
1. the hottest
2. the ugliest
3. the sweetest
4. the most interesting
5. the most expensive
6. the best
7. the worst

LISTENING PART 3
1. C
2. B
3. A
4. B
5. C

PUSH YOURSELF B1
1. is as clever as
2. is as high as
3. wasn't as warm as
4. isn't as good as
5. isn't as expensive as
6. isn't as easy as

READING
1. C   4. F
2. D   5. E
3. A   6. B

SPEAKING
1. 're wearing
2. 've got
3. think
4. sure
5. Perhaps/Maybe
6. probably
7. don't think
8. looks
9. Maybe/Perhaps
10. could be

WRITING
Exercise 1
Paragraph 1: C
Paragraph 2: D
Paragraph 3: A
Paragraph 4: B

Exercise 2
1. On the less positive side
2. So do I recommend the tent?
3. it depends on what you want.
4. then it is not a good buy
5. I fell in love with
6. It's the coolest tent
7. But for me, the best thing

UNIT 14
VOCABULARY
Exercise 1
1. athletics
2. basketball
3. cricket
4. rugby
5. tennis
6. football

Exercise 2
1. F football
2. F football
3. T
4. F basketball
5. F athletics
6. T
7. T
8. F tennis

Exercise 3
1. pitch
2. referee
3. red card
4. sent off
5. rules
6. lose

Exercise 4
1. g
2. b
3. e
4. a
5. f
6. c
7. d

Exercise 5
1. home matches
2. away matches
3. Season tickets
4. live matches

Exercise 6
1. play
2. do
3. play
4. go
5. go
6. do

GRAMMAR
Exercise 1
1. can
2. must
3. has to
4. can
5. needs to
6. can
7. mustn't
8. don't have to
9. don't need to
10. can't

Exercise 2
1. practise
2. will play
3. have played
4. taught
5. were living
6. is working
7. will

PUSH YOURSELF B1
1. always
2. After
3. finally
4. Suddenly
5. afterwards
6. unfortunately
7. Fortunately

LISTENING PART 5
1. H
2. A
3. E
4. G
5. D

READING
Exercise 1
A

Exercise 2
1. D
2. A
3. B
4. C
5. B
6. E
7. D
8. A
9. E
10. B

SPEAKING
1. c
2. a
3. f
4. b
5. d
6. e

WRITING
Exercise 1
1. Richard was playing his guitar when his aunt arrived with a box.
2. As Nick was driving along the street, it started to snow.
3. The sun was shining when Lucy's race began.
4. Two children were walking through the park when a little kitten started to follow them.
5. While the family were swimming in the sea, some birds started to eat their picnic.

Exercise 2
1. One afternoon, Richard was playing his (favourite) new guitar when his (favourite) aunt arrived with a large box.
2. One evening, as Nick was driving along the dark street, it started to snow.
3. Last Saturday, the sun was shining when Lucy's important long-distance race began.
4. Yesterday, two young children were walking through the park when a sweet little kitten started to follow them.
5. Last weekend while the family were swimming in the sea, some annoying birds started to eat their delicious picnic.

WORKBOOK AUDIOSCRIPT

STARTER

Track 02
1 T, R, K, S, H, I, U
2 H, S, I, N, C, E, E

Track 03
1 The first of May twenty eighteen
2 The thirty-first of August 1992
3 The twentieth of September 2004
4 The fifteenth of March twenty twenty-five

Track 04
Man:	Good morning, welcome to the Art School.
Woman:	Thanks. I'd like to join one of your evening art courses.
Man:	OK. Which one?
Woman:	It's the Chinese writing course. I can speak the language, but I want to learn to paint the writing. It's so beautiful.
Man:	Yes, it is. Very beautiful. So I need to ask you some questions to fill in this form.
Woman:	OK.
Man:	What's your first name, please?
Woman:	It's Lucy. L-U-C-Y.
Man:	OK. And your surname?
Woman:	Mansfield. That's M-A-N-S-F-I-E-L-D.
Man:	Thank you. And what's your date of birth, please?
Woman:	It's the second of June, 2001.
Man:	Great. Next question … What's your nationality?
Woman:	Well I live and work here in England, but actually I'm American.
Man:	OK. Good, only two questions now. Can you tell me your address?
Woman:	Yes, it's 58 Charnwood Road.
Man:	How do you spell that?
Woman:	It's C-H-A-R-N-W-O-O-D.
Man:	Fine. And lastly, your phone number please.
Woman:	Right, it's 0795301244.
Man:	Thanks. Now. I'll give you some information …

UNIT 1

Track 05

Man: The best thing about my working life is that every day is different. I travel a lot, but when I'm at home I like getting up early. The first thing I do is to take my dog for a walk. I think that's the perfect start to a day – being outside in the sun. Then I take the dog home and go out to the café near my house for a coffee. Back home again, I have a shower, get dressed and go to the computer to start work. After answering some emails, I talk to people about the jobs I'm doing with them, then write. At the end of the day, my favourite thing to do is go swimming at the pool near my house.

Woman: I don't like to get out of bed quickly in the morning. When I hear the alarm clock at about seven o'clock, I wake up and my husband brings me a cup of green tea – my favourite drink. He always gets up before me. I feel awake after the tea, so then I'm ready to get up and go for a swim in the sea – our house is next to the beach. I usually go for a walk along the beach after my swim, too. Then it's time to go to the computer and start my day's work. But before I start, I always speak to my friends and family on the phone.

UNIT 2

Track 06

Listening Part 1

Narrator: For each question, choose the correct answer.
Now we are ready to start. Look at question one. What weather does Maria's island usually have in March?

Man: What's the weather like on your island at the moment, Maria?

Woman: It's warm and sunny, which is lovely. But it's very different from the weather we usually have in March. Most years there are strong winds and lots of rain during this month.

Man: Really? Well we've still got snow here in the mountains.

Woman: Oh great!

Narrator: Now listen again.

Narrator: Two. Where is the man's uncle travelling now?

Man: My uncle's having a great time travelling around the world.

Woman: Really? Where is he at the moment?

Man: He left his home in the USA in April, and then went to South America for six months last year. But at the moment he's in Africa. He loves it there, and is driving across a desert this week. He'll come to Europe after that, I think.

Woman: Sounds great.

Narrator: Now listen again.

Narrator: Three. In which month does Monica stay with her grandparents?

Man: What do you do in the summer holidays, Monica?

Woman: I stay in the city in June and July – I work in a shop. Then I go back to my family in the country in August. I stay with my grandparents and help on their farm. What about you?

Man: I work in my aunt's hotel in June, July and August.

Narrator: Now listen again.

Narrator: Four. Where is Richard working this week?
Woman: Are you enjoying your job in the national park, Richard?
Man: It's fantastic. We do something different every week. Last week we worked on the island in the lake, but now we're cleaning the waterfall in the river. Other staff are cutting the long grass on the hill this week so we can put some animals there next week.
Woman: Wow! That's amazing.
Narrator: Now listen again.

Narrator: Five. What is Jessica's friend, Lucy, doing in the forest?
Man: Are you going for a run today, Jessica?
Woman: No, because I usually run with Lucy, and she's busy. She's taking her son for a walk.
Man: Is she? Why don't you go with her? Where are they going?
Woman: In the forest. She invited me, but I'm going to go for a ride on my bike instead.
Narrator: Now listen again.

Narrator: That is the end of Part One.

UNIT 3
Track 07
Anna: What did you do on Saturday, Ryan?
Ryan: I went to my cousin's house, on the coast. It was good to get out of the city because it was so hot.
Anna: I know. The temperature was 38 degrees! I stayed in the city and didn't go out. I downloaded a TV series and watched that.
Ryan: Cool! So which series was it?
Anna: A science-fiction series called *White Sky*. Do you know it?
Ryan: Yes, but I don't like that kind of series very much. I prefer crime drama.
Anna: Really? I think that's so dull – every series is the same!
Ryan: Not really! Some are quite scary, and some are really clever. So did you do anything else on Saturday?
Anna: Yes, I played a video game with my dad. I thought it was a bit boring, but he enjoyed it.
Ryan: I played a new video game with my cousin and it was brilliant!
Anna: Didn't you go to the beach?
Ryan: Yes, a bit later in the day. I went swimming in the sea and then sat and chatted to some friends in the café.
Anna: Sounds good. I didn't see my friends on Saturday – we just chatted online.

UNIT 4
Track 08
Listening Part 2
Narrator: For each question, write the correct answer in the gap. Write one word or a number or a date or a time. You have ten seconds to look at Part Two.

Narrator: You will hear the secretary of a running club telling new members about the club.
Woman: Good morning, everyone. It's always great to welcome new members to the running club. I'm the club secretary and my name's Daniella Black. You'll find my email address on our website. The club gets together one evening every week, on Tuesdays. I post information about the runs on Sundays. As it's summer now, we're still meeting at seven o'clock. However, that will change next month. In the autumn and winter we meet at five thirty. We do two practice runs each week: one is 12 kilometres, and there's a shorter run for beginners and children that's six kilometres. You can choose which run you want to do. When the weather's good, we run through the forest, but if it's wet we run on the paths through the park. We also have a special club day every year. This year that'll be on June 18th at Jack's Hill. Last year we had a barbecue at the house of a club member, and this year we're going to have a picnic. So does anyone have any questions?
Narrator: Now listen again.

Narrator: That is the end of Part Two.

UNIT 5
Track 09
Daniel: I went on my first cruise last month. I'm a journalist for a student magazine, and a cruise company invited me to go on one of their ships. The company wants more young people to try cruises.

The cruise ship I went on was enormous: it had 15 floors, like a high building, and there were over 2,800 passengers on it. It was a two-week cruise from Turkey, around Greece and ending in Italy.

I got on the ship and went straight to my room. I took everything out of my suitcase, put my suitcase under my bed and went to look around the ship. There were 10 restaurants, and during the cruise, I tried them all! The food was fantastic. You could choose from lots of different types, and there were different menus in the restaurants every day.

Before I left, I was worried about being bored on the cruise, but I soon stopped thinking that. In fact, there was too much to do! We stopped at a new place nearly every day, and there were tours at each one. It was very tiring. And on the boat there were swimming pools, a running track, a gym and exercise classes.

I was surprised about the age of people on the ship because they were not all very old! Most of the people on the cruise were between the ages of 40 and 60, but there are also some young families and a few people the same age as me. It was really easy to make friends, too, because you sat with the same group of people each night for dinner, and you soon got to know everyone very well. I will certainly go on a cruise again!

UNIT 6

Track 10

Listening Part 5
Narrator: For each question, choose the correct answer. You have fifteen seconds to look at Part Five.

Narrator: You will hear Pippa talking to her friend Mario about desserts in a restaurant. Which dessert does each person want?
Mario: Right, Pippa, we have to order desserts over there, at that food bar. I'll go and order for everyone.
Pippa: Great, thanks, Mario.
Mario: So what does everyone want, Pippa? I'll write it down.
Pippa: Well I'd like the fresh mango – my favourite fruit.
Mario: OK, and David, will he have fruit too? He usually does.
Pippa: Yes, but not the pears. He wants the strawberries – with cream, not ice cream.
Mario: OK. I love strawberries too but coconut rice is on the menu – the best dessert in the world! I'll have that.
Pippa: OK, Mario. Now, Helen couldn't decide between the chocolate cake and the ice cream but chose the cake in the end.
Mario: Right. And Sarah?
Pippa: She'd like the baked pears – she usually has coconut rice here but she wants to try something new.
Mario: OK. What about Paul? He doesn't like desserts much, does he?
Pippa: Not usually, but he'd like the yoghurt and honey. You can have biscuits with it, but he doesn't want any.
Mario: Great. That's everyone. I'll go and order.
Narrator: Now listen again.

Narrator: That is the end of Part Five.

UNIT 7

Track 11

Johannes: I can't believe how many clubs this university has, Carla!
Carla: I know – there are 286 on this list! It's impossible to choose!
Johannes: But I think it's really important to do club activities as well as studying. If you study all the time, you just get bored and you don't learn as much.

Carla: I totally agree, Johannes. But how can we choose from so many?
Johannes: OK, so do you want to do some exercise? Or do some art? Or social clubs, where you can just have fun hanging out with people? There are clubs for the course subjects, too, like the history club or IT club.
Carla: I'm not interested in those – we spend enough time studying them! I'd like to do some exercise so I can keep healthy … but not running or tennis … something different …
Johannes: Right, well these look exciting … snow sports, or flying club …
Carla: Oh look – what's this one: the 'parkour' club?
Johannes: Oh yes … I've done that. But I hated it – it was really hard. It's a bit like what you do in a gym, but without any equipment, and you do it outside – you run and jump over walls and stairs in the street, things like that.
Carla: Really? That sounds good. I think I'll try that. What about you, Johannes? Do you want to do exercise or art, or something else?
Johannes: Well, I want to do some volunteering – you know, work for no money, helping people. A group of students from our university goes and helps at the hospital. They visit sick children and take them presents, or play board games with them, or just hang out with them.
Carla: That's a great idea, Johannes. And you want to be a doctor, so it will help you with your job in the future.
Johannes: That's right.

UNIT 8

Track 12

Listening Part 4
Narrator: For each question, choose the correct answer.
One. You will hear a woman talking about her home. What sort of home is it?
Woman: It's not very big but it's on two floors and it's got three bedrooms. It's a traditional type of building in this area, and is about 100 years old. The best thing is the views from all the windows: you can see fields and the river, and mountains in the distance. We're a long way from the nearest city or town.
Narrator: Now listen again.

Narrator: Two. You will hear a man talking to his wife about a sofa.
What are they discussing?
Man: It'll be great to have a new sofa.
Woman: Yes, I can't wait for it to come. It'll look great under the window.
Man: Actually I think it'll be too high for there. It'll be better on the wall opposite.
Woman: But the bookshelf's there. I don't want to move that.
Man: Let's wait until it's here. Then we can decide.
Narrator: Now listen again.

Narrator: Three. You will hear a woman talking to her friend about her flat.

Why doesn't she want to live in it any more?

Woman: I've decided to look for another flat.
Man: Really? Because of your new job?
Woman: Well it will take me longer to get to work now. But that's not it. The problem is that my cousin is going to come and live with me and we'll need another bedroom.
Man: That's nice – and it will be cheaper for two of you to live together.
Woman: I hope so.
Narrator: Now listen again.

Narrator: Four. You will hear a man telling a friend about a problem in his apartment building.
What is there a problem with?
Woman: Did you get home OK last night?
Man: Well, I was trying to get from the garage in the basement up to my floor last night. I got in and pressed the button for the third floor and nothing happened. It was so annoying. I had to walk up the stairs with all my shopping.
Woman: Oh dear.
Narrator: Now listen again.

Narrator: Five. You will hear a woman telling her friend about her parents' new house.
What does she like best about it?
Woman: I went to my mum and dad's new place at the weekend.
Man: So what's it like?
Woman: Well, the garden's lovely but the kitchen is very small.
Man: So you don't like it much?
Woman: Oh, I do, especially the living room. It has a lovely view out over the park.
Narrator: Now listen again.

Narrator: That is the end of Part Four.

UNIT 9

Track 13

Listening Part 3

Narrator: For each question, choose the correct answer. You have twenty seconds to look at Part Three.

Narrator: You will hear Laura talking to her friend Otto about Marla, the place where they live.
Narrator: Now listen to the conversation.
Laura: Otto, you've lived in Marla for a month now. What do you think of it?
Otto: Well actually, Laura, I know it's a small town, but it's the biggest place I've ever lived in! Our last house was in a little village on an island.
Laura: I've never lived in a city, have you?
Otto: No, but I'd like to – it'd be great to have all those shops and cinemas …
Laura: Yes, it would be great. I'm so bored here in Marla. And I'd really like to be able to go to the theatre.
Otto: I like it here.
Laura: What do you like about Marla?
Otto: Lots of things. For example, I know nearly everyone in my street already, and they all smile and talk to me when they see me.
Laura: That's nice.
Otto: And of course, the mountains around Marla are amazing.
Laura: Yes, they are. They're a great place to do lots of activities, like climbing – I know you love doing that.
Otto: Exactly. And there are lots of other things to do – I'm planning to get a mountain bike soon – I think that will be fun.
Laura: That's a good idea, Otto. Actually, my brother does a lot of activities. You should meet him – I think you'll get on very well with him.
Otto: I'd like that, Laura.
Narrator: Now listen again.

Narrator: That is the end of Part Three.

UNIT 10

Track 14

Listening Part 2

Narrator: For each question, write the correct answer in the gap. Write one word or a number or a date or a time. You have ten seconds to look at Part Two.

Narrator: You will hear an advertisement for a new department store.
Woman: Your new Richards Department Store will soon be open! The fantastic new store is in Victoria Square. It's right in the city centre, and very easy to get to on public transport – only a five-minute walk from the underground – and the station is beside the store.

The store will open in June. The first day is the 15th, when it'll open at 10 o'clock. From the 16th of June, it opens at nine o'clock, which will be the normal opening time. It will be open Monday to Saturday, and will close every night at half past eight. Last shoppers can enter the store at eight o'clock.

The new store has two floors of clothes above our large supermarket on the ground floor. Above the clothes you'll find furniture, and then our amazing restaurant and café. That's up on the fourth floor.

If you come in the first week we open, we will give away a free pen to every customer and all the bags will be half price. So come and shop!

Narrator: Now listen again.

Narrator: That is the end of Part Two.

UNIT 11

 Track 15

Listening Part 1

Narrator: For each question, choose the correct answer.
Now we are ready to start. Look at question one.
Where is Anna going next week?
Man: Are you doing anything next week for the holidays?
Woman: Yes, I'm going to see my grandpa.
Man: Oh – the one who lives in the mountains, or the one who lives by the sea?
Woman: The one from the mountains, but I'm not staying with him there. We're going to meet in the city because we both want to see some exhibitions.
Narrator: Now listen again.

Narrator: Two. What is Alejandro going to buy?
Woman: Have you decided what you want to buy yet, Alejandro?
Man: Yes – I'm not going to get the jacket. I haven't got enough money.
Woman: The jeans are quite expensive, too …
Man: But there's a big discount on them, so I'll get them, but not the belt. I don't need that.
Woman: OK.
Narrator: Now listen again.

Narrator: Three. In which month does Antonio's English course start?
Woman: So when does your English course start, Antonio?
Man: Next month. I chose the June course because I wanted to do my other exams before it, and they're all in the last two weeks of May. The course is every weekday for the whole month.
Woman: So will you have a holiday after that, in July?
Man: Yes, if I have the money!
Narrator: Now listen again.

Narrator: Four. What time does the shop close?
Man: What's the matter, Gina?
Woman: I've started making a cake but there aren't any eggs!
Man: Oh dear – I had them for lunch! I'll run to the shop down the road – it stays open until half past six, doesn't it?
Woman: Actually it shuts at six o'clock, and it's quarter past now.
Man: Sorry!
Narrator: Now listen again.

Narrator: Five. What kind of music will there be at tonight's concert?
Man: I'm going to a concert tonight.
Woman: Oh? Is it to see that famous musician who plays the violin?
Man: No, it's someone new who plays the trumpet.
Woman: Oh right. I'm surprised you're going – I thought you only liked guitar music.
Man: The guitar's great, but I love seeing people play other instruments really well too.
Narrator: Now listen again.

Narrator: That is the end of Part One.

UNIT 12

Track 16

Listening Part 4

Narrator: For each question, choose the correct answer.
One. You will hear a woman asking her friend James about college.
What did James do this morning?
Woman: What were you doing at college this morning, James?
Man: I was finding out about schools in our city for a history project. I found some great photos and newspaper articles, as well as a useful book, so I wrote lots of notes! It's important for me to get a good mark for this essay, so I don't fail the history course.
Narrator: Now, listen again.

Narrator: Two. You will hear a woman talking about school. What was her favourite subject at school?
Woman: Mr Richards taught my favourite subject at school. He was a great teacher because he wanted everyone in the class to take part in our performances, even the students that didn't want to act. He asked them to sing a song, for example, or to paint the walls around the stage. He always made his lessons a lot of fun.
Narrator: Now listen again.

Narrator: Three. You will hear a man talking to a friend about an exam. Why did their friend Tom fail the exam?
Man: Tom didn't pass the biology exam.
Woman: Tom didn't? That's unusual for him. Was he ill?
Man: He was fine, but he said he wrote too much, and then he didn't have time to answer all the questions.
Woman: What a shame. You both did so much work to prepare for that exam.
Man: Oh well, he can take it again in September.
Narrator: Now listen again.

Narrator: Four. You will hear a girl talking to her dad about university. What does the girl's dad suggest that she does?
Woman: My maths teacher wants me to do a maths degree.
Man: Is that what you want to do?
Woman: Yes. I was thinking about doing physics but I enjoy maths more, so I've decided to do that.
Man: Great. Why don't you look at different universities and see which offer the best courses for you?

Woman: I'll do that today.
Narrator: Now listen again.

Narrator: Five. You will hear a woman talking to a friend about her job. Why does she like her job?
Man: Are you still enjoying your job at the farm?
Woman: Yes – I'd like to earn a bit more one day, but the work's brilliant. I know much more about farming now than when I started – college certainly doesn't teach you everything you need to know! I don't see the manager much, but the other staff are lovely.
Man: Great!
Narrator: Now listen again.

Narrator: That is the end of Part Four.

UNIT 13
Track 17
Listening Part 3
Narrator: For each question, choose the correct answer. You have twenty seconds to look at Part Three.

Narrator: You will hear Jo talking to her mum about her mum's Grandpa Bill.
Now listen to the conversation.
Jo: Mum, look at this old book!
Mum: Where did you find that?
Jo: Well, I was looking for my blue jewellery box in the cupboard in the living room. I found this instead. I'm not sure why it wasn't on the bookshelf.
Mum: That book belonged to my Grandpa Bill.
Jo: I never knew him. What was he like?
Mum: Lovely. He didn't talk much, but he smiled all the time. But he didn't like big groups of people, so never came to family parties.
Jo: Is he the grandpa with the horse?
Mum: Yes, but it was old so I didn't ride it. Grandpa read lots of books, and he baked bread. I loved making different kinds with him.
Jo: And what about his job? Wasn't he a factory worker?
Mum: For many years he was. He liked it, but he wanted me to be a doctor, and wasn't happy when I became a teacher!
Jo: So where did he meet his wife, your Grandma Annie?
Mum: She worked in a theatre, selling tickets …
Jo: And he met here there?
Mum: That's right. He invited her to the cinema, and soon after that they got married in the town hall.
Narrator: Now listen again.

Narrator: That is the end of Part Three.

UNIT 14
Track 18
Listening Part 5
Narrator: For each question, choose the correct answer. You have fifteen seconds to look at Part Five.

Narrator: You will hear Steve talking to a friend about his family and sports. What sport does each person do?
Woman: This is a great picture of you with your team, Steve!
Man: Thanks!
Woman: Have you played cricket all your life?
Man: Yes, since I was seven.
Woman: Does your sister play too?
Man: She thinks cricket's really boring. Her sport's volleyball and she's very good at it – better than she was at basketball. She doesn't play that now. She's got a match tomorrow, actually.
Woman: Are all your family going to her match?
Man: My brother can't because he's got a competition.
Woman: He runs, doesn't he?
Man: Yes. He's got races this morning and the long jump this afternoon.
Woman: What a sporty family!
Man: Yes! It's probably because of my granddad. He was a rugby player.
Woman: Oh yes. Does he still play?
Man: No, but he loves tennis and badminton.
Woman: Really? And what about your parents?
Man: Mum spends a lot of her free time at the pool.
Woman: Right. Is your dad sporty?
Man: Not very. He played basketball with us when we were younger, and he's always liked kicking a ball around in the park with friends. He still plays football sometimes.
Woman: That's nice.
Narrator: Now listen again.

Narrator: That is the end of Part Five.

LINKS TO STUDENT'S BOOK VIDEO AND PUSH YOURSELF AUDIO

Starter Unit	Page 10	Grammar on the move	www.cambridge.org/OW_Key_Vid1
	Page 11	Grammar on the move	www.cambridge.org/OW_Key_Vid2
Unit 1	Page 16	Grammar on the move	www.cambridge.org/OW_Key_Vid3
	Page 19	Grammar on the move	www.cambridge.org/OW_Key_Vid4
	Page 25	Real world	www.cambridge.org/OW_Key_Vid5
Unit 2	Page 28	Grammar on the move	www.cambridge.org/OW_Key_Vid6
	Page 31	Grammar on the move	www.cambridge.org/OW_Key_Vid7
	Page 37	Real world	www.cambridge.org/OW_Key_Vid8
Unit 3	Page 42	Grammar on the move	www.cambridge.org/OW_Key_Vid9
	Page 43	Grammar on the move	www.cambridge.org/OW_Key_Vid10
	Page 51	Real world	www.cambridge.org/OW_Key_Vid11
Unit 4	Page 54	Grammar on the move	www.cambridge.org/OW_Key_Vid12
	Page 56	Grammar on the move	www.cambridge.org/OW_Key_Vid13
	Page 63	Real world	www.cambridge.org/OW_Key_Vid14
Unit 5	Page 66	Grammar on the move	www.cambridge.org/OW_Key_Vid15
	Page 68	Grammar on the move	www.cambridge.org/OW_Key_Vid16
	Page 75	Real world	www.cambridge.org/OW_Key_Vid17
Unit 6	Page 80	Grammar on the move	www.cambridge.org/OW_Key_Vid18
	Page 82	Grammar on the move	www.cambridge.org/OW_Key_Vid19
	Page 89	Real world	www.cambridge.org/OW_Key_Vid20
Unit 7	Page 92	Grammar on the move	www.cambridge.org/OW_Key_Vid21
	Page 101	Real world	www.cambridge.org/OW_Key_Vid22
Unit 8	Page 105	Grammar on the move	www.cambridge.org/OW_Key_Vid23
	Page 106	Push yourself B1	www.cambridge.org/OW_Key_track070
	Page 107	Grammar on the move	www.cambridge.org/OW_Key_Vid24
	Page 113	Real world	www.cambridge.org/OW_Key_Vid25
Unit 9	Page 118	Grammar on the move	www.cambridge.org/OW_Key_Vid26
	Page 120	Grammar on the move	www.cambridge.org/OW_Key_Vid27
	Page 127	Real world	www.cambridge.org/OW_Key_Vid28
Unit 10	Page 131	Grammar on the move	www.cambridge.org/OW_Key_Vid29
	Page 134	Grammar on the move	www.cambridge.org/OW_Key_Vid30
	Page 139	Real world	www.cambridge.org/OW_Key_Vid31
Unit 11	Page 143	Grammar on the move	www.cambridge.org/OW_Key_Vid32
	Page 144	Grammar on the move	www.cambridge.org/OW_Key_Vid33
	Page 151	Real world	www.cambridge.org/OW_Key_Vid34
Unit 12	Page 156	Grammar on the move	www.cambridge.org/OW_Key_Vid35
	Page 158	Grammar on the move	www.cambridge.org/OW_Key_Vid36
	Page 165	Real world	www.cambridge.org/OW_Key_Vid37
Unit 13	Page 168	Grammar on the move	www.cambridge.org/OW_Key_Vid38
	Page 171	Grammar on the move	www.cambridge.org/OW_Key_Vid39
	Page 177	Real world	www.cambridge.org/OW_Key_Vid40
Unit 14	Page 180	Grammar on the move	www.cambridge.org/OW_Key_Vid41
	Page 189	Real world	www.cambridge.org/OW_Key_Vid42

ACKNOWLEDGEMENTS

Page make up
EMC Design Ltd